THE HEROES
OF THE GREEKS

C. KERÉNYI

THAMES AND HUDSON

Professor Kerényi wrote this book
between 1952 and 1959
for and on the suggestion of Thames and Hudson
as a companion volume to their The Gods of the Greeks
by the same author.
The German text has been rendered into
English by Professor H. L. Rose

Copyright © 1959 Thames and Hudson Ltd

First published in Great Britain in 1959 by Thames and Hudson Ltd, London
First paperback edition 1974

Published in paperback in the United States of America in 1978 by Thames and Hudson Inc., 500 Fifth Avenue, New York, New York 10110

Reprinted 1997

Library of Congress Catalog Card Number: 77-99200

British Library Cataloguing-in-Publication Data:
A catalogue record for this book is available from the British Library
ISBN 0-500-27049-X
Printed and bound in the United States of America

TO THE POETS OF THE FUTURE

For the earth begets them again
As it has ever begotten them.

Faust II, iii 3

CONTENTS

LIST OF PLATES   *Page* xi

PREFACE   xxi

INTRODUCTION   I

BOOK ONE

    I   Kadmos and Harmonia   25

   II   The Theban Dioskuroi   34

  III   Danaos and his Daughters   40

  IV   Perseus   45

   V   Tantalos   57

  VI   Pelops and Hippodameia   62

  VII   Salmoneus, Melanippe and Tyro   69

VIII   Sisyphos and Bellerophontes   75

  IX   Phrixos and Helle   85

   X   Oidipus   88

  XI   The Spartan Dioskuroi and their Cousins   105

  XII   Meleagros and Atalante   113

BOOK TWO: HERAKLES

    I   The Theban Tales   128

        1   Stories of Herakles' Ancestry   128

        2   The Hero's Birth   131

        3   The Tales of his Youth   136

II The Twelve Labours   *Page* 140

    1 The Nemean Lion   140

    2 The Hydra of Lerna   143

    3 The Hind of Keryneia   146

    4 The Boar of Erymanthos   148

    5 The Birds of Lake Stymphalos   150

    6 The Stable of Augeias   151

    7 The Horses of the Thracian Diomedes   154

    8 The Bull of Minos   158

    9 The Girdle of the Queen of the Amazons   159

    10 The Cattle of Geryoneus   163

    11 The Apples of the Hesperides   172

    12 The Hound of Hades   177

III Deeds and Sufferings after the Twelve Labours   183

    1 Kallinikos   183

    2 The Madman   185

    3 The Sinner   187

    4 The Servant of Women   192

    5 The Rescuer of Hera and of Deianeira   197

    6 The End of Herakles' Earthly Life   201

BOOK THREE

    I Kekrops, Erechtheus and Theseus   209

   II Jason and Medeia   247

  III Orpheus and Eurydike   279

  IV Tereus, Eumolpos and Kephalos   287

   V Amphiaraos and the Heroes of the Theban War   294

  VI Atreus and his Dynasty   302

 VII The Prelude to the Trojan War   308

VIII The Heroes of the Trojan War   *Page* 319

  IX   Iphigeneia and her Brother and Sisters   331

   X   Telephos   337

  XI   Protesilaos and Laodameia   342

 XII   Achilles and the Aftermath of the Trojan War   347

GENEALOGIES   363

SOURCES   381

INDEX   413

LIST OF PLATES

ARV Sir John Beazley, *Attic Red-Figure Vase-Painters*, 1942

ABV Sir John Beazley, *Attic Black-Figure Vase-Painters*, 1956

Bl. Frank Brommer, *Vasenlisten zur griechischen Heldensage*, 1956

KADMOS KILLS THE DRAGON. In the background,
the local goddess Thebe and the spring-nymph Krenaie.
See p. 30   *Plate* 1
    Trendall, *Paestan Pottery* (1936), p. 24

SCENE IN THE UNDERWORLD. THE SOULS OF THE
UNFULFILLED BUSIED IN FILLING A BOTTOM-
LESS VESSEL. In the foreground, Oknos (the Delayer),
a folklore figure of descriptions of the other world. He is
plaiting a rope of rushes, which is eaten by an ass behind
his back, another picture of life without fulfilment. *See* p. 43   2
    After Cook, *Zeus* III, Plate xxxvi

DANAE AND PERSEUS IN THE OPENED CHEST.
Before them stands Diktys, net in hand. *See* p. 48   3
    In Syracuse; after *Athen. Mitt.* xli (1916), opposite p. 8

PERSEUS AND THE FOUNTAIN-NYMPHS. *See* p. 49   4
    Rumpf, *Chalkidische Vasen* (1927), p. 10

PERSEUS SLAYING THE GORGON MEDUSA. *See*   5
p. 51
    Hampe, *Frühgriechische Sagenbilder in Böotien* (1936),
    p. 58

PERSEUS AFTER BEHEADING MEDUSA. *See* p. 51   6
    ARV 365, 53

ANDROMEDA, PERSEUS AND THE SEA-MONSTER
(KETOS). *See* p. 52   7
    In the Antikensammlung at Berlin, after a reproduction
    by the Staatliches Museum

PELOPS, HIPPODAMEIA AND THE FALL OF
MYRTILOS. In the background Nemesis, goddess of
retribution. *See* p. 66   *Plate* 8
From Capua, after *Monumenti dell' Istituto*, X, 25

THE MARRIAGE OF ANTIKLEIA. *See* p. 78   9
From Ruvo, after a reproduction by the Antiken-
sammlung at Munich; *cf.* Furtwängler-Reichhold III,
204

THE MADNESS OF SALMONEUS. *See* p. 74   10
ARV 396, 24. Courtesy of the Art Institute of Chicago

THE PUNISHMENT OF SISYPHOS. On either side, the
king and queen of the underworld. *See* p. 79   11
ABV 383, 12

BELLEROPHONTES BEFORE IOBATES. *See* p. 82   12
From Campania, after Bloesch, *Antike Kunst in der
Schweiz*, plate 49

PHRIXOS AND THE RAM PURSUED BY INO. This
episode is not described in my text. *See* p. 86   13
ARV 779, 1

OIDIPUS ON THE ARM OF THE HERDSMAN
EUPHORBOS. *See* p. 93   14
ARV 634, 4

OIDIPUS SOLVES THE RIDDLE OF THE SPHINX.
See p. 98   15
ARV 296, 12

OIDIPUS KILLING THE SPHINX. Besides the deities,
Athene and Apollo, the artist (the 'Meidias painter') has,
after his fashion, added other heroic figures to the scene,
Kastor, Polydeukes and Aineias. *See* p. 99   16
ARV 83, 48

KASTOR AND POLYDEUKES GREETED BY LEDA
AND TYNDAREOS. A work by Exekias.   17
ABV 145, 13

HERAKLES SUCKLED BY HERA in the presence of
Athene. *See* p. 134   18
Bl. 40, D 1

THE INFANT HERAKLES STRANGLING THE
SERPENTS. *See* p. 134   *Plate* 19
ARV 386, 39

HERAKLES ESCORTED TO SCHOOL. The grey‑haired
figure with the lyre has written alongside the name Ger . .
pso . . . evidently a compound of *geron* (old man) and
rhapsodos (reciter of epic); Gerapsos or Geropsos may be
the name of the 'aged singer'   20
ARV 576, 16

HERAKLES AT SCHOOL. *See* p. 135   21
Bl. 63, B 7

THE YOUNG HERAKLES OVERCOMING NEREUS.
Unless the painter means some adventure previous to the
voyage to the Hesperides (*see* p. 172), the story is otherwise
unknown   22
Bl. 89, B 7

HERAKLES AND THE SEA‑GOD. Unless the same
adventure as in the foregoing picture is meant, this is another
unknown tale. Herakles has wrenched his trident from the
sea‑god, with whom he had previously drunk. A Nereid
hurries by in fright   23
In the Museo di Villa Giulia, Rome, after a repro‑
duction by the German Archaeological Institute,
57, 653

HERAKLES AND GERAS. This story, otherwise un‑
known, is alluded to for us by vase‑paintings. Geras, 'old
age', is probably no more than a modified form of Thanatos,
Death, whom Herakles fought in so many legends   24
In the Museo di Villa Giulia, Rome, after a repro‑
duction by the German Archaeological Institute,
57, 682

HERAKLES AND THE LION. *See* p. 141   25
ARV 167, 32

HERAKLES AND THE HIND WITH THE HES‑   26
PERIDES. *See* p. 142
Bl. 44, A 17

HERAKLES TAKES THE GOLDEN ANTLERS. Before
him stands Apollo, Athene behind him to protect him.   *Plate* 27
See p. 148
    Bl. 43, A 7

HERAKLES WITH THE BOAR. A variation of the often-
repeated scene with Eurystheus in his jar. *See* p. 150   28
    Bl. 28, A 14

HERAKLES WITH PHOLOS THE CENTAUR. *See*   29
p. 149
    Bl. 105, A 33

HERAKLES AND THE STYMPHALIAN BIRDS.
See p. 151   30
    Bl. 122, A 3

HERAKLES AND THE SEA-MONSTER. *See* p. 161   31
    After Brommer, *Marburger Winckelmann-Programm*,
1955, Plate 3

HERAKLES AND THE AMAZON ANDROMACHE.
In the legend of the Amazons, this name occurs only on
this vase-painting   32
    After Bothmer, *Amazons in Greek Art* (1957), Plate V

HERAKLES AMONG THE AMAZONS. *See* p. 161   33
    Bl. 15, D 1

HELIOS SHOT AT BY HERAKLES. *See* p. 168   34
    Bl. 39, A 2

HERAKLES AND GERYONEUS. *See* p. 168   35
    Bl. 37, C 2

HERAKLES IN THE CUP OF THE SUN. *See* p. 168   36
    Bl. 113, A 1

HERAKLES WITH THE HESPERIDES. *See* p. 176   37
    Bl. 41, B 12

HERAKLES BEFORE ZEUS WITH THE APPLES OF
THE HESPERIDES. Apollo and Artemis stand in the
background, to welcome their former enemy. The head of
the lion-skin is drawn incorrectly. *See* p. 177   38
    Probably Etruscan; after Noël des Vergers, *Etrurie*,
Plate IV

HERAKLES CHAINING KERBEROS. *See* p. 181   *Plate* 39
Bl. 54, B 1

HERAKLES AND THE KERKOPES. *See* p. 194   40
ABV 370, 137

THE SHOOTING-MATCH AT OICHALIA. *See* p. 189   41
Bl. 32, A 1

THE FIGHT FOR THE TRIPOD. *See* p. 191   42
After Rumpf, *Chalkidische Vasen*, Plate 171

NESSOS CARRIES OFF DEIANEIRA. *See* p. 200   43
Sherd from an ancient Attic vase after *Bull. corr. hell.*,
76 (1952), 347

HERAKLES LEAVING THE FUNERAL PYRE. *See*
p. 203   44
ARV 805, 1

HERAKLES JOURNEYING TO OLYMPOS. *See* p. 203   45
From the subterranean shrine at Paestum, after *Abhandl.*
Heidelb. Akad., Phil.-hist. Klasse 1957, 2, Plate 16

DIONYSIAC APOTHEOSIS OF HERAKLES, who
holds the *kantharos*; Athene offers him a flower   46
After Lullies-Hirmer, *Griechische Vasen* (1953), p. 30

KEKROPS AND PALLAS ATHENE BEFORE THE
SACRED OLIVE. In the background one of the daughters
of Kekrops, before her the mysterious basket, covered with
a cloth. *See* p. 212   47
Bl. 155, B 4

THESEUS MEETS SKIRON, PHAIA AND SINIS. *See*
p. 220   48
Bl. 127, 13

THESEUS ON THE TORTOISE. *See* p. 221   49
After Zanotti-Zancani, *Heraion* II, 307

THESEUS MEETS KERKYON AND THE MARA-
THONIAN BULL. *See* pp. 222, 226   50
Bl. 125, 5

THESEUS AND PROKRUSTES. *See* p. 222   *Plate* 51
   Bl. 127, 13

RECEPTION OF THESEUS IN ATHENS; a ceremonial
welcome, *cf.* p. 223. Athene in person is the first to receive
him   52
   Bl. 127, 14

ARRIVAL OF THESEUS IN THE PALACE OF
POSEIDON. Poseidon stands behind the powerful Triton
who has brought the boy. *See* p. 229   53
   Bl. 127, 14

THESEUS BEFORE AMPHITRITE. She hands him the
headband for his garland. *See* p. 229   54
   Bl. 127, 14

THESEUS AND THE MINOTAUR. On this picture the
monster is called Taurominion. *See* p. 232   55
   From the collection of Jacob Hirsch, in possession of an
   art-dealer in 1957

THESEUS AND ARIADNE ON NAXOS. Athene holds
Theseus back from the sleeping Ariadne. It is not yet the
bridal-night, as there is a boy lying at the bride's feet, after
the Naxian custom, by which the *pronymphios hypnos* ('the
sleep before the bridegroom') is his. In the air Iris, messenger of the gods, is hurrying to call Dionysos. *See* p. 233   56
   Bl. 130, B 5

THESEUS CARRIES OFF KORONE. It is more likely
that the names written alongside the female figures are out
of place and that Theseus is carrying off Helen. The other
man is Peirithoos. *See* p. 235   57
   ARV 25, 3

THESEUS FIGHTING THE AMAZONS; his opponent
is Hippolyte. *See* p. 241   58
   ARV 724, 2

THESEUS AND HERAKLES. *See* p. 239   59
   After Beazley, *Attic Red-figure Vases in American
   Museums* (1928), p. 136

PHINEUS ON HIS COUCH. Behind him stands his wife; the name Erichtho was written alongside her. *See* p. 259 *Cf.* Furtwängler-Reichhold I, 209 ... *Plate* 60

THE SONS OF BOREAS AND THE HARPIES. *See* p. 259 61 In the Museo di Villa Giulia, Rome, after a reproduction by the German Arch. Inst., 57, 660

JASON SPEWED UP BY THE DRAGON. *See* p. 265 62 ARV 286, 93

MEDEIA'S REJUVENATING MAGIC. The man who stands opposite her may be Jason. *See* p. 273 63 ARV 194, 17

ORPHEUS AMONG THE THRACIANS. *See* p. 281 64 ARV 703, 1

THE DEATH OF ORPHEUS. According to this picture, the singer was not torn to pieces with bare hands, but carved up with a sword. *See* p. 285 65 ARV 646, 15

POLYNEIKES AND ERIPHYLE. *See* p. 297 66 ARV 408, 119

VISIT OF THE GODS TO PELEUS AND THETIS. Thetis is sitting in the nuptial hut, Peleus receiving the visitors, Chiron, Iris, Chariklo, Demeter, Dionysos being visible. *See* p. 312 67 ABV 76, 1

THE THREE GODDESSES BEFORE PARIS. Hermes introduces them. *See* p. 316 68 After Clairmont, *Das Parisurteil in der antiken Kunst* (1923), Plate 3. ABV 87, 16

PARIS COMING HOME FROM IDA. Artemis stands behind him, Hekabe embraces him, Hektor offers his hand, Priam receives him on his throne. One of the two female figures in the background is Kassandra. *See* p. 317 69 ARV 246, 4

PELEUS BRINGS ACHILLES TO CHIRON. *See* p. 318   *Plate* 70
    ARV 434, 1

ORESTES AND IPHIGENEIA BEFORE THE TAUR-
IAN TEMPLE. In the temple stands the idol of the
goddess; Iphigeneia carries the temple-key on her shoulder.
The second man is Pylades. *See* p. 335   71
    ARV 875, 1

ACHILLES AND TROILOS. The powerful figure behind the fountain is Achilles, the small ones in the
foreground Troilos and Polyxena. *See* p. 348   72
    In the Museo di Villa Giulia, Rome, after a repro-
    duction by the German Arch. Inst., 57, 659. *Cf.*
    Kunze, *Archaische Schildbänder* (1950), 140ff

ACHILLES AND PENTHESILEIA. *See* p. 352   73
    ARV 582, 1

ODYSSEUS AND NEOPTOLEMOS. *See* p. 356   74
    ARV 282, 28

THE BATTLE OVER THE CORPSE OF ACHILLES.
In the foreground stand Aias and Glaukos, in the background Athene and Paris, who is drawing his bow. *See*
p. 354   75
    Mon. Istit., I, 51

MENELAOS BRINGING HELEN HOME AGAIN. *See*
p. 360   76
    After Ghali-Kahil, *Les enlèvements et le retour d'Hélène*
    (1955), Plate IV

MYTH is a universal postulation of Greek existence. The entire civilisation, along with all the commissions and omissions, was still the old original one, except that it was gradually evolving. Man was still aware of the mythic and sacred source of count‑less forms of life, and felt very close to that source. The whole Greek race considered itself to be heir and assign of the Age of the Heroes; retribution was still exacted for wrongs suffered in primaeval times; Herodotus begins his story of the great battle between West and East with the abduction of Io, and the Persian War is a continuation of the Trojan.

Jacob Burckhardt

PREFACE

THE BOOK WHICH I NOW OFFER TO THE PUBLIC is
again full of matter, even more so than was my *Gods of the
Greeks*. It continues indeed the narrative of that learned Greek
islander of our times into whose mouth the story of the gods was
put, and complements it at every point where that ran into the
story of the heroes. But we may as well take the opposite route,
starting from the heavy destinies of these demi-gods who were
often for that reason all the more suffering men, and so passing
on to the playful existence of the 'easily-living' gods. Here it is
not the world of the gods, but a whole world which will be
revealed; sometimes it will seem familiar to us, sometimes
strange, and handled from this side perhaps for the first time. It
is a world which lies between the mouth of the Guadalquivir
and the Caucasus, over a space of time beginning about
1500 B.C. and lasting for at least two thousand years. It carried
the glory of great gods and goddesses in the shape of their sons,
who were venerated as heroes.

It is a part of that history which we may call our own, in the
sense of the common inheritance which enables us to remember
and adopt it. On the basis of the results of psychologists I doubt
if it be possible to eliminate such a portion of history entirely,
and as a historian I would account it a falsifying of the general
history of mankind to wish to suppress the knowledge of it. I
do not for a moment believe that I have presented it in a final
form. That is why I have dedicated it to future poets; be it

theirs to transmute it, as a once present truth of the mind, belonging to the history of European literature and religion, into a new form, more fitting than is possible in a work of classical scholarship.

This book does not try to adorn its subject. That has been done by Gustav Schwab's *Schönste Sagen des klassischen Alter-tums*, which for so long has conformed to the dreams of youth, and by other such descriptions in other languages, whatever their titles may be—for instance, Kingsley's *Heroes*. It is careful not to mask the ancient tradition, so brilliant in its realism. A concealment of tradition can arise even from an honestly meant scientific spirit, a justifiable desire to know, which does not recognise the bounds set to it by this very tradition. The desire to know can be directed to what is traditional, to details and connecting links, which may be daily enlarged by discoveries and decipherments; it may try to illuminate and vivify the whole intellectually, and then it has every right to claim the title 'scientific'. At the same time, the temptation is all too often present to proceed to ask how the tradition arose, and here we generally come into collision with the unknowable, for it is rare for the process of an origin to be handed down to us. This is most especially true of the material of the stories of gods and heroes.

The tradition is found in texts and in art-monuments. To occupy oneself with the history of this form of tradition is important for the recognition of what is really traditional. But it implies a vast departure from the tradition itself, in the direction of theories of origins and reconstructions of lost works, to arguments which in the last analysis depend on what cannot be proved. Such hypotheses and attempts at reconstruction, even when they do not turn into a play of fancy cut off from anything concretely present, can easily conceal concrete matter.

My aim has been to proceed resolutely to the contents of the myths. This could be done, so far as it was possible, by living with the texts, keeping in sight the inexhaustible works of the vase-painters and sepulchral art (since graves were the sites of a long-surviving worship of heroes), not for the sake of interpretation, but of the atmosphere. This entailed bringing the traditional material into a state of liveliness and detachment, from which the forms of the heroes could emerge as it were of themselves in their original outlines. Here the development of the art of story-telling since Virginia Woolf, has given much encouragement even to a scientific writer. Every hero is, when treated along with his cult, Virginia Woolf's Orlando, and many comparisons between heroes and deities had to be left as uncertain as the mythological self-identifications of Thomas Mann's young Joseph.

The smooth level of narration from one point of view has long ago been ended in great literature. A form which lets the ancient narrators—even several of them, alongside of or after one another—and the reflective re-tellers of the tales all have their say should be developed also in scientific literature, without even attempting to produce the effect of an original narrative work, but only trusting to the self-maintenance of a most ancient narrative material. To test this self-maintenance during years of work at selecting, releasing and fitting together the concrete human content, first on myself, then on others, attracted me, I confess, as a scientific experiment, and I found it at the same time an attempt at living humanism, which always is somehow connected with the Greeks. We must find the right attitude towards Greek heroic mythology also, on the basis of a picture neither simplified after the fashion of a school-master nor tidied in the manner of *belles-lettres*, or concealed or veiled in any way at all.

The dedication to the Poets of the Future is not meant to cancel out the dedications of particular chapters which were presented as festival gifts—that of 'Kadmos and Harmonia' to Walter F. Otto, that of 'Perseus' to C. G. Jung, and that of 'Sisyphos and Bellerophontes' to Thomas Mann—to each of those three great encouragers of my labours in mythology on their eightieth birthdays.

It gives me especial pleasure that the translation is due to Professor H. J. Rose, the author of a well-known *Handbook of*

Greek Mythology. I feel all the more obliged to him because I know that he cannot agree with all the ideas and conclusions in this book. Surely this translation bears witness to the existence of a veritable *res publica doctorum virorum* in classical scholarship, although not to any identity of opinion between translator and author.

C.K.

Ascona, Switzerland

INTRODUCTION

IF GREEK MYTHOLOGY were confined to the gods and at any rate to myths of the origin of the human race, the heroes would have to remain on the verge of it. But the gods demand the heroes, and these still belong to mythology. Thence they spread to the time which deals no longer with 'stories' but with 'history'. An essential difference between the legends of heroes and mythology proper, between the myths of the gods and those of the heroes, which are often entwined with them or at least border upon them, consists in this: that the latter prove to be, whether more or less, interwoven with history, with the events, not of a primaeval time which lies outside of time, but with historical time, and bordering on it as closely as if they were already history proper and not mythology. We cannot on principle deny factual existence, historicity, to the heroes. They appear before us as if they had in fact existed and only exceptionally achieved the status of gods, on Olympos in the case of Herakles, otherwise in the underworld. But even if they were once historical persons, they exist in their 'legends' in a manner which takes them out of 'history'. We cease to be quite fair to them when we prove their 'historicity'. They forfeit thereby their mythological aspect, which connects them with the gods and by virtue of which they, like the gods, act as Prototypes. Their existence is a special kind of quasiexistence, which is both less and more than the ordinary existence of human beings—more, because it includes also their posthumous life in cult.

They were not always distinguished, not even, for instance, by heroism; that is why English 'hero' is not a satisfactory rendering of Greek *heros*, though it must be used for want of a better word. Far more than by any peculiarity, the heroes in all their legends are marked by their substantiality, by a remarkable solidity, which they share with the divine figures. The gods of many mythologies unconnected with the civilisations of the Near East and the Mediterranean occupy this middle position between gods like those of the Greeks and human beings. This solidity is one which has been preserved in the poetical representation to which the heroes were continually liable, to such an extent that an Alexander, Caesar or Napoleon, completely transformed by the arbitrary imagination of some writer, is more conceivable than a Perseus or an Oidipus, who is quite different. Indeed a transformed Alexander the Great is less so, because he had already passed into the ranks of the heroes in antiquity. To the 'heroes' of history, historical time belongs. They are embedded in a single period of time, which is determined by innumerable contemporary happenings and which cannot be altered. Even a completely 'new' Caesar or Napoleon would have his outlines therefrom, and would be recognisable by his temporal outside. The unchangeable part of the heroes of mythology, on the other hand, is an unalterable kernel which is always to be found in the same hero. Ralph Waldo Emerson's dictum is true also in the factual sense belonging to the history of religion: 'The hero is he who is immovably centred.' He may resemble other heroes in one or several traits; there are heroic types, as there are types of ordinary men. But in the central point of his traits which makes him one the hero remains unique. The reduction of the hero, solid in his uniqueness, to a possibility performed in man and in his world, the proof and definition of his archetypal character, must remain the task of a special treatment, which could be properly undertaken only from the point of view of psychology and philosophy, though hardly without the historical foundation which is supplied by a description of the tradition concerning the heroes of the Greeks that is conscious of its limitations. However, the philosophical style of expression cannot be wholly avoided in this introduction, and a 'Myth of the Hero' will emerge.

The hero, as he meets us in his 'legends' assuredly embodies, even more than the gods of the Greeks, a teaching concerning mankind. His purely human characterisation is fully possible, but there falls a glory upon him, which from the point of view of the history of religions, for which the divine is the datum serving as its starting-point,[1] we may term the glory of the divine, the word 'glory', 'radiance' or 'splendour' being of course used metaphorically, yet in a way which is as well justified as when we speak of the 'glory' of a work of art, and are understood by all who possess—what is common to mankind but distributed in various proportions—the power to perceive it. The glory of the divine, which falls on the figure of the hero, is strangely combined with the shadow of mortality. This results in a mythological character, that of a peculiar being, to whom belongs at least one story, the narrative concerning just that hero and no other. If the mythological character is replaced by one purely human, the legends of heroes become tales of warlike men, to whom the epithet of 'hero' applies only in that sense, divorced from cult, in which Homer uses it, approximately 'noble gentleman', and thus mythology, even the mythology of heroes, finds its limit.

This occurs in the epic poems concerning the journeys and campaigns of whole companies of heroes, such as the voyage of the Argo or the War of Troy. All this, and certainly also the expedition of the Seven against Thebes and a number of lost pre-Homeric epics, has become heroic poetry, with an atmosphere of its own, even when its heroes belong to the heroes of mythology. Like every mythology, that of the heroes has its connection with cult. Heroic poetry is, so far as we know it, unconnected with cult. The hero with his cult is more differentiated from the hero of Epic than from the hero of Tragedy, which after all presents an act of cult. There is no

boundary in the matter, but there is one between the atmo-
spheres. The description of the heroes in Greek mythology must
also submit to such a differentiation, if it is not to become in the
end a mere table of contents of heroic poetry and so either strip
off its peculiar atmosphere (besides, it will not wish to arouse
interest in accounts of battles), or else confuse it with another.
Here the voyage of the Argonauts and the expedition of the
Seven constitute a middle stage, by the fashion in which they
are handed down, the one by the learned poet Apollonios of
Rhodes, the other in Tragedy, and this must not be excluded
in a re-telling of the heroic mythology. A re-telling of purely
heroic poetry, which could communicate the content of both
the poems connected with the name of Homer, the 'Iliad' and
the 'Odyssey', to men of today, seems to me possible, indeed
necessary, but not in this book.

To the hero belonged his cult, a peculiar form of reverence,
not to be confounded with hero-worship in Carlyle's sense. It
was veritable cult, straightforward, strict ritual observance, a
perfectly natural tribute to the hero, not a manner of exalting
him. On a smaller scale it was like the reverence which was
paid on a larger one to the gods of the underworld, the lords of
the departed. The divine, whose glory the hero bears among the
dead, produces from the realm of the dead, far more than from
the figure of an ordinary mortal who has joined the dead, that
deep awe which—as W. F. Otto, with truth on his side, says
of it—we describe too one-sidedly as fear, whereas it is also the
most solemn and exalted feeling.[2] The sacrifice for gods of the
dead and for heroes was called *enágisma*, in contradistinction to
thysía, which was the portion especially of the celestial deities.
It was offered on altars of a peculiar shape; they were lower
than the ordinary altar, *bōmós*, and their name was *eschára*,
'hearth'. Through them the blood of the victims, and also
libations, were to flow into the sacrificial trench. Therefore they
were funnel-shaped and open at the bottom. For this kind of
sacrifice did not lead up to a joyous feast in which gods and
men took part. The victim was held over the trench with its

head down, not, as for the celestial gods, with its neck bent back and the head uplifted; and it was burned entirely. These are the characteristic traits of these rites, which however did not form a rigid, unalterable ceremonial; for example, in many places the sacrifices to Herakles combined these gloomier methods with the brighter ones, and in Attica the bulls were offered to him in the same manner as to the Olympians. And in other ways too, these and other less gloomy details bore witness to the joy of the Greeks even in this cult.

The heroes, although their cult belongs to the complete picture of them, would certainly not have attained to any importance for us through it alone; nor would they from their surviving tombs, although they are impressive enough, as those within and without the Cyclopean walls of Mycenae or those, of truly 'heroic' appearance in their vast and uncouth layout, which have been found near Eleusis, on the road from the Peloponnesos to Thebes, and were supposed to cover six of the famous Seven. Not even the names which are connected with the foundations of cities, with ruling families, noble lineages, and whole tribes would have sufficed for a more general importance, not to mention the large number of heroes who are mere names to us, or remained nameless. Scientific interest would exist for them all, in so far as they belong to the general picture of Greek culture; but the human importance lies in the traditional stories which had their cult for a background.

It often seems as if the tales of gods and heroes alike were to be referred to 'folktale motifs', as if they were further develop-ments of a few primaeval folktales, to which they could be easily reduced. This appearance (apart from its being decep-tive) is fitted, more than anything else, to distract attention from their humanly absorbing content. 'Motifs' or 'narrative formulae', if handled for their own sakes, are merely the results of abstraction and reduction. They do not exist and are not active of themselves, but only in 'stories', which are more than motifs and formulae. Folktales are in truth full of motifs and of formulae, and although this does not completely exhaust them, yet they can be largely reduced thereto. In this as in other things they betray their relatively late date. The earliest folktales and the earliest collections of them all lie before us in texts of relatively, indeed absolutely, recent times. To assume 'folktales' as older forms of the legends of gods and heroes on the analogy of these texts is one of the illogicalities of a historical method which has not been thought out. Still, these very texts furnish us with a basis, the only one we really possess, for reflecting on the character of those forms of narrative which are called folk-tales in English, *Märchen* in German. Anyone who has done so conscientiously enough[3] must recognise the comparatively late date of folktales even in their characteristics. The teller of such tales turns against the tragic reality of human existence and the limitations from which it suffers, and opposes it with an anti-tragedy. Consciously or unconsciously the teller of folktales is a denier and an anti-tragedian, and his creation, with reference to that which he denies, is secondary. The primary, that which is denied, is in myth. The folktale ends most willingly with a wedding or other fulfilment. When this occurs, for instance in the story of Perseus, the reason for the folktale flavour of this particular myth lies in the fact that it was probably in a relatively late form from the Mycenaean age that it reached the poets who, for us, are the first to take notice of it. In the tale of Theseus or the story of Peleus (both names of the same type), we can still almost observe the process of the myth turning into a folktale, for in the one case the tragic ending, the death of Theseus at the hands of Lykomedes, is entirely without motive, but does occur, while in the other it is softened, in that the wedding with a goddess was considered, alike in the myth and in the folktale derived from it, to be a piece of good fortune which out-weighed all the tragical results.

The stories of heroes in mythology are akin to another form of narrative, one which has similarly tragical features. In Old Norse it is called 'saga', a word which has been adopted into English and, in the form *Sage*, into German also. We can comprehend the saga in the concrete example of Old Icelandic literature, which presumably goes back to the oral family chronicles of the noble houses that emigrated to Iceland. Like André Jolles, we must define the saga as a 'simple form', as the folktale also is, but with greater veracity: as the formative principle of that very *genre* which shaped and maintained the world in saga. That great Germanist characterises saga as follows:

> 'Arising from the occupation of the mind with family, kin, and blood-relationship, it built a world from a genealogy, which remained the same in a hundred many-hued varieties, a world of pride of ancestry and of the father's curse, of family property and family quarrels, of abductions of women and adultery, blood-revenge and incest, loyalty to kin and hatred of kinsfolk, of fathers and sons, brothers and sisters, a world of inheritance.'[4]

This sketch reminds us indeed of resemblances, especially of the story of the dynasty of Atreus, but also of differences which we will encounter in Greek stories of heroes. Part of the difference is that we are confronted in Greece with no such solid, self-consistent, independent tradition about the heroes, no such real family tradition, as that of the Icelandic sagas. We must collect fragments, and that always at second hand. It is true that it is often the hand of some great poet, above all of Homer. A world of original heroic mythology preceding the Homeric epics can, however, be inferred; this justifies us in asking whether the mythological tradition concerning the heroes is on Greek soil really what the sagas are in Iceland, rather than a peculiar phenomenon of the history of humanity.

If we pass through the famous gate of the stronghold and royal seat of Mycenae, which has to decorate its gable and to crown it a pillar flanked by lions (a symbol of the cult of the great goddess, the Lady of Wild Beasts, and possibly the place of her epiphany in the form of a bird), the first thing we notice is a great burial-ground. It is surrounded by slabs of stone

arranged parallel to each other. With this surround the deep
pit-graves of the earlier kings were walled in in the fourteenth
century B.C., after the gate and the mighty Cyclopean fortifications of the stronghold had been built. This was a mark of the
veneration of their predecessors, who perhaps were not even the
ancestors by blood of the future rulers, on the part of the
succeeding generations, the veneration of the House of Perseus,
if we may adopt without proof the names from the mythology
of the heroes, by the House of Atreus. Schliemann, when he
excavated the grave-circle, found there an altar, which had
served, in the manner above described, for hero-cult. From the
time in which no kingdom belonged any more to the royal
castle we know of two surviving cults of heroes in connection
with Mycenae, both outside the city: that of Perseus himself,
but not of the kings who perhaps were considered as his
descendants, as Perseidai, testified to by tradition, and that of
the Atreid Agamemnon, known from the discovery of the
place where he was venerated.

Schliemann, however, found no gravestone on which the
name of any departed royalty honoured within the ring-wall
could be read. In those days indeed no one expected written
evidence from so early a date. Yet, when not long ago a second
ring of similar graves was discovered and excavated outside the
walls of the fortress, and grave-stelae were found which bore
carvings, scenes of hunting and fighting with powerful beasts,
yet not a single inscription, the silence of the stones began to be
significant. No discovery from elsewhere justifies us so far in
concluding that this silence is mere accident; it is, rather,
characteristic. We now know the Mycenaean script; its monuments have been found in the palace of Nestor at Pylos, in
Mycenae and to name here only this central point of the
legends of heroes, in Thebes. Plutarch tells us of this script,
which the Greeks of historical times thought more like
Egyptian hieroglyphics than their own letters. The Spartans,
who were masters of Boiotia under Agesilaos about 380 B.C.,
opened a tomb at Haliartos, in which it was said Alkmene,

the mother of Herakles, lay, and found there a bronze tablet with writing of that kind, but far more modest grave-gifts than those which have come to light from the tombs within the stone circle at Mycenae.[5] In not one of the many graves of Mycenaean date which have been opened by archaeologists has an inscription been found. The inscribed tablets which have been discovered in palaces and houses are lists of property, of sacrifices and tributes belonging to gods and men. For Crete and Mycenae it seems as if the observation which I have already expressed[6] and may now be repeated in the words of Oswald Spengler still holds good: 'In the whole mass of the Cretan finds there is no indication of historical, political or even biographical consciousness, such as reigned particularly among the people of the Egyptian culture from the earliest days of the Old Kingdom on.' At all events, it has left no trace of an impulse towards immortalising in writing in the Mycenaean burials, carefully though they were arranged and guarded.

The immortalising, however, was there, though not through writing. The magnificent beehive tombs outside the city were built from the fifteenth to the thirteenth century B.C. The shaft-graves, though so richly provided with costly funeral offerings, are not only proof of a cult of the dead in Mycenae, a precursor of the Greek hero-cult in historical times, but in their very dumbness they testify to a cult of memory, to a trust (if we may say it in the language of the historical Greeks, which was already spoken in the stronghold of the grave-circles) in the goddess Mnemosyne. According to much later evidence of a belief which surely rested upon an ancient cult of the dead, the departed themselves had a personal trust in her, and hoped to drink from her fountain in the underworld. He who remembers himself corresponds to the remembrance in which he lives on; that surely would be Mnemosyne's greatest gift. We have, for Mycenaean beliefs concerning death, no such evidence as those little gold tablets on which we find directions for the attain-ment of this greatest gift; but we cannot fail to provide Mnemo-syne with a period of time which was not exclusively one of more or less dim family memories, and in which the daughters of that great goddess already had their part. The excavation of Nestor's palace at Pylos furnished, in my opinion, the proof that a very human epic poetry, very attached to material things, came before Homer and extended across the confused times at the turn of the millennium until it reached him.[7]

How far writing had already supported both memory and the art of the poet, however, can no longer be exactly stated. Written records certainly did not stand in the foreground in that age which I have therefore called the age of Mnemosyne. And if in that very point we must note a resemblance to the Icelandic sagas, it seems to us that the dark family history of the Atreidai is not at all characteristic of Greek hero-mythology as a whole. Many figures of heroes and heroines bear a brighter, a divine radiance, which might even belong to former deities. We do not know how far the kings of Mycenae attempted to resemble the gods, and how far their cult of the dead gave expression to this attempt. The archaeological discoveries[8] so far tell us unambiguously that Greek hero-cult is the continuation, not of a general cult of the dead in Mycenaean times, but of the Mycenaeans' cult of the royal dead. If that contained a theo-morphism, the extent of which is unknown to us, this meets with an anthropomorphism in the myths of the gods, to which an ivory group of two goddesses and a divine child bears testimony already in the manner of Greek mythology.[8a] This meeting may have arisen in the mythology of the heroes. The divine passed into the human, and the human was exalted to divinity; and so the hero-myth arose. Originating in man himself, it got its nourishment from the double kingdom of Mnemosyne, the realm of the dead, to which the cult at the graves was directed, and the past, which remained present through memory and won to an ideality which could distinguish only godlike men.

Here I made just one assumption concerning the origin of the cult of heroes among the Greeks. If we are inclined to see in the godlike splendour of the men to whom that cult belonged the realisation in death of a striving native to man's nature, then the fitting means of expression for that is to speak of a contradictory figure which should admit of all variations of hero-mythology, of the figure of the god-man in its countless variations in the countless stories. In that case, the presupposition of the tales of heroes would be this human characteristic, that man is capable, even in the bond of a tribe or a family, of knowing the unique, which will not fit in with it. The origin of the peculiarity and uniqueness of a being brought into the world by his mother as something astonishingly new, which never was there before, the immediacy of the intrusion into the world resulting in a unique career, appears in heroic mythology as a divine origin. Of this we may speak in philosophical language as of a revelation of the being in man, and add that all revelations of this being have passed into forms, wherever they appear, both in history and also in mythology, to which alone our present consideration belongs. The expression 'god-man' I have chosen, independently of its Christian significance, on the basis of the Greek data; its sense is not the redemption of man, but rather a high conception of him, which vainly seeks for its like in the whole history of religion. For the general conception, which is meant here, and its post-Christian expression, we may cite Carlyle:[9]

> 'The essence of our being, the mystery in us that calls itself "I"—ah, what words have we for such things?—is a breath of Heaven: the Highest Being reveals himself in man. This body, these faculties, this life of ours, is it not all as a vesture for that Unnamed? "There is but one Temple in the Universe", says the devout Novalis, "and that is the Body of Man. Nothing is holier than that high form. Bending before men is a reverence done to this Revelation in the Flesh. We touch Heaven when we lay our hand on a human body!" This sounds much like a mere flourish of rhetoric; but it is not so. If well meditated, it will turn out to be a scientific fact; the expression, in such

words as can be had, of the actual truth of the thing. We
are the miracle of miracles—the great inscrutable mystery
of God.'

In this manner Carlyle laid the foundation for his exalted
reverence towards heroes, which for him formed the basis of
Christianity—an Arianic Christianity it is true, and therefore
not wholly unlike antiquity in conception; a reverence for
heroes which—it must be said in his own words—is a 'heart-
felt, prostrate admiration, submission, burning, bondless, for a
noblest godlike Form of Man'. 'Is not that,' he adds, 'the germ
of Christianity itself? The greatest of Heroes is One—whom
we do not name here!' The legends of the Greek heroes on the
other hand are as little elevated as their hero-cult. They are,
rather, astonishingly realistic and anything but ethically idealis-
ing, when they describe the human characteristics of their
heroes. Carlyle is poles asunder from them. Greek hero-myths
are concerned with the origins of cities, families, and tribes, and
at the same time are concerned with the 'god-man'; in this way
their peculiar loftiness is determined. Between these two
themes the stories of the discoveries and acquisitions of economic
and technical advances play a minor part. The concept of the
'culture-hero' introduced by ethnologists belongs to mythologies of a different quality to that of Greece, indeed it would be
violent to drag him into it. A culture-hero would be a hero
reduced to a single function, and the very humanity of the
Greek heroes refuses to endure any such reduction. Herakles,
if one wanted to emphasise the 'culture-hero' element in him,
would become at most a hunting hero, an enemy of wild
beasts, an Orion, though Orion too was something more than
that. The analysis of the deeds of Herakles is enough to show
us something different; it is only the late interpretation of them
which fits in with this simplification. Two of the great achieve-
ments that were necessary for human culture, corn and fire, are
accredited to gods and Titans, Demeter, Hermes, Prometheus;
the working of metals, to gods and primaeval beings sprung

from the earth—Hephaistos, the Daktyls and the Kabeiroi. Only the bringer of wine is a 'god-man', Dionysos, who it is true is the god-man among the gods.

The mythology of Greek heroes, although it is equally con-cerned with god-men and with foundations, is characterised by the fact that its emphasis, its peculiar stress, is laid on the side of the human and by no means on the importance of a foundation. In India, for instance, the divine is emphasised and exalted in a crude way, when this country's heroes, by measure-less development of power, allow the god who has taken human form to become manifest. For the heroic mythology of the Greeks nothing is more characteristic than that the divine element is taken for granted, and its epiphanies are the most natural thing in the world. The stress is laid rather on the human side in all its manifestations, not least in the burden of destiny and suffering which the heroes endure. With this manner of emphasising the human element, the mythology of the heroes takes a new direction from the very beginning, which characteristically leads into Tragedy. The legends of heroes lead us from the solemn, self-explanatory hero-cult to the Tragic stage, the place of ever new excitements produced by the old material. If we try to find a Greek expression for this particular material of mythology (for Greek has no word answering to Norse *saga* or German *Sage*), we have recourse to that used by Asklepiades of Trogilos, who in the time when tragic poetry in Athens was waning set it forth in a prose work and called his book *Tragodumena*, that is to say 'materials of Tragedy'. All these stories, even those which as it happens were never worked up by tragic poets, deserve this title; they were always potential tragedies.

In this material we have to do not only with little dramas whose archetypal scheme contains a necessary group of persons, as in the tales of the gods; fundamentally we always find a certain drama which deals with the destiny of the 'god-man', a drama with countless variations. Besides him there stand ready also other *dramatis personae*, who do not always make their

appearance, especially the mother of the god-man, who conceived him by a god, also the god's substitute, the hero's
earthly father, and often an inferior brother, even a twin. But
there is no rule for the tasks or the stages which he must pass
through or the exploits which he must accomplish in order to
be a hero. Destiny and development are not identical. Emerson
has uttered and Rilke has confirmed the truth about the hero in
the sentence already quoted, 'The hero is he who is immovably
centred.' We must continually recall this sentence to mind
when we occupy ourselves with the legends of heroes. The glory
of the divine rests upon the immovable in him, but is shadowed
by his destiny. He carries out the tasks apportioned to him by
fate by means of that immovable element, to which his cult
still bears witness in his death. It is the rarest of exceptions (as
in the case of Herakles) if he does not fall a victim to death; he
is always in contact with it, death belongs to his 'shape', and
the cult testifies to the last, destined turn of the hero-life, for it
is after all a cult of the dead.

The cult and the myth of the hero contain Tragedy in germ,
not only as regards its material, its formative principle and its
significance, but also in time. Attic Tragedy attaches itself to
the cult and the mythology of heroes. There is no break here,
no gulf between them. There is an unbroken continuity of
intellectual activity, which, with regard to the mythology of the
heroes, that hero-cult by narrative, may already be styled an act
of cult. Tragedy is no less an act of cult than the sacred proceedings of the worship of heroes. It is a great and solemn action
belonging to the cult of Dionysos, full of the sufferings of the
heroes. Thus there remains only this question: do the heroes
belong to Dionysos and Dionysos to them? The fixed connection between the cult and narrative in honour of the heroes
and the dramatic action which we call Tragedy, in honour of
Dionysos, is there and itself testifies to an aspect of the god
through which he answers our question. For he was the hero
among the gods. Thus the women of Elis invoked him with
'Come, hero Dionysos.'[10] If we were certain that in this context

'hero' signified merely 'lord', even so we should have to bestow our attention on the circumstance that the distinctive name with which, in Homer, men with no claim to a cult are addressed is here applied to a god in his worship, and withal to a god whose connections with the realm of the dead and with death itself are made certain, if only by the story of his birth. Whether he was born of Persephone, goddess of the under-world, or of the Theban princess Semele, while she was already burning with Zeus' lightnings,[11] it was a subterranean birth, or a birth in death. As the healing god Asklepios was taken from his mother Koronis on her funeral pyre by Apollo, so was Dionysos raised by Zeus from the deadly blaze. It is the story of birth in fire, of the birth of a god who comes from death and is touched by it. Asklepios also must die; his birth, how-ever, was one worthy of the god of healing. And Semele also was a *herois*, a heroine (so the festival at Delphi was called at which she was honoured with secret rites),[12] Dionysos had to bring her up from the underworld.[13] But he, too, died.

The birth of a god in the grave, even without the theme of burning, must have been a very old story, since it was told also of Perseus, the hero and founder of Mycenae, as his birth-legend. He was born in an underground room, a chamber of bronze, in which, as in a sepulchre, his mother had been imprisoned for ever. Thence the voice of the baby made itself heard in the court of the palace. The scene of the story is Argos, the royal castle opposite to Mycenae. For us, it gives life to the stone ring of graves in the Mycenaean citadel, as if the ancient narrators thought of the chamber of bronze as built there in the depths of the earth. But the death of Dionysos was attributed to Perseus. He killed him, it was said, in trying to exclude his worship, or so the tale is motivated later.[14] He threw the god into the deep waters of Lerna. However, the story of the enmity between Dionysos and Perseus is itself meant to provide a motive for something, namely the belief which was prevalent in the region round Mycenae and Argos that Dionysos had to do with the underworld, the entrance to which was

supposed to be at Lerna, a prehistoric town in the neighbourhood of those named. As at Elis, so here there was a festival at
which the god was summoned from the underworld. In Elis
the women's song bade the 'Heros Dionysos' rush on his bull's
foot into his temple. In Lerna, Dionysos was called upon as
Bugenes, the Son of the Bull.[15] He was summoned with a
trumpet-call, an unusual ceremony in Greece (all this comes
to us as an echo from an earlier world, surely that of Mycenae),
and a lamb for the Pylaochos, the 'Keeper of the Gate', was
sunk into the depths of the waters. The lord of the underworld,
otherwise known also as Hades, was called 'Keeper of the
Gate' or 'Closer of the Gate' (Pylartes). According to the
legend of the bringing up of Semele from the underworld,
Dionysos descended thither at Lerna to fetch up his mother; in
the story of Perseus, he was thrown in. But to whom did the
trumpet-call belong if not to someone whose home was there
and who waited for the summons to appear again among the
living?

If he was invoked as 'Heros', this also points to a like close
connection with the realm of the dead, and this is but to say the
least of it. The philosopher Herakleitos said something of
greater import. He found everywhere examples of the One
which reveals itself in opposites. He *takes* these examples, he
does not construct them, for how, in that case, could they be
examples which prove anything? From the visible world: 'The
sea is the purest water, and the impurest; to fish it is drinkable
and very salvation, but to men undrinkable and deadly.' 'The
road upwards and downwards is one and the same.' And from
the invisible world: 'Hades and Dionysos are the same.'[16] It is
the same lesson (a lesson for us, not for his contemporaries)
which art-monuments convey to us, above all that vase-painting
of the archaic master Xenokles, who tells us after his fashion
how Dionysos, *kantharos* in hand, welcomes, or takes his leave
of Persephone.[17] But archaic gravestones from the neighbourhood of Sparta let the secret out most clearly;[18] recently also a
large find of clay tablets[19] brings the same identity before our

eyes. The god sits on a throne, with the same wine-cup, the *kantharos*, in his hand, or else a pomegranate, which he has offered to Persephone to eat; the Queen of the Underworld sits beside him. Other signs, the serpent, the dog, the horse, once also the youthful-looking head, the offering which little human figures are bringing to the divine pair, all tell us unmistakably that his Hades and Dionysos in one person represents the 'Heros'. And more than this: one of the grave-stelae bears the name of the Spartan sage Chilon and shows us that the representation is not of *a* hero in general, but the recently buried dead heroised, and (this is the most important information) heroised as Dionysos.

It seems that Dionysos was once in Greece a lofty mark for theomorphism. It was not apotheosis in general without passing into a definite form which was sought after, but identity with this god, the husband of the Queen of the Underworld and the Lord of the realm of the dead. Probably this was to begin with a royal aspiration, not taken over by Homeric poetry which shut the door against Dionysos. It is to be assumed in the first place in regions where Dionysos was held to be king of the underworld, especially in the Peloponnesos, which was much less penetrated by the spirit of Homer than the island world or Athens. But even the most inconspicuous traces which this striving has left behind betray its meaning, for instance the vine-branches on which the Athenians laid their dead in their graves.[20] But some traces the custom has left behind whose similar meaning could easily escape us, namely the burial of wine-cups with the dead. To it we owe treasures of vase-paintings and in general the greater part of our knowledge of this art. Ancient sepulture, that limited kind of hero-cult, is full of the Dionysiac element until the latest times. Everything about it alludes to and conjures up the blessedness bestowed by the god after the unavoidable sufferings of life, which are merely increased by warlike deeds: by the god Dionysos, who had his share of suffering and death. He was the Heros among the gods, whom once the kings strove to follow. There was a song sung for him also, concerning the kid which as a sacrificial victim represented him in his passion.[21] That song was called *tragodia*, the Song on the occasion of the Young Buck-goat, and into it, into Tragedy, the sufferings of the heroes were introduced by bolder and bolder poets.

His myth, which originally included the destiny of all living things, plants, beasts and men, took on traits, in the Theban legend of his birth, which characterise the myth of the god-man. His epithet *Bugenes* at Lerna still indicates his descent from deities in bestial shape, and his Theban mother Semele still bears the name which designated the goddess of the under-world in Phrygia.[22] But she has now become merely a princess, the chosen bride of the king of the gods. We do her no wrong when we see in her an earthly maiden; she belongs to the lengthy series of mothers of heroes, beloved of gods, who take the foremost place yonder in the other world, as the 'Odyssey' describes it.[23] Genealogical poetry especially reckoned them up and glorified them one after another; 'or like her who . . .' thus the praise of each of them began, and the praises became a poetic *genre*. Odysseus, apart from the meeting with his own mother, seems to have wished to tell only of them. If he says nothing about Semele, it is an impressive silence, which admits of two opposed explanations. Either the poet excluded the god's mother as he did the god himself, or he shows by his silence the validity of that story according to which Dionysos did not long leave Semele in the underworld. According to the holy legend of Thebes, she conceived and bore the god in her father's house as a mortal mother who died in giving birth, and thus in Kadmos' palace the myth of gods passes into a hero-myth. There, in Dionysos, son of a mortal woman, the figure of the god-man, uniting divinity and mortality, showed clear for a moment.

But such were the births of heroes everywhere. A being of divine descent was born, though not in death like Semele's son, yet in the end for death, for the underworld, in order after-wards to be active from his grave and receive veneration at his grave. An inspection of the hero-legends of the Greeks which treats them as a mythology connected with hero-cult leads us unforcedly and consistently to the origin of Greek Tragedy. Nothing concerned Dionysos so closely as the destiny of a hero who passed through suffering and death into cult. The solution of the old problem presents itself almost obviously from the viewpoint set forth here, and at the same time guarantees its correctness. The viewpoint is won from the tradition, which is now to be set forth in detail, a start being made with the tale of Kadmos and Harmonia, for the myth of the gods passes into that of the heroes in Kadmos' palace not only through the legend of Dionysos' birth but also through the story of this divine pair. Kadmos and Harmonia had no hero-cult in Greece and their story is rather poor in human details; let it therefore be stated to begin with who they probably were.

They were accounted a hero and heroine, who, however, had found their place of rest not among Greeks but in distant Illyria. It was natural enough to tell of their transportation to the Islands of the Blessed, if only because their hero-tombs were nowhere honoured in Greece. Their metamorphosis into serpents would indeed be the obvious form of survival in cult for a hero and heroine, or else—this is the other possibility—in that shape they were connected still more closely with the underworld. And so, very probably, it happened. If they received no hero-cult, yet they had the cult of a pair belonging to the underworld in an even more solemn form. In the centre of their cult stood their wedding. This was celebrated on Samothrace in the mysteries. The other site of like mysteries was Thebes, and it is not easy to decide how far this cult on Theban soil was influenced from Samothrace and to what extent the mysteries of the Thracian island, testified to only by comparatively late buildings, took their form from Thebes. Three of the secret names of the gods of the mysteries, Axieros, Axiokersos and Axiokersa, are Greek, while the fourth, Kadmilos or Kasmilos, is a diminutive form of Kadmos. One of the two witnesses to whom our very succinct source appeals[24] is the historian Dionysodoros, most likely he of Boiotia, who could have information about the Theban divine names. In Thebes, apparently, the divine pair of the mysteries were paraphrased as Axiokersos and Axiokersa, 'those who are worthy of marriage',[25] and of these very names we are told that they meant Hades and Persephone. Many vases found in the Theban sanctuary of the mysteries relate to a marriage-festival, and we must not assume that in that Kabirion there was celebrated the marriage of other deities than on the island of the Kabeiroi, Samothrace. The shrine lay outside the city; but in the holy ruins of the palace of Kadmos, on the Theban citadel, the Kadmeia, there stood a very old statue of Dionysos Kadmos.[26] No other than he was the worthy bridegroom in Thebes; Dionysos and Hades in one person called Kadmos in the hero-legends, Axiokersos in the mysteries; and no other than Harmonia was the worthy bride, otherwise called Persephone. The tale about it, how they found one another and celebrated their marriage, is handed down to us, however, as a hero-legend.

Neither this nor any other unavoidable interpretation in what follows is intended as an end in itself, but only as a help for the reader to master the material, which is evasive, especially in the oldest stories, and reduced by its very age. The genealogical tables in the Appendix serve to give a general view. In them, as elsewhere, there will be found a certain selection among the traditional names, for only too often these have been invented by the genealogists or taken from petty local traditions. The references to the sources have—as in my *The Gods of the Greeks* —been numbered consecutively throughout. To avoid breaking up the text too much, however, the figures from 1001 to 1999, and again from 2001 on, have been divested of their thousands; to offset any confusion that might arise therefrom, each page of the sources list itself has the numbers of the relevant text pages superposed. In the case of texts which have already been retold in *The Gods of the Greeks*, the references to sources refer to that work. No page-references are given to *The Heroes of the Greeks* itself, since with the help of the Index, everything that has to do with one figure in several passages can readily be found. Specialists will see that my handling of the material includes criticism of the philological literature on the passages in question (including the interference with the text of Pindar, Nem. 3. 22); the general reader will not be disturbed thereby.

In this re-telling of the mythology of the Greek heroes, pictures have again served as sources alongside the written tradition. However, as a text in pictures, even though scattered throughout the book, they are never to be thought of as illustrations, but as variants.

It is important to remember that they stood alone on the vases, and related the myth in a medium other than language and without the help of words. No doubt they were individual variants, just as the *ductus*, the 'handwriting' of the painter could not remain without individuality. But it would be too one-sided to call them the painters' 'own invention'. For while treated from a different angle, they set forth the indispensable other condition of the material expressed in different medium. To particularise the place where this condition produced con-spicuous new traits, if and to what extent it was in a 'picture-book' that was there before the vases, and to what extent it was on the vases themselves—is a matter we must leave for a treat-ment of the painters and their works which shall go beyond the present state of our knowledge of vases, for the future science of vases in fact.

The present-day method of treating our growing treasure of such paintings we owe to the guidance already given us con-cerning the individuality of the painters, as revealed by their styles, and concerning the current state of the pictorial tradition; and especially to the following three works of classification: Sir John Beazley's *Attic Black-Figure Vase-Painters* (1956) and *Attic Red-Figure Vase-Painters* (1942), and Frank Brommer's *Vasenlisten zur griechischen Heldensage* (1956). The sources of the illustrations are given in the List of Plates at the be-ginning of the book (pp. xi–xviii) and use these three works of classification wherever they apply. It is only in the case of pictures which fall outside them that an independent source is given. Against these notes are also entered the pages of the text which tell the relevant story.

The author wishes to extend his special thanks to the museums whose reproductions have been placed at his disposal, as well as to the German Archaeological Institute in Rome.

BOOK ONE

CHAPTER I

Kadmos and Harmonia

THERE IS NO CITY IN GREECE, outside Mycenae, which had gathered together so many legends of heroes on its site and in its neighbourhood as Thebes, and no hero was so honoured of gods and men as Kadmos, after whom the citadel of Thebes was called Kadmeia. He belongs to the fifth genera⁄ tion of the primaeval kings, the founders of countries and cities, who were sprung from the marriage of Zeus in bull⁄ shape, with Io in the form of a cow.[27] The many threads which connected him with the gods were admiringly reckoned.[28] His great⁄grandfather was Zeus, Poseidon his grandfather, Ares and Aphrodite his wife's parents. His daughter Semele became the mother of Dionysos and ascended with her son to heaven.[29] Another of his daughters, Ino, also became a goddess, turning into Leukothea, the 'white goddess'. Besides Dionysos, Kadmos had likewise, in her son Palaimon, otherwise named Meli⁄ kertes, a divine child as grandson. Both children found their way into the tales of the gods.

All this results in a vast web of genealogical tales surround⁄ ing Kadmos. They were doubtless the work of Theban genealogists, who wished to secure for him this prominent position in the world of the gods ruled over by Zeus. He was made out to be descended from a race in which Zeus had twice celebrated his marriage in bull⁄shape, the first time with Io. She was, as we know from the legends of the gods, the daughter of Inachos, the river⁄god of Argos. Hence she originated from the district in which Mycenae and the other strongholds of the Argive land were to arise. Driven from place to place in the shape of a cow, she fled from her father's river to the Nile, and there bore Epaphos to Zeus; Epaphos became the ancestor of that line concerning which there will be some⁄ thing to say in the story of Danaos and his daughters. The genealogists included Kadmos also in this line. He is said to have reached Boiotia on the track of a cow and founded the town of Thebes there. Beautiful Europa likewise was a member of that same line; Zeus in the shape of a bull carried her off to Crete in the well-known tradition, but to Boiotia in the less familiar one.

Whether wandering on her track or on that of an ordinary cow, Kadmos appears in this fabric of two bull-marriages, which is nothing else than the story preliminary to the birth of Dionysos, the god in bull-form who was worshipped as Son of the Bull, as a herdsman. But Kadmos appears thus also in the story of the Titans.[30] In those days, the lordship of Zeus over the world of the gods was as yet nowise assured. The dragon Typhoeus had cut out his sinews and hidden them in a cave. In this tale Kadmos appears as a herd-boy. He charmed the dragon with his herdsman's pipe, and thus got back the sinews and gave them to Zeus again. This affair took place in Kilikia, in the eastern land, wherein according to the genealogy, Kadmos' brother Kilix was supposed to be reigning.

A herdsman of primaeval times, on the track of a cow which yet was no ordinary cow but the bride of a god and carrying the emblem of the moon—thus the form of Kadmos arises from the east, and in his house in Thebes, Dionysos was to be born. It remains obscure—probably it was kept secret— whether he himself begot a divine child. In the circle of the Kabeiroi, who had their secret worship on the island of Samo-thrace, but also in Thebes, one of the gods was called Kad-milos, that is to say 'little Kadmos'. He was no other than Hermes in that shape in which the Athenians often repre-sented him, in agreement with the sacred legend of the Samo-thracian mysteries, namely as an ithyphallic herm.[31] Why was this Hermes styled 'little Kadmos', if he was not Kadmos' divine son? Even in late times the very intimate associations of the messenger of the gods with the first king of Thebes were still known, though it is true that it was said then that Hermes' relation to Kadmos was the same as Apollo's to Hyakinthos.[32]

The story of Kadmos' journeyings embraced many countries.

Agenor, who was made out to be his father, a great-grandson of Io and according to his name a 'leader of men', was sovran of Phoenicia.[33] His sons were called Kadmos, Phoinix and Kilix, and his daughter, Europa. According to the older narrators, she was rather the daughter of Phoinix,[34] and Kadmos was perhaps her brother in this case also. After the abduction of Europa, her father sent out his sons to look for his stolen daughter. They were not to return home until they had found their sister again. In this way the wanderings of Kadmos began. He was the only one and the real one who took the search for the girl seriously. Of Kilix we are told that he turned back to become king of Kilikia, country near to Phoe-nicia, to which Phoinix gave his name.

Kadmos journeyed further and reached the country of the Thracians. Concerning this part of his wanderings the tale was told principally on the island of Samothrace, where the same language was spoken as in Thrace. According to some he gave up the search for Europa here, according to others he found here another Europa.[35] How this is to be understood we are not told, but in the Thracian stories Kadmos was known by no means as a lonely wanderer, for he is supposed to have taken his mother with him on his quest. She bore the lunar name Telephassa or Telephae, 'she who illuminates afar', or Argiope, 'she of the white face'. Here another brother of Kadmos appears, Thasos, who gave his name to the island adjacent to Samothrace.[36] It is the picture of a mother with two sons, which appears in these stories as if it hovered over the coastal and island landscape of the Thracian Sea.

On Samothrace the three had other names as well.[37] The mother was called Elektra or Elektryone there; her sons bore the names Dardanos and Eetion or Iasion. Between these brothers, however, there stood as a third figure not only their mother; they had a sister, Elektra having a daughter, as Telephassa had Europa. This daughter was Harmonia, Kadmos' destined bride. According to the Samothracians she was begotten of Zeus; and as Zeus carried off Europa, so

Kadmos did Harmonia. Perhaps that is why it was said that he found another Europa on Samothrace. Elektra sought for her daughter, as Demeter did for Persephone and as Tele/ phassa in company with Kadmos sought for Europa. So Kadmos, who had gone forth to look for his sister, found his bride on Samothrace.

It was also said that the first marriage on earth in which the gods took part and to which they brought their gifts was celebrated here, on the island of the mysteries.[38] There was even a tale of how the love began;[39] Kadmos had had himself initiated into the mysteries and during the celebration caught sight of Harmonia among the young women. This is a pretty tale, but certainly not a very old one, and it is the model, if it is not the imitation, of one still better known. Philip of Macedon in like manner saw the young Olympias for the first time at the Samothracian mysteries, and she was the future mother of Alexander the Great. It was not till after his marriage with Harmonia on Samothrace that Kadmos received the oracle from Delphi which sent him further on to accomplish his exploit as a founder in Boiotia.[40]

But there was another account,[41] and with it we pass into the sequence of those tales in which Thrace plays no part or no large one; Kadmos was not accompanied by his mother on his search,[42] but by an armed band.[43] With his followers he marched through the lands and on his way consulted the oracle of Delphi. The answer is transmitted to us actually in verse, and it allegedly ran somewhat thus:[44]

'Kadmos, Agenor's son, heed thou my words.
Rise with the dawn, go forth from noble Pytho
In common dress, bearing a hunter's spear,
Through Phlegyan land and Phokis, till thou reach
Herdsman and herd of Pelagon, born to death.
Meet him, and of the lowing kine take one
That hath on either flank a moon/like orb;
Make her thy guide upon the beaten path.

A clear sign I will tell thee, thou shalt know it;
Where first that hornèd beast that dwells in field
Shall kneel her down upon the grassy ground,
There make thou sacrifice to dark-leaved Earth
Cleanly and holily. Thine offering made,
Found on the hill a town of spacious streets,
First sending Ares' dreadful guard to death.
So shall thy name be known of men to come,
Thy consort be a goddess, blessèd Kadmos.'

It is not to be alleged of this oracle that it is very old, but still
the verses were composed assuredly on the basis of an ancient
tale. Kadmos found the cow with the lunar emblem which he
was looking for in the possession of a herdsman born of clay
(his name, Pelagon, was apparently understood as equivalent
to *pēlogonos*, 'sprung from clay or mud'),[45] and bought it from
him. The country into which the cow led him[46] was then
named Cowland (Boiotia).[47] The beast let itself be driven
through the whole land, and where it dropped from weariness,
it lay down on its right side. This also was a predicted sign.
Thereupon Kadmos made his offering ready. He sent out
some of his following to look for a spring, since water was one
of the necessaries for a sacrifice.[48] But the men he sent did not
return; they had been killed by the dragon which guarded the
fountain, for there was one in the neighbourhood, known as
Areia, 'spring of Ares'. This formidable serpent had its
dwelling over it in a cave; it was the offspring of the war-
god,[49] to whom belonged the hill on which the Kadmeia, the
acropolis of the future Thebes, was to rise.

So Kadmos was confronted with the deed which only he
could accomplish, whether he really came from abroad or, as
some would have it,[50] was the son of a native primaeval man,
Ogygos the child of Earth,[51] whom the genealogists then made
out to have for his father the hero of the country, Boiotos.[52]
There he stood, on ground for which no people had as yet
arisen before his deed in founding the city—at the beginning

of the world, as it were, in primaeval loneliness. For he must perform his feat quite alone. Like a god, on the earth which was unpopulated and dwelt in only by some few primaeval men, he went to meet the dragon. Pelagon, 'born to death', in whose possession he had found the lunar cow, was also a primaeval man, born from clay, whose existence had indeed modified the loneliness of the primitive conditions but not altered it essentially. As a lonely traveller, not like a hero accompanied by a company of heroes, is how the oracle also represents Kadmos, his only weapon being a hunting-spear.

However, he accomplished the deed quite in the manner of primaeval conditions, when there were no weapons as yet; Kadmos slaughtered the serpent with a stone.[53] There were some narrators[54] and some vase-painters who could not imagine him without his sword in his hand, but Assteas of Paestum painted him naked, with his traveller's cloak on his back and a little pointed cap. He holds two hunting-spears in his left hand, but makes no use of them; he is hurling the stone with his right hand against the gigantic serpent. Stones will play a part in the continuation of the story also. Most painters and poets, not seeing the divine element in Kadmos himself, were agreed that goddesses and gods supported him in accomplishing his deed. Athene, they tell us, helped him[55] and advised him to use the dragon's teeth for seed; she even sowed them for him.[56] All this happened, some believed, according to the will and plan of Ares.[57]

And indeed the outcome of this extraordinary affair in no way contradicted the war-god's meaning. From the dragon-seed there sprung armed warriors, five or more, a whole threatening host for the lone Kadmos who had called them into being. But they did not notice him, for being just born from the earth they had hardly yet opened their eyes. The hero then cast stones at them, and the warriors thought they were attacked by one another. Fighting broke out and they killed each other, only five remaining alive, Udaios (man of the ground), Chthonios (man of the earth), Pelor (giant),

Hyperenor (more than man), and Echion (serpent-man). They were collectively known as the Spartoi, i.e. 'sown men', and famed as the 'golden-helmed seed'.[58] Their descendants, the ruling family of the Thebans, still designated themselves as earth-born and bore a spear on their bodies as a birthmark.[59]

Thus the unarmed man created the kernel of an armoured and armed people of warriors. But his action as founder, the founding of a world on the hills of Thebes, where the dragon bore rule no longer, was completed by his marriage with Harmonia, daughter of Ares and Aphrodite. This is clear, not from the name Kadmos, as if we must catch from it an echo of the word *kosmos*, Greek for the ordered universe, but from the name of the bride, Harmonia, and from the wedding itself, which followed at once. Only those who would tell the foundation-legend completely in the spirit of the god of Delphi made out that Kadmos must first serve Ares for a great year (eight ordinary years) by way of penance, as Apollo likewise had to atone for his killing of a dragon.[60] Harmonia, as her name implies, was harmony itself, the Uniter, a second Aphrodite and at the same time daughter of the god of war. And she united herself to Kadmos as no other goddess, certainly not the great love-goddess, ever did to any hero. Only the marriage of Dionysos, the hero among the gods, with Ariadne when she was already called Aphrodite Ariadne, could be compared to this union. True, the Samothracians named Zeus and Elektra as the parents of Harmonia, and perhaps that was even what the Thebans really thought, since one of the seven gates of their city was named after Elektra.[61] But who knows if Aphrodite also was not meant by Elektra daughter of Atlas, and therefore a younger Aphrodite was no less signified by Harmonia? The two names and the two traditions were also reconciled in a tale[62] to the effect that Kadmos brought Harmonia with him from Samothrace, from the house of Elektra, for Elektra had taken over Aphrodite's daughter, the fruit of her notorious *affaire* with Ares,[63] to bring her up. The Thebans also knew a story according to which Harmonia knew a great deal about matters which had happened among the barbarians, as if she were one of the princesses come into Greece from distant parts, like Medeia in Corinth.[64]

All the gods came to her wedding,[65] leaving their heavenly abodes for her sake, and the Muses honoured the bridal pair with their singing;[66] it was such a festival as seldom happened in the legends of the heroes. A second time was a marriage on earth thus celebrated, when Thetis wedded Peleus, again a goddess with a hero. Zeus, on this occasion, it is said, feasted at the same table as the fortunate Kadmos.[67] In the wedding procession the pair were brought in by a remarkable team, as can be seen on an old vase-painting; a boar and a lion were yoked to their carriage. King Pelias later wanted the same for his daughter Alkestis, and Apollo helped Admetos to harness the beasts, who agreed so ill with each other.[68] Such a combination was suitable to the wedding procession of Harmonia, the Uniter. Apollo, who contrived it, walked in beside the carriage. And the Muses sang; we are often told what they sang then,[69] 'What is fair is ever dear'—'A thing of beauty is a joy for ever', a poet translated it after more than two thousand years. Kadmos' victory was a fair deed, but fairer still was the bride, fair-haired Harmonia with the eyes of a heifer.[70]

It was known also what wedding presents the gods brought her,[71] also what Kadmos gave his bride,[72] the gift that was to prove fatal to later generations. One wedding-present was a *peplos*, a sort of cloak; another was a necklace, presented to Kadmos by Aphrodite and wrought by Hephaistos,[73] the corresponding piece to the wedding gift which Europa received from Zeus.[74] This also was a token of the incomparably high rank of the marriage, although no pure good fortune came of it. Where Dionysos is near, Tragedy is near also. Four daughters and one son were born to Kadmos and Harmonia; of these, Semele was to be smitten by the lightning of Zeus,[75] Agaue in horrible madness to tear her own son to pieces,[76] Autonoe one day to gather up the bones of her son

Aktaion,[77] and Ino to venture to leap into the sea with her son Palaimon.[78] The palace of Kadmos was destroyed when Semele burned, before he and Harmonia disappeared. The kingship of Thebes fell to his only son, Polydoros, 'him of the many gifts',[79] and the line was continued through that ill-starred succession, Labdakos, Laios, Oidipus.

The story was told[80] that Kadmos and Harmonia left Thebes on a carriage drawn by calves—a divine pair about whom it cannot be known when they turned into snakes. Did this transformation, worthy of true deities of the underworld, already happen in Thebes, before they set out on their journey to the north-west,[81] or was it not till they reached the Illyrians, over whom they ruled and whom they were to lead against the Greeks as far as Delphi? Long after, the Illyrian tribe of the Encheleis still carried snakes as their standards, and this custom may have been connected with the account of the sovranty of Kadmos and Harmonia over those tribes of the northern Balkan peninsula. Allegedly, they reached the Adriatic on their team of cows at the point where the little harbour town of Budva now stands (it was formerly called Buthoe,[82] in commemoration of the 'swift cows' of the Theban king and queen). There was also a son born to them there, Illyrios, who gave his name to the Illyrians, of whom the story was told that a snake cherished him in its coils and made him strong.[83]

In Illyria also, the graves of Kadmos and Harmonia were shown, and two serpent-shaped stones[84] which were supposedly their memorials. But it was also said that they quitted the earth. Zeus, or—according to those who put the war-god, as Aphrodite's husband, in the foreground—Ares,[85] transported them to the Islands of the Blessed,[86] not Kadmos alone, but Harmonia as well, both in serpent-form.[87] Like the well-known divine pair on the Spartan gravestones (a pair composed of Dionysos, as hero and king of the underworld, and his consort), they doubtless sit enthroned among the dead, but to the living there appears a pair of snakes.

CHAPTER II

The Theban Dioskuroi

THE MARRIAGES OF ZEUS made beauty, order and memory rule in this world. His marriage with Eurynome, a daughter of Okeanos and Tethys, established the rule of beauty, for the Charities were the offspring of this union. His wedding with Themis, the law of nature, a great goddess, who bore Zeus the three Horai, the queens of ripeness and right times, made strong the regularities which form the natural order of the world. His union with Mnemosyne, who pre-sented him with the nine Muses, increased memory by the arts of her nine daughters. Since the wedding of Zeus with Hera, heaven has ruled over us men and in that rule a god and a goddess take part as man and wife. The first marriage on earth, the model for the rest, was that of Kadmos and Harmonia. The sons of Heaven came to Harmonia's bridal. String music, the notes of Amphion's lyre, first made the walls of Thebes, the city between the two rivers, arise.[88]

The Thebans, and not they alone of the Greeks, knew many tales concerning divine twins,[89] of brothers who were unlike or even hostile. I would merely touch upon the Theban tale of Melia and her two brothers before telling the story of the twins Amphion and Zethos. Melia, as her name implies, was a nymph of the manna-ash, like the mothers and wives of the first men,[90] a being sprung from the earth,[91] but also the goddess of a spring and reckoned a daughter of Okeanos.[92] She had two brothers, Ismenos, which is the name of one of the two rivers of Thebes, and Kaaithos or Kaanthos, a very old-fashioned name, the proper form of which the tellers no longer knew. Both were sons of Okeanos. Through them, fratricide came into the world, for they quarrelled over their sister.[93] Ismenos seems to have been her favourite,[94] and there-fore his brother killed him. The story is also told thus:[95]

Apollo, who had the surname Ismenios, carried Melia off, and Kaanthos, like Kadmos, was sent by his father to look for his sister. Then, when he found her in the god's possession, he set fire to Apollo's shrine, the Ismenion. Melia bore Teneros the prophet, after whom the plain was named on which the Thebans' temple of the Kabeiroi stood.

This was a trio like that on Samothrace, the island of the Kabeiroi, two brothers with a sister, with the nymph of the manna-ash, the primaeval woman, over whom they both strove, who was carried off and sought for, and who was the cause of fratricide or, in the later form of the tale, of the burning of a temple. But in the hero-mythology of the Thebans there was yet another pair of brothers, two young heroes with their mother. Antiope, daughter of Asopos, one of the river-gods of Boiotia, could boast that she had lain in the arms of Zeus. She bore him twins, Amphion and Zethos, who were to found the seven-gated city, for 'without walls they could not dwell in Thebes of the wide dancing-places, strong though they were'.[96] According to the story alluded to in these words of the 'Odyssey', the city must have been an unfortified place around the Kadmeia, the former palace of Kadmos, as the inhabited places were in Crete around the palaces of Knossos or Phaistos in the days of king Minos.

The beauty of Antiope was famous;[97] it was the beauty of the moon when she looks upon us with her full face, for that is what her name means. The sun-god's consort at Corinth bore the same name.[98] If the story speaks of an earthly father of Antiope, at least it gives him the name Nykteus, 'he of the night'. In a late and purely human tale it was not Zeus who was her lover, seducing her, it was said, in the shape of a satyr,[99] but a king named Epopeus,[100] which signifies the sky-god looking down on us; for the Corinthians, who called their lofty citadel Epope,[101] this was Helios, but elsewhere it meant Zeus. It was no mortal woman who brought the King of Heaven the Theban Dioskuroi, the sons of Zeus, as Leda did Kastor and Polydeukes in Sparta,[102] two riders on white colts.[103] Amphion and Zethos were born in a cave on Kithairon, on the Attic side of the mountain, between the places called Oinoe and Eleutherai. Their mother left them there.[104] A spring issued from in front of the cave, and there a herdsman bathed the divine twins. They did not find their mother again till they were young men. This is how the story was put on the stage by Euripides, in a famous tragedy entitled 'Antiope'.[105]

It has not come down to us complete, but we can still reproduce its contents. It began with the story told by that herdsman to whom Antiope had entrusted the twins on Kithairon. In the tragedy she was the daughter of King Nykteus, who bore rule in Thebes after the death of Pentheus, the grandson of Kadmos, who was torn in pieces. Being with child by Zeus, Antiope had to flee from her father. She wandered over Kithairon until she came to Sikyon on the far shore of the Corinthian Gulf. There Epopeus was king, and in him Antiope found a protecting husband. Nykteus in his fury took his own life, after laying on his brother and successor, Lykos, the 'Wolf', the task of bringing Antiope back. Lykos captured Sikyon, killed Epopeus and took his niece prisoner. Antiope had to return over Kithairon, the mountain of the Kadmeian maenads, where perhaps also Zeus had met her in satyr-shape, as a slave, to the land over which Lykos ruled. On the way, she bore her sons by night in that cave, and handed them over to the shepherd.

In the tragedy, the herdsman told this tale in front of the very cave, in which the twins had grown to young manhood. He had not yet dared to tell them all, seeing that he tended the herds of the king, under whose wife, the imperious Dirke, Antiope now lived the life of a slave. Now Amphion entered, holding the lyre which Hermes, son of Maia and half-brother of the divine twins, had invented and given him. He proceeded to sing of Heaven and of Earth, the universal mother,[106] for that radiant youth lived only for song. Zethos was of a different disposition. He returned from hunting and rebuked his brother for his idleness. Each spoke in praise of his own way of life, Zethos for that of warfare and activity, Amphion for that of music and contemplation. They were dissimilar brothers, these divine twins, although not hostile like those who quarrelled over their sister. The sage, gentle Amphion was here again the one ready to yield, and he followed his brother to the hunt.[107] But on that day Antiope had escaped from her servitude while her mistress, Dirke, was gone with the Kadmeian women into the hills as a maenad to worship Dionysos.

The fugitive met the glorious youths before the cave. She recognised them as the sons whom she had borne to Zeus and addressed them as their mother.[108] It was in vain; the twins could not recognise the bride of Zeus in this tormented woman, and Zethos repulsed her when she wished to seek refuge in the sheltering cave. For Dirke was entering with the rout of maenads,[109] probably to get a bull from the herdsman to sacrifice to Dionysos. There she met her escaped slave, and in her rage ordered the young men to bind Antiope to the bull dragging her with her own hands to the place where she hoped to find the beast. At this moment the old herdsman came running up. He stopped the twins, who were hesitating, undecided (probably only Zethos had taken part in the foregoing scene), and testified that Antiope was really their mother. The brothers ran after the women, freed Antiope, caught Dirke and bound her to the bull. The queen was consequently dragged to death. Lykos too was overthrown; with the help of the herdsman they enticed him into the cave and would have killed him there if Hermes had not bidden them stop. He brought the commands of the Father; the sovranty belonged to the sons of Zeus, and Lykos was to hand it over to them voluntarily, to burn Dirke and strew her ashes into the spring of Ares. From then on the spring and the brook, which beyond all others furnished Thebes with pure water, were called Dirke.

Zethos was to be protector of the city and Amphion to

hymn the gods. His lyre-playing and his song set the stones in motion, also the trees, which left their ground and offered themselves to the carpenters. Hermes foretold it, and it was said that Thebes originated as a fortified place thus; the moving stones arranged themselves at the notes of the lyre into a wall with seven gates—seven, probably because Amphion's lyre already had seven strings.[110] That was the harmony in this foundation, which also led to the creation of a cosmos. But Amphion's further destiny was less in accord-ance with it.

For he took to wife Niobe, most beautiful of brides, a daughter of Tantalos, king of Lydia, as Hermes foretold; and we all know[111] what ill-fortune befell Amphion through her. The daughters whom Niobe bore him were killed by Artemis, the sons by Apollo. One of the daughters was again called Melia,[112] and as Kaanthos became an enemy to Apollo because of that Melia of whom we spoke at the beginning, so it was with Amphion too. From anger and revenge for the children who had been shot down he tried to storm the god's temple, and was slain by Apollo.[113] He and Zethos were buried in one tomb,[114] though both brothers were reckoned immortal divine riders. From the Thebans they had the cult of heroes, not of gods.

Antiope did not remain on Theban soil. Being a goddess, she ruled a wider region. Perhaps she had originally been a wandering divine woman, like Io or Europa. It was thought therefore that Dionysos had driven her mad and punished her with wanderings, because Dirke was trying to do him honour when she met her death on account of Antiope. It was also told[115] that in Phokis, the hero Phokos, after whom the region was named, met her in her wanderings, cured her of madness, and took her to wife. The common tomb of Antiope and Phokos was shown near the town of Tithoreia in Phokis.[116] When the sun entered the sign of the Bull, the Tithoreians always used to steal earth from the grave of the sons of Antiope and strew it on the grave of their mother, a custom which proved the connection of Antiope with a divine bull, whether Zeus or Dionysos, even after her death. The Tithoreians believed that if they were successful in their theft, their land would be blessed with fruitfulness that year more than the land of the Thebans.

CHAPTER III

Danaos and his Daughters

THE TALES OF HEROES and their woes which have Thebes for their scene are very far from being ended yet, but we must now begin with stories which are staged in other cities and districts, especially in Argos. These too begin with Io, and also with names such as Melia and Niobe. Melia, the nymph of the manna-ash, appears in Argos connected with Inachos the river-god, father of Io. To this pair was born the primaeval man Phoroneus,[117] with whom, in one connection or another, Niobe the primaeval woman herself was associated. It is not told of Io that she was the daughter of Melia and not of Inachos only. She was supposed then to be the great-grand-mother of Agenor and Belos, the two sons of Poseidon and Libye, after whom the African district of the same name was called. At the beginning of these tales the narrator stands with one foot on the plain underneath the towering citadel of the country and city of Argos, the Larissa, where the Inachos flows, and the other far away, where the Nile (also called Aigyptos in earlier times) comes up from the south and empties into the Mediterranean.

Once more we find twins and brothers unlike each other as the subject of the story;[118] Danaos and Aigyptos, the sons of Belos, whose name reproduces the Phoenician Ba'al, 'Lord'. The Greeks, or at least some of them, were called Danaoi in old days, and that is the plural of Danaos. Melia is named among others as the wife of this Danaos. She was a daughter of Agenor.[119] One tradition made the twins Danaos and Aigyptos the immediate descendants of Io.[120] The river-god Inachos of Argos, the wandering Io, the nymph of the manna-ash, Melia, the primaeval woman Niobe and the representa-tives of peoples and countries have been put together into a genealogy. The unlikeness of Danaos and Aigyptos consisted

I KADMOS KILLS THE DRAGON

2 SCENE IN THE UNDERWORLD;
THE SOULS OF THE UNFULFILLED BUSIED IN
FILLING A BOTTOMLESS VESSEL

in this, that the one had only daughters, the other none but sons; Aigyptos fifty sons, Danaos fifty daughters. Belos had divided his kingdom so that Danaos got the western half, Libye, Aigyptos originally the eastern, Arabia.[121] Then the brothers fought with one another and we are told that Danaos with his daughters was afraid of the sons of Aigyptos. So he built the first fifty-oared ship[122] and fled with his band of daughters to their common land of origin on the banks of the Inachos.

Those fifty were no ordinary girls. In one description[123] they appear as beings whose voices were not female, who practised sports with war-chariots and sometimes hunted in the sunny woods, sometimes gathered dates, cinnamon and incense. They had already armed themselves for battle against their cousins, the sons of Aigyptos, who desired them as wives.[124] Or did they merely fit out the ship, which they alone had to row? It is a picture of fifty Amazons, although they are never so called, fifty warlike, man-hating women, such as those were who bore the name of Amazons and were to fight against Herakles and Theseus in their day. Their number reproduces the fifty months of a four-year festival cycle, half a 'great year'. The second half of it had only forty-nine months, as also forty-nine of the daughters of Danaos remained true Danaids. Their victory over their suitors and persecutors involved a horrible deed only here on earth; in heaven the successive moons triumphed over the darkness of night without spilling blood.

In Argos, the name of which signifies 'the bright land', the young women finally arrived with their ship, fleeing before the dark sons of Aigyptos. Their arrival and its immediate consequences were put on the stage by Aeschylus in his tragedy 'The Suppliants'. According to him,[125] the then king of the plain of Inachos was Pelasgos, a son of the earth-born Palaichthon, the hero 'Ancient Earth'. He and the inhabitants of Argos were prepared to protect the Danaids and their father against the pursuing Aigyptiads. According to others,[126] Danaos demanded of king Gelanor the return to himself of the kingship of Argos, since he was the descendant of Inachos, the river and primaeval king. On the day on which the people were to decide concerning his demand, a wolf attacked the leading bull of the herds of Argive cattle, fought with it and defeated it. So the people saw in the bull their own king, in the wolf the stranger, and accepted the decision of the gods. Danaos received the sovranty and by way of thanksgiving founded a temple to Apollo Lykios, Apollo of the Wolves. Ostensibly, he did not deny his daughters to the pursuing sons of Aigyptos, but apportioned the fifty to their fifty cousins. This was the ultimate result in Aeschylus also, though at the end of 'The Suppliants' the Egyptians are still rejected. But the Danaids with their father contrived a horrible ruse. Danaos gave every maiden a dagger;[127] the bridal night came and forty-nine brides murdered each her bridegroom. The heads of the murdered men were cut off and cast into the deep water of Lerna, which ever since then has sprung from as many heads.

Hypermestra, the only one who was softened by the proximity of a young man, fell in love with him and did not assassinate him, and so became by her husband Lynkeus the ancestress of great heroes, Perseus and Herakles. But by that very act she showed herself faithless to her father and sisters. Danaos cast her into prison the next morning and had her brought to trial.[128] Aeschylus' 'Danaids' was devoted to her hearing. Not much more is preserved of this tragedy than of the 'Egyptians', the gloomy second member of the trilogy, in which the horrible deed was done. In the 'Danaids', then, Hypermestra appeared as an offender against her sisters and her father, but Aphrodite in person came before the court and informed all who were to judge the case of her universal power. Pure Heaven, she said in effect,[129] longs to fill Earth with love, Earth is seized with desire for love, the rain from Heaven makes her fruitful and thus she brings forth the plants and animals by which men are nourished. This is the great eternal example which the love-goddess brought forward on Hypermestra's behalf. The young man she had saved had already

taken refuge in the neighbouring village of Lyrkeia at dawn of
day; his name was really Lyrkeus, not Lynkeus like the sharp-
sighted son of Aphareus, of whom we shall hear later. He
made fire-signals from Lyrkeia,[130] and his loving Hypermestra,
now free, answered them from the lofty citadel of Larissa.
Thus Lyrkeus became king of Argos after Danaos.

It is also said that Athene and Hermes, by command of
Zeus, purified the remaining Danaids from the taint of
murder,[131] and that their father Danaos himself thereupon put
them, or more correctly only forty-nine of them, at the finish of
a racetrack,[132] as prizes for the runners. Before high noon he
had a son-in-law for each of them. Or, were they all (except
Hypermestra and another of whom we shall speak shortly) put
to death by the one survivor of the brothers?[133] This also was
alleged, and their forms, in the artists' pictures of the other
world, entered the House of Hades as examples of the eternally
unfulfilled, of those who never reached the *telos*, the com-
pletion, whether that be consummation of marriage or initiation. In the underworld they everlastingly carried water in
broken jars, or they poured it into a jar with no bottom. The
'Danaids' jugs' which are never full, passed into a proverb.[134]

There remains only the fate of that Daniad who bore the
name Amymone, 'the Blameless'. Aeschylus made her the
heroine of a satyr-play which ended the tetralogy that began
with the 'Suppliants'. As the tale is told us in this merry piece,
it seems as if the bloody deed of the Danaids never took place,
or at least as if Amymone could have had no part in it. Danaos
had just arrived with his daughter at Lerna, on the Gulf of
Argos, at the spot now known as Myli from its water-mills,[135]
and her father sent Amymone out to get water for the sacrifice
which he meant to offer. At that time Poseidon was still angry
because Inachos, when he and Hera disputed the possession
of the land, had adjudged it by his verdict to the queen of the
gods.[136] She, after all, had been the sovran of that district ever
since the days of Phoroneus the primaeval man, who had been
the first to do her honour, and so she remained, ruling from her

famous shrine in the neighbourhood of the city of Argos, between Tiryns and Mycenae. Poseidon had to give way here as he did in Attica also, in competition with Pallas Athene. And as he was therefore angry, a spring was hard to find. Amymone fell asleep from weariness, so the story is told in the style of the Pompeian paintings, and was caught sight of by a prying satyr. Or, if it was desired to show her more like an Amazon, she threw her hunting-spear at a buck and hit a sleeping satyr.[137] Being hurt, he attacked her. So, whether she hurt him or was taken merely by surprise, the girl screamed for help, and Poseidon hurried up. He threw his trident at the satyr and became the real and victorious bridegroom of the Danaid. She bore him Nauplios, founder of the harbour-town Nauplia, which still stands opposite Lerna.[138] The god bestowed a splendid morning-gift on the young wife, the future water-nymph. She herself was allowed to pull the trident out of the rock, and in that place there sprang forth the triple fountain Amymone, the most beautiful of the countless springs of Lerna. An ancient poem said:[139] 'Argos was waterless, the daughters of Danaos made Argos abound in waters.'

CHAPTER IV

Perseus

THERE WAS A VERY OLD STORY which told of a girl
of the Danaoi and named her simply Danae accordingly;
originally the daughters of Danaos were also called Danaai,
that is Danaan girls or women, and that is the plural of Danae.
But this was *the* Danaan girl, the chosen of all Danaan women,
their most perfect representative, so perfect that she could
become the earthly bride of Zeus and the mother of the hero-
founder of Mycenae. The story begins with the account of her
father and his brother, the grandsons of the Danaid Hypermestra and Lyrkeus.

It is the tale of twin brothers who were enemies,[140] Akrisios
and Proitos. They were to have ruled jointly over Argos, but
quarrelled with one another even in their mother's womb. They
had hardly grown to manhood when they fought for the kingship. On the road from Argos to Epidauros there stood a
pyramid decorated with shields, a gigantic tomb,[141] the monument of the famous war between the brothers, during which, it
was said, the round shield was first invented. According to
one tradition, the battle which was fought there remained undecided,[142] and therefore the kingdom was divided between
the two brothers; Akrisios bore sway in Argos, Proitos in
Tiryns, the neighbouring castle with its fortifications made by
the Kyklopes. According to another tradition,[143] Proitos was
defeated and emigrated to Asia Minor, where he took to wife
the daughter of the king of Lykia, that Anteia or Stheneboia
who was to become notorious through her love for the hero
Bellerophontes, and with the help of his father-in-law he came
back. From there, it is said, came also the seven Kyklopes, who
built the indestructible walls.[144] The story of the three daughters
of Proitos who would not honour Dionysos and so were
driven mad by the god has been told among the tales of the

45

gods.[145] But his son Megapenthes seems to have played a part like that of Dionysos' Theban persecutor Pentheus. The allegation that Proitos was the real father of Danae's son, that the uncle seduced his own niece,[146] we may neglect. Against it stands the tale of the loves of Zeus and of Akrisios' only daughter, Danae.[147]

Akrisios, king of Argos, had but this one child born to him; therefore he inquired of the oracle of Delphi how he might have a son. The god replied that he should never have a son, but that his daughter would, and that his daughter's son would be his bane. Returning from Delphi, Akrisios caused a chamber of bronze to be made in the court of his palace, subterranean like a tomb. Into this he shut his daughter with her nurse. Danae must bid farewell to the light of heaven.[148] She was buried for ever in darkness, in order that she might bear no son. Meanwhile it was the King of the gods himself who desired the Danaan maid; Zeus, changed to a golden rain, poured through the roof of the subterranean chamber. The maid caught it in her garment, and from the rain came forth the King of Heaven. The tomb became a marriage chamber, and a son of Zeus was born.

That is the tale of the conception of Perseus. Danae bore her child and fed it with the help of the nurse secretly. As to what happened after the birth, there is no agreement between the narrators, the dramatists and the vase-painters who continued the story. According to some, Perseus was perhaps some three or four years old when king Akrisios, overhead in the hall of his palace, heard the voice of a child at play coming to him from the depths. The child was playing with a ball, so a vase-painting indicates, when it shows little Perseus with the toy in his hand. He cried out when the ball rolled away from him. The king had Danae brought out from the tomb of bronze. The nurse must die, since it was she who had communication with the upper world, to enable her to feed the girl. In the court of the palace stood an altar to Zeus, as was proper. At this altar Akrisios made his daughter tell him who the child's father was. She answered, 'Zeus', and was not believed. Akrisios had the mother and child shut up in a chest, a closed ark, and had it cast into the sea. Thus both, devoted to death, were afloat on the waves.

According to other tellers of the story, this happened earlier, just after the birth of the hero. He was born in the darkness of the bronze tomb and straightway shut up in the blackness of the ark. When, in the fair-wrought chest the wind that blew and the stir of the water made her heart sink for fear, while her cheeks were all bedewed, she cast a loving arm about Perseus and said, 'My child, what pain is mine! But thou sleepest, and slumberest with a mind at rest in this comfortless vessel, and in the darkness of its fastenings of bronze thou shinest, a beam of light in the black gloom. The salt depth of the wave that passeth over thy locks thou regardest not, nor the noise of the wind, as thy fair face lies on the purple cloak. If terror were terror to thee, surely thou wouldst lend thy little ear to my words. Sleep on, babe, I bid thee, and let the sea sleep, let our measureless mishap sleep, and may some change come, father Zeus, from thee. If I pray in too bold words and beyond justice, forgive me.'[149]

This is how Simonides lets us hear the words of the humble prayer of the god's beloved from the gloomy ark, and see the glory that shines about the divine child. Another poet, Aeschylus, shows us on the stage in his satyr-play 'The Net-drawers', how the chest was sighted from the island of Seriphos.[150] A fisherman called Diktys, the 'man of the nets' saw the floating object from the shore. 'What's this? What shall I call it? Some sea-monster, grampus or shark or whale, do I see? Lord Poseidon! Zeus of the sea! what an unexpected gift you send us from the water! Whatever the thing is, it comes no nearer. I must shout and bawl.' Diktys called for help. A large net was thrown and the chest brought to land. In the satyr-play, when Diktys appeals for aid, instead of country people, shepherds and fishermen, it was Sileinoi who appeared and they are there when the chest is opened—a crowd of the

worthless, half-divine and half-bestial dwellers in the hills and
fields, bald-headed, flat-nosed, with faces painted red. Little
Perseus laughed at them from the chest.[151] This laugh was in
itself a proof of his divine origin. Danae is horrified at first at
the change in her plight and amid lamentations reveals the
secret of who she is and whose son the child is. The fisherman
does them both reverence, takes them into his hut and passes
them off as his kinsfolk,[152] which they really were through the
Danaids, for Diktys was a descendant of Nauplios, the son of
Poseidon and Amymone daughter of Danaos.

The lord of Seriphos was not Diktys but his brother
Polydektes. Again, the brothers were unlike, fisherman and
king, and while not twins (by one account they had the same
mother only),[153] yet they were a pair. The 'receiver of many',
i.e. Polydektes, which is the same as Polydegmon, one of the
many names of the king of the underworld,[154] belongs to the
'netman'. What the one caught had to be the prey of the other.
Thus Danae became the prisoner of Polydektes, and so arrived
with her child in the underworld for the third time. She lived
henceforth in the king's house as his slave.[155] It was also alleged
that she was married to Polydektes,[156] while Perseus was
brought up in the temple of Athene as a ward of the goddess
at whose birth there had happened something like that which
took place when Perseus was conceived; a golden rain fell
from heaven.[157]

When the hero had grown to manhood and might have been
able to free his mother, Polydektes arranged an *eranos*, that is to
say a banquet to which every invited guest must bring with
him a certain gift. He gave out that a wedding-present for
Hippodameia, daughter of Oinomaos, was to be collected;[158]
obviously the king was posing as an intending suitor of that fair
bride, of whom the whole world was then talking, and of
whom we shall soon hear more. To Polydektes' *eranos* each
person taking part had to contribute a horse. Perseus, the son
of the slave-woman, assuredly possessed none. If, as other
narrators would have it,[159] Danae was still living in Diktys'

hut, the hero had been brought up in the poor circumstances of the fisherman, and what other aim could the king have had save to humiliate Perseus deeply? He no doubt assumed that the young hero in the fisherman's cottage could not bring this gift, but for very shame would quit the island and abandon the mother he had so far protected.

Notoriously, fishermen do not breed horses, so how could Perseus have brought one with him? Consequently, he said stubbornly to the king, 'I will bring you the Gorgon's head', and the king answered, 'Bring it.' The Gorgon Medusa has the body of a horse in a very old representation of her; according to the oldest narratives she was a mare, bride of Poseidon at one of his marriages which he entered upon in the shape of a stallion.[160] Thus Perseus promised nothing else than the desired gift, a horse, but a much more unusual one, harder to get and apparently impossible. For the mare which he offered bore the Gorgon face, the look of which made everyone stiffen in death. Polydektes too may have been thinking of just that when he accepted the hero's offer.

Perseus already repented of what he had promised; he retired to the furthest point of the island and lamented, and he did well to lament. If Danae was not yet in the king's power, the danger was now present that this would happen if her son did not keep his word. The freeing of his mother from the might of the 'receiver of many' was at stake. Then Hermes appeared to the hero,[161] or was it Athene who came first to his help? In the pictures of ancient artists she stands by him in front of Hermes. But who could lend him the winged shoes, or at least one of them, as we read in Artemidoros, the interpreter of dreams,[162] so that he could leave the island and come into the neighbourhood of the Gorgons, if not Hermes? This probably was how it happened in Aeschylus,[163] in the tragedy entitled 'The Daughters of Phorkys'. The dramatist simplified the journey of Perseus through the realms of thrice-three goddesses and probably left out the first three, the spring-nymphs.

These, the Naiads, were, however, probably the first who

helped the hero in his desperate situation. They lived in a cave
on the island of Seriphos, as they had their dwelling elsewhere
also in the stalactite-filled caves of the Greek mountains; and
they were in possession of the means which Perseus needed to
fulfil his undertaking. Later he could give them back the three
invaluable things. Whether they now approached the hero or
he visited them in Athene's company, they were his deliverers.
On an ancient vase-painting we see the nymphs receiving the
hero, one bringing him the winged shoes, another the cap of
invisibility, the third the wallet, *kibisis*, for the Gorgon's head.

Thus equipped, Perseus hastened away like a swift walker
through the air,[164] over the sea and Okeanos, like the sun.
Tradition tells us that[165] the Sun himself bore the name of
Perseus. On the other side of Okeanos, near the Garden of the
Hesperides, where the realm of Night begins, was the dwelling-
place of the Gorgons.[166] Three, or perhaps only two, grey-
haired goddesses, daughters of the old man of the sea, Phorkys,
the Graiai, kept watch before them.[167] Neither sun nor moon
ever shone upon them.[168] A landscape of pathless forests and
rocks had its beginning there;[169] it was also called Kisthene,
the Land of Rock-roses, and could be reached equally well
from the east.[170] It was the land of darkness, in which all the
lights of heaven vanish and from which they all appear again,
for it borders on east and west alike. It is conceivable that even
Pallas Athene did not know the way through that district to
the Gorgons, for the younger deities did not know all things
whereof the older ones, such as the Moirai and the Graiai, had
knowledge. Perseus must first approach the grey goddesses if
he wished to find the way to the Gorgons.

The Graiai kept watch turn about,[171] for they had but one
eye and also but one tooth between them. Would they have
caught sight of their visitor with this eye even through the
darkness if he had not worn the 'cap of Hades', the cap which
made him invisible? There he was, and he waited close at hand
for the daughters of Phorkys to change watch, at the entrance
to their cave, perhaps the same which hid the Gorgons within

it.[172] As they relieved guard, one Graia passed the single eye to the other, and for so long they were both blind. Perseus had been waiting that moment; he snatched the eye from their hands and would not give it back until they told him the road to the Gorgons. Under that strong compulsion the sisters did so, but when did the hero then give the eye back? Was it when he had discovered that the entrance to the cave led to the Gorgons? Did he toss it to the Graiai only on his flight? Did he, as some would have it,[173] fling it into Lake Tritonis as he flew away? What a cry of woe must those primaeval goddesses have raised! But this came afterwards; beyond a doubt, the 'Phorkides' of Aeschylus was full of their wailings. For us there remains but one line of the piece, 'Boar-like he passed into the cave.'[174]

In this cave the three Gorgons were sleeping. Only one of them was mortal, Medusa,[175] the Mistress, as we might translate her name. His fortune, or Athene, must guide Perseus' hand; the hero must feel for the head of Medusa and keep his face turned away,[176] so as not to see her mask-like visage. We are also told that[177] the goddess showed him the Gorgon's head in a bright shield which she had given Perseus or herself held for him.[178] He came armed with a *harpe*, a sword shaped like a reaping-hook, which also was a divine gift, and with this old Titanic weapon he cut off Medusa's head.

She was with child by Poseidon and had in her womb the hero Chrysaor and the steed Pegasos, both of whom sprang out from her severed neck. The hero hid the head in the *kibisis*.[179] Now he must flee, for the two immortal sisters of Medusa awoke and pursued him. The air was the scene of the struggle between Perseus and the Gorgons; on old vase-paintings we see them both flying after the hero, and on one he is actually mounted on Pegasos, being the first to ride him, before Bellerophon.[180] It was impossible to catch him, for on his feet he had the winged shoes and his sword hung from his shoulder; thus a continuator of Hesiod describes him as represented on the shield of Herakles.[181] He flew with the speed of thought, his back protected by the terrible head of

Medusa. He carried the *kibisis* slung around him and had the cap of Hades on his brow; the darkness of night spread around the hero.

Perseus was soon beyond the region in which the Gorgons lived, and which bordered on the lands of all peoples who themselves, it is said, dwelt beyond the countries of ordinary mortals. He feasted with the Hyperboreans in the north,[182] and in the south he flew over the land of the Ethiopians. There, on a rocky coast (it is said[183] that it was in Palestine near Jaffa) he caught sight of a fair maid. She had been exposed there in chains. This sight is a peak not only of the story of Perseus but also of the history of Greek drama, for Euripides gave form to the scene in his 'Andromeda'. This at once gives us the name of the maiden. They tell us that the god in whose honour plays were acted, Dionysos, was himself so enchanted with the piece that he could not be separated from it, or so Aristophanes the comedian jokingly says.[184] It began with a great monologue by Perseus, who supposed that he had caught sight from the air of a figure of a maiden, the work of some artist, not a living girl.[185] The monologue soon passed into a most moving dialogue between the hero and heroine, with the words of Andromeda,[186]

> 'Take me hence, stranger, take me as thy servant,
> Or wife, or slave, whatever is thy will.'

The lord of the Ethiopian country was Kepheus.[187] His queen, the proud Kassiopeia, had angered the gods of the sea, in that she entered into a competition of beauty with the Nereids and boasted that she had emerged victorious. Her punishment was that Poseidon sent a flood over the country and a monster, to which her daughter Andromeda must be exposed. So an oracle advised and so it was done. Perseus flew up and slew the monster. An ancient vase-painting shows us Perseus fighting the boar-headed horror, which is rising from the sea, by flinging stones with both hands; Andromeda hands him the stones, the hero having freed her from her bonds.

He took her away from her parents also, who were loath to see
her depart, and from her sullen bridegroom, by name Phineus,
a name which we shall meet again in the story of the Argonauts. It is said of this Phineus that he was a brother of Kepheus, who wished to marry his niece. Perseus was thus again
confronted with an enemy whose appearance, as described
in the tales of the Argonauts, resembled the Graiai. Here
the Gorgon's head helped him; the hero drew it from the
kibisis,[188] and Phineus and his men were turned to stone;
Perseus carried Andromeda through the air to Seriphos. But
all four characters who met in this Ethiopian tale finally
reached heaven as constellations, Kassiopeia and Kepheus,
Andromeda and Perseus.[189] Athene promised it at the end of
the tragedy, but the poet would not have put such a prophecy
into the mouth of the goddess if people had not already
believed they saw the hurrying figure of Perseus in the skies.

Having cut off Medusa's head and put it into the *kibisis*, and
having freed and won Andromeda, Perseus returned to
Seriphos. It seems to have been described in another tragedy
of Euripides, the 'Diktys', how the hero found his mother and
her protector, Diktys the fisherman, as suppliants at an altar,[190]
to which they had been obliged to flee for refuge from the
violence of Polydektes. But now the young hero reappeared
sooner than they could have believed. Even the *eranos* to which
Perseus had promised to contribute the head of the Gorgon
instead of a horse was not yet over.[191] The guests, none of
whom could bring anything more than ordinary horses, were
still assembled when Perseus appeared with his gift, flying
through the air on his winged shoes and with Medusa's head
hanging from his shoulders in the wallet. No one would believe
that the hero had kept his promise, least of all king Polydektes.
He called the people together,[192] presumably to convict
Perseus of deceit. Apparently the young man was not popular
on Seriphos. Perseus appeared before the assembly of the
Seriphians, took the head out of the *kibisis* and showed it to the
assembled people by way of proof. Since then Seriphos has

been one of the rockiest islands in the Archipelago, for they all turned to stone. The hero dedicated the Gorgon's head to the goddess Athene, who has worn it on her breast ever since. The *kibisis*, the winged shoes and the cap of Hades he gave back to the nymphs. Diktys became king of Seriphos, but Perseus left the island and went home to Argos with Danae and Andromeda.

Akrisios was no longer in power there.[193] Fearing death from his grandson, he had gone from his native castle to Thessaly, to another stronghold also called Larissa. Perseus went after his grandfather, found him and wanted to be reconciled to him. There was a tragedy of Sophokles on that subject, 'The Larissaians'. The festival of reconciliation was held and Akrisios was ready to return to Argos.[194] At the celebration of the peace the young men of Larissa were playing with the discus, and Perseus could not resist it; he took the sun-like round in his hand, as Apollo did with the like tragic result, and sent it flying. It flew through the air and struck Akrisios—only on the foot, but it was a mortal wound. So the grandfather died at the hands of the grandson, and the hero's glory passed into darkness. Darkness follows the rays of the sun in heaven also; how much the more the deeds of a divine child on earth, even if he were a true child of the Sun!

In those days the lord of the castle of Tiryns with its gigantic stone walls was Megapenthes, only son of Proitos. According to one story he took vengeance for the death of his uncle Akrisios and killed Perseus on his return;[195] but this tale is lost, and only the name of Megapenthes informs us that he was a man 'of great sorrows' and perhaps, like his three sisters, he strove against Dionysos and in the end, like Pentheus the Theban 'man of woe', was punished by the god. It is also said that he exchanged kingdoms with Perseus, since the latter was ashamed of having slain his grandfather and would not return to Argos any more.[196] Thus henceforth Megapenthes ruled in his stead in the Larissa of Argos and Perseus in Tiryns. From there he fortified the rocky strongholds of Midea and Mycenae.

The Mycenaeans later honoured him as their founder-hero and forgot the heroine Mykene, a daughter of Inachos,[197] who had once been as famous as Tyro or Alkmene,[198] and gave her name to the strongest castle in that region. But they could tell no story of any importance of the way in which the foundation took place under Perseus. In one account he took hold of his sword-sheath and finding that the chape, *mykes* in Greek, was lost, he founded *Mykenai* on that spot.[199] Others remembered the famous fountain under the Cyclopean walls of the fortress and were of opinion that Perseus, being tormented with thirst, had picked a mushroom, also called *mykes*, whereupon the spring arose, at which the hero refreshed himself and for very joy founded the city.[200] Presumably he then led the water from outside under the walls into the deep fountain, Perseia.

He was also supposed to be the founder of a great family, all kings. Andromeda allegedly had already borne him a son named Perses, the ancestor of the Persian kings, who later, when they laid claim to the land of the Hellenes, invoked Perseus as their ancestor.[201] In Mycenae he had several sons and one daughter; of the former, Alkaios and Elektryon were the grandfathers of Herakles, the daughter was Gorgophone, grandmother of the Spartan Dioskuroi. But Perseus won no such great renown as his great-grandson Herakles because, so it was said,[202] he too was one of the persecutors of Dionysos and committed a deed of violence against him. Did he, with his opposition, replace Megapenthes or Megapenthes him?

It was told in Argos that Dionysos arrived there over the sea with Ariadne and attended by mermaids. Perseus fought with them and killed many of his female followers. At Argos they showed the monument of Choreia, 'the Dancer', the name of a maenad,[203] and the grave of the mermaids (Haliai), who came with the god.[204] Vase-paintings show Perseus fighting with Dionysos' following. He held up the Gorgon's head against their hordes, and another story said that he turned Ariadne into stone before she and her garland reached heaven.[205] According to this tale the two heroes, Dionysos and

Perseus, both sons of Zeus, at last concluded a peace.[206] A temple with a sacred precinct in Argos was dedicated to the Cretan Dionysos, and there allegedly Ariadne lay buried.[207] One old tale even insisted that[208] Dionysos was killed by Perseus and thrown into the waters of Lerna, which formed a gate of the underworld. From those depths the god used to reappear, summoned back by the sound of a trumpet.[209] But did not the god of himself tread the path to the underworld at Lerna, to free Semele?[210] Persecutor and persecuted were not unlike each other in this one deed at any rate—the freeing of their mothers. Perseus had a hero's tomb before the city of the Mycenaeans, on the road to Argos,[211] and there received their worship.

3 DANAE AND PERSEUS IN THE OPENED CHEST

4 PERSEUS AND THE FOUNTAIN-NYMPHS

5 PERSEUS SLAYING THE GORGON MEDUSA

CHAPTER V

Tantalos

THE NAME OF NIOBE occurs more than once at the beginning of the history of mankind.[212] In Argos, it is connected with the primaeval man Phoroneus, in Boiotia with Alalkomeneus, who brought Pallas Athene up. In Thebes she was considered the wife of Amphion. There it was said that this presumptuous and horribly punished woman was the daughter of Tantalos, king of Lydia, a country in Asia Minor, to which his story now takes us.

Tantalos came at the very beginning, quite as much as Alalkomeneus or Phoroneus and even the Theban Dioskuroi to some extent. He was the father of Broteas, who to judge by his name was the first ancestor of mortals, *brotoi*, and was the first to carve an image of the Mother of the Gods on the rocks.[213] And he was the father also of Pelops, after whom a large portion of Greece was called the Peloponnesos, 'Pelops' island'. Two sons of Pelops, Atreus and Thyestes, founded the second dynasty of Mycenae, which was even more renowned as a royal line than the first one, the family of Perseus. Thus an important thread takes its beginning in Lydia, Tantalos' kingdom in Asia Minor, on the mountains of Sipylos, whose heights dominate Smyrna and on which Niobe was later pointed out turned to stone. A tarn there bore the name of Tantalos,[214] and there was a story of another in which his city was sunk.[215] His much-admired tomb[216] stood on Sipylos, although this was not the only spot where heroic honours were paid him. Argos believed[217] it possessed his bones, and the little town of Polion on Lesbos had built him a hero-shrine.[218] It is said that he with his son Pelops founded on the Sipylos range the first city of that region, if it was not the first in the whole world.[219]

He was held to be a son of Zeus,[220] but Mount Tmolos in

Lydia was also named as his father.[221] His mother was Pluto, 'the Rich', a daughter of Kronos,[222] and, as a Berekynthian nymph,[223] certainly also daughter of the Berekynthian Great Mother, if she was not that goddess herself under a name which fitted the giver of great wealth. From ancient times, Lydia was famous for its gold; gold was hidden in its mountains, in Tmolos above all, and the rivers carried gold in their sands. No name was more fitting to the greatest goddess of this country than Pluto. The wife of Tantalos was variously named, one name being Dione. She was supposed to be a Pleiad, a daughter of Atlas, and bore the same name as one of the great consorts of Zeus.[224] Through her the genealogists connected Atlas, an old god of the race of the Titans, with the king of Lydia.

The realm of Tantalos is supposed to have extended further than this one country; it included also Phrygia, the range of Ida, and the plain of Troy.[225] On the island of Lesbos, where allegedly he had a hero-shrine, there was also a mountain which bore his name.[226] This name was Greek and signified 'adventurer',[227] one who could dare the greatest venture of all. The wealth of Pluto's son became proverbial,[228] and the poets played with the resemblance in sound of his name and that of their heaviest weight of gold, the talent, connecting the 'talents of Tantalos' with each other.[229] Like the sinner Ixion,[230] he sat at the table of the gods,[231] and although accounted a man,[232] was no mortal; the everlasting duration of his punishment will show this. He climbed heaven to reach the banquet of the gods,[233] and invited them to come to him in his beloved city of Sipylos.[234] But the meal which he had prepared for the gods was of such a kind that the poets did not wish to believe it nor like to tell of it,[235] at least, not the Greek poets. Later Romans found it to their taste.[236] But it must be told, for it was Tantalos' venture and to some extent originated in the stories of the gods, which declared[237] that originally the baby Dionysos underwent what was done to the vicarious victim, kid or calf, for he too was cut in pieces and boiled.

This was the sacrificial feast to which Tantalos had invited the gods. He dared to set before them something which involved a much greater sin than the deceit of Prometheus whereby he founded the great sacrificial ritual of the Greeks. Tantalos' sin was that he prepared for the gods' meal no vicarious beast, but the best he had to give,[238] his own son, and this sacrificial meat he had ready for them. He butchered little Pelops,[239] cut him up, had his flesh cooked in a cauldron,[240] and intended, so later generations believed,[241] thus to test the omniscience of his guests. The gods knew of it and refrained. The old narrators found it horrible enough that anyone should present such a sacrifice to the Heavenly Ones in earnest and not, for instance, only as in play, by offering a beast. Rhea, the great goddess, who had also gathered the limbs of the infant Dionysos,[242] put the portions together again and made the child arise from the cauldron.[243] Hermes of course could also have recalled him to life,[244] or Klotho the Moira, who had not yet determined his death.[245]

It was, so to speak, a rebirth. The cauldron remained pure, unstained by cruelty, and the boy rose up more beautiful than he was before.[246] His shoulder shone like ivory.[247] The story was told that one deity had in fact tasted of his flesh at the point that now shone. Most alleged that it was Demeter, made inattentive through the loss of her daughter;[248] being an allusion also to the fact that Demeter, in her character of goddess of the earth, had a claim to the body. This was why Pelops ever after had an ivory shoulder, which the gods had put in place of the one devoured, and for that reason his descendants too were distinguished by a birthmark, either an unusually white shoulder[249] or a star on the same part.[250] Poseidon at once fell in love with Pelops and carried the beautiful boy off; he lifted him on his chariot and brought him with his golden team to the palace of Zeus. This is supposed to have happened before Ganymedes arrived there.[251] Only evil tongues could allege that the child had been devoured, when he was not brought back to his mother.[252] But later the gods sent the young man

back to short-lived human-kind;[253] after sinful Tantalos he
was to become a famous ruler upon earth.

For various sins were laid at Tantalos' door, sins indeed, but
perhaps only veiled accounts of his great venture, the too exact
carrying out of a sacral performance, in this shape a horrible
deed, which was to recur among the descendants of Pelops.
Such stories as the following were told of the sins of Tantalos:
as guest of the gods, he had not been able to hold his tongue,[254]
but betrayed to mortals what he should have kept quiet,[255] the
secrets of the Deathless.[256] In another account, he let his
friends actually share the enjoyment of the food and drink of
the gods, their nectar and ambrosia,[257] and this again was a
theft, not unlike that of Prometheus.

He was likewise involved in the misdoings of others. Among
the Cretan Tales was one concerning a golden dog belonging
to Zeus.[258] Pandareos, son of Merops, one of the forefathers of
mankind,[259] stole this marvellous creature, brought it to
Sipylos and handed it over to Tantalos to keep safe.[260] But
the receiver played the thief false. On the golden dog being
reclaimed from Tantalos, he denied having had it and confirmed his denial by a false oath. Zeus punished them both; he
turned Pandareos into stone and flung Tantalos down with
Sipylos on top of him. According to others it was not Zeus
but Tantalos who was the kidnapper of Ganymedes,[261] or at
least he played some part in the boy's disappearance.[262] But he
was not punished for this. An ancient song also accused him
of no greater crime than that,[263] when Zeus was ready to fulfil
any wish of his, as his beloved guest, he asked for the life which
the gods live. Angered at this, the Olympian did indeed grant
the wish, but caused a stone to hang over Tantalos' head, so
that he could get no enjoyment of all that was available to him.

The scene of his punishment was certainly the whole space
of the world to begin with, not only because the same story is
told of him as of Prometheus, that he must hang with hands
bound to a rock,[264] or bear up the sky, like Atlas;[265] we are
told in so many words that he floated between heaven and

6 PERSEUS AFTER BEHEADING MEDUSA

7 ANDROMEDA, PERSEUS AND THE SEA-MONSTER

8 PELOPS, HIPPODAMEIA AND THE FALL OF MYRTILOS

9 THE MARRIAGE OF ANTIKLEIA

earth,[266] and he got the epithet of 'wanderer in the air'.[267] In this condition, so Euripides understood it, he had the sun over his head like a fiery stone.[268] But there were also other very ancient punishments which had their place in the spaces of the universe and were transferred to the underworld only in later tellings of them; for instance the punishment of Ixion[269] or Tityos,[270] not to speak again of Prometheus, the only one who was freed from his pains. Tantalos belonged to those whose penance was eternal.

Poets and painters depicted his lot, when they described the underworld. He stands, says Homer,[271] in a pool, with the water reaching his chin. He is tormented with thirst and cannot drink, for if the old man bends down to drink, the water disappears as if it were sucked away, and the black earth shows at his feet. Tall trees let their fruit hang down over his head, but if the ancient tries to grasp it in his hand, a gust of wind tosses it up to the clouds. The painter Polygnotos added the threatening rock.[272] The picture of the underworld on a Tarentine vase shows us the king in his long robes fleeing from the stone. He is the shadow-picture of the too daring and too wishful for all times.

CHAPTER VI

Pelops and Hippodameia

THAT PORTION OF the European and the Greek continent which is named after Pelops, the son of Tantalos is connected with the rest of Greece by a single narrow strip of land,
the Isthmus. As one could get around by sea, starting from
Corinth, and thus arrive in the same city again, though in a
different harbour, it has always given the impression of being
a large island, a separate country. It is, however, cut up by
many mountain ranges and in antiquity it was divided among
so many tribes that one must think: 'That must have been no
common hero and ruler for anything so manifold to be considered a unity under his name!' His renown has remained, but
not the memory of any single people whose eponym he might
have been. The sceptre which the master-craftsman Hephaistos
so skilfully wrought for Zeus, and which later Atreus, Thyestes
and Agamemnon, the princes of the second Mycenaean
dynasty, carried as the mark of their lordship over Argos and
many islands, was sent by the Olympian to Pelops through
Hermes.[273] He was thought of as the first ruler of this great
realm; it was even believed that Hermes was his father, his mother
being Kalyke, 'the bud', a nymph of the region of Elis.[274]

But what was his exploit as a founder, which could be
compared with Kadmos' slaying of the dragon, or Amphion's
lyre-music, or even with the building of the walls of Tiryns
and Mycenae? No walls due to any action of his were shown;
rather the story was told of a foundation which was to assemble
more Greek peoples at the expiration of every four years in a
common festival than the Peloponnesos contained. The tale of
this foundation begins with Oinomaos, king of Pisa, lord over
a fertile district on the western edge of the peninsula, on the
lower part of the valley of the river Alpheios. To judge by his
name, he should have been a gentle monarch, as 'king of

wine'. The king of Aitolia, Oineus, whose name was similar, had a brother unlike himself, Agrios, 'the wild', whereas Oinomaos' savagery was in himself. Even that Oineus or Oinopion who was mentioned in the history of the gods[275] showed himself rather cruel than gentle towards Orion. Oinomaos was accounted a son of Ares the war-god.[276] In his days snow fell abundantly on the hill which the visitors to Olympia know as the Hill of Kronos. Herakles named it, for while Oinomaos ruled it was nameless as yet.[277]

The story went[278] that king Oinomaos, son of Ares, had a daughter called Hippodameia, 'she who tames steeds', whom no man could get as his wife. Two reasons were assigned for the association between the father and daughter, which were unnatural under human relationships. According to one, Oinomaos was himself in love with Hippodameia, according to the other, an oracle had foretold that he would be killed by his son-in-law. Whether Oinomaos' passion remained un-satisfied or, as others would have it,[279] he was already united to his daughter as her husband, he killed her suitors. His weapons and his horses he had got from Ares, two mares called Psylla, 'the Flea' and Harpinna, 'she who snatches', the latter having the same name as Oinomaos' mother.[280] Both were as swift as the Harpies,[281] swifter than the wind.[282] He made a show of being ready to give his daughter to anyone who could beat him in a chariot-race,[283] the goal of which was the altar of Poseidon at the Isthmus,[284] and the race-track the whole country, the lordship over which was no less at stake than the winning of Hippodameia. It was at the same time a case of bride-stealing, like that of Persephone, only the other way about, for Hippodameia was to be freed from her Hades-like father and husband. The suitor was to take her with him in his chariot, while Oinomaos pursued the fugitive pair. If the suitor was not caught, he won the maid to his wife, other-wise he was put to death by her pursuing father. In this way Oinomaos had already murdered many suitors. He cut their heads off and put them up over his palace; the number of the slain already amounted to twelve. The no less significant total of thirteen is also mentioned[285] (there are twelve months in a year, but thirteen in a leap-year), and it seems as if Oinomaos' time was thus expired. Many narrators did not confine them-selves to this limit, but listed the names of still more un-fortunates.[286]

The limit was set by the son of Tantalos, the 'dark-faced' prince, as his name may be understood. Pelops had hardly returned from the gods and the dark down was scarcely spring-ing on his chin,[287] when he wanted Hippodameia for his wife. We hear that he went in the darkness to the shore of the grey sea and called upon his divine lover.[288] Poseidon at once appeared and heard his prayer: 'If the dear gifts of Her of Cyprus earn aught of thanks, stay thou the bronze spear of Oinomaos, bring me on the swiftest of chariots to Elis and let me meet with victory. For he hath slain thirteen men and delays his daughter's wedlock. But this great danger meeteth with no coward; since die we must, why should one vainly spend a nameless old age, sitting in the shadow, with no share in aught noble? Nay, this exploit shall be my portion, only do thou grant wished-for accomplishment!'

The god gave him a golden car with winged steeds, and on it he flew over the sea from his eastern abode in Sipylos to his future country in the west.[289] His words testified to a hero who deserved his victory, and so it came about for him, since, as already said, Oinomaos' time was expired. Hippodameia her-self was ready for a real marriage-journey, and beside her stood her helper. The vase-paintings show him youthful, the maker of the marriage, appropriately to his name, for that was Myrtilos, derived from *myrtos*, myrtle, that plant which is beloved of Aphrodite but hated by virginal goddesses. Pelops, so the story was told in his Asian fatherland,[290] had vowed a statue of myrtle-wood to Aphrodite if he might be wedded to Hippodameia; and now Myrtilos was present, a son of Hermes,[291] who served Oinomaos as charioteer, and caused the bridegroom to win.

The story is worthy of a son of Hermes, although it is told us with additions which fit a commonplace faithless servant. Thus we are informed that Pelops promised Myrtilos, who was in love with Hippodameia, the bridal night in return for his help,[292] while others put that promise into the mouth of the bride herself,[293] for Hippodemeia at once fell in love with Pelops when she caught sight of him and wanted to assure his victory at all costs. Allegedly too, half the kingdom was promised to Myrtilos.[294] But he seems to have been much rather the *daimon* of marriage, to whom the first night belonged in a special way, and, like his doublet Hymenaios,[295] who did not survive the marriage, he died during the triumphant journey of the pair, allegedly thrown from his chariot by Pelops.[296]

But here we have anticipated too far. From a tragedy of Sophokles, entitled 'Oinomaos', there are preserved to us the words of Hippodameia, describing the loveliness of Pelops, the magic which streamed from his person and the consuming lightning of his eyes.[297] Euripides in describing the arrival of Pelops in his 'Oinomaos' represented him as regretting his purpose when he caught sight of the severed heads over the palace gate.[298] From here on the best tellers of the story are the vase-painters, who take up the thread and show us the further course of events in pictures.

Oinomaos made his agreement with the new pretender, as he always did, with a libation on the altar of Zeus Herkeios in the courtyard of his palace. The heads of the murdered suitors Pelargos and Periphas looked down upon the solemn rite. The agreement was made with Hippodameia also, that she should belong to the bridegroom only if he was not caught. Thereupon both got into the chariot. Oinomaos stayed behind yet, to make sacrifice of a ram; the time needed for the offering he was accustomed to allow the suitor by way of a start.[299] A vase-painting shows us that the light-coloured ram was not intended for Zeus, as some supposed, but for a goddess to whom human sacrifices were welcome, for the stiff idol of

Artemis watched over the procedure, which at the same time anticipated the sacrifice of the young man. After completing the ritual, the king mounted his chariot, which Myrtilos had ready for him.

The horses of Ares might perhaps have caught even those which Pelops had got from Poseidon, for the pursuit went right across the whole country, but Myrtilos' ruse had decided the victory in advance. He had not put the linch-pins into the wheels of the chariot, or only waxen ones.[300] Then, when the wheels began to part from the chariot, Myrtilos jumped out, and Oinomaos, entangled in the reins, was dragged to death.[301] But it was also said[302] that he had the *coup de grace* from Pelops, a superfluous deed of blood, to which was added something worse still, the murder of Myrtilos, which was a sin against Hermes and of dire consequence for the House of Pelops.[303] It was alleged as a motive for this murder that Myrtilos claimed by violence the price of his help.[304] His fall from the chariot in which Pelops and Hippodameia rode is to be seen only in a vase-painting, and the vase-painters testify also that the victorious couple, after their goal on the Isthmus was reached, drove all round the land of Pelops, hovering over the sea. This is how it could be stated[305] that the Myrtoan Sea, which washes the east coast of the Peloponnesos, got its name from the charioteer's fall.

Another story was[306] that Zeus destroyed the detestable palace of Oinomaos with his thunderbolt. The one pillar which was left standing after the fire stood, marked by a bronze tablet, for long afterwards in the sacred precinct which was henceforth to bring the Greek races together for festival con-tests, the precinct of the King of the Gods, in the Altis at Olympia. There also tales were told of older contests, the races of the five Idaean Daktyls, the eldest of whom was called Herakles and instituted the sport;[307] likewise of a wrestling-match between Zeus and Kronos for sovranty, and of the victory of Apollo over Hermes and Ares.[308] But it is not with-out reason that the poets celebrate the 'racecourse of Pelops'[309]

and *his* contests.[310] For after the victory of his chariot over that
of Oinomaos he was Lord of Olympia and was later honoured
as a hero among all the shrines which were to rise there.

The hero-tomb which was erected to him after his death in
the middle of the Altis[311] was only a 'makeshift grave', a
cenotaph at which to worship him. The bones of Pelops were
preserved in vineyards of the territory of the vanished city of
Pisa, near the temple of Artemis Kordaka.[312] At his 'makeshift' tomb, however, close to the temple of Hera, a black ram
was yearly sacrificed.[313] No one who ate of the flesh of that
creature might enter the temple of Zeus,[314] but before every
sacrifice to Zeus the hero was remembered with an offering of
which nothing was eaten.[315] Then, when the temple of Zeus,
whose prostrate columns we gaze upon in wonder today, was
built, its eastern gable bore figures which immortalised the
scene before the chariot-race of Pelops and Oinomaos. On one
side stood the king with his queen, Sterope, Pelops and
Hippodameia on the other, and the Olympian in the middle.
The two chariots and their attendants, including Myrtilos,[316]
completed the scene, the preliminaries to the exploit of
foundation.

Hippodameia for her part founded, out of gratitude to the
Queen of the gods, a festival of Hera, which also recurred
every four years, and included a race for girls. Chloris is named
as the first to win it;[317] she was a daughter of Amphion and
Niobe, the only one who was spared, and she became the
mother of the long-lived Nestor. But the name of Hippodameia betrays the fact that she personally had to do rather
with horses and chariots. And this name at least was preserved on the west gable-end of the temple of Zeus in a scene
from the story of a Hippodameia who allegedly was not the
same, but the bride of the Thessalian hero Peirithoos, whose
wedding was the occasion of the fight portrayed on the pediment, that between the Lapithai and Centaurs. Certainly
there were Centaurs here also, in the neighbouring mountain
range of Pholoe, and perhaps Lapithai too, if that was what the

inhabitants of the Lapithos range opposite were called. But if anything of the kind took place at the wedding of Pelops and Hippodameia, this was already forgotten in late antiquity.

The story tells of six sons of the heroic pair,[318] among them Atreus and Thyestes who inherited the sceptre that came from Zeus. Two daughters are also named, Lysidike, the future mother of Amphitryon, and Nikippe, afterwards mother of Eurystheus. Again, we hear of thirteen sons,[319] who founded cities, countries and royal families in the Peloponnesos and on the Isthmus. Only one had no issue, Chrysippos, 'he of the golden steeds', as his name signifies, a double of Pelops. His story will take us back to Thebes. It is said that Hippo-dameia treated him as a stepson,[320] had him murdered by Atreus and Thyestes, and was therefore obliged[321] to flee from Pelops to the stronghold of Midea. From there her bones were brought to Olympia and buried in her shrine, which only women might enter and they only once a year. It was not easy to approach her and learn more of her august figure.

10 THE MADNESS OF SALMONEUS

11 THE PUNISHMENT OF SISYPHOS

CHAPTER VII

Salmoneus, Melanippe and Tyro

AS WE HAVE ALREADY SPOKEN of Oinomaos and lastly also of his wife Sterope, whose name signifies 'lightning', we have now to tell of Salmoneus, the founder of the city of Salmona on the banks of the river Alpheios, near Pisa, who wanted to handle thunder in a sinful manner. Salmoneus belongs to the same series of dark kings in the tales of the heroes as Oinomaos, and even passed into the ranks of the exemplary sufferers of punishment, like Tantalos and Sisyphos, his brother, whose story will be told shortly. His ancestry went back to Deukalion, son of Prometheus, and Pyrrha, daughter of Epimetheus, the two survivors of the most famous deluge,[322] unless it be that his grandfather Hellen, after whom the Hellenes were named, was after all no son of Deukalion but of Zeus and Pyrrha.[323] In that case Salmoneus too must have been descended from Zeus.

His father bore the name of the king of the winds, with the difference that the other Aiolos was called Hippotades,[324] this one simply Aiolos. He is said to have given their name to the race of the Aiolians. But his grandson had the same name, and either Aiolia on the Propontis or the Aiolian Islands in the west were called after him. This youngest Aiolos was a nephew of Salmoneus. Salmoneus' sister, who bore to Poseidon him and his twin brother Boiotos, the eponym of the inhabitants of Boiotia, was Melanippe. Her story became famous by two tragedies of Euripides, and must be told before that of Salmoneus, the more so as the same thing occurred to his daughter Tyro as to Melanippe: the ancient narrative of the exposed divine twins, founder-heroes, as also the Theban Dioskuroi were.

The elder king Aiolos of Thessaly became, like Boreas the north wind and lover of mares,[325] a lover of a daughter of

Chiron the Centaur. Her name was Hippo or Hippe, a word which signifies a mare. The story is also told that she had originally the shape of a girl and bore some other name. She was ashamed of her pregnancy, fled into the wilderness, and in order that her father should not see her as a woman in child-birth, the gods changed her into a mare.[326] This daughter of Chiron was distinguished for her gift of seer-craft, and told too much of what she foresaw,[327] the death of Asklepios, whom Chiron reared,[328] even the destiny of her father himself.[329] It was said that owing to her freedom of speech she was changed by Zeus into the shape of a beast, namely a vixen.[330]

She was changed at the very moment, we are assured,[331] when she had borne a daughter. The girl was given the name of Melanippe, the 'black mare', and this surely lets us see that in her family the horse-shape was more original than the human. She found a lover in Poseidon, who was so fond of taking equine shape and having stallion-weddings.[332] She bore him the twins Aiolos and Boiotos. One of the two tragedies of Euripides, 'Melanippe the Wise' (a once famous piece, but now lost with its companion 'Melanippe the Captive'), gave a full account of the matter.[333] When Aiolos, in consequence of a homicide, was obliged to spend a year in voluntary exile, this happened to his daughter: Melanippe hid her twins from her father on his return home in a byre, where the bull guarded the sucklings and a cow gave them milk. The herdsmen saw the wonderful sight and informed the king. They believed that a cow had dropped human offspring. Aiolos was horrified and asked his old father Hellen what he should do.

Hellen advised him to burn the unnatural births, and there-upon Aiolos ordered his daughter to trim the sucklings for sacrifice, for she had a reputation for wisdom and understood all sacral procedures. Thereupon Melanippe the Wise rose up against the men and in a cunning speech told them of the beginning of things, as she had been taught concerning it by her mother, the Centaur's daughter. She proclaimed the com-mon origin of plants, beasts and men, a doctrine which the followers and devotees of Orpheus preserved[334] and which is here, through the appeal to the daughter of the wise Centaur, traced back to Chiron himself. According to this there can be no such thing as an unnatural birth. Suppose (Melanippe did not omit even this possibility) some seduced girl had exposed the children, then again to burn them would be to commit a murder and no sacrifice.[335] Thus, or somewhat thus, spoke the embodiment of women's cleverness on the stage. But it was apparently not she but her prophetic mother who rescued the twins; she appeared in the shape of a female Centaur and foretold the children's future as founder-heroes.

In the other tragedy, Melanippe was a prisoner and had come to Metapontum, the city in south Italy. There her sons were being brought up to be men of valour. The details can no longer be told and they would take us too far from Salmoneus, in whose house a like event was to take place. This was staged by Sophokles, but it kept so close to the old tale of the divine twins who were exposed that the Romans, if they read the tragedy, could recognise in it the childhood of their own founder-heroes, Romulus and Remus. And perhaps there were even writers who actually recognised the common element and emphasised it in their re-telling of the legend of the foundation of Rome still more than it discloses of itself. The modern re-teller of the story of Tyro, the milkwhite daughter of Salmoneus must, on the contrary withstand the temptation, lest he land on the banks of Tiber, who according to well-informed tradition[336] was the loving husband of the mother of the Roman stock. He must stay on the Enipeus.

That was the name of the river on which Salmoneus' kingdom lay, first in Thessaly, in the country of his father Aiolos, then in the Peloponnesos, in the district of Elis, where he founded his own city. Enipeus means 'the roarer', a name which any noisy stream and even the sea itself might have. Poseidon had it as an epithet.[337] Tyro was in love with the river Enipeus, the fairest river on earth.[338] She often walked on the banks of the lovely water, which Poseidon had chosen for the shape of his epiphany, to love the maid. A purple wave rose mountain-like out of the river and hid god and maiden, and he loosed her virgin girdle and poured sleep over her. But when the god had accomplished the works of love, he clasped her by the hand and spake her name, saying, 'Be of good cheer, woman, at this our love-play, for in the course of the year thou shalt bring forth glorious children, since the beds of the Deathless are not without fruit. Tend them and rear them; but now, get thee home and refrain from naming me, for I am Poseidon Earthshaker.' Thus spake he, and plunged under the waves of the sea.

Tyro bore twins and did not dare keep them. She put them into a wooden chest which could both serve as a cradle and float on the water; it was a hollowed-out log which became famous.[339] In this the children were entrusted to their paternal waters, for their mother did not nurture them but handed them over to the Enipeus. They floated on the water, which brought them to a place on the bank where a herd of horses was grazing. The beasts rescued the children; one of them, who got the name of Neleus, was suckled by a bitch belonging to the shepherds,[340] and the other by a mare.[341] As the beast trod on this one's face and made a dark spot which he ever afterwards bore, the boy was named Pelias, 'Grey-face'.[342] At last one of the herdsmen found them both, brought them up and also preserved the hollowed log with everything that the mother had given her exposed children.

Tyro's face was white, as if she lived on milk only.[343] Her name itself expressed this, being the very word by which to this day cheese is known in Greece—the white, soft gift of the sheep. The princess' body was soft,[344] and her beautiful hair full of the charm of love.[345] A harsh stepmother was hers in the person of Sidero, 'the iron woman', as Salmoneus' second wife was called. Suffering under her harshness she appeared in Sophokles' tragedy 'Tyro'. Twenty years had passed since the exposure of the twins, and that milkwhite face was marked with black from the stepmother's blows.[346] The lovely hair was cut short, so that the luckless princess should feel the more abased, like a filly with her mane shorn.[347] And in the early morning she had to fetch water from the fountain. There two young men met her, and not far off was the herdsman, carrying their little property in a bag, and also a hollowed log. But their companion, appeared only at the last, to make the recognition possible.[348] Sidero was there earlier, the persecutor of her stepdaughter, but was obliged to flee to the temple of Hera from the young men, who took the tormented Tyro under their protection. Neleus drove off Salmoneus, who hurried to his wife's help, and Pelias killed the wicked queen at Hera's altar.[349]

That he was not straightway punished for this by the Queen of the gods was no doubt thanks to his father Poseidon, who at the last moment stretched his sheltering hand over Tyro and her sons. Not till later did punishment fall on Pelias, in the course of the story of the Argonauts. But Sidero was hardly a favourite of Hera, if she acted in the same way towards the goddess as Salmoneus did towards Zeus. What good kings were like in the days of the hero-legends and what they achieved is described for us in the words of Odysseus, where he compares the fame of Penelope to that of such a king,[350]

> 'That ruleth over many mighty men,
> Upholding righteous dooms. For him dark earth
> Bears wheat and barley; fruit-trees heavy-laden,
> And ewes that lamb and fail not, and the sea
> Teeming with fish because he ruleth well,
> And under him the people prosper still.'

Such kings were conscious of the exalted position to which the gods had called them, but also of the higher power which stood over them. Of course there were others, who 'strove to be Zeus',[351] and one of these was Salmoneus.

He claimed for himself the sacrifices which were due to the King of the Gods,[352] and he attempted, by driving about in his chariot on the banks of the Alpheios, actually to thunder and lighten.[353] He threw torches among the people, who hated him[354] and they also fell into the fields.[355] He drove his team over bronze bridges, to mimic the voice of the thunder.[356] Or he had bronze cauldrons fastened to his chariot and dragged them about.[357] That at least fitted the satyr-play which Sophokles staged. On a vase-painting we see the mad king chained and getting free again from his chains. Finally Zeus struck him down with his lightning, and Salmoneus became one of those everlastingly punished in the House of Hades. According to the most celebrated mention of him, in Vergil's description of the underworld, it would appear that even down there he still dashed about in his chariot with his torches, without ever being able to stop, just as Herakles in the under-world had everlastingly to aim with his bow.[358] But that was not Herakles himself, but only a phantom of him, for he himself had reached Olympos, while for Salmoneus there remained nothing else for the future but this image of his wild career.

Tyro, after her deliverance, became the wife of her uncle Kretheus, one of the sons of Aiolos, and bore him three sons, Pheres, Aison and Amythaon. She was thus the mother of five founder-heroes and the ancestress of great families. Her twins, it is true, did not agree together very well.[359] Pelias was king of Iolkos in Thessaly, Neleus founded the city of Pylos in the extreme south-west of the Peloponnesos, and took to wife Chloris, daughter of Niobe and winner at the first festival of Hera at Olympia.[360] Thus he became the father of Nestor, the oldest of the heroes who fought in the War of Troy. A son of Pheres was Admetos, whom Apollo served as a herds-man.[361] Aison was the father of Jason, who led the expedition of the Argonauts from Pelias' city of Iolkos to Kolchis. Amythaon's sons included Melampus, 'blackfoot', who purified the daughters of Proitos, Danae's grandfather, from their madness.[362] But the story of Bellerophon will bring us back also to Proitos in the strong castle of Tiryns.

CHAPTER VIII

Sisyphos and Bellerophontes

'As is the race of leaves, so that of men.
Of leaves the wind strews some upon the earth,
Others the springtime forest putteth forth,
And so of men, these grow and these decline.'

IT IS IN HOMER[363] that the younger Glaukos begins the story of
his ancestry with these words. He descended from Sisyphos,
son of Aiolos, grandfather of Bellerophontes, whose grandson
he himself was. So it is fitting to begin our story with Sisyphos,
who will then quickly lead us (for there is nothing much to
tell of the elder Glaukos, Sisyphos' son) to the history of
Bellerophontes, the greatest hero and slayer of monsters, alongside of Kadmos and Perseus, before the days of Herakles.
There was even a tragedy which made Sisyphos the violent
husband of Tyro;[364] but he was a man of cunning rather than
violence, the subtlest of all mankind.[365]

He belonged to those primaeval inhabitants of the earth who
could still look on at the first deeds of the gods, like that remarkable old man at Onchestos in Boiotia who cultivated a
vineyard and spied upon little Hermes with his stolen cattle.
He betrayed him to his brother Apollo, as we know from the
history of the gods.[366] Sisyphos lived at Ephyra, in that corner
of the Isthmus where Corinth was to arise, which city he was
supposed to have founded.[367] If anyone wanted to make his
way from Phlius, a spot further inland, hidden behind great
hills, to the Saronic Gulf, he could easily be spied upon from
the towering rocks which bore the name of Akrokorinthos,
and that was what happened to Zeus. In Phlius he carried off
Aigina,[368] daughter of the river-god Asopos and the future
mother of Aiakos, for whom the King of the Gods was to turn
into men the ants of the island of which she became the

eponym.[369] The island lay in the Saronic Gulf and in those days was still called Wine Island, Oinone. Asopos looked for his daughter and arrived at Sisyphos' rocky eyrie. Sisyphos could inform him, but would say nothing until the river-god caused a spring to gush forth for him up among the towering rocks.[370] The deep well in its old curb is the only one today which has remained to us up there from antiquity. For this price Sisyphos betrayed the abductor.

Thus the unwelcome spy drew the wrath of the gods upon himself.[371] Zeus sent Thanatos, Death, against him. He too was espied in good time. We should like to know how Sisyphos outwitted Death, but the story is lost to us. He contrived to do so and threw Death into strong chains. From that moment, no one died on earth, until Ares the war-god set Death free and handed over Sisyphos to him. The cunning man contrived to make one condition before departing for the nether world, to speak once again with his wife, queen Merope. He secretly ordered her to send no more sacrifices down to the king and queen of the realm of the dead. These then were surprised in the underworld when for a long while they got no more libations from above. It seems from this tale that Sisyphos was not only a primaeval man but also a primaeval king and lord of almost the whole earth. He contrived so to befool Persephone, queen of the nether world,[372] with cunning words that she let him go in order that he might let the sacrificial gifts, the flesh and blood of the victims, come abundantly once more. So Sisyphos took leave of the House of Hades, of Zagreus, son of the infernal Zeus and of Persephone,[373] and of all the secrets of the world below. He bade them farewell for ever, in words which could be heard in Aeschylus' satyr-play, the 'Runaway Sisyphos'.[374]

Now that he has escaped Death for the second time, we may insert here the famous tale of how the arch-rascal and the master-thief, Sisyphos and Autolykos, dealt with each other. Autolykos was a son of Hermes. The god of thieves begot him on one of Apollo's loves. He had taken the place of his elder

brother by night with Chione, the 'Snowmaiden' in a hiding‑
place on Mt Parnassos, where the snow often falls.[375] Thus the
'Wolf itself' (for that is the meaning of Autolykos) was born,
and he honoured his father Hermes above all gods. From him
he got his talent for theft and clever perjury.[376] He could make
anything invisible that he touched with his hand.[377] He knew
how to make white ḅeasts black and black beasts white; he
would take the horns off horned beasts and put them on the
heads of those that had none.[378]

At that time, and it must have been the time of primaeval
men, when the population was scanty, the herds of both
rascals pastured on the wide region between Parnassos and
the Isthmus. Autolykos could never be caught when he went
thieving; Sisyphos saw only that his herds kept growing
smaller and the other's larger. Then he thought of a ruse. He
was one of the first who mastered the art of letters, and so he
engraved the initial letters of his name on the hooves of the
cattle. But Autolykos found a way to alter this too,[379] because
he could alter everything belonging to the beasts. Then
Sisyphos poured lead into the hollow of the hooves, in the
shape of letters which produced in the footsteps of the cattle
the sentence 'Autolykos has stolen me.'[380]

It was only after this piece of evidence that the master‑thief
owned himself defeated. It was a contest in cleverness, and
Autolykos thought so highly of the winner that he im‑
mediately concluded an agreement of friendship and hospi‑
tality with him. It is not quite clear who was responsible for
what took place in his hospitable house. A so‑called 'Homeric'
drinking‑cup shows pretty undisguisedly Sisyphos in the bed‑
chamber of his host's daughter, the arch‑rogue sitting on the
bed and the girl with her spindle. Did he secretly have
relations with the beautiful Antikleia? It would have been
quite worthy of him. But also it would be a thought worthy of
Autolykos to offer his own daughter to the man who had out‑
done him in cleverness, so that they might produce the
cleverest of all.[381] Thus Antikleia became the mother of

Odysseus; it was not by Laertes, whom we know as the father from the 'Odyssey', but from Sisyphos that she conceived the man of many wiles, if we believe this story; Laertes took her when she was already with child.[382] A vase-painter of Magna Graecia has preserved for us the scene in which the young man displays his bride, in an interesting condition, to his astonished followers. For he was not even deceived; Autolykos, in this picture, shows him the name of Sisyphos on a leaf, somewhat larger than a laurel-leaf. It was the evidence which their guest, who loved letters and was responsible for the pregnancy, had left behind. The final victory in the matter was won by Aphrodite, who is also in the picture and is entrusting Odysseus to the care of his foster-father, the still young Laertes.

Sisyphos also had a son by his queen Merope; he was Glaukos, the elder bearer of this name, which means 'the sea-green one' and would fit a deity of the sea, as would also his Poseidonian tastes, for the lord of the sea had a predilection for horses and for horse-shape. About half-way from the Isthmus to the region of Parnassos, in Potniai, Glaukos possessed a stud of horses whose race showed plainly their relationship to the Harpies and Gorgons, for they had to be fed on human flesh, and ended by tearing their own master in pieces at the funeral games of Pelias, king of Iolkos.[383] The story was told in a tragedy of Aeschylus, the 'Glaukos Potnieus'.[384]

Sisyphos too died at last, from the weakness of old age.[385] This form of death he could not escape. Concerning his grave it is said[386] that it lay on the Isthmus, but only a few Corinthians knew where. He was one of the heroes honoured on the Isthmus, and allegedly founded the Isthmian Games[387] in memory of the dead Melikertes.[388] The hero Sisyphos had a statue erected to him there; we can read his name on the pedestal. On the other hand, his famous punishment pictures the eternally vain endeavour to roll away from himself the lot of all mortals. In the underworld he eternally rolls the rock:

'With thrusting hands and feet he ever drave
The stone towards the hill⁄crest, but whene'er
The height was almost passed, the cruel stone
By might compelled rolled down again to earth.'[389]

Vase⁄paintings show us the hill⁄top looking like the rocks of
the Akrokorinthos. Sisyphos always recommences his useless
task, while the sweat streams from his limbs and dust defiles
his head.

Of his line the only survivor was the son of the elder
Glaukos, grandfather of the younger, who tells of him in the
'Iliad'; this was Bellerophontes. If this genealogy, according to
which his grandfather was Sisyphos, had not been im⁄
mortalised by the beautiful verses of Homer, he would have
been accounted simply a son of the sea⁄god, be his name
Glaukos or Poseidon. His mother bore the name of the
goddess Eurynome,[390] a queen of the sea[391] and a great consort
of Zeus in primaeval times,[392] or actually Eurymeda,[393]
which is a feminine form of Eurymedon, 'wide⁄ruling', also
meaning the lord of the sea.[394] He seems to be a heroic child
sprung from the sea even as son of Glaukos the 'sea⁄green'.[395]
Soon he became the slayer of an original enemy named
Belleros, and so Bellerophon or Bellerophontes, understood as
'Belleros⁄killer'.

There is nothing more to be said of this enemy except that
he must have been there from the beginning and have had that
name, if Bellerophon got his universally famous appellation
from his victory over him, as Hermes his surname Argei⁄
phontes after the killing of the many⁄eyed Argos. Before this
victory the young hero is said to have had some other name,[396]
for instance Hipponoos, a name which connects him with the
noble steed, *hippos*. Or he bore the very same name as the
brother of his famous mount Pegasos, a son of Poseidon, who
is connected with no story whatever, outside of genealogies and
the tale of his birth. No wonder that it was so, if his original
name was soon to give place to that of Bellerophontes and the

hero in his boyhood and young manhood was still called Chrysaor. This name, which means 'golden-sworded', comes in a genealogy at the place which usually belongs to Bellero-phontes,[397] for this Chrysaor was also a son of Glaukos, the son of Sisyphos.

We know the story of his birth. When Perseus cut off Medusa's head, she was with child by Poseidon of a hero and a winged stallion, Chrysaor and Pegasos. They leapt out through the neck from the body of their beheaded mother. From this moment on we hear no more of Chrysaor, the rest of the tale concerning the stallion only. Pegasos drank from the spring Peirene,[398] as the double fountain in Corinth was called, which sprang from the Akrokorinthos rocks from over-head and from below at the beginning of the road leading to Lechaion, the port on the Corinthian Gulf, and to Poseidon's temple. In the name Pegasos itself the connection with a spring, *pege*, is expressed. Hippukrene, the 'fountain of the horse' on Helikon, was supposed to have sprung up from under his hooves,[399] and the like tale was told of Peirene itself.[400] It was easy to attach such stories to him, the son of Poseidon. He seems to have been so fond of visiting Peirene because of its nearness to his father's sanctuary, and perhaps also for his brother's sake, by whom in the end he let himself be caught, the immortal horse by his mortal brother.

Bellerophontes was the mortal brother, whether or not he was the same as Chrysaor, for he too was a son of Poseidon, one of the many that were born on earth to the god. And he asked his father for a winged horse, which Poseidon granted to his son.[401] But it was not easy to catch and hold the beast as he drank, for the bridle had not then been invented. So the hero endured much in his desire, until the virgin Pallas brought him the bridle of gold, in a dream that straightway was waking truth. And she said, 'Sleepest thou, prince of the house of Aiolos? Come, take this charm for the steed and show it to the Tamer thy father as thou makest sacrifice to him of a white bull.'[402] Up sprang the young man; he had been sleeping at the altar of the goddess to get advice from her in his troubles. His hand grasped the golden wonder, for there it lay. He ran with it to Polyidos the prophet, the same who found the likeness for the marvellous calf in Minos' herds and revived the little child, Glaukos of Crete, in the honey-jar.[403] Now at his bidding Bellerophontes, having made sacrifice to Poseidon, raised an altar to Athena Hippia. Thus Pegasos became his property, sent him by Poseidon, but led to him and bridled by Athene.[404] The hero mounted the divine steed and danced with it the war-dance in full armour, to the goddess' honour.[405]

Certainly it was very soon after this that he became 'Bellerophontes', 'the slayer of Belleros', and this name made his former one pass into oblivion. Still, like Apollo after the slaying of the dragon Delphyne,[406] he also had to do penance and must have himself purified. The tale of how he committed murder and so defiled himself has not been preserved, but we do know[407] that the hero by way of penance quitted Corinth and betook himself to Tiryns. There king Proitos was on the throne and purified him. Proitos must by that time have been an old king, being great-uncle of Perseus, the slayer of Medusa. This no doubt is why some believed[408] that there was another of the same name whose wife was that Anteia of whom we shall have more to tell presently. But legends of heroes trouble themselves but seldom with the age of their characters, and almost everlasting youth was characteristic of heroines. This Proitos was certainly Proitos of Argos, he who had striven with his brother Akrisios in their mother's womb and later quitted the disputed kingdom and emigrated to Asia Minor. From there, from the land of Lykia, he came home with a princess for his wife and seven Kyklopes, to build the strong castle of Tiryns. And as Akrisios had withdrawn to Larissa in Thessaly, Proitos as chief king was sovran of the whole land of Argos, from which his three daughters and his son Megapenthes later tried to exclude Dionysos. But this story has not yet got so far; Proitos was still reigning in full power and might.

In his capacity as great king he cleansed Bellerophontes from homicide and kept the royal scion of Corinth with him in Tiryns. But not for long; his wife Anteia (or Stheneboia, as the tragedians call her), the princess from Asia Minor,[409] fell in love with the handsome rider of Pegasos. It is the story which was to play itself out also in the family of Theseus, and not there only, to the great joy and immortal renown of a narrator even in these latter days, who has taken up the familiar threads after nearly three thousand years. The queen tried to seduce the young man, but failing in this she said to her husband: 'Proitos, or die or slay Bellerophon, Who would enjoy me, all against my will.' The king was angry, but did not dare to kill his guest himself; he sent him to Lykia, to his father-in-law, who according to the tragedians was called Iobates, but according to other and probably the earlier narrators was that very Amisodoros[410] who had reared the Chimaira.[411] To him Proitos sent Bellerophontes with fateful written characters on a sealed tablet.

For nine days the king of Lykia feasted him, and nine bulls were killed for that festival. On the tenth day the king read his son-in-law's letter and saw that he was to give Bellerophontes over to death. Therefore he gave him the task of killing the monster which he had among his cattle. Presumably it, like the marvellous coloured calf in Minos' herds with which Polyidos the prophet had to do,[412] had been dropped by one of his own beasts.[413] The creature was a goat; a young goat which had seen but one winter was called *chimaira* in Greek. Under this name the monstrous Lykian beast too was remembered, although it had the body and the head of a goat only in the middle, being lion in front and serpent behind, a three-headed creature which breathed fire.[414] Bellerophontes mounted his own marvellous steed Pegasos, flew up aloft on him, and shot the Chimaira from above with his arrows.[415] Vase-paintings show him, however, rather with a spear or with Poseidon's trident in his hand.

Thereupon, the king sent him a second time to his death,

against a people beloved of the gods, the Solymoi.[416] But Bellerophontes defeated them. The third time he was sent against the Amazons, and as he was returning victorious from that struggle also, the best Lykian champions awaited him in ambush. None of them returned home, for all were killed by Bellerophontes. Then the king recognised in him the offspring of the gods, kept him with him, gave him his daughter to wife, and ceded half his kingdom to him. Bellerophontes begat two sons and a daughter on this younger sister of Anteia; the daughter was Laodameia, who was to bear Sarpedon to Zeus, though it was elsewhere said that Sarpedon was, like the Cretans Minos and Rhadamanthys, a son of Zeus and Europa.[417] As Lykia was thus connected with Crete and as the person of Pelops, the hero of Olympia, connected Lydia with the Peloponnesos, so Bellerophontes connected another Asian country, or rather two, Lykia and Karia, with the kingdom of Argos, which included Corinth also.

Riding on his winged horse, he had his home both here and there. In Euripides' tragedy 'Stheneboia' it was described how the hero, after slaying the Chimaira, came flying to Tiryns, to take vengeance on Proitos' wife. She was in the very act of making an offering to Bellerophontes as to one dead, for she still loved him.[418] The hero made a pretence of yielding to the queen's passion, took her on Pegasos' back, as if he would fly with her to his kingdom of Karia, and let her fall into the sea by the island of Melos.[419] Or had he become really reconciled to her and still angry only with the treacherous Proitos? On a vase-painting which shows the fall of Stheneboia, Bellero-phontes is covering his face with his hand. A fall from Pegasos, like the fall of Phaethon, whether or not he was guilty of that loving woman's fall, was soon to be his lot also.

According to the story,[420] he wished to mount up to heaven on his steed and intrude upon the counsel of the gods. How he arrived at this design was shown on the stage in another tragedy of Euripides, the 'Bellerophon'. His experiences had convinced the hero that the old saying is true, that the best of

all is never to be born.[421] And are there gods[422] at all? Possess-
ing as he did his marvellous steed, he wished to investigate the
matter for himself. Thus disillusioned and doubting, he was
seen on the back of Pegasos on his flight to heaven, uplifted
above the stage.[423] But did Bellerophontes need disillusionment
and doubts to risk the adventure of a flight to heaven? Was it
bitterness or hot-headedness that made him storm the skies?
The divine stallion threw his foolhardy rider,[424] who fell, as
the older narrators already knew, on the plain of Aleion the
Plain of Wandering, far off in Asia Minor, where he avoided
the company of men.[425] Limping, he mourned for the lot of
mortals, while the undying Pegasos carries the thunderbolt for
the King of the Gods[426] or serves the goddess Eos,[427] who
brings the morning and carries off young men. He was taken
up to Olympos, to the ancient mangers of the divine steeds.[428]

CHAPTER IX

Phrixos and Helle

ATHAMAS WAS ANOTHER SON of the great ancestor
with the name of the wind-god, Aiolos. The story of this
brother of Salmoneus and Sisyphos belonged partly to the
legends concerning Dionysos. For his second wife he had
Kadmos' daughter Ino, an aunt of the god of whom it is said[429]
that he was brought up as a girl in Athamas' house. How the
story ended then with the madness of Athamas and his queen
and how she with her little son Melikertes or Palaimon leaped
into the sea and became the goddess Leukothea is known from
those narratives. We know also that Ino as the second wife of
Athamas was an evil stepmother to Phrixos and Helle, the
king's children by his former wife. This is not to be told at
greater length, the more so as the picture of the brother and
sister voyaging through the air on the back of the ram, whereby
one saved his life and the other fell off, is best connected with
the tale of Pegasos' journey.

Athamas, the eponym of the Athamanes, founded the city
of Halos in Thessaly,[430] but was also accounted king of
Boiotia.[431] In like manner, Salmoneus was at home in two
districts, in Thessaly and in the Peloponnesos. In Thessaly the
story was told that[432] a goddess named Nephele, 'the Cloud',
came to king Athamas and chose him for her husband. She
was not that cloud of which it was alleged that Zeus sent it in
the form of Hera to Ixion,[433] who begot on it Kentauros, the
father of the Centaurs. According to this tale, Nephele bore
Athamas two children, Phrixos, 'the Curly', and Helle,
which might also be the name of a young doe or roe. But the
king turned away from the goddess and took an earthly wife.
Then Nephele returned to heaven and punished the whole
land with drought. Athamas sent messengers to Apollo's
oracle to learn what was to be done about it. This story is also

told in this way,[434] that it was queen Ino who moved the women of the country secretly to roast the seed-corn, and thus was responsible for the infertility of the fields; and, still according to this version, she bribed the messengers who were sent to Delphi to say that the oracle commanded Nephele's children to be sacrificed.

Euripides in particular staged the tale in this form in his tragedy 'Phrixos'.[435] Probably the original story went on to say that young Phrixos offered himself as a victim to drive away a drought from the land.[436] In the town of Halos it was long the custom to sacrifice the eldest son of the family of Athamas to Zeus Laphystios, if he entered a particular sacred building, the meeting-place of the leading men.[437] Now, we know from the story of Pelops that the human sacrifice was completed by the simultaneous offering of a ram. Here a ram, not merely light-coloured, as in the case of Pelops, but golden-fleeced, came to the rescue. As Pegasos was the fruit of one of Poseidon's unions in stallion form, so this marvellous creature was the offspring of the same deity by a marriage in the shape of a ram.[438] Zeus sent it to save the brother and sister,[439] for Helle was to be sacrificed with her brother, possibly of her own free choice, since Phrixos offered himself of his free will; or was it the case that neither had any suspicions when Athamas, intending to sacrifice them, sent for them? They lived with the king's herdsmen, and the king bade them fetch the first ram that came to hand with them as a victim.[440] But this ram was the marvellous beast, and it informed the brother and sister of Athamas' intentions and rescued them.

Another story was[441] that their heavenly mother Nephele had got the ram with the golden fleece as a present from Hera, and sent it to the aid of her children. They mounted the back of the intelligent beast and it flew with them through the air in the direction of the distant eastern land of Kolchis. It was the girl's fate to get only as far as the narrow sea which divides our continent from Asia Minor, and which to this day is known as the Hellespont, the Sea of Helle, because Phrixos' sister fell into those waters. It was her wedding with Poseidon, or so the vase-painters represented it.

The ram addressed her horrified brother and gave him courage.[442] Phrixos reached Kolchis, the land of Aietes, son of Helios, who received him hospitably and gave him his daughter Chalkiope, 'bronze-face', to wife. But the ram was intended from the beginning to be sacrificed; Phrixos offered it to Zeus Phyxios, the rescuer of fugitives. Its golden fleece he presented to king Aietes, the brother of Kirke and Pasiphae, whose acquaintance we have made in the history of the gods in connection with the Sun-god's kin. Another daughter of his was Medeia, whose name has become famous and notorious, famous by reason of the golden fleece, notorious for her murderous deeds and her sorceries. The fleece was hung up in the shrine of Ares on an oak; it was for its sake that Jason and the Argonauts came on their venturesome journey to Kolchis.

This happened after Phrixos was dead; he died at a ripe age in Aietes' palace.[443] Chalkiope bore him four sons, one of whom entered upon the inheritance of his father's house in Halos after Athamas and Ino were punished with madness.

CHAPTER X

Oidipus

WHAT WAS LEFT after Kadmos in Thebes when he and Harmonia had taken on snake-form and entered into the realm of Beyond? There remained the burned bower of Semele in what had been his palace and was to become a temple of Demeter.[444] In that bower Zeus had shown the might of his lightnings,[445] and there he had taken Dionysos to himself from the burned body of his mother. In that place a piece of wood had fallen from heaven and replaced the child for mortals.[446] Polydoros, Kadmos' son and successor, gave it a casing of bronze and called it Dionysos Kadmos. A vine surrounded the unapproachable spot with its tendrils.[447] Ivy, the god's other sacred plant, garlanded the infant Dionysos[448] and what stood for him. According to his name, 'he of the many gifts', Polydoros might have been a little Dionysos too; but he was also called Pinakos,[449] 'writing-tablet man', because his father Kadmos had introduced the Greek letters from Phoenicia. His son Labdakos[450] actually bore the name of a letter, Lambda, which follows K in the alphabet. But there is little to tell either of him or of his son, especially as their time was occupied by the story of the Theban Dioskuroi.

And what remained after these, after Amphion and Zethos, the sons of Zeus and Antiope, except their hero-tomb from which the men of Tithorea tried every year to steal earth? Niobe had united herself to Amphion and the tale of the hapless mother and her children is but too well known. No less sorrowful was the family history of Zethos; but this belongs to another and separate form of narrative, which is founded on the common possession by human beings and birds of one gift of the Muses, in that both can sing. The form of birds was not strange even to the Muses themselves.[451] It was related of Zethos' wife[452] that she was a daughter of Pandareos, like those

12   BELLEROPHONTES BEFORE IOBATES

13   PHRIXOS AND THE RAM PURSUED BY INO

14 OIDIPUS ON THE ARM OF THE HERDSMAN
EUPHORBOS

two who were carried off by the Harpies.[453] But she, whose name was Aedon, 'the Nightingale', had accidentally killed Itylos, the son she had borne to Zethos.[454] An Attic vase-painter shows us the scene, in which she murdered the child in his cot. She did it in a state of unsound mind; by another account, the misguided woman wanted to kill, not her own son, but a little nephew, out of jealousy against her sister-in-law.[455] In her agony she thereupon wished to quit the world of human kind, and was transformed into a nightingale. It is she who laments for Itylos, if his name was not Itys and he was not the son of Prokne, of whom we shall hear in the story of Tereus.

Zethos died of grief, and the Thebans called Laios, son of Labdakos, to the throne.[456] 'Laios' signifies, in a shorter form, the same as Laomedon, namely 'king of the people'. He was a baby one year old when Labdakos died, and the two dark brothers, Nykteus and Lykos, who have played their part in the story of Antiope, got possession of the kingship.[457] In the time of Amphion and Zethos, Laios was still living with Pelops, and thus the Theban stories got a connection with the events which transpired in Pisa. There appears Chrysippos, as the most veritable son of Pelops, indeed his double, a very child of the Sun, whose name means 'he of the golden horses', and who shared much of his father's destiny. He also, like Pelops, was carried off, and his kidnapper was Laios.

Both were endangered by murderous intentions, the Lydian prince in the house of his father Tantalos, who set him before the gods as their food, Chrysippos through the cruelty of his stepmother Hippodameia and his own brothers Atreus and Thyestes, who are said actually to have murdered him.[458] The stories know him only as a boy, who never lived to marry, but was kidnapped early—by Zeus himself, according to a poetess[459]—like another Ganymedes. But his kidnapping by Laios was better known through a tragedy of Euripides; the son of Labdakos, as the poet represented him on the stage in his 'Chrysippos', was the 'inventor' of homoerotic passion.[460] As Pelops' guest-friend, he was instructing the handsome boy in chariot-driving.⁴⁶¹ There was also a story that he did not carry him off from Olympia, but from Nemea, and took him on his chariot to Thebes.⁴⁶² This, it is true, could not be possible if the Nemean Games were not founded till the time of Laios' grandsons. Pelops, then, the story goes on, got back his son by force of arms. A vase-painter shows us the scene of the kidnapping; Chrysippos stretches out his arms to his father from Laios' four-horse chariot. Another artist even showed Hippodameia in the background, desperately crying for help, as if she were not the boy's stepmother. According to this, the kidnapping took place in Pelops' house. Another tradition⁴⁶³ tells us that Laios went five days' journey abroad to fall in love with Chrysippos and carry him off; that was the distance from Pisa and the holy ground of Olympia to Thebes.

Pelops' curse accompanied the kidnapper; he might never beget a son, or if he did, by that son he should be slain.⁴⁶⁴ It was said also ⁴⁶⁵ that Chrysippos for very shame took his own life. There is yet another telling of the tale;⁴⁶⁶ Atreus and Thyestes, the elder brothers, caught the kidnapper and brought him and the boy back. Then Pelops had mercy on Laios' love for Chrysippos; only Hippodameia wished to persuade the elder sons to murder the youngest, who was not her child. When these would not take her advice, she made her way by night into the bedroom of Laios where he was sleeping with Chrysippos, drew the lover's sword, wounded the boy with it and left the weapon in the wound. Chrysippos lived just long enough to save Laios by his evidence and to denounce the murderess. Thereupon Pelops divorced Hippodameia and banished her. You already know the other version of the story, according to which Atreus and Thyestes committed the murder. The curse of Pelops followed them also⁴⁶⁷ and their race was not much more fortunate than that of Laios.

A tragedian transported the suicide of Chrysippos to Thebes,⁴⁶⁸ at a time when the son of Laios had long been on the throne there. As king of Thebes, Laios had chosen as his consort the daughter of a great-grandson of Echion the 'snake-man', one of the dragon's seed and grandson of Pentheus the 'man of woe', son of Agaue, 'the August'. Her name was Epikaste, or as she is much more commonly called, Iokaste. It was under the latter name that she achieved such notoriety, even to the latest times, as hardly any other of the queens who were mothers and wives of heroes. It is said that she combined both relation-ships to one and the same hero. Also through her, her brother Kreon got the sovranty over Thebes for a while. Here again there is a report[469] that Laios slew his father-in-law Menoikeus. It was Iokaste's destiny to become the source of royal power in Thebes.

But Laios should not have begotten a son on her. Three times the oracle of Delphi warned him[470] that Thebes could be saved only if he died without issue. Laios was incapable of forming a firm resolution,[471] and the consummation of the marriage took place when the bridal pair were, so to speak, afflicted with madness.[472] So we are told in Aeschylus' tragedy, the 'Seven against Thebes', which was preceded by two plays now lost, the 'Laios' and the 'Oidipus'. In the first, presumably, the story was told how Laios, who had not taken the oracle's advice, yet later exposed the child which he had begotten on Iokaste,[473] thus drawing down on himself the wrath of Hera and eventually of the god of Delphi.[474] Apollo always left his consultants free to follow the better course, which he advised them, or the worse, if they so chose. It needed more to arouse the wrath of the god; the violent death of Chrysippos in the house of Laios at Thebes may have given rise to his abhor-rence, for he was the protector of boys and tender youths. It was enough to anger Hera if the boy, kidnapped and withheld by force, was to replace his wedded wife for the king. She sent the Sphinx, the monster of which we have to speak presently, against the Thebans from Ethiopia. Chrysippos took his own life, and thereupon Laios decided to journey to the god at Delphi and inquire of him yet a fourth time; that is one form of the story,[475] and perhaps it is to be connected with the 'Seven against Thebes', and thus attributed at least in part to Aeschylus. To him, Laios was not the 'inventor' of homoerotic passion, but the evil lover in whose possession the beloved boy came to a bad end. Teiresias, the wise Theban prophet, who knew that the king was hated by the god, advised against the journey and bade him rather make sacrifice to Hera, god-dess of marriage. Laios would not heed the seer, but set out on the way which he must follow at first to the south,[476] through a narrow cross-road between Kithairon and Potniai.[477]

The tale of the oracle and of Laios' journey is told in another form also, in the words of Iokaste at the beginning of Euripides' 'Phoenissae', with which he continued his 'Chrysippos'. Laios had lived for many years with Iokaste in a childless marriage[478] when he decided to question the oracle regarding offspring. The god replied to him:

'Beget no child against the will of heaven;
For if a son be thine, that son shall slay thee,
And all thine house shall tread the road of blood.'[479]

Laios should have been content with this and given up all thoughts of offspring, but being overcome with lust and wine he afterwards begat a son[480] and at once had him exposed. Long years afterwards, impelled by evil apprehensions, he set out to learn of the oracle if the exposed child was still alive; he took the shortest way to Delphi through the region of Phokis,[481] and there arrived at a narrow cross-road.

The third, and the simplest, account of the oracle is con-tained in that tragedy whose greatness overshadowed all others that were written before or after it on this subject and made them almost wholly forgotten, the 'Oidipus the King' of Sophokles. The king and queen of Thebes, Laios and Iokaste, received a warning from Delphi that their son would slay his father,[482] and that was why the child was exposed. Later it was pretended that an oracle in the Pythia's own verses could be produced, though indeed it has no such archaically simple tone, but contains the whole preliminary history.[483] That is the only reason for giving it here, before our tale goes on to the fate of the exposed child:

'Laios, Labdakos' son, thou askest the blessing of offspring.
I will give thee a son of thine own, yet destiny willeth
That at the hands of thy child thou die, for so hath allowed
Zeus, Kronos' son, who heedeth the bitter curses of Pelops,
Robbed by thee of his son, who invoked these evils upon thee.'

The earlier narrators paid attention, probably, more to the person of Oidipus and less to the preliminaries of his exposure. To judge by his name, the hero was 'swell-foot', and the tellers of the tale gave themselves trouble enough to explain this remarkable name and make it credible that it really had something to do with the feet of the exposed child. Otherwise, one could easily think of one of the Daktyls, one of the earth-born sons of the great Mother of the Gods. In the oldest times proper names which had not even the periphrasis 'swell-foot' were in use, when the peculiarity of the Daktyls was alluded to, consequently one of them might have been called simply Oidyphallos;[484] but in the days when the story of Oidipus is told us, this seems to have been no longer usual.

The child was exposed in winter, in an earthenware pot; this was the account given in Aeschylus' 'Laios'.[485] A vase-painting shows him sitting naked on the arm of Euphorbos, who found him. Not till later are his swaddling-clothes mentioned,[486] and to increase his helplessness his feet are represented as pierced either with a gold pin[487] or with an iron spike,[488] so that he was 'swell-foot' all his days. A superfluous cruelty on the part of the narrators hides what they would not credit and what was formerly indicated, the ancient Daktyl-nature of the red-headed[489] man of whose fits of furious anger we shall soon hear more.

But his story begins exactly like that of other exposed heroes and divine children. It was even alleged[490] that he was a son of Helios. Something like the stories told of Perseus and once of Dionysos himself[491] was narrated of him, namely that he was thrown into the water in a chest,[492] either in the Corinthian Gulf or the Euripos, the strait which separates Euboia from Boiotia. The chest floated about on the sea so far that Hippodameia herself could pick up and rear the foundling, as if he, like Chrysippos, were a son of Pelops;[493] for in this version he killed Laios to protect or avenge his supposed brother, and got possession of Iokaste when she came to Pisa for her husband's funeral. He is even represented as a rival of Laios and as murdering him for that reason. These are far-reaching branches of the story, in which new and old are mingled and the ancient thread is quite lost.

According to one old account, the chest with the infant got no further than the neighbourhood of the city in which Polybos, a son of Hermes, bore rule.[494] Was this Sikyon, Corinth, or Anthedon?[495] Queen Periboia was washing her clothes by the seashore when the chest came to land there.[496] On a 'Homeric' cup, as it is called, we see Hermes handing the child to the queen, and Periboia setting him on the lap of the king. Oidipus grew up in the house of Polybos in the belief that he and Periboia, or Merope as she is also named,[497] were his parents. But the well-known story is that he was exposed, not on the sea, but on Mount Kithairon, where the herdsmen of Thebes from one side and those of Sikyon on the other could meet. If Laios' herdsmen exposed the child, those of Polybos might find him, and so it happened, on Hera's meadow, as Euripides represents it.[498]

Or indeed, the child was never exposed at all—so we are told in the 'Oedipus Rex'—[499] but the Theban herdsman handed him over to one from Corinth, to be brought up as his own son. He presented him to his childless king;[500] Oidipus himself tells the story in this tragedy[501] of how, when he had become the first citizen of Corinth, a drunken guest at a banquet reproached him with not being the king's son, how his foster-parents, when he enquired of them, repudiated the slander, and how he secretly set forth to ask the god at Delphi; and further, how the god did not answer his question, but threatened him with the awful doom of becoming his mother's husband and his father's murderer. Therefore he did not dare return to Corinth, but took another route, through Phokis, passing a narrow cross-road, where he was to murder an unknown man.

And so the tale, whether we begin from Laios or Oidipus, brings us to a narrow cross-road, wherever it may have lain, between Thebes and Delphi, in Phokis, or to the south of Thebes, between Kithairon and Potniai. There the father and son were to meet, without recognising one another, an ill-starred father and a son no less unfortunate, who should have avoided each other and had even done everything possible to shun the encounter. It was not necessary to the story that they should know the fate which awaited them; it is equally conceivable without the intervention of an oracle. The narrators, who believed in oracles, got hold there of something which from the very beginning had formed the kernel of this tale of unintended and yet perpetrated patricide. Oidipus had no idea in any form of the story that his route through the narrow cross-road would meet that of his father. Also Laios' anxiety lest he be dethroned by his son needed no oracle, for its prototype was found in the history of the gods, in the tale of Uranos and Kronos, a very ancient tradition, common to the Greeks and the Asians from an early date. By means of the prophecy the narrators gave shape to a very ancient fear, and the exposure resulted from that fear, not from Apollo's foretelling, though of course not without his knowledge, if he was already the god of the Delphic oracle. Man so often runs into something terrible through fear of the terrible.

And thus this very human happening occurred; the son's path crossed that of the father in a narrow pass where it was not possible to make room. 'Traveller, give way to the king!' cried Laios' herald to the stranger,[502] as Laios was driving through the narrow place in his chariot. Oidipus' rage boiled up; he strode forward on his way without a word.[503] One of the king's horses trod on his foot,[504] and the old king also struck him on the head from the chariot with the forked goad which he used to drive his team. Thus the measure was fulfilled.[505] In anger, and not knowing whom he was striking, as is explicitly told us,[506] he smote his father dead[507] with his staff,[508] and the herald as well.[509] Aeschylus preserves another detail of the picture of the anger which possessed him; he bit the corpse of his victim and spat the blood out.[510]

A very ancient form of the story is referred to by a late narrator, that one who informs us[511] that Oidipus was then gone out to steal horses and that Laios when he met him was accompanied by his wife Epikaste. But he shuns the point of the story and alleges that after the murder Oidipus took refuge in the hills, as is usual to this day in Greece, and did not touch Epikaste. How, then, could she in the later course of the narrative have willingly taken the slayer for her husband, after being witness of the murder, if she had not then and there become the prey of the robber? Surely, in that old telling of the story, everything happened in the same outbreak of rage; the son struck his father dead and took possession of his mother, the unknown queen, thus attaining through her the kingship of Thebes as well.

Doubtless the poet of the 'Odyssey' also knew it, as he tells us the tale thus: Epikaste became the wife of her son, who took her when he had killed and taken the spoils of his father, but the gods straightway made all known to men. And he, in woe, was still king of the Kadmeians in lovely Thebes, through the cruel counsels of the gods. But she went to the house of Hades, the mighty guardian of the gate, fastening a rope sheer from the high roof, in the gripe of her grief. To him she left behind many woes, even those which a mother's avenging spirits accom⁄plish.[512] Oidipus' children also must have discovered it; according to the older narrators they were not the offspring of Epikaste but of a second wife, who bore the beautiful name of Euryganeia, 'she who shines joyfully far and wide'.[513] Indeed yet another name was traditionally borne by a wife of Oidipus, Astymedusa,[514] which would fit any and every queen. It is quite possible that both names mean the same woman. Oidipus himself fell, the Iliad tells us, mightily on the field of battle.[515]

Homer says not a word about the wisdom by which Oidipus had to win the throne of Thebes after the murder of Laios, in the best-known form of the story, but speaks as if the Kadmeians had never been plagued by the monster on the neighbouring height of Phikion, the Phix, or, in the more intelligible form of her name, the Sphinx, the Strangler. If Oidipus, as the later teller of the old tale of his horse-thieving expedition would have it,[516] returned to his foster-father Polybos with the plundered horses or mules, and had not taken possession at once of the queen and also of the kingdom, he must have journeyed to Thebes later, to free the city from the Sphinx. After the death of Laios Kreon, brother of Iokaste, ruled there. He and the elders of the city were in great anxiety ever since the winged lioness or bitch with the head of a virgin had invaded the neighbourhood of the town.

As already mentioned it is said that his visitation had assailed Thebes already in Laios' lifetime. Hera had sent the Sphinx from Ethiopia against the Kadmeians, because they tolerated their king's passion for Chrysippos. Or Dionysos might have sent the ravenous lion-virgin against his natal city, which would not honour him. This Euripides seems actually to have alleged,[517] though elsewhere he states,[518] what must have been the view of the sufferers themselves, that the underworld had sent the Sphinx up against Thebes. To Thebes' bane, the mother of so many monsters, the serpent-goddess Echidna, had borne her[519] after mating with her own son, the dog Orthos.[520] The Sphinx took her seat on the hill which was named Phikion after her, if she did not perch on a pillar in the Kadmeians' market place, to pick out her victims. In this position she appears, but also on the hill. We see her also carrying off young men and strangling them, and so she was to be seen on the throne of Zeus wrought by Pheidias.[521] An old account says that she carried off Haimon, son of Kreon, the handsomest and tenderest youth in all Thebes.[522] Thereupon Kreon made proclamation that Iokaste and the kingdom should be his who overcame the Sphinx.

Originally no doubt the hero who would kill her must go against her to the hill Phikion. Thus a vase shows us Oidipus raising his club to strike, not pondering over any riddle, as he faces the lion-virgin. According to the well-known account, the Thebans used daily to assemble to puzzle over the riddle which the Sphinx set them, and when they could not solve it, she always seized one of them.[523] She had got the riddle from the Muses[524] but here she resembled the Sirens more than the Muses; certainly she was not originally the 'wise virgin',[525] rather the artful one who had learned her one ruse. On an engraved stone of the best classical date we see her getting her wisdom from a book-roll, or reading it aloud. She sang her riddle like an oracle,[526]

> 'On two feet, yet on four, there treads the earth,
> Yea, and on three, a creature of one name.
> Alone it changes shape of all that walk
> On ground or fly in air or swim the sea.
> But when it goes supported on four feet,
> Then is the speed the feeblest in its limbs.'

The Sphinx may well have been proud of her riddle, and also it confused people; for they likewise did not understand that riddle which was carved, as a sage's warning, on the porch of Apollo's temple at Delphi, 'Know thyself.' The answer to that is, 'Know that thou art man.' We see Oidipus (as more than one vase-painter represents him) sitting in front of the Sphinx and pondering. 'What does she mean by "yea, and on three"?' And he cried,[527]

> 'Of Man thou tellest. When he goes on mould
> Four-footed first he creeps, a babe new-born;
> In age a staff, third foot, must him uphold,
> All heavy-necked, with curvèd eld forlorn.'

When the Sphinx heard this, she did what the Sirens did when anyone failed to succumb to their singing. Just as they threw themselves, winged creatures though they were, into the sea and thus committed suicide, so also did the winged lion-virgin cast herself down from her rocks[528] or from the column on the Theban acropolis.[529] We see too on a vase-painting how Oidipus puts her out of her misery with a light spear.

Thus Oidipus became a sage, and also the most foolish of all the kings in the world. He received as the prize of his victory (so the best-known version has it, which does not make Iokaste present at Laios' murder), his own mother to wife and begat on her four children, the sons being Eteokles and Polyneikes, the daughters Antigone and Ismene, all to become famous through the misfortunes of the House of the Labdakids. Oidipus, wise in appearance only, had no idea of this. Doubtless he recognised himself in the strange creature which the Sphinx meant by her riddle, but not what man is, not the tricks played him by the fate to which he, unlike the fateless gods, is delivered over. It was human destiny which fulfilled itself in him and that destiny was made plain in time. For not all who had exposed the child, or were supposed to have done so, but did not, were dead.

Also there was the one really wise man in Thebes, the seer Teiresias, whose blind eyes saw through the errors of Oidipus as they formerly had those of Laios. But when he was forced to speak by the king himself, many years had passed under the government of the foolish pair, the mother and the son, and a plague made the Thebans feel that all was not well with their State.[530] Teiresias had something in common with Oidipus (his name signifies one who interprets *teirea*, that is signs). He had become blind in his youth, as the hero who had taken his mother to wife was to become in the prime of life. It was told of him too[531] that he was the descendant of one of the Spartoi, Udaios, the 'man of the ground'. His mother was named Chariklo, like the wife of the wise Centaur Chiron, and belonged to the train of Pallas Athene. Thus Teiresias in his youth saw what he should not have seen. The goddess, delighting in her horses, was travelling about in Boiotia and stripped off her clothing to refresh herself with a bath. This she did once in Hippukrene, the 'horse's well' on Helikon, in the stillness of noon and in loneliness.[532] Teiresias, on whose cheeks the first down was showing, was hunting there alone with his hounds at the holy place. Impelled by unspeakable thirst, he ran to the spring, poor wretch, and unintentionally he saw that which it is not lawful to behold. He had seen the bosom and the flanks of Athene, but might never see the sun again; the goddess put her hands over his eyes and blinded him.[533] But for love of her lamenting attendant Chariklo she dedicated him prophet, purified his ears so that he could understand the voices of birds, and gave him a staff of cornel wood with which he could walk like a sighted man.

Another story of the blinding of Teiresias had the like meaning; there again he caught sight of something which he ought not to have beheld. When he was a young herdsman,[534] so the tale runs, at a cross-roads[535] on Kithairon,[536] or on Mount Kyllene, in the region where Hermes with the pair of snakes on his staff was at home,[537] he saw two serpents coupling. This adventure, which one would think was nothing extraordinary in the life of a herdsman in Greece, must have had a special meaning for ancient times, if later days made it into the starting-point of a veritable divine jest. Teiresias, so we are told, had killed the female snake as she was coupling,[538] and in that very instant was himself turned into a woman. As such he lived for the next seven years and experienced the love of man.[539] After the seven years he again saw a pair of snakes at the act of love; this time his blow struck the male and he was immediately turned into a man again. At that time Zeus and Hera were disputing with each other as to whether the male or the female kind got more pleasure of love. They chose Teiresias as their umpire, and his decision ran thus:[540]

'Of ten, the man enjoyeth but one part,
Nine parts the woman fills, with joyful heart.'

Hera was furious at this pronouncement and punished him with blindness. Zeus bestowed on him in compensation the gift of prophecy and caused him to live for seven generations of men. But we are not told that his gift made the sage happy. He sighed, it is said,[541]

> 'Ah, father Zeus, a lesser lease of life
> Would thou hadst granted me, and wits no more
> Than other men's. No honour hast thou done me,
> No, not the least, with this my length of days
> To seven generations thus prolonged.'

Blind and gifted with divine wisdom, he was obliged to live through the destinies of Kadmos and his descendants, six generations of them, and alone of all men to keep his intelligence even in the underworld. This gift Persephone granted him.[542] Odysseus visited him later in the realm of the dead and let him, still carrying a prophet's golden staff, be the first to drink from the blood which filled the sacrificial pit. Teiresias recognised him and addressed him without having drunk the blood,[543] and after doing so, foretold him all his future destiny.

He also saw the fate of Oidipus, which was fulfilled even as Teiresias prophesied it.[544] When that unhappy man could but perceive that he had become the husband of his mother and the brother of his children, he deprived himself of eyesight.[545] That was the penalty for those who had seen what it was not allowed them to see; as Teiresias had seen the goddess, or the snakes at their deed of kind, so he had seen his mother. It was also said[546] that he did not blind himself, but the old brothers-in-arms of Laios did so when they meant simply to punish the murderer of their lord and never knew that he was also Laios' son. People tried to give ever-new turns to the old narrative. In the 'Phoenissae' of Euripides, Iokaste herself appears as still an aged queen-mother, many years later than the exposure of her shame, on tottering feet,[547] and kills herself over the corpses of her two sons, who have slain one another,[548] thus drinking the woes of her agonising maternity to the very dregs. According to all earlier handlings of the story, she hanged herself at once when her shame was revealed.

The blind Oidipus vanished from the eyes of the Thebans. In order that the pure light of the sun should not be polluted by his presence,[549] he was kept in hiding, as it were in a dungeon, by his family, either Kreon[550] or his sons.[551] No longer in his right mind,[552] and more than ever subject to furious outbreaks of rage, he submitted. He forbade his sons ever again to set the royal dishes before him, the story continues;[553] and when fair-haired Polyneikes nevertheless did so, putting pious Kadmos' silver table before him and filling the golden goblet with sweet wine, the blind man perceived it; he took it as an insult, his soul was overcome with grievous evil, and he put a curse on both his sons, that they should divide their paternal inheritance between them with iron.[554] When on the other hand they once forgot[555] to send their father the royal portion of a victim, the shoulder-piece, and instead sent him a haunch, he perceived that too, flung the piece to the ground, and cursed his sons again; he directed to Zeus and the other gods his prayer that the two might pass together into the underworld, either slain by the other's hand.

Oidipus in the 'Phoenissae', appears from his palace-prison like a ghost,[556] to see the fulfilment of his curses. The imprison-ment in his own palace, in an underground chamber where according to a late account he died,[557] was only one form of his sufferings. In this Euripidean tragedy Antigone, the elder and stronger of his daughters, leads him away from the battle-field, where for the last time he had caressed the three beloved bodies, the corpses of Iokaste, Eteokles and Polyneikes.[558] It was his destiny to become a vagabond too,[559] and she led him on the road to Kolonos, Poseidon's rocky hill and the threshold of Athens and of the underworld, the holy spot where, according to a pronouncement of the Delphic oracle, he was to end his life.[560]

In Sophokles' last tragedy, the work of his old age, the 'Oidipus at Kolonos', we meet this pair. The younger daughter Ismene was soon to join them on the way which they had long trodden, even before the strife of the brothers. They roamed begging through the land, for the aged Oidipus was no longer the fiery-tempered man he had been; he asked for little and was content with even less when it was given him.[561] He was become the suffering hero, who after his death should be the treasure and defence of those in whose land he found his rest. This was to happen there in the *petite patrie* of Sophokles, on the territory of the demos Kolonos, at a rocky hill. There the goddesses who avenged a mother, the Erinyes—also called the Eumenides, the Benevolents, by the Athenian people—had their inviolable grove. That was the goal of Oidipus' woeful journey, and there he found grace.[562]

He entered with confidence the grove which might not be entered. He knew that here he had to await the announcement of his coming, disappearance by earthquake, thunder and lightning.[563] He entrusted himself and the secret of his grave, which was to be no ordinary grave but should hereafter protect the Athenians, to the lord of the land, Theseus. Theseus sent for him in all haste, when Zeus gave the first signal with his thunder.[564] It roared like an unceasing thunderstorm, peal on peal, flash on flash, and now the blind man became the guide of Theseus and his two daughters, who had followed him there. With unhesitating tread he followed the Guide of Souls, whom he seemed to see, for he named him, Hermes, and also the goddess of the realm of the dead, whom he dared not name.[565] At the edge of the gulf he halted;[566] through it steps of bronze formed the approach to the very roots of the rocks. The countless roads which lead to the underworld met here; and here, between a hollow pear-tree and a stone tomb, Oidipus sat down, threw off his soiled garments and had himself washed and clothed by his daughters as the dead should be. And with them he raised the lament at departure when the thunder of Zeus of the nether world sounded. This too passed and all were silent. With a shudder they heard the voice of a god, 'Ho there, ho there, Oidipus, why must we wait for you?'[567] Only Theseus might see what happened then;[568] he remained standing there a long while and covered his face; Oidipus had vanished.

Probably Aeschylus told much the same story; it was said of him[569] that he had divulged something in his 'Oidipus' which belonged to the Mysteries of Demeter. Those Mysteries were the Mysteries also of her daughter, the goddess of the realm of the dead. According to the older narrators, Oidipus did not get to Kolonos; he wandered in his sorrows, after he had robbed himself of the light of his eyes, for a long while in the wild mountain scenery of Kithairon,[570] where he had been exposed and where in his anger he had unwittingly slain his father. In that region also his grave was shown. His kin, so the story went, wished to bury him in Thebes,[571] but the Thebans would not allow it; he was, as it were, marked out by his misfortune. So the burial took place in another district of Boiotia, called Keos. But mishaps befell that village and the inhabitants believed that the cause of them was Oidipus' grave. Finally he was buried in Eteonos, also a village situated in Boiotia and later called Skarphe. It was night when they buried him there in secret, not knowing that the spot was in a sacred precinct of Demeter. When this became manifest, the Eteonians asked the god of Delphi what they were to do, and Apollo replied, 'Disturb not the suppliant of the goddess.' So he remained buried there, and that is why the place is called Oidipus' shrine.

On vase-paintings we see young men and young women approaching the monument. Do the artists mean the sons and daughters of Oidipus, or were these other young people, perhaps even young husbands and wives, bringing an offering to the hero whose sorrows were to bestow blessings, not indeed on his own kin, but on strangers who honoured him? The tomb, marked by a column, bore the inscription,[572]

> 'Mallow above and asphodel I bear,
> My lap holds Oidipus, king Laios' heir.'

15 OIDIPUS SOLVES THE RIDDLE OF THE SPHINX

16 OIDIPUS KILLING THE SPHINX

17 KASTOR AND POLYDEUKES GREETED BY
LEDA AND TYNDAREOS

CHAPTER XI

The Spartan Dioskuroi and their Cousins

KASTOR AND POLYDEUKES (still better known perhaps in their Latin form, Castor and Pollux) are the names of a pair who to this day signify for us the inseparable union of brothers. They were not the only ones to be known as *Diòs kûroi*, 'sons of Zeus'; Thebes knew and honoured Dioskuroi among the heroes who founded her, twins whose father was the King of the Gods, the sons of Antiope. Yet when we hear of *the* Dioskuroi, it is especially the twin brothers, sons of Leda, who are meant. We know of them and likewise of their mother from the history of the gods.[573] They were also named the Tyndaridai, or still earlier Tindaridai, allegedly after an earthly father called Tyndareos. The appellation 'sons of Zeus' may be hidden in this name also, expressed in a tongue which was spoken earlier in Greece.

The story of Kastor and Polydeukes, so far as it belongs to the legends of the heroes, must therefore start with king Tyndareos. For these legends have a liking for the genealogical tree which connects the heroes with one another through earthly fathers and mothers and a widening circle of kin. It was said, then,[574] that Gorgophone, daughter of Perseus, 'she who slew the Gorgon', so named in memory of her father's victory, was married first with Perieres, one of the sons of Aiolos, king of Messenia at Oichalia, as Andania, the site of the later mysteries, was then called. To Perieres she bore Aphareus and Leukippos, whose transparent name signifies 'one who has a white horse'. But she is said to have been the first wife[575] to marry another husband after the death of the first. In her second marriage she became the wife of Oibalos, who to judge by his name was a Daktyl-like primaeval being of Lakonia, the 'copulator', whose father according to some was Kynortas, 'arouser of dogs', a brother of Hyakinthos.[576] Tyndareos was a son of Oibalos and Gorgophone, or, by another tradition which knows nothing of all this genealogy,[577] of a fountain-nymph, Bateia, 'the thicket'.

After this the genealogy of the Dioskuroi takes root, through Tyndareos, on Lakonian soil, and so it should for a king of Sparta, which Tyndareos was to become, and for the Spartan Dioskuroi whom his wife bore. True, it is not said that he bore undisturbed sway over Lakonia.[578] For a time he was driven out by his half-brother Hippokoon; Herakles later restored him. He took refuge in the western part of the Greek mainland. According to most accounts the king there was Thestios, a descendant of Pleuron, founder of the city of the same name among the Kuretes of Aitolia. But it is quite possible that according to other accounts Thestios likewise had founded cities, Thestia in Aitolia and earlier still another Thestia in Lakonia.[579] According to the Spartans, Tyndareos never moved to Aitolia and Thestios at all, but to the Lakonian town of Pellana.[580] In Aitolia, Thestios was already the father of a famous daughter, Althaia, of whom we shall have to speak in the story of Meleagros. His other renowned daughter was allegedly Leda, although the tale is told that Thestios' wife Panteidyia, 'the all-knowing', conceived her not by Thestios but by Glaukos son of Sisyphos.[581] It was not easy to find a father and a family tree for a primaeval woman such as Leda, to judge by her name, must have been.

We all know the famous tale[582] of how Leda conceived the Tindarids in Lakonia; Zeus loved her in the shape of a swan under the height of Taygetos, over which those great white birds flew. In the Messenian Gulf, opposite the Lakonian coast, rises the little rocky island of Pephnos; there the twins, Kastor and Polydeukes, came into the world. The island was not supposed to be the birthplace of their sisters Helen and Klytaimnestra. We may remember the vase-painting[583] which represents the sons of Leda as young men, while the egg from which Helen was to be born lies between them on the altar, a scene which is laid in Tyndareos' royal residence, whether that was in Pellana or in Sparta. Pephnos on the other hand is hardly more than a reef, and only heavenly children could find their birthplace there; certainly no woman would visit that rocky island to bring forth her child. That mother must have had wings and laid eggs, like the sea-birds and Leda's heavenly double, the goddess Nemesis. In such shape she, the daughter of Night, by whichever of the two names we like to call her, doubtless brought her sons into the world, and we shall hear later that even their wings were not quite forgotten.

In antiquity the round cap, *pilos*, which the Dioskuroi wore whether on horseback or holding their steeds by the curb was explained[584] by saying that they got it from the egg out of which they had crept. Hermes, according to later accounts,[585] brought the divine children from Pephnos to Pellana. On the little island were shown their bronze statues, no more than a foot high, although they too, like the Kabeiroi, were also called Great Gods, and the tale was told[586] that the flood which swept over the rocks in winter time never washed these figures away. The Spartans were content with two beams, fastened together in the shape of the letter H, or two slender amphorae, around each of which in the representations a serpent often entwines, when they wished to be reminded of their beloved Tindarids.

Messenia, the neighbouring country to Lakonia, also had its divine twins. They were the cousins of the Spartan Dioskuroi. Gorgophone in her first marriage bore Aphareus, and he took to wife Arene, sister of his half-brother Tyndareos.[587] But he was no more, or no less, the father of his sons than Tyndareos was the begetter of the Dioskuroi. The real father of the twins whom Arene bore was said to be Poseidon;[588] especially the gigantic Idas was allegedly begotten by the lord of the sea. But Lynkeus, 'lynx-eye', was also an extraordinary being, for his sharp sight pierced into the depths of the earth.[589] The story of the Lakonian Dioskuroi must include their Messenian cousins, for they were not long in coming to blows with each other.

It was said of Idas[590] that he was the strongest man on earth. He fought Apollo himself for a beautiful maid, Marpessa, daughter of Euenos king of Aitolia,[591] of whom the same was reported as of Oinomaos, both being sons of Ares, namely that he would give his daughter only to one who beat him in a chariot-race. But Euenos always won, decapitated the men he defeated and ornamented his palace with the heads. But Idas carried Marpessa off from the dances which the virgins were performing in honour of Artemis on a meadow; the meadow was called Ortygia, 'quail meadow', like the birthplace of the goddess. Idas had got the swiftest of horses from his father Poseidon, and Euenos pursued him in vain. When the king saw the maid's abductor escape with his booty at the river Lykormos, he killed his own team and plunged into the river, which henceforth was called Euenos, 'well-bridled'.

After that, Marpessa was nearly lost to her strong bridegroom, for one still mightier appeared and tore Idas' bride from him. The maid lamented like the female fulmar in the arms of Apollo.[592] This happened after Idas had arrived in Messenia with his booty.[593] He was not slack, but bent his bow against the god;[594] it was said that Idas' shots never missed.[595] But Zeus did not let the shot be discharged; he sent Hermes[596] or, according to the representation of a vase-painter, his messenger Iris, and ordered the choice to be left to the girl. Marpessa chose her earthly bridegroom, for she was afraid that Apollo would leave her when she grew old. This is how late narrators account for her choice,[597] not considering any longer how annihilating for a mortal maid Apollo's embrace must seem. Marpessa behaved no otherwise than if it was Death himself who had her in his power. The daughter whom she bore to Idas bore the nickname of Alkyone, 'fulmar',[598] in memory of the bitter complaints of her mother in the arms of the god. Otherwise she was known as Kleopatra, 'famed for her father', and became the wife of Meleagros.

Wife-stealing was a definite form of marriage, consecrated by the carrying off of Persephone in primaeval times, but particularly usual in Lakonia. In this the Spartan Dioskuroi set the example to all mortals. Allegedly they had as cousins not only a male but a female pair of twins, the daughters of Leukippos, Tyndareos' other half-brother. But perhaps the girls had no mortal father but were called Leukippides in the sense of celestial 'white fillies'. Apollo was thought to be their father,[599] and they were given names which fitted two phases of the moon, Phoibe, 'the pure' and Hilaeira, 'the serene', appropriate respectively to the new and the full moon. Phoibe is said also to have been priestess of Athene, Hilaeira of Artemis.[600] Later they possessed their shrine in Sparta, near the house which was held to be the sacred dwelling of the Dioskuroi.[601] The Leukippides were carried off from the sacred precinct of Aphrodite, where they were playing with their companions when Kastor and Polydeukes lifted them on to the chariot. According to the representation of an Attic vase-painter, the goddess of love and Zeus were present and approved the rape, by which two divine pairs concluded a marriage after the Spartan fashion.

This started the enmity between the two divine pairs of brothers. The Leukippides, the story goes,[602] were originally betrothed to their Messenian cousins under an oath; but the Dioskuroi bribed Leukippos with larger presents so that they might carry off their cousins. Idas and Lynkeus pursued the kidnappers, caught up with them at Aphareus' tomb, and so the story came to its tragical end. According to the older tellers of the tale,[603] the enmity began otherwise. The four cousins made a raid in common on the territory of the Arkadians, which marched with theirs to the north, Kastor and Polydeukes coming from Lakonia, Idas and Lynkeus from Messenia, to steal cattle. They returned with abundant booty and entrusted the division of it to Idas. He quartered a cow and made the proposal that whoever could eat his quarter first should have half the spoil, and the next to finish should take the other half. Thereupon the gigantic Idas swallowed first his own quarter and then also that of Lynkeus, and thus the

Messenian brothers drove home the whole of the captured herd; they had played a foul trick on the Dioskuroi.

The sons of Leda took part also in many other adventures, never separating from one another, Kastor as a horsemaster, Polydeukes as a boxer.[604] We shall meet them again on the voyage of the Argonauts. But the picture of the Tindarids is not complete unless there stands between them the shining figure of a woman, their beautiful sister or actually the great goddess, the Mother of all the gods. Rock-carvings at the town of Akrai in Sicily testify to the service of the Dioskuroi to the great Mother, Rhea-Kybele. They served their sister Helen in setting her free from the fastness of Aphidna in Attica. This belongs to the history of Theseus, who carried off the daughter of Zeus. The end of the story of the enmity between the cousins and at the same time of the earthly life of the Tin-darids[605] came much later, after the marriage of Peleus and Thetis.

Paris had already set out, encouraged and protected by Aphrodite and accompanied by Aineias, the son of the goddess, to carry off Helen anew. Tyndareos was no longer king of Sparta, but his son-in-law Menelaos. He carelessly enough, soon left his beautiful wife alone with the Asiatic guests. Paris and Aineias, on arrival in Lakonia, first visited the Dioskuroi, the ever-ready guardians of their sister. This was the will of Zeus, who himself no doubt brought it to pass that the brothers should be got away from all that was happening in Sparta and Lakonia. At the feast which was given to receive the guests Idas and Lynkeus were also present. They cracked their rude jests and spoke of the marriage by capture of the Dioskuroi as if they had undertaken it merely to avoid having to pay Leukippos any dowry for his daughters.

'Very well,' replied the Tindarids, 'we will make up for it now, and give him a rich present of fine cattle.' And off they went, to get the herds of Idas and Lynkeus from Messenia. Polydeukes went ahead to drive off the cattle, while Kastor hid in a hollow oak to ambush their cousins, who they guessed would come after them. They had left their sister unprotected and handed over to the seductive arts of the Trojan prince, who in her brothers' absence attained his end.

The Messenian twins also did not stay long at the feast. Lynkeus hurried homewards up Taygetos, which divides Lakonia from Messenia. From the summit his all-penetrating vision caught sight of Kastor where he lurked in the tree. He told his brother, and Idas took Kastor unawares and speared him. After his murder the cousins took to flight, but Poly-deukes was in the neighbourhood (in one version of the story, he too was hidden in the oak) and pursued them both. He caught up with them at Aphareus' tomb, and there the end came. The Messenians tore their father's headstone out of the earth; Polydeukes' spear gave Lynkeus his death-wound, but the gravestone was flung at and struck him, and after the stone came Idas while he was still stunned. But Zeus hurled his thunderbolt between the two and smote down the giant.

There, with none to lament them, the bodies of Aphareus' sons burned. Polydeukes ran to his brother and found him at the last gasp. He raised his voice to Zeus and besought his father that he might die also. Zeus approached him and said,[606] 'Thou art my son; this man thy mother's husband begat on her afterwards with mortal seed when that hero embraced her.' And he gave Polydeukes his choice, either to live henceforth on Olympos or to pass one day under the earth with his brother, the next with Kastor in the celestial palace with the gods. What Polydeukes chose was to share light and darkness too, for ever. And so they both dwell for one day with Zeus, the next in their hero-grave at Therapne, across the Eurotas from Sparta, where also a shrine was built for Helen. They inhabit[607] their dark subterranean mansion when they do not enjoy the light of heaven.

It was told[608] and also believed that they live in heaven as bright stars, and they were recognised[609] in the constellation of the Twins. A star frequently decorates the crown of their *pilos*; often it is even-encircled by the moon, as if the two

Dioskuroi represented the two hemispheres of the sky, or at least as if their round caps did so.[610] Certainly at all times they became for their worshippers more than other heroes; they were deities of the heavens, setting as the stars do, yet confined to no grave, but swift riders, who course through the air from above and intervene wherever men in distress invoke them, as helpers and deliverers in the emergencies of the battlefield, but still more often in the perils of the sea.

If they bring aid to a ship in danger during the winter gales, they do not appear as horsemen, but as the gods of earlier days often revealed themselves, in the shape of winged celestial beings. The mariners, so it is told us,[611] cry and pray to the sons of great Zeus with sacrifice of white lambs, as they take their stand on the aftermost stern, which the great wind and the wave of the sea have flooded; and they at once appear, flashing through the air on their speedy wings, and straightway they make the blasts of the cruel winds to cease and lay the waves of the foam-white brine on the seas, fair omens to bring surcease of toil. And the mariners rejoice to see them, for they have rest from their grievous labour.

CHAPTER XII

Meleagros and Atalante

L E D A ' S   S I S T E R , or rather she who of all the Aitolians was worthiest to pass for a sister of the primaeval woman,[612] Althaia, took her name from the mallow which grows in the swamps. Her husband was Oineus, king of Kalydon, who was named from wine, *oinos*. Kings with names like these had traits very reminiscent of the underworld, particularly Oinomaos, who decorated his palace with the severed heads of Hippodameia's suitors. It is told of Oinopion, king of Chios, who made the hunter Orion drunk and then blinded him,[613] that he hid underground in a bronze chamber. He was accounted also a son of Dionysos,[614] or else of a notable toss-pot called Oinomaos.[615] Oineus had none of these traits, but he had a brother called Agrios, 'the wild', of whom it was told[616] that he afterwards drove Oineus out; and it was said of Oineus himself that he killed his own son Toxeus, 'the bow-man', because he neglected his father's vineyard and leaped over its ditches.

According to one of the genealogies,[617] Oineus was descended from Aitolos, eponym of the Aitolians. He in turn was accounted a son of Endymion by a fountain-nymph,[618] though elsewhere we hear only of the loves of Endymion and Selene. The love of the moon-goddess for a primaeval being seems to be a very old account of the origin of the human race. According to another genealogy,[619] Oineus was descended from Deukalion, whose son Orestheus was Oineus' grand-father. Orestheus, 'mountain-man', possessed a bitch of which it was told that she brought forth a stick. Orestheus buried the stick and it soon was made clear that it was the first grape-vine. Therefore the bitch could be no other than the hound of heaven, Sirius, which ripens the vine. Orestheus' son (Orestheus was not called Mountain-man to denote that he lived inside the mountains but probably because he, with his bitch, lived the life of a hunter) was named Phytios, 'planter', and his son in turn was Oineus.

According to other narrators,[620] wine was not known to men until the reign of king Oineus. A he-goat repeatedly disappeared from his flocks for a while and seemed to be sated when it returned. The goatherd went after it, and found the he-goat at a grape-vine, the sweet fruit of which it was devouring. The name of the goatherd is traditionally Orista,[621] a malformation of Orestheus or Orestes; he is also called Staphylos, and allegedly the grape-cluster is called *staphyle* after him.[622] Oineus made wine from the grapes and called it by his own name. The water that was mixed with wine for the first time was drawn from the river Acheloos, and the poets never forgot this.[623]

But who had taught Oineus how to use the intoxicating drink aright? The tale is told[624] that Dionysos had entered the king's house, not to visit him, but Queen Althaia. Oineus pretended not to notice the god's intentions, and left the city to make a sacrifice outside it. In Athens the same thing was the custom; the Queen, the wife of that archon who bore the epithet of King, separated herself from her husband while she awaited the visit of Dionysos. The grape-vine and the instructions what to do with it and with wine were the gift of the grateful deity to Oineus. That the goat which devoured the vine was sacrificed is not told us in these stories, but we know that it was from many traditions concerning the religion of Dionysos.

From her *affaire* with Dionysos, Althaia, it is said, had a daughter, Deianeira, who to judge by her name should be a maiden hostile to men, and a dangerous wife; we shall hear more of her in the history of Herakles. Althaia bore Oineus several sons,[625] and it was said of the most famous of them that his father was Ares, whom Althaia had entertained on the same night as Oineus; for it was not easy to believe that Meleagros was of other than divine origin.[626] From his birth onwards another piece of wood was to play a part in the House of Oineus, but it was very different from the stick of which wine was the blessed gift.

The story goes[627] that the three Moirai appeared at the birth of Meleagros. They entered the chamber in which Althaia had been delivered of her son. The first of them, Klotho, sang, 'He shall become a man of noble spirit'; Lachesis, the second, sang of the hero he was to become; Atropos, the third, gazed into the fire on the hearth, in which a log was burning, and sang: 'He shall live as long as the brand is not wholly consumed.' Thereupon Althaia sprang out of bed, caught the brand off the fire, and hid it in a chest,[628] no one knew where, in the palace. But the boy got the name Meleagros, which means one whose thoughts are on hunting, in the oldest Greek speech, which did not yet run its vowels together.

In Oineus' kingdom the divine huntress Artemis was a great deity. Yet Oineus, the Wine-man, had once forgotten her.[629] We are told[630] that on the occasion of a harvest-festival he entertained all the gods, but had offered no beast to her at the great sacrificial feast. He had done himself great harm, for the goddess was angered and let loose a wild boar in the king's fertile fields. The beast was so huge[631] that no single hunter, not even Meleagros, could put an end to it. Men must be assembled from many cities, and even so the boar sent many of them to the funeral pyre. At last Artemis made the hunters fight with one another, and thus the Kalydonian hunt became only the beginning of the punishment which the goddess inflicted on the House of Oineus.

To hunt the boar there came to Kalydon before all others Meleagros' uncles, Althaia's brothers, from Pleuron, the near-by city of the Kuretes. In Aitolia these formed an entire people, whereas in Crete none but three divine youths, who had danced their war-dance around the infant Zeus, bore the name of Kuretes.[632] It is even said that heroes from all over Greece came to the Kalydonian hunt.[633] No one stayed at home of all the heroes then alive, with the sole exception of

Herakles, who had his labours to attend to; it was said later[634] that he was then serving Omphale. The Dioskuroi, Kastor and Polydeukes, came with their Messenian cousins Idas and Lynkeus; Theseus came from Athens, Iphikles, Herakles' half-brother, from Thebes, Jason, Admetos, Peirithoos, Peleus and his father-in-law Eurytion arrived from Thessaly, Telamon from Salamis, Amphiaraos from Argos, Ankaios and Atalante from Arkadia, and others as well. The two last named however were those who brought bane with them.

Ankaios brought it for himself. To judge by his name, he was a wrestler who broke his opponent's ribs in his powerful embrace; along with another of the same name he had taken part in the voyage of the Argonauts. The story was told of the other Ankaios[635] that he had been forewarned that he should never drink the juice of his vineyard. At that time he was at home in Samos, had already planted a vineyard, and the first vintage was just being gathered. He sent for the soothsayer, pressed out with his hand the juice of a bunch of grapes into his cup, and lifted it to his lips. The soothsayer then uttered the famous adage, 'Much lies between the cup and the edge of the lip.' Ankaios' lips were not yet moistened when a shout was raised that a boar was laying his vineyard waste. He set down the cup with the grape juice, rushed off to dispatch the boar, and was killed by it. The Arkadian Ankaios too seems to have had a bad omen, for his arms were hidden at home.[636] He set out in a bearskin, armed only with a double axe, and met his death at the tushes of the Kalydonian boar. Bleeding from many wounds[637] he lay under the feet of the gigantic beast. On Roman sarcophagi the double axe is carried at the Kalydonian hunt by the death-god, under whose sign this adventure assuredly stood.

The participation in the adventure of the beautiful huntress Atalante was to be fatal to Meleagros and the House of Oineus. In her person Artemis herself likewise appeared at the boar-hunt, for surely no one who did not belong to her could have laid it low. Even as a spoil it remained her property. Atalante was anything but an ordinary mortal. Later no one knew where she was buried; an epigrammatist says merely that it was 'apart'.[638] Rather was there a story that she lived forever in the shape of a beast, a lioness, even as Artemis was 'a lion unto women'.[639] As her father there was named either Iasios,[640] also called Iasion,[641] the Cretan hunter,[642] or else Schoineus,[643] 'the man of rushes'; for Atalante was not confined to any particular stretch of country, or at most to those frequented by Artemis. Now her haunts, besides mountains, were swamps. A swamp surrounds Kalydon, and there were swamps everywhere in the place where Schoineus founded a city with the name Schoinus, 'rush-town'.[644]

It was said that[645] Atalante's father had expected a son before she was born, and that when the baby proved to be a girl, he did not perceive that his daughter was as good as a son, but had her exposed on the hill Parthenion, according to one story.[646] A she-bear then adopted the child; this was appropriate to the circle of Artemis,[647] where the great goddess and her little doubles were considered to be she-bears and were called so. Hunters found the child and brought her up. According to another story, she left her father's house of her own accord, to avoid being forced into marriage,[648] and retired to the wilderness, where she hunted alone. Once she had an experience similar to that of Artemis, who was pursued by the two gigantic boys, sons of Aloeus;[649] Atalante was attacked by two centaurs, and killed them both with her arrows.[650]

Still, she was not spared by love, as even Artemis was not quite spared.[651] The fair-haired huntress' beauty[652] attracted suitors after her even into the woods,[653] although she had imposed a severe condition. Atalante was the best runner in the world, and she offered to race her followers for marriage or death. She gave the suitor a start and promised to yield to him if he could get to the goal before her; otherwise she had the right to kill him with her arrows when she caught up with him.[654] It is not recorded how many men she shot; she stripped

naked, as young men did, for the race, and no one could with‑
stand the temptation.[655] But Hippomenes also was beautiful,
a descendant of Poseidon, like Hippolytos, and with a similar
name; 'impetuosity of the stallion' is what it means, as Artemis'
love was 'stallion let loose'. Hippomenes, who was cunning,
ran on, but he had three golden apples in his hand, and that
decided the race.

The golden apples came from Dionysos' garland, and
Aphrodite brought them to the young man;[656] there shone an
irresistible love‑magic from them.[657] When Atalante caught
sight of them, she was seized with amorous madness.[658]
Hippomenes threw the golden apples at her feet. Was she really
charmed with their sheen, like a little girl? She snatched at
them, picked them up, and her bridegroom had by that time
reached the goal. Atalante followed him into a dark grove,[659]
in which stood a hidden forest sanctuary, like that in the Lucus
Nemorensis on the Lake of Nemi, to which Artemis carried
off her beloved Hippolytos and where the hunters, in later
times, used to bring her a branch with the apples hanging on
it as an offering.[660] The shrine in which Atalante was united
to Hippomenes belonged to the Great Mother of the Gods,[661]
who, as we know, was also called the Great Artemis.[662] She, it
is alleged, punished the two lovers by turning them into a lion
and lioness and harnessing them to her car; a late story, but one
which still gives the lovers immortality, for they everlastingly
take part in the triumphal progress of the Mother of the Gods.
It is well known, so people declared in those times, that lions
live chastely with each other and mate only with leopards,
so by their transformation Hippomenes and Atalante were
doomed to everlasting chastity.[663]

Earlier, the tale was told of another wooing of Atalante, the
wooing by her cousin Melanion.[664] He has even been confused
with Hippomenes,[665] and perhaps not without reason. It is
the same love‑story, only the divine maid in this version has
from the beginning a more kindly aspect. The young man's
name seems also to be older than Hippomenes or Hippolytos;

it is sometimes written Melanion, sometimes Meilanion, and so cannot be certainly translated. Children in Athens were told, in the time of Aristophanes, how[666]

> 'Once on a time there was a lad,
> Melanion was his name,
> He didn't want to marry,
> So to the wilds he came,
> And lived among the mountains,
> And hunted after hares,
> And kept a dog besides,
> And plaited cunning snares,
> And home again he wouldn't go.'

The continuation of the story was probably that he caught sight of Atalante in the mountains, and courted her with the present of a fawn.[667] He courted her long; his wooing was famous for its length. In this version too he had rivals,[668] but he won, for he laboured longest for the maid, enduring all the hardships of a hunter's life.[669] They could tell of his union with her too,[670] and could name a son whom Atalante bore to Melanion; his name was Parthenopaios,[671] 'son of the maid', and he went later to Thebes with the Seven.

When Atalante appeared in Kalydon for the hunt, there was much excitement among the men. Oineus entertained the assembled heroes for nine days,[672] but they would not have a woman with them when they undertook that dangerous chase. It was probably an old sacral custom that the men should go entirely by themselves to hunt. This was the first time that any woman had wanted to take part in their hunting. But Melea-gros, as Euripides told the old story on the stage, courted Atalante from the first moment that he set eyes on her,[673] and compelled the heroes to begin the hunt on the tenth day.[674] Ankaios was one of those who opposed him most, and he fell a victim to the boar. This was not the only ill-luck which happened at that hunt; Peleus accidentally hit his father-in-law Eurytion with his spear, and another hunter beside Ankaios was killed by the boar. Finally the greatest disaster took place.

The hunt lasted for six days,[675] and on the sixth the two together, Atalante and Meleagros, dispatched the boar. She was the first to hit the beast with an arrow, and he gave it the death-blow. Now the flesh was to be divided and a great feast to follow, as was usual among men when they went hunting. The head and hide of the boar belonged to him who had dispatched it,[676] but Meleagros gave these parts to Atalante. This was more than his uncles, Althaia's brothers, could endure. They took their stand on the rights of the kin which they represented.[677] A quarrel broke out therefore; the spoils were torn from Atalante, the quarrrel became a fight and Meleagros killed his uncles. Word was brought to Althaia that her brothers had been laid low by her son and that the strange girl was in triumphant possession of the spoils.

The fight between Meleagros and his mother's brothers was early portrayed. A story was told of a war between the Aitolians of Kalydon and the Kuretes of Pleuron,[678] and the more the teller of it was at the same time an epic poet, the more he forgot Atalante as the origin of the quarrel and said nothing of the brand, not yet burned, which was in the possession of Althaia, the woman of Pleuron. As we hear the tale in the 'Iliad' from old Phoinix,[679] the angry mother dropped on her knees on the ground, her bosom wet with her flood of tears, smote the earth with her hands and called on the rulers of the underworld, Hades and Persephone, thus wishing the death of her own son.

When Meleagros heard of this, the epic poet continues the story,[680] he was enraged at his mother, retired from the war, and lay beside his wife, the beautiful Kleopatra, daughter of Idas and Marpessa. Even in this version, which knows nothing of Atalante and the brand, he was susceptible to womanly charms. In vain did the elders of Kalydon[681] entreat him to go forth against the enemy, in vain did his father, his mother and his brethren do the same. He let the

Kuretes break into the city and force their way even to his house. Not until their stones were falling on the roof of the bedchamber in which Meleagros lay beside the fair Kleopatra, and his wife besought him with tears to preserve her from the degradation of slavery, did he put on his armour and drive the enemy from the town.

But the Erinyes in Erebos had heard the mother's curse.[682] Apollo with his deadly arrows met the hero in the battle.[683] The god's hand made the magic power of the brand of no avail and superfluous. Originally it was not so; thus it was told from time immemorial and thus an old tragedian proclaimed it from the stage,[684] 'For he escaped not the chill of death, but the swift flame devoured him when the brand was destroyed by his dread mother's evil contriving.' That was what Althaia had done; she had taken the meticulously guarded brand out of the chest and thrown it into the fire on the hearth. As it fell to ashes, Meleagros collapsed on the battlefield,[685] or, in the oldest version,[686] while he was still jointing the boar, beside the corpses of his mother's brothers.

The women of Kalydon ceaselessly lamented the hero who died in his prime. In their endless lamentations they turned into the birds which men called *meleagrides*, otherwise known as guinea-fowl.[687] Where a man who had died young is seen on an Attic gravestone as a dreamy hunter, in a certain way Meleagros is still there; his story is recalled to memory, not in its details but as the tale of an early, undeserved death. In the underworld he was the only one before whose ghost even Herakles was afraid,[688] and when Meleagros tearfully told the story of the Kalydonian hunt, tears came for the first and only time to the eyes of the greatest of the heroes, the son of Zeus and of Alkmene.

BOOK TWO

Herakles

THE HERO AMONG THE GODS WAS DIONYSOS.
His conception and birth in the house of king Kadmos of
Thebes as the son of Zeus and the princess Semele were the
true conception and birth of a hero. They might have led to a
heroic life-history if Dionysos had not been after all a god, a
god who in this fashion entered, through his mother, into a
more intimate relation with mortals than all other deities,
Asklepios excepted. This birth, moreover, was held by many
to be but one of three, coming between his first birth from
Persephone and his third from the thigh of Zeus, and therefore he was known among the informed as 'the thrice-born'.[689]
These other births made him much greater than a hero. As a
god he was born of Persephone, and he was raised to the status
of a new god by Zeus himself. Such events were unique in the
history of the gods.

In the case of Herakles there happened something only half
similar. He entered upon mortal life, begotten by Zeus upon a
mortal mother. He had to pass through a long course on earth
before he could celebrate his entry into Olympos. Dark
shadows fell upon him before his final glory. Those Greeks
were probably best advised who, like the inhabitants of the
island of Kos,[690] burned a sheep at evening as a hero's offering
and next morning sacrificed a bull to him as to a god. According to the inscriptions and traces of sacrifices that have been
found in the excavation of his shrine on Thasos, the inhabitants of that other great island behaved in much the same way.
Herodotos the historian believed that he had met the same god
there as he had become acquainted with in Phoenicia among
the Tyrians.[691] Therefore he strongly approved of the twofold
manner of sacrifice. But he can hardly have been right when he
tried to separate the god and the hero, as if they were different

persons; at that rate we should have to distinguish between Dionysos son of Persephone and Dionysos son of Semele. Here again we must recognise the one in the other.

The Sikyonians, it is alleged,[692] at first offered sacrifice only to the hero; but they soon learned better and brought him both kinds of offering. The information that Herakles was a god they owed to one who was in a position to decide, that Phaistos who came to them as a stranger, probably from Crete, and becoming king in Sikyon, journeyed to the great southern island and took over the sovranty there.[693] He was supposedly a son or a grandson of Herakles himself as one of the Idaean Daktyls, who were likewise of Cretan origin. An account was given also of another descendant of Herakles as a Daktylos Idaios in Crete, one Klymenos of the Cretan town Kydonia.[694] And it was as a Daktyl, not as the son of Zeus and Alkmene, that, so it is said,[695] he came from Crete and, with his brothers, originated the first race at Olympia, an ancient site of the cult of Hera.

In this capacity, as a Daktylos, he was worshipped by the Tyrians, the Ionians in Asia Minor,[696] the Koans and certainly also by the Thasians. Tradition has it[697] that the first half of the Koan rites honoured Herakles the Daktylos. It also was fitting for a Daktylos that he was served on Kos as a deity of marriage.[698] The peculiarities of a Daktylos marked the beginning of the road which he trod. He was accounted one of the brotherhood of beings of primaeval days, sprung from the earth and phallic, as one of the sons of the Mother of the Gods, but a particular one, a single, incomparable divine servant of a goddess. It was, however, not quite right when the poet Onomakritos[699] made him out to be a Daktylic servant of Demeter. That described rather the beginning of the life-story of Oidipus, a life-story which, as we know, ended in a sacred precinct of Demeter and in the underworld. Herakles exalted himself to the son-ship of Zeus by his service to Hera, the great goddess of marriage.

The divinity of this servant of a goddess is attested by the rites which on Kos and in Sikyon form a unity although in two phases. His connection with Hera is shown, not only by his office as a god of marriage on Kos, but also by his very name, Herakles, with its obvious meaning 'he to whom Hera gave glory'. How this glory became his portion is to be told in what follows. He had also brought divinity with him into the tales of the son of Zeus and Alkmene, as which the whole world was to know him. The wise poet who styled him *heros theos*, 'the god-hero' was certainly right.[700] Probably hero-tales were told also of other, earlier gods, but none was so manifestly the god among the heroes as Herakles.

CHAPTER I

The Theban Tales

I

STORIES OF HERAKLES' ANCESTRY

IT IS PERHAPS no great exaggeration to say[701] that the Thebans honoured no other god with so many processions and sacrifices as Herakles. They were very proud that not only Dionysos but Herakles too had been born among them. This happened, so the genealogists reckoned, in the reign of Kreon the uncle of Oidipus. A Theban hero, like Oidipus, was also Amphitryon, the earthly father of Herakles; and Alkmene, mother of the son of Zeus, was also worshipped as a Boiotian heroine. The genealogists made them both descended from Perseus, since Herakles was otherwise known as a Tirynthian hero and belonging to the kingdom of Argos and Mycenae.

The sons of Perseus ruled over three strongholds in the land of Argos, Mycenae, Tiryns and Midea. One of these sons was named Alkaios or Alkeus. His son was the above-named Amphitryon, again according to the genealogists. Herakles is said to have been known as Alkeides from his grandfather, but the name alludes rather to the valour, *alké*, of the hero. Some also claimed to know that Herakles himself had been earlier called Alkaios,[702] or simply Alkeides,[703] but was later renamed by the Delphic oracle.[704] His mother Alkmene had likewise the word 'valour' in her name. Elektryon is given as her father, a second son of Perseus, and therefore she was spoken of as 'the maid of Midea' after the third family stronghold of the Perseids.[705] Her son was called 'the Tirynthian' after the fortified city of Tiryns.[706] It is said that her husband Amphitryon did not remove from Tiryns to Thebes until after the birth of Herakles.[707] This occurred after the death of

Elektryon. Then the third son of Perseus, Sthenelos, acquired the kingship over Mycenae and Tiryns, and left that of Midea to Pelops' sons Atreus and Thyestes. After Sthenelos, his son Eurystheus became king of Mycenae and Tiryns,[708] thus being himself also a Tirynthian and overlord of Herakles,[709] even if, as was later generally alleged, the latter was born in Thebes. The events which led to the birth of the hero, however, merely began in the realm of the sons of Perseus.

Before the Greek mainland, and to the west, opposite the district of Akarnania, lie the islands of the Taphians or Tele-boans, 'those whose cry is heard afar'. Over them ruled king Pterelaos. By grace of Poseidon he could not be conquered so long as he remained in possession of a golden hair.[710] The sea-god was his grandfather, and his great-grandfather on the mother's side was Mestor, a son of Perseus. The six sons of Pterelaos, who were savage pirates,[711] on one occasion appeared before Mycenae and demanded the kingship from Elektryon, who had eight sons beside his daughter Alkmene. Thus he rejected the offspring of his brother Mestor. Thereupon they drove off his cattle, and as so often in heroic times, a fight over the cows started. In this there fell seven of the sons of Elek-tryon (the eighth was too small) and five sons of Pterelaos. The remaining Taphians retired to their ships, which they had lying off the west coast of the Peloponnesos. They left the cattle with the king of Elis, Polyxenos. Amphitryon bought them back from him. Elektryon had entrusted the kingdom and his daughter to him, his nephew, and was about to set forth himself against the Teleboans, to avenge his sons. But then ensued a fresh misfortune, again in connection with the cows which Amphitryon had ransomed and brought back. The details are not handed down, only that Amphitryon became furiously angry.[712] Or was it pure chance that he hurled his throwing-stick at one of the cows? The stick glanced off the beast's horn, when it struck, and killed Elektryon. Therefore Amphitryon had to undertake the campaign against the Teleboans, and might not touch Alkmene, the bride entrusted to him, until her seven brothers were avenged. This was the condition which she herself imposed after the death of her father. The conceiving of Herakles, son of the King of the Gods, by this virgin princess, was thus prepared.

But first of all, as those narrators knew who laid the con/ ception and birth in Thebes, Amphitryon must find a new fatherland for himself and for Alkmene. His uncle Sthenelos banished him from the realm[713] after he had killed Elektryon, whether in anger or by pure mischance. So the young couple came to Thebes, where Kreon purified Amphitryon from the homicide. Alkmene remained his virgin wife as long as his vow of revenge was unfulfilled. But this might not be for some time. Thebes was then plagued by a fox,[714] a dangerous creature which had its earth on Mount Teumessos; and as it ran so fast that it could never be caught, it carried off what it liked from the town. Every month the Thebans exposed a child for it, in order to induce the beast to spare them.[715] Amphitryon also could not have dispatched it, for he was engaged in collecting an army against the Teleboans. So he had recourse to Kephalos, the Attic hero, whose wife Prokris had brought Minos' hound, a gift of Zeus to Europa,[716] from Crete.[717] Just as no one could catch the fox of Teumessos, so nothing could get away from this hound. It followed the fox on the plain of Thebes, and Zeus turned them both into stone. Amphitryon then set off with Kephalos, Panopeus of Phokis, and Heleios, the youngest of the sons of Perseus, against the Taphians. It was their good fortune that Komaitho, daughter of Pterelaos, fell in love with one of the commanders, either Amphitryon or the handsome Kephalos,[718] and robbed her father of the golden hair which made him invincible. With this to help him, Amphitryon succeeded in avenging Alk/ mene's brothers and so returned to her victorious.

But the wedding/night with his virgin wife, the great/ granddaughter of Danae, was not reserved for him. Zeus came to her in the shape of Amphitryon; with a golden goblet in his hand and a necklace like that which he had given to

Europa,[719] the King of the Gods entered her bedchamber.[720] She questioned him about his victory over the Teleboans, and the god, in her husband's shape, informed her of how revenge had been achieved; the goblet was the token of it, for it had been a present from Poseidon to the first king of the Taphians.[721] The marriage was consummated, with Zeus in the place of the mortal victor,[722] in a night of which it was told that it was three times as long as ordinary nights. As it was said of the first night when Hermes went stealing that the moon rose twice,[723] so it would seem that she rose three times on that occasion, wherefore Herakles, the fruit of the night of Zeus and Alkmene, was called *triselenos*, the child of the triple moon.[724]

Whether Amphitryon returned that same night,[725] or not till the next,[726] Alkmene conceived twins, one son of Zeus and the other of Amphitryon, named Iphikles, 'famed for his strength'. But it is also said that the victor was not received by his wife as he had expected to be, for she said to him, 'You came yesterday, made love to me and told me of your doings',[727] and showed him the goblet to prove it. Then Amphitryon realised who had taken his place (they say the seer Teiresias helped him also to read the riddle),[728] and did not touch the bride of the god.

2

THE HERO'S BIRTH

It is not easy, as the narrative proceeds, to keep to the old story of how Hera, as Herakles' name implies, made him glorious. But as ancient artists, for instance at Paestum, where the Sele runs into the sea, decked the temple of the Queen of the Gods with the exploits of Herakles, we must, after all, believe that she too could take delight in the hero's deeds. In the traditional accounts it looks as though on nearly every occasion she was his bitterest enemy. This state of things began immediately before the birth of the hero, when Alkmene's time was drawing

near. On the day when she was to bear Herakles, Zeus became
the victim of Ate, of infatuation, and proclaimed aloud to all
the deities,[729] 'Hear me, all ye gods and all ye goddesses, that
I may utter what the heart in my bosom bids me. This day
Eileithyia of the birth-pains shall bring to the light a manchild
who shall bear sway over all that dwell around, being of the
blood of those men who spring from me.' But Hera pretended
that she did not believe him and induced him to swear 'That
verily he shall bear sway over all them that dwell around who
this day shall fall between the feet of a woman, being of the
blood of those men that are of thy race.' Zeus marked not the
deceit of her mind, but swore a great oath. Hera sprang forth
and left the peak of Olympos, and came in haste to Argos,
where she knew the mighty consort of Sthenelos, son of
Perseus, was with child, and the seventh month was come. And
she caused the child to come forth, though all untimely, and
stayed the childbirth of Alkmene, causing the Eileithyiai to
halt. When all this was done, she brought word to Zeus that
the man who was to rule over all Argives was born—Eurystheus, son of Sthenelos. Vainly did Zeus catch Ate, the
goddess of infatuation, by the hair and fling her far away from
Olympos, down to mankind. He could not take back his oath.

It seems that Herakles nevertheless saw the light on that same
day, but it was Eurystheus, with his name meaning 'the
widely powerful', a name which might have adorned the king
of the underworld, and not he, who became great king of that
kingdom of Argos and Mycenae, and Herakles remained his
vassal, although according to this version he was born in
Thebes. Eileithyia sat in the vestibule of the palace in which
Alkmene lay in labour.[730] With her were the three Moirai,
with their knees crossed and their hands firmly folded over
them. Then a weasel suddenly ran across,[731] the startled goddesses lifted their hands high, and what had been fastened
became open. Or perhaps it was not a weasel, but the 'weasel-
girl', Galinthias or Galanthis (*galê* is a weasel), a playfellow of
Alkmene, who thought of this trick for herself. It was she who

ran out from the birth-room to the goddesses in the vestibule, and cried, 'According to the will of Zeus, Alkmene is delivered of a boy, and you have nothing more to do.' The goddesses, astonished, opened their hands, and in that instant Alkmene bore Herakles. Then the goddesses, who had been thus befooled, changed the cunning girl into the creature which, as was long after believed, conceives through its ear and bears through its mouth. Hekate took her as her sacred attendant. Herakles established the cult of Galinthias in his house, and the Thebans yearly sacrificed to her before every festival of the hero. They also alleged[732] that the victims of her deception were not goddesses, but wicked witches, who were out-manœuvred by Historis, 'the knowing one', a daughter of Teiresias, with the false report that Alkmene had borne her child. But the weasel, owing to its alleged powers of conceiving through the ear, was to become an allegory for the Virgin Mary.

Herakles was born on the second day of the moon,[733] and after him (a night later, as many declared),[734] his twin brother Iphikles. He was a doublet of his brother only in name, a Herakles like him, until the latter became famous not only for his strength but with the help of Hera. There is hardly any story of Iphikles, except that he, as if Zeus had robbed him of understanding, left his home and his parents and gave himself willingly into the service of Eurystheus.[735] It is said that later he much regretted this, but we hear nothing further about it. It was not he who was Herakles' favourite companion, but Iolaos, who is said to have been the son of Iphikles, and whom the Thebans honoured no less than the Argives did Perseus.[736] As regarded Herakles, Zeus and Hera were in agreement;[737] Eurystheus was indeed to have the sovranty over Tiryns and Mycenae and Herakles to be in his service, until he had accom-plished twelve labours for him, but after that the son of Zeus should win the immortality which was due to him after his deeds.

But the story still departs very far from this. There is also the tale that Alkmene, through fear of Hera's jealousy, exposed the little Herakles immediately after his birth, on a spot afterwards known as the Plain of Herakles.[738] Pallas Athene and Hera passed that way, ostensibly by accident, but it was not unintentional on the part of the virginal goddess, with whom the *alké*, the warlike courage, of Alkmene's son allied him closely. She expressed her admiration for the sturdy child and persuaded Hera to offer him her breast. However, he sucked at it so strongly that the goddess could not bear the pain and threw the baby from her; but the milk of the Queen of the Gods had already made him immortal. Athene, well content, brought the child back to his mother. According to another account,[739] however, what happened was that while Hera was asleep, Hermes brought the baby Herakles to her celestial abode and put him to her breast, and when she cast him from her in pain and her milk continued to flow, the Milky Way came into being.

Such were the events in heaven, but in the palace of Amphitryon other things were happening. According to an old story,[740] it was immediately after the twins were born; according to a later one, not till they were both ten months old.[741] The picture of a divine child between two serpents may have been long familiar to the Thebans, who worshipped the Kabeiroi, although not represented as a first exploit of a hero as in the following tale. The door of Alkmene's chamber, in which the newborn children lay in their saffron-dyed swaddling-bands, stood open. In crept two serpents, sent by the Queen of the Gods, and with gaping jaws threatened to devour the babes. But he who was to reach renown through Hera, the son of Zeus, lifted his head and tried himself in fight for the first time. With his two hands he seized the two serpents and strangled them until the life left their terrible bodies. The women who were the helpers at Alkmene's childbed were paralysed with fear, but the mother sprang up and would herself repel the monsters' violence. The Kadmeians ran up armed, Amphitryon, sword in hand, first of them all; but he halted, struck still with surprise, horror and joy, when he saw the unheard-of daring and strength of the child. He at once sent for Zeus' distinguished seer, the soothsayer Teiresias, from the near-by palace, and he revealed to him and to all the people the future destiny of the boy, the many unruly beasts he was to slay by land and sea, how he was to fight by the side of the gods against the Giants, and what reward was to be his in the end.

Nothing would be easier than to go on here with the list of Herakles' instructors, as the later tellers of the story used to do,[742] alleging that he learned from Amphitryon how to drive a chariot, archery from Eurytos, fighting with weapons from Kastor, wrestling from Autolykos, and so on, as if Herakles had been no more than a prince, of divine origin indeed but not a divine being, not one who resembled other heroes only in appearance, since they were never exalted to Olympos, but like Oidipus passed into a grave in the bosom of Mother Earth. But even in the tales of his life as Amphitryon's son and later as son-in-law of Kreon, the outbreaks of his superhumanly savage nature could not be kept secret.

He was to learn his letters from Linos, of whom it was said that he was the first to introduce them into Greece. Of this Linos everyone knew that he was a son of Apollo,[743] or of the Muse Urania,[744] and that he died young by violence, and that therefore all singers and harp-players lamented for him at banquet or at dance.[745] One version of his violent death was that Kadmos killed him, because he, Kadmos, wanted to be the first to introduce writing among the Hellenes.[746] According to another and later account, Linos had to teach Herakles the art of writing and of harp-playing, and went so far as to chastise the unteachable hero-child.[747] A vase-painter has sketched the scene for us; the young hero is breaking the chair on which he had sat over his teacher's head. For that reason, we are told further,[748] Amphitryon sent him out to the pastures; there among the herdsmen he grew, till at eighteen he was four cubits tall. The fire of his eyes revealed his divine nature. He never missed his mark when he shot with his bow or hurled his spear. A great piece of roast meat and a basketful of black bread was his daily ration.[749] He lived in the open air and slept out-of-doors.[750] But this already refers to the life of the hero, in his wanderings, not among the herdsmen on Kithairon, where that may have been simply the most natural thing to do.

In the shrine of Apollo Ismenios in Thebes there was shown a tripod, said to have been dedicated by Amphitryon[751] in commemoration of his son Alkaios[752] having held the post of the laurel-crowned young priest, an annual office in Thebes. The strife of Herakles with his brother for his Delphic tripod, on the other hand, is preserved in art-monuments much older than this tale. This fraternal quarrel, however, came much later in the course of the hero's life and will be told then. We have now to pass to the tales of events in his youth, in Thebes or in the mountains around it. There he was to accomplish his first heroic deed and display his Daktylic nature for the first time.

3

THE TALES OF HIS YOUTH

Kithairon, on the foothills of which the Theban herdsmen pastured their beasts, was the scene of many stories of gods and heroes. It was there that Zeus and Hera met for their sacred wedding; there Semele's sisters roamed after Dionysos; there Amphion and Zethos, the baby Oidipus too, were exposed; there Antiope and the old, suffering Oidipus wandered. Between Kithairon and the other mountain of the gods in Boiotia, Helikon, lay the town of Thespiai, where later Herakles, we are assured,[753] possessed a very old-fashioned sanctuary as Idaios Daktylos. In the days when the young hero was living with the herdsmen, king Thespios bore rule there. The tradition is uncertain whether the lion which ravaged his herds and those of Amphitryon came from Kithairon[754] or

18 HERAKLES SUCKLED BY HERA

19 THE INFANT HERAKLES STRANGLING THE SERPENTS

20 HERAKLES ESCORTED TO SCHOOL

21 HERAKLES AT SCHOOL

Helikon.[755] In historical times there were no more lions there; Herakles was to free the land from that scourge.

He went about unarmed between the mountains; but concerning his famous club, without which posterity can hardly conceive him, tradition has it[756] that he pulled it out of the ground on Helikon, a wild olive, roots and all. Herdsmen often carried such club-like sticks as they moved around; these served them as the simplest kind of weapons for hunting, no less than the well-known curved shepherd's staff which they threw at hares. Herakles dedicated this his first club, or his second or his third, for here again there are several traditions,[757] to Hermes Polygios, or more correctly Polygyios, 'of the many limbs', a sign that so mighty a staff was especially suitable to a Daktylic being such as Hermes was when he bore that epithet.

Herakles set out against the lion and arrived at king Thespios' house. The king received him hospitably and gladly, and wished to have grandchildren by the hero, as Autolykos had by Sisyphos.[758] He had fifty daughters and he caused them all, one after another, to sleep with his guest. One only resisted the hero, and so was all the more closely attached to him. The others bore sons, one or two of them even twins,[759] (these children of Herakles later colonised the island of Sardinia),[760] but she, having resisted him, became his priestess for life,[761] the first of the virgin priestesses in the temple of Herakles at Thespiai, and virgin priestesses are always the wives of the god they serve. Afterwards, he also dispatched the lion, and covered his head and shoulders with its hide;[762] we know that characteristic costume, concerning which, it is true, there is another tradition,[763] that it was taken from the Nemean lion. But that is another story, of which we shall hear later.

From his adventures between Kithairon and Helikon, Herakles turned back to Thebes. He was now eighteen years old—so the later narrators made out, hardly being able any longer to conceive of an ageless hero of early days,[764] and provided with his club and his lion-skin. On the way he fell in

with ambassadors[765] coming from the Boiotian city of Orchomenos, a Minyan town, ruled at that time by king Erginos.
Years before, Thebans had killed his father, in anger over some
trifle, at the festival of Poseidon at Onchestos.[766] The duty of
revenge devolving on Erginos, he besieged the Thebans and
laid a heavy tribute on them; they were to send the Minyans a
hundred cows a year for twenty years. These twenty years were
not yet up; Thebes was quite defenceless,[767] and the feeble
Kreon was ruling there. The ambassadors were coming to
collect the tribute when Herakles met them, and their attitude
certainly was not conciliatory.

How the meeting between them and the young hero went
off is not told us, but only the result of it; Herakles cut off their
noses and ears, hung them around their necks and sent that
tribute to Erginos. Thereupon the Minyans came again from
Orchomenos to wreak vengeance; Herakles went out single-
handed against their host, or so the oldest form of the story
says.[768] Provided with arms by Pallas Athene,[769] he defeated
the Minyans and freed Thebes. In return, Kreon gave him his
daughter Megara to wife,[770] and Herakles brought her home
to the sound of flutes,[771] to Amphitryon's palace. No one could
guess how horribly it was to end. Kreon handed over the
sovranty of Thebes to him.[772]

Amphitryon, according to one version,[773] had fallen in the
battle against the advancing Minyans, but according to
another he lived in his palace with Megara and his grandchildren, after the hero left them.[774] The Thebans later on did
him honour in his hero-tomb, together with Iolaos,[775] son of
Iphikles, his grandson and Herakles' favourite; it was he who,
according to another tradition, led the fifty sons of Herakles to
Sardinia. The remains of his palace at Thebes, which the
architect-heroes Agamedes and Trophonios, sons of Erginos,
built for him, were also shown.[776] It was even thought that
Alkmene's marriage-chamber could still be made out in the
ruins. Indeed, the Boiotians claimed also to possess the tomb
of Alkmene at Haliartos, until the Spartans, having captured

the Kadmeia, opened it and transported its modest contents, including a tablet with Mycenaean characters on it, to their own city.⁷⁷⁷ These assuredly were old hero-tombs of Myce-naean date which the Thebans and their neighbours ascribed to the relatives of Herakles.

But the tellers of the tale had somehow to get Herakles to Tiryns, after attaching him by so many ties to Thebes; he must come to the Mycenaean kingdom where he was king Eurys-theus' vassal. There the goddess bore sway who was known as Hera of Argos from the name of the whole district. Her temple, on an imposing mountain terrace between Tiryns and Mycenae, belonged to no single town, but she also had her temple in Tiryns, where she and not Pallas Athene was con-sidered the lady of the castle. With this castle, the servant of the goddess, Herakles of Tiryns, was also Eurystheus' subject. We have already heard of the ruse by which she is said to have brought about this subjection. This was an old story, but not so old as the connection of Hera with Herakles, which perhaps was even older than that between the Queen and the King of the Gods. In an age when Zeus had not yet won the great goddess of Argos to wife, she might have put her divine servant, to whom she wished to give glory, at the disposal of the king of her country, even without a trick. King Admetos of Thessaly got a divine servant in the very person of Apollo,⁷⁷⁸ and he too was an earthly potentate with a name which might signify the king of the underworld.

It is said that Eurystheus sent to Thebes for Herakles,⁷⁷⁹ or Herakles himself had a fancy to inhabit the Cyclopean walls of Tiryns,⁷⁸⁰ and must pay for it with his Labours. The Theban stories are not finished, but we must now start on those of Tiryns, or of Mycenae, for Eurystheus had his residence in Mycenae and thither Herakles must return after fulfilling each command of the king, to get a further commission.

CHAPTER II

The Twelve Labours

I

THE NEMEAN LION

ON THE NORTHERN EDGE of the plain of Argos, no great distance from Tiryns and Mycenae, rise the mountains over which the road to Corinth leads. The highest, which looks oddly like a table half overset, is the Apesas, on which Perseus made sacrifice to Zeus for the first time;[781] the waters of a deluge on which he had floated still reached that height, according to an old tale. Under Mount Apesas lies the wide valley of Nemea, with many caves in the neighbourhood. One mountain there actually was called Tretos, 'the pierced'.[782] In this region a lion had his lair and made all the mountain district unsafe. A god had sent him against the inhabitants of the land as a punishment; they were the descendants of the primaeval man Phoroneus. So we are told in a simpler story,[783] and even this much seems more than is necessary. Was not a lion alone, without having been sent by gods, a sufficient task for a hero?

The details of the twelve Labours of Herakles were told from ancient times by so many poets, named and unnamed, and so adorned, that it is not surprising that we hear a different tale about the origin of this savage creature also. According to some,[784] the serpent-goddess Echidna[785] was the mother of the lion by her own son, the hound Orthos. The Nemean lion was thus brother to the Theban Sphinx. Hera brought him from the eastern land of the Arimoi to her own country. According to another version,[786] the beast was originally at home with Selene, the Moon-goddess; she shook it off, and so it fell down upon Mount Apesas.

It is clear also from the accounts of the fight between Herakles and this marvellous beast that no weapon could wound it.

Such details may be accounted mere decorations, and they were still further elaborated; nevertheless, the lion, against which only a Herakles could prevail, had assuredly something special about him. He may have embodied death and the underworld particularly. The lions which ancient artists put over graves remind us of this, his representative capacity, even if they did not intend to portray the lion of Nemea. Allegedly, Herakles himself after his victory over the Orchomenians set up a lion before the temple of Artemis Eukleia,[787] a name which signifies that the goddess, herself a 'lioness to women',[788] is a deity of the underworld. As a hunter, Herakles did not exterminate ordinary beasts of the earth, like Orion,[789] nor appear in the role of lord of the underworld as a hunter-god; what he hunted was apparently death. He overcame and caught weird beasts which belonged to gods, even definitely to gods of the underworld. When, after his victory over the Nemean lion, he laid its skin and head over his own head and shoulders, that which had formerly threatened mortals with death became a promise of their deliverance.

The story goes[790] that Herakles, when he set out against the lion, entered the little town of Kleonai on the borders of the wood of Nemea. The later version has it that Molorchos, who was his host, was a poor peasant, a day-labourer,[791] but in the original tale he probably was a primaeval man, founder of the city of Molorchia.[792] The lion had killed his son, and now he wished to offer his only ram in honour of his guest. Herakles bade him wait for thirty days; if by the thirtieth day he had not returned from his combat with the lion, the ram was to be sacrificed to him as to a hero, but otherwise, to Zeus the Deliverer. From Molorchos he learned how he was to attack the lion; it must be a wrestling-match, even if Herakles, as old pictures show him, used sword and spear, or, as was told later,[793] first stunned the beast with a blow of his club. He had to force his way into its den, which allegedly had two openings, one of which Herakles blocked.[794] It took him the whole thirty days to do all this, not to get from Kleonai to Nemea, which is quite near, but presumably to reach the depths where the monster had his dwelling. Or was it merely the sleep which overtook him after he had strangled the lion that lasted so long? The tale is told of that sleep,[795] and we should not forget that Sleep is the brother of Death. The carvings on the metopes of the temple of Zeus at Olympia, which represent the Labours of Herakles, show the hero still almost half-asleep, in memory of that dangerous slumber. But when at last he awoke on the thirtieth day, he crowned himself with wild celery, like one come from the grave, for graves were garlanded with this plant.[796] Later, the victors at the Nemean Games, and after them, those at the Isthmian, wore the same garland.[797]

Molorchos, the story goes on, was just about to sacrifice the ram to the hero as a funeral offering when Herakles appeared. He was carrying the lion on his back. The ram, according to this version, was sacrificed to Zeus Soter, the god who rescues, but it could have been the victim which Herakles received there later. He stayed with Molorchos for one night more, and early in the morning took the road to the south and journeyed over the pass towards Argos. From there he sent his host a mule, which he had promised him, and did him as much honour as if they were connections by marriage.[798] He came with the lion to Mycenae, Eurystheus' residence,[799] and the king was so terrified at the hero's uncanny exploit that he forbade him in future to enter the city with his booty. It would be enough for him to appear before the gates. According to this tale, Eurystheus even then had a bronze vessel fixed under the earth and crept into it whenever Herakles came near. He communicated with him only through his herald Kopreus, the 'dung-man'.

The hero stripped the lion of its invulnerable hide after cutting it off with the creature's claws,[800] but Zeus, to do his son honour, transported the monster to the skies as a memorial, where it became the Lion in the Zodiac.[801]

2

THE HYDRA OF LERNA

Near the city of Argos to the south, but also not far from Mycenae and Tiryns, on the narrow strip of land between Mount Pontinos[802] and the sea, there are veritable abysses covered over with the fresh water of the many springs which issue from the foot of the limestone range. The story of the Danaids is connected with these springs, but the depths beneath them with the destiny of Dionysos, who when he was killed by Perseus came to the underworld through them, to rule there and when summoned back, to return thence through them. The underworld was the near neighbour of the land of Argos in Lerna's bottomless waters. The sentinel on the border, on the entry to the realm of the dead, was the serpent which Herakles had to overcome after the Nemean lion.

The serpent, too, was said to have the serpent-goddess Echidna for her mother,[803] but she had no special name, and therefore it became usual that the word Hydra, that is 'water-snake', meant her and no other. She, the murderous 'bitch of Lerna' (for she was called that too)[804] had in common with her elder brother Kerberos, the other monster of the underworld, a plurality of heads. He was her elder brother only in their genealogy,[805] but his office of watcher over the dead remained in men's memory far more than that of the Hydra; this peculiarity of the water-snake of Lerna was soon forgotten. True, it was said that her breath killed men.[806] It was believed also that she could be exactly located, in the roots of the plane-tree by the triple spring Amymone.[807] Gigantic planes with gigantic roots and gigantic hollows grow in such places in Greece. The gigantic water-snake, so the story was told,[808] grew up in the swamp and ravaged the herds and the countryside.

As Kerberos is now called three-headed and now five-headed,[809] it is equally hard to give a fixed number for the heads of the Hydra. The five to twelve which are shown in pictures stand for the nine,[810] or fifty,[811] or a hundred[812] of which the poets speak. It is also stated that only one head, in the middle of the other eight, was immortal,[813] and late artists even represented one head of the Hydra as of human shape. In this they departed from a very old tradition, for the picture of the innumerable serpent-heads springing from a common, shapeless body, comes into the history of Herakles from a very old mythology. To the ancient picture-makers of Mesopotamia who were the first to fix the type, its meaning was certainly not in doubt. They expressed in that manner the difficulty of overcoming the enemy they made their heroes do battle with, and that enemy, however he might be named, could be nothing else than death. The hopelessness of the struggle, except for Herakles the unique, was also expressed in the Greek narrative by making two heads grow up in place of every one that was struck off. Herakles himself needed a helper if he would dispatch the monster, and in this Labour had a younger hero, his Theban nephew Iolaos, at his side.

Only this much is preserved of the tale of the adventure.[814] The hero came with Iolaos, driving in his war-chariot, to the neighbourhood of the very ancient town of Lerna, and found the infernal serpent in her lair by the spring Amymone. He shot fire-arrows into the lair and so forced her to crawl out. She had hardly crept forth when he attacked her. The Hydra coiled around one of the hero's feet. On old pictures we see Herakles attacking the serpent, not with his club but with a sickle-shaped sword. But every time he struck off a head, two living ones grew in its place. Besides, there was a gigantic crab in that place and it bit the hero's foot. He had to begin by killing that guardian of the spot, and not till then did he call Iolaos to his aid. The young hero used up almost a whole forest to cauterise the wounds of the snake with burning brands, so that she could grow no new heads. Now Herakles could cut off the immortal head also. He buried it by the road which led from Lerna to Elaius. He dipped his arrows in the poison with which the serpent's body was filled. The giant crab got into the sky as the next sign of the Zodiac to the Lion; Hera exalted him thither.[815] It is the point at which, according to the doctrine of astrologers, the souls of men descend to lower regions,[816] for the subterranean half of the sky begins at the sign of the Crab.

It appears as if uncertainty prevailed among the tellers of the tale whether Herakles was bound to perform twelve Labours for Eurystheus, or to spend twelve years over the performance of his works, ten Labours being enough for that.[817] The time for purification and service amounted to one great year, that is, eight ordinary years, for the gods. So it was with Apollo,[818] so also, allegedly, with Kadmos, and so, according to one reckoning, with Herakles himself, for he is said to have accomplished the first ten Labours in eight years and one month.[819] Twelve is the number of the months and of the signs of the Zodiac; and we have already heard that Herakles himself fixed in advance the time required to deal with the Nemean lion at thirty days. This may have been an older and more Oriental conception, of which the celestial equivalents of the crab and the lion still remind us. The number twelve proved strong enough to oust the list of ten Labours which undoubtedly was once canonical.

Eurystheus, so the story goes, would not recognise two of the twelve Labours, and, for a start, not the victory over the serpent of Lerna, because in it Iolaos had helped the hero.[820] Such excuses were put into Eurystheus' mouth late and not even consistently; but it is a fact that two of the Labours had not the same object as the two already told and eight others, namely the fight against Death. In this struggle it was the wish of Eurystheus that Herakles should succumb; but in that case the Labour of Lerna was one of the ones that counted.

3

THE HIND OF KERYNEIA

High mountain ranges separate the land of Argos from Arkadia to the west, the Parthenion and the Artemision. Their names (respectively 'Virgin Mountain' and 'Artemis' Mountain') remind us of the great virgin goddess who bore sway there. Artemis had her temple on a peak of the massif of Artemision and there had the title Oinatis, 'she of Oinoe' ('the wine village'), from the last little town and furthest outlying region which still belonged to Argos. Thither Herakles was now to journey, for Eurystheus set him as his third task[821] to bring the golden-antlered hind alive to Mycenae. It belonged to the goddess of Oinoe, but tried to hide even from Artemis on the rocky hill of Keryneia in Arkadia.[822] It ranged the whole wild region of Arkadia and also the goddess' mountains in the neighbourhood of Argos. From there it is said to have visited and laid waste the peasants' fields,[823] but assuredly it was not merely for that reason that it became the third monster in the series of those hunted by Herakles, after the Nemean lion and the hydra of Lerna.

Hinds had no antlers even in those days, and if one of them actually had golden antlers it was no ordinary beast, but a divine being. It is also told[824] that a companion of Artemis, the Titaness Taygete, after whom Mount Taygetos was named, was obliged to take the form of this hind, because she had accepted the love of Zeus. That was how Artemis punished her. According to others,[825] she meant thus to save her. But when Taygete had later on enjoyed the attentions of Zeus, by way of atonement she dedicated the hind into which she was to have been turned to Artemis Orthosia.[826] It is not easy to differentiate between the divine beast, the heroine, and the goddess. When Artemis was pursued by the outrageous giant twins, the Aloadai, she was herself the hunted hind.[827] A divine creature with golden antlers, the hind of Keryneia, let itself be hunted by Herakles—that is the right expression here. The difficult, dangerous and uncanny thing about the hind was not its unusual wildness,[828] which would enable it to offer resistance to the hunter, as many believed, but that it fled and the pursuer could not stop trying to make this strange game his prey. The danger lay in the pursuit, which took him beyond the known region of hunters into another country, from which no one ever came back. Therefore, Herakles was to catch the hind, not shoot it down, which would have been easy for so great an archer, and which he actually did in one much too novel variant.[829] It was again no common hunt that he had to engage in.

The hind began by running away from him out of Oinoe into Mount Artemision, then further through the whole of Arkadia to the river Ladon. As the hero was neither to kill nor hurt it, he followed it for an entire year.[830] Where the creature he pursued led him in all that time we are told in Pindar's ode about the branch of wild olive which Herakles brought to Olympia to be the garland of the victors, and we learn of it from an ancient vase-painting. In Istria, the poem states,[831] Artemis met the pursuer; there, at the most northerly extremity of the Adriatic Sea, by the mouth of the Timavus, the goddess had a sacred grove of which it was told that deer lived peaceably with wolves in it.[832] She was called Reitia by the inhabitants of that country, the Veneti, and that can be a translation of Orthia or Orthosia. Pursuer and pursued arrived there through the country of the Hyperboreans,[833] Apollo's holy people, whom the name Istria designated for the Greeks, as well as the peninsula at the Timavus. From that other-world region Herakles brought the slip of the wild olive to Olympia, which till then was treeless. An old vase-painting, however, shows us that he penetrated still further in his pursuit beyond the world's end, even to the Garden of the Hesperides. The hind stands beneath the tree of the golden apples, guarded by two women, the Hesperides. According to this picture the hero took the homeward path, escaping from the dangers of remaining in the other world; according to another, his booty was the golden antlers.

The Garden of the Hesperides lay a great way from the Arkadian river Ladon, and yet bordered on it, as the under-world at Lerna bordered on Argos; those were regions outside the world we live in, regions which the narrators but gradually brought into our world. Ladon was the name both of the river and of the serpent that watched over the tree of the golden apples.[834] The hind wanted to swim through the waters of the Ladon, and so, by this account, was not yet arrived beyond the world[835] when Herakles came up with and caught her. Only very late narrators believed that he shot her. The hero tied his prey's feet together, as a group of statues from the temple of Apollo at Veii shows, took her on his shoulder and journeyed back with her through Arkadia. There he en-countered the divine brother and sister, Apollo and Artemis, the god of the other world and the goddess of the lands of mountains and swamps, which lead to the other world. There was nearly a fight between the brothers, both sons of Zeus, as almost happened again later over the Delphic tripod. We see on art-monuments that Apollo tried to take the hind from the hero by force. Artemis accused him of killing her sacred animal, but Herakles excused himself by stating that he was forced to do what he did, and showed her that he was taking the hind alive to Mycenae, or according to certain pictures, only her antlers; the goddess therefore forgave him.

4

THE BOAR OF ERYMANTHOS

The most original district belonging to Artemis, her dancing-place on the lofty mountain-crests, and as dear to her as Taygetos,[836] was Mount Erymanthos in the north-western corner of Arkadia, where it borders on the regions of Achaia and Elis. Hither Herakles was sent with his fourth commission, to get the boar. When the goddess turned a wrathful countenance upon a country, as in the story of Meleagros, she would send a raging boar which laid waste the farmers' fields. Nothing of the kind is told us here, but only that the inhabitants of Psophis had reason to complain of the Erymanthian boar.[837] But this again was not why Herakles was to catch it and bring it to Mycenae alive; it would have satisfied the countrypeople if he had destroyed the beast.

Once more the hero journeyed through the whole of Arkadia, and arrived first at the forests of Pholoe, the high ground between the valley of the Alpheios and Erymanthos. This district was inhabited by Centaurs, of like nature and habits to the semianimal neighbours of the Lapithai of Thessaly. There were also Lapithai in the neighbourhood, but Herakles had nothing to do with them. He was hospitably received by the Centaur Pholos, who lived there in a cave.[838] His host set roast meat before the hero, while he ate raw meat himself. In one version, the wise Chiron was present also,[839] the most righteous of the Centaurs.[840] He had retired before the Thessalian Lapithai to the Peloponnesos, and now lived at Cape Malea instead of on Pelion. Did Herakles ask for wine as well, or was this, too, a part of Pholos' hospitality?[841] He opened the common winestore of the Centaurs, which he had to keep in a great *pithos* or storejar. It is even said that this wine was a gift of Dionysos,[842] intended by the god for the hero himself;[843] a dangerous gift, for evidently the Centaurs did not yet know its nature. Old vasepaintings are fond of the scene in which Herakles draws from the great vessel, as yet untouched.

The scent of the wine now attracted the remaining Centaurs, and the drinkingbout of the Centaurs soon changed into a battle with them, another favourite subject of artists and narrators. It is stated that the fighting ranged from the heights of Pholoe to Chiron's cave at Cape Malea, for thither Herakles pursued the Centaurs with his poisoned arrows. One arrow, aimed at Elatos, went through him and struck the divine Chiron. The hero vainly tried to heal him with Chironian medicaments; the poison of the Hydra was too strong. Being wounded on the knee, the wise Centaur could neither recover nor die, wherefore he retired with his incurable wound to his cave and suffered there until he could be offered to Zeus in place of the tormented Prometheus.[844] Then at last Chiron died and Prometheus was freed. The good Pholos also died by an arrow of Herakles. He pulled the poisoned missile out of the corpse of a Centaur and marvelled at the tiny thing which could destroy so large a being; it fell on his foot and killed him too. Herakles buried his friend and went his way to Mount Erymanthos.

There he started the boar from its lair, drove it into the snow on the heights, caught it in a snare, threw the beast across his shoulder and travelled back with it to Mycenae. Then occurred the long-prepared scene which again the vase-painters were fond of representing. The hero, with the wild boar on his back, sets a foot on the rim of the buried jar into which Eurystheus had crept; the coward's head and arm are alone visible, for he was as much afraid of the boar as of death.

5

THE BIRDS OF LAKE STYMPHALOS

In the north-eastern corner of Arkadia lies the swampy lake of Stymphalos. It was surrounded once by shady woods.[845] The number of the birds which inhabited it was beyond all calcu-lation;[846] when frightened, they darkened the sun.[847] In the underworld, the souls, innumerable as they, came to the swampy Acheron, 'as many as the birds that flock to the coast from the high seas, when the cold season chases them across the waters and sends them to sunny lands. . . .'[848] 'One after another thou mayest see them, like a strong-winged bird, swifter than raging fire, hastening towards the shore of the sunset god.'[849] In these words of a tragic poet, the western shore where the Sun-god sets means the realm of the dead. Here the birds remind us of it.

Their pictures decorated the temple of Artemis Stym-phalia,[850] the ruler over these swamps. Maids with the feet of birds were portrayed there also, and signified the Stymphalian birds as the deadly Sirens of the marsh. They were man-eating birds, according to the story concerning these inhabitants of the marsh,[851] and Ares had reared them.[852] Their feathers were so sharp that they wounded anyone on whom they fell.[853] To say that they damaged fertile fields[854] is here again an under-statement. Once more Herakles was set the task of facing something deadly and frightening it away. He was to drive off the birds from Lake Stymphalos.

He climbed an elevation on the edge of the swamp[855] and startled the birds by making a great noise. The story goes[856] that he used a bronze rattle for this, and that was enough in itself to rid the lake of the birds. On old vase-paintings we see the hero aiming at them with a sling or fighting them with a stick, but his weapon against them was above all his bow.[857] Such birds as he did not shoot flew away to the Island of Ares in the Black Sea. There the Argonauts in their turn had later to do with them.[858] Carved on a metope at Olympia is Herakles showing his booty to Pallas Athene, who by one account had to advise him in connection with this adventure. Presumably he then brought the deadly birds to Mycenae, as proof of his deed.

6

THE STABLES OF AUGEIAS

His next task awaited Herakles on the west coast of the Peloponnesos. Augeias, king of Elis, a son of Helios, was ruling there. His name signifies 'radiant', and it was also told of him[859] that sunbeams shone from his eyes. In his herds of cattle he seems to have possessed the wealth of the Sun-god, but his kingdom, there on the western coast, was rather a realm of the setting sun, a lordship over the underworld, than one over the land of Elis. Eurystheus sent the hero to him,[860] and the task that was given him reminds us of the other side of the subterranean kingdom, its dirt alongside of its riches. The dung of the cattle filled the byres, and it was stated[861] in this instance also that this bred a pestilence in the whole land. Herakles was now to clear away the filth. His task was made the harder by his being obliged to complete the work in one day.

But it is also told of him that his taskmaster was not only Eurystheus but rather Augeias as well.[862] In one version,[863] Augeias promised him part of his kingdom as payment for the work. It looks as if the hero was to get the king's daughter along with part of the kingdom. But if the work was not completed in one day, presumably he must become Augeias' slave for ever, to remove the droppings from the byres. A daughter of Augeias, Epikaste by name, is reckoned among the wives of Herakles.[864] That old form of the story, according to which he was cheated out of her hand also and for that reason fought with Augeias later, is lost to us; other narrators say[865] that Herakles did not inform the king that the task had been imposed upon him by Eurystheus, and bargained on his own behalf for a tenth of the cattle if he could succeed in cleaning the byres. The witness to this contract was Phyleus, the king's son. On a metope at Olympia we may admire the vigour with which he wields a broom or a spade, but according to later narrators he cut through the foundation-wall of the building and led a river, or even two rivers, Alpheios and Peneios, through the byres. The impossible task in which Augeias would not believe was accomplished. When in addition he heard that this work had been imposed on Herakles by Eurystheus, he would not keep his word. According to this version, which assuredly is not the oldest, the king denied that he had ever promised anything, and a certain Lepreus, 'itchy', actually advised him to throw the hero into chains.[866] The quarrel was to be settled before a court of law;[867] Phyleus appeared as a witness against his father. Augeias became angry and drove his son and Herakles out of the

22 THE YOUNG HERAKLES OVERCOMING NEREUS

23 HERAKLES AND THE SEA-GOD

country, before the case was decided, a *casus belli* which later
led the hero to attack Elis.

On his way back to Mycenae he visited king Dexamenos in
the city of Olenos. The king's name, 'receiver', can equally
well denote a hospitable mortal as the king of the underworld,
who is otherwise known as Polydektes or Polydegmon, 'he
who receives many'. Moreover, Dexamenos was not, according
to all ancient accounts, a human being and the father of the
girl whom Herakles was to rescue, but a Centaur, whose
intention was to carry her off.[868] This Centaur with whom the
hero had now to do was also called Eurytion,[869] a name which,
like Eurytos, signifies a good shot and clearly marks a being of
the realm of the dead, Geryoneus' herdsman. Oriental artists
represented Centaurs as archers and thus expressed the connection of these wild and violent creatures with death. In
Greece it was said[870] that no Centaur employed the bow.

The Centaur Eurytion, the story goes, also had no bow. The
hero entered the house of the king of Olenos at the very
moment when the wedding of the princess with Eurytion was
being celebrated, for he had forced himself upon them as her
bridegroom.[871] Or, the marriage was being celebrated with a
proper bridegroom, but Eurytion was one of the guests and
tried to carry off the bride.[872] Herakles struck the Centaur dead
and saved the girl, but not to keep her for himself. It is only in
that version which calls the bride Deianeira even in this connection that he, as Dexamenos' guest, had already possessed
her.[873] But he promised to come back to her to take her home
as his wife. In his absence, Eurytion forced them to accept him
as her bridegroom; at the moment when the Centaur with his
brethren wanted to take the bride away, Herakles appeared, as
he had promised, and again showed himself a slayer of Centaurs, as previously in the story of Pholos and Chiron.

In Mycenae he reported that he had accomplished his work
for the king of Elis, but in vain; Eurystheus would not accept
it, and reproached the hero with having undertaken it not for
him alone but also for Augeias.

7

THE HORSES OF THE THRACIAN
DIOMEDES

The order in which the twelve Labours were recounted was not always precisely the same. Still, the narrators seem to be in agreement to this extent at least, that the first task of Herakles was the fight with the Nemean lion and that for his first six Labours he was assigned on each occasion a region of the Peloponnesos around the land of Argos, the kingdom of Mycenae and Tiryns. Only from the seventh Labour onwards did Eurystheus exact from him longer and longer journeys to distant lands. As to what happened on all these journeys, over and above the assignments, more and more stories were told. Thus, to begin with, the journey to Thrace, the object of which was to bring the dangerous horses of king Diomedes to Mycenae. This undertaking is now to open the second series of the Twelve Labours.

The horses of Diomedes ate human flesh, and it was later alleged[874] that they were the same which had torn Glaukos, son of Sisyphos, to pieces at the funeral games of Pelias. It is indeed hard to decide if the four horses, which on a gem have a man given them to eat—in the 'bloody manger', as a tragic poet puts it[875]—belonged to Glaukos of Potniai or the Thracian king. An ancient vase-painting shows them winged. Assuredly they were related to the Harpies, Gorgons and Erinyes, and were more at home in Thrace, the land of Boreas the north wind, who mated with mares,[876] than anywhere else. But the king of the underworld was also *klytópolos*, 'famous for his steeds',[877] and horses brought the heroes to him. So when anyone is shown seated on a throne or lying on a couch and at the same time a horse's head peeps in at the window, there can be no doubt that we have to do with the honour done a dead man. Whether solemnly harnessed to the hearse of a hero on very old sepulchral vases, or furiously tearing him to pieces in the tales of later narrators, they are always the horses of death, and that, too, is how the strange story of the man-eating steeds is to be understood.

Diomedes, who possessed the horses of death, was a son of Ares the war-god. He was lord of the Thracian tribe of the Bistones. Eurystheus sent Herakles to him to get his horses. The hero went his way through Thessaly and visited king Admetos at Pherai; the tale is immortalised by Euripides in his play 'Alkestis'. Admetos, the 'unsubduable', himself bore a name of the king of the underworld, and he was the ruler whom Apollo served for a year. The god guarded Admetos' herds[878] and watered his famous steeds,[879] the best in the world.[880] He also helped him to win Alkestis, the most beautiful of the daughters of Pelias, king of Iolkos.[881] Pelias had made it a condition for her suitors[882] to yoke a lion and a boar to the wedding-coach. Apollo had achieved this already at the marriage feast of Kadmos and Harmonia, and he did it again for Admetos.[883] It was also told[884] that when the bridegroom opened the marriage-chamber, it was full of snakes, allegedly a punishment sent by Artemis, to whom the king had forgotten to sacrifice. Perhaps it is a trace of an older tale in which Admetos and Alkestis celebrated their wedding in serpent-shape, as was fitting for a royal pair of the underworld.

But in this story, the continuation of which the arrival of Herakles in Pherai composes, Apollo promised to placate Artemis; indeed, he befooled the Moirai, who were present at the marriage-feast. He gave them wine till they were drunk,[885] and asked a wedding-gift of them. Then the tipsy Moirai doubled Admetos' short life, on one condition—that[886] on the day when he should have died, another, say his father, his mother or his wife, should voluntarily depart this life in his stead. That day soon came, and it is that day which Euripides portrays for us.

On that day Apollo left the house of Admetos, which Thanatos, Death, entered.[887] He was come to fetch queen Alkestis, for no one else, not even his aged father or his old mother, would die for Admetos, but only his young wife. She now takes leave of her husband and her two little children. The palace is full of sorrow and lamentation; and at that moment Herakles arrives.[888] The king does not let his guest know who is dead, but leaves him to drink at his ease. Alkestis has already been carried out to burial, and Thanatos, Death, is waiting for her behind the sepulchre,[889] to drag the dead queen away with him. Not till then does the hero learn what has happened. He runs after the funeral procession and in a wrestling-match tears Death's prey from him.[890] In the famous conversation in the house of Agathon, the tragedian, which the great Plato has immortalised,[891] mention is made of a version according to which the gods of the underworld themselves let Alkestis go, so amazed are they at her voluntary arrival in Hades. But the old tragedian Phrynichos[892] described the wrestling, body to body, of the hero with Death.

From Admetos, Herakles journeyed on to the cruel Diomedes, son of Ares, one of the most terrible death-gods. It is said of him that he kept his savage horses fastened with iron chains to their bronze manger and fed them on the flesh of unfortunate strangers.[893] To tame them, Herakles threw their master himself to the steeds to devour and brought the beasts with him to Mycenae. Eurystheus is said to have dedicated the horses to Hera, and their breed to have lasted until the time of Alexander the Great.[894]

Other narrators connect this story with the foundation of the Greek city of Abdera in Thrace. According to them, Herakles travelled on shipboard in the company of a whole host of followers;[895] he captured the steeds from their guardians and drove them from the country of the Bistonians down to the sea. Diomedes and the Bistonians pursued him; the hero thereupon left the horses in charge of his favourite, Abderos, joined battle with the pursuers, and put the Bistonians to flight. Meantime Abderos fell a victim to the horses, who dragged him to death, or tore him in pieces as was their custom. Herakles buried Abderos and founded the city of Abdera at his hero-tomb.

We see that in this way the story of the heroes passes into

24 HERAKLES AND GERAS

25 HERAKLES AND THE LION

26 HERAKLES AND THE HIND WITH THE HESPERIDES

narratives of the campaigns of whole companies of them. It was also told how Herakles, after this Thracian exploit, joined the Argonauts;[896] but he did not long remain with them, for as soon as they landed at a bay on the Sea of Marmora, he lost his young follower, the beloved youth Hylas, to the fountain-nymphs.[897] While he was desperately seeking him, the ship Argo sailed on with a favouring wind.[898] Then Herakles, according to the one story, made his way on foot to Kolchis and took part in the winning of the Golden Fleece,[899] but according to the other,[900] went back to the Labours which his destiny compelled him to accomplish for Eurystheus.

It was much more fitting for Herakles (in Euripides he says it is his *daimon*, that is, his personal destiny)[901] to fight all three sons of the death-dealing Ares, in Thrace, Macedonia, and Thessaly—Lykaon and Kyknos as well as Diomedes—than to take part in the Argonautic expedition, which was to make famous the name of another hero, Jason. The tale of his victory over Lykaon is not preserved, but a continuator of Hesiod sang of the fight with Kyknos.[902] To judge by his name, Kyknos, 'the swan', ought to belong to the servants and favourites of Apollo. He lived in a grove of Apollo at Pagasai in Thessaly,[903] and assailed the worshippers of the god who passed that way going to Delphi with their hecatombs.[904] In this account, therefore, he was anything but a servant of Apollo. His father Ares was bodily present to help him, with his charioteers Deimos and Phobos, Fear and Rout. Herakles fought against Kyknos, accompanied on his war-chariot by Pallas Athene, who held victory and renown in her hand.[905] His bold charioteer was the hero Iolaos, but the horse harnessed to the chariot was the divine steed Arion,[906] which Poseidon had begotten on Demeter.[907] Herakles had not stolen it but got it as a present[908] or a loan,[909] and returned it to Adrastos.

The result of the fight is sometimes told thus: Ares did indeed help Kyknos, and a thunderbolt from Zeus separated the combatants.[910] But according to most narrators, Kyknos was killed by the hero and Zeus interposed his lightnings only when his two sons, Ares and Herakles, were fighting one another.[911] On an ancient vase-painting the Old Man of the Sea and Poseidon at one side, Apollo and Dionysos at the other, look on at the fight which blazed up over the corpse of Kyknos and was stilled by Zeus in person. In the story as told by Hesiod's continuator the King of the Gods does not inter-fere. Herakles is warned in advance by Athene that Ares will enter the struggle on his son's behalf, and he wounds the god in the thigh with his spear; his charioteers bring the wounded Ares to Olympos. Herakles takes the arms of Kyknos, whom his father-in-law Keyx later buried, but Apollo has the grave swept away by the river Anauros.[912]

Kyknos belongs rather among the birds, as do his father-in-law Keyx and the latter's wife Alkyone. *Keyx* and *alkyone* apparently mean in Greek respectively the male and the female fulmar. Originally they were, it is said, a human couple, with whom Herakles was in friendly association. They were, how-ever, so overweening as to address each other as Zeus and Hera, and for a punishment they were transformed into birds.[913] The tellers of the story have also contrived to make the swan, Apollo's sacred bird, of which it was believed that its song was to be heard only when it perceived its death approaching,[914] into the murderous son of the war-god. But they could have found no better opponent for him than Herakles, who became master also of the death-dealing steeds of Diomedes and took them with him to Argos.

8

THE BULL OF MINOS

According to most accounts, Eurystheus sent Herakles first to Crete to get the bull, and not till afterwards to Thrace to bring back the horses. Allegedly, king Minos was in possession of the bull, but should not have been, for it was the very same of which we have already spoken in the Cretan Tales,[915] the one with which Pasiphae fell in love. In the account handed down to us,[916] there is only this much difference concerning him—that he no longer plays the part of the queen's lover. He arose from the waves, says the tale, and Minos had previously promised to sacrifice to Poseidon that which should come out of the sea.[917] But the beast was so handsome that Minos sacrificed another bull instead and sent this one to his herds of cows.

Up to this point the tale is identical with the history of Pasiphae, as brought on the stage by Euripides in his 'Cretans'. There, however, Minos' punishment consists in the morbid desire for the bull which Poseidon aroused in the queen.[918] But it was told that Poseidon inflicted yet a further punish- ment;[919] the bull went mad, and it needed Herakles to get rid of it. Therefore Eurystheus sent the hero to Crete, to bring the bull alive to Mycenae. Here Minos himself helped him.[920] Ancient vase-paintings show how the bull was caught, with a rope which Herakles throws around the beast's muzzle and foreleg, or without a rope, when he meets the bull head-on. At length he stunned it with his club and brought it to Mycenae, where he let it go. For a long time the untamed beast wandered about the Peloponnesos, but at length it crossed the Isthmus and came to Marathon, where Theseus caught it again and finally sacrificed it to Apollo.[921]

This was rather an exploit for Theseus. If it is true that in earlier days only ten Labours of Herakles were recounted, it certainly was this and the next one which were the later additions.

9

THE GIRDLE OF THE QUEEN
OF THE AMAZONS

Admete, daughter of Eurystheus,[922] wanted the girdle of Hippolyte, queen of the Amazons. Herakles therefore was sent to the land of Pontos, in Asia Minor, on the Black Sea, where the Amazons lived by the river Thermodon. They were a people consisting of warlike women. Of their children they raised only the girls, and they cut off their right breasts, so that they should not be encumbered when shooting with the bow and hurling the spear; they suckled their daughters from the left breast. Hippolyte their queen was the bravest of them all, and as a sign of this she had been given the girdle by her father Ares. Herakles took a whole company with him when he set out on this enterprise, and[923] among his followers were Theseus, about whom we shall have more to say presently, and Telamon,[924] the hero of the Salaminians and Aiginetans. It was like another voyage of the Argo, and it was even said that all the Argonauts took part in it.[925] According to some accounts, this journey even involved a Trojan war, that which Herakles waged against Laomedon, king of Troy, with a host of Tirynthians and with Iolaos and Telamon.[926]

There was an old tale[927] about the deceitful Laomedon, who possessed famous horses, a present from Zeus.[928] Of him something like the same story was told as of Admetos. He too, the 'lord of the people'—for that is what his name means, and the king of the underworld is ruler over a great people—had Apollo in his service as a herdsman,[929] and with him Poseidon, who built the walls of Troy.[930] The gods served him in human form[931] and competed[932] in establishing the city, but then Laomedon cheated them out of their wages, and added a threat[933] to bind them hand and foot, sell them abroad and even cut off their ears. What he had promised as a reward, either to both or, probably, to the winner in their competition in service, was assuredly his famous steeds, and it was for these horses that Herakles too came to Troy with his six ships.[934]

For, so the tale goes on,[935] Poseidon, on being cheated after building the stronghold, sent a sea-monster against the land of the Trojans, and Apollo sent pestilence. His oracle advised[936] that Laomedon's daughter Hesione should be given over to the monster. In royal robes[937] she was exposed on the shore and Laomedon promised to her rescuer the divine horses of which he had cheated Poseidon. Herakles undertook the task; the

Trojans, with Pallas Athene's help, built him a shelter on the beach, into which he could retire when hard pressed.[938] An ancient vase-painting shows the monster, a gigantic fish with open jaws, which the hero enters, his curved sword in his right hand, to cut out the gigantic tongue. Hesione looks on in all her grand attire. It was also stated that Herakles leaped into the creature's gullet,[939] indeed that he abode for three days in its belly and came back bald-headed.[940] Thus he killed the monster.

But Laomedon would not give the steeds to him either, and abused the hero.[941] The result was the first destruction of Troy; the streets of the city were empty when Herakles moved on.[942] Of his men, Telamon particularly distinguished himself,[943] and got Hesione as his wife by way of a gift of honour.[944] Laomedon and his sons were shot down by Herakles[945] except the youngest, whom Hesione rescued, ransoming him from the hero for her gold-embroidered veil. Till then the youth had been called Podarkes, 'swift-foot', or so we are told,[946] but afterwards Priamos, from *priamai*, 'I ransom'. He became king, and in his old age he witnessed the second overthrow of Troy.

According to older accounts,[947] the voyage against the Amazons followed on this victory, but the later ones[948] reverse the order. To fulfil the task set by Eurystheus, Herakles landed with his host at Themiskyra, at the mouth of the Thermodon. The Amazons were not unfriendly to the men, and Hippolyte was inclined to make a present of her girdle to Herakles.[949] A vase-painter shows the scene between the hero, who sits quietly, and the Amazon in her Scythian trousers; she is handing the girdle to him amicably. Or had the capture of her sister Melanippe already occurred,[950] and was she to be freed at the price of the girdle?[951] But it is told that Hera then appeared in person, disguised as an Amazon,[952] and roused distrust against Herakles and his followers among the female nation, asserting that the strangers intended to kidnap Hippolyte. According to this tale, the heroes and the Amazons did come to blows, and in the fighting, Herakles killed the queen and took the girdle from her dead body. That is how the relief on a metope at Olympia shows her, dying on the ground.

According to those narrators who hold that the first hero to fight the Amazons was Herakles, and Theseus was one of his followers, the latter was now given as his meed of honour the Amazon Antiope,[953] as Hesione was given to Telamon. According to others, Theseus took the queen of the Amazons prisoner,[954] made prize of her girdle[955] and presented it to Herakles. But it is also alleged that the Amazon whom he carried off for himself and by whom he had his son Hippolytos was Hippolyte, not Antiope.[956] But this story has its proper place in the history of Theseus. The girdle was preserved in Mycenae,[957] if it was not rather in the temple of Hera, whom Admete served as priestess.[958]

There were tales also of the return voyage of the heroes, one of them very old and connected, not with the easy task against the Amazons, but with the heavy one at Troy.[959] It was told that[960] on the very day when Herakles turned his back on Troy, Hera moved Hypnos, the god of sleep, to rock Zeus to profound slumber. She herself aroused a mighty storm and drove the hero to the island of Kos, far from all his friends. Of his six ships he lost five.[961] The inhabitants of the island greeted him with volleys of stones.[962] He landed at night and dealt with king Eurypylos, 'him of the wide gate', obviously a name for the lord of the underworld. Having killed him,[963] he had still to fight his son Chalkodon, 'him of the bronze teeth',[964] and was wounded by him. Only Zeus could now rescue his son[965]—from whom, in reality? The name has revealed to us already the God of Death.

The inhabitants of the city of Antimacheia on Kos told the story in rather more detail.[966] After Herakles landed at Cape Laketer from his one remaining ship, saving only his men and their arms, he met a herd of sheep and their shepherd, Antagoras. He is said to have been Chalkodon's brother.[967] Antagoras, who perhaps originally was Antaios, 'he who encounters', is, surely, but another and less transparent name for him. Herakles asked the unknown shepherd for a ram, but the son of Eurypylos challenged him to wrestle. The wrestling soon passed into a fight, for the Meropes, the inhabitants of Kos, helped Antagoras, while Herakles' companions were for defending him, their leader. And they were the first to be worsted; the hero himself had to give in. He took refuge with a Thracian slave-girl and disguised himself in women's clothes until he could overcome the Meropes. Dressed in parti-coloured female attire, he then celebrated his marriage with the daughter of the king, Chalkiope, 'bronze-face'. Ever since then, the priest of Herakles at Antimacheia wore women's clothes and a female headdress at the sacrifice, and so did every bride-groom at his wedding. This was not the last time that Herakles dressed like a woman; a story about it shall be told later, for he was thus travestied when he served Queen Omphale; female attire and women's tasks suit the servant of a goddess, who in the oldest stories probably was neither persecuted by Hera nor in need of rescue by Zeus.

As the end of this tale is told by Homer,[968] the King of the Gods awoke and saw his son in difficulties. He would have thrown Hypnos into the sea and made an end of him, had not the winged god taken refuge with his mother Night, who coerces all gods. Zeus respected her and would not grieve her. But he hung Hera up on a golden rope in the air, with two anvils on her feet. No god could deliver her, and when one of them, Hephaistos, tried to do so, the Olympian threw him from the threshold of the celestial palace far down to the earth.[969] His son he rescued and guided home to Argos of the horse-pastures.

10

THE CATTLE OF GERYONEUS

To take the cattle of Geryoneus, Herakles was sent to the farthest west. He must cross Okeanos and reach the island of

Erytheia,[970] the isle of the red sunset-glow, where the herdsman Eurytion and the two-headed dog Orthos, brother of Kerberos and of the Hydra of Lerna,[971] guarded the cattle in their misty byres. They were purple-red cattle,[972] and their owner was Geryoneus, from whom Herakles was to seize them and drive them all the long way to Argos. It is said of Geryoneus that he was the son of Chrysaor and the Okeanid Kallir-hoe,[973] of Chrysaor, 'the golden-sworded hero' who sprang along with Pegasos from the neck of Medusa when she was beheaded.[974]

Such a father was appropriate to him, for he was no herdsman but, as art-monuments show him, a helmed and armoured warrior with shield and spear. His name, Geryoneus or Geryones, means 'the shouter', and shouting and fighting went together.[975] When the wounded Ares screams, it is like the battle-cry of nine or ten thousand fighting men.[976] His herds-man Eurytion with his bowman's name, borne also by the Centaur in the adventure at Dexamenos' house, was a son of Ares.[977] Geryoneus is described as having three heads,[978] but poets and vase-painters alike[979] agree in giving him three bodies, at least from the trunk up; he fought with six arms and possessed wings as well,[980] so that like the Harpies, Erinyes or some bird of prey he could pounce on his victim. His shield-device was an eagle. His red cattle pastured at sunset. There he stood on watch, perhaps shouting out of the sunset and calling men who had the desire to do battle and capture herds to their death.

According to the oldest narratives, Herakles certainly did not need to go very far, no further than the west coast of the Peloponnesos, to get on board the only vessel by which he could reach Geryoneus' Red Island. Perhaps it was at Pylos on the south-west coast, where Neleus, with his significant name, 'the pitiless', bore sway; he was the son of Poseidon and Tyro, whose story has already been told. Later accounts[981] made out that Neleus and his sons, save only Nestor, tried to seize the cattle of Geryoneus when Herakles was driving them home,

27 HERAKLES TAKES THE GOLDEN ANTLERS

28 HERAKLES WITH THE BOAR

29 HERAKLES WITH PHOLOS THE CENTAUR

and therefore the hero gave Nestor the kingship of Pylos. But
another story was to the effect that the city gate was shut when
Herakles arrived before Pylos, without cattle and certainly not,
as was alleged later,[982] to have himself purified, for then the
gods would not have personally troubled themselves to bar his
entrance. The name Pylos, which is shared by another town on
the same coast—and that one actually had a shrine of Hades[983]
—meant for the narrators, who no longer had before them the
splendour of Nestor's palace, the gate of Hades, *Hadou pylai*.
It was an old tale, already alluded to by Homer,[984] that
Poseidon, Hera and Hades[985] (other poets add Ares and
Apollo)[986] stood by Neleus when Herakles assailed Pylos;
Zeus and Pallas Athene helped the hero. He wounded Hera
on the right breast with his three-barbed arrow and caused her
incurable pain.[987] He struck Ares down thrice with his spear,
and the third time he pierced him through the thigh.[988] Also
he wounded Hades in the shoulder with his arrow, 'in Pylos
among the dead', so it is expressly told.[989] Paieon, the physician
of the gods, healed him on Olympos.[990] Neleus and eleven of
his twelve sons fell.[991]

According to another and perhaps still older version,[992]
Herakles had to deal with only one son of Neleus at Pylos,
Periklymenos, 'the very famous'. By him also nothing else is
meant than is signified by the sons of Eurypylos on Kos. The
story ran that he was really the son of Poseidon, and had
received from his father the gift of taking many shapes. Sometimes he appeared as an eagle, sometimes as an ant, again as a
bee attended by a whole swarm, sometimes as a snake. He was
in the shape of a bee when he settled on the boss of the yoke of
Herakles' team. According to the later version of the tale,
Herakles recognised him by the help of Athene and shot the
bee off. The original version was perhaps that this expert in
transformations was not killed after all, but got away in the
shape of an eagle.[993] Herakles had still a long way to go before
he could reach Geryoneus and his cattle, even when he had
forced the Gate, Pylos.

According to the later tellers of the story, the journey took him through the regions of North Africa to the far-famed Pillars of Herakles, which he erected on that occasion. Some also declared[994] that it was on this journey, as he travelled through Libya, that the giant Antaios met him. Antaios, as his name tells us, was simply 'he who meets', and in speaking of appearances of ghosts they would say that they 'met' someone. Demeter, in her capacity as lady of the dead, who were called Demetreioi, was known as Mother Antaia,[995] and above all, Hekate, the queen of the spectres which she used to send,[996] was so called; she also could 'meet'. Concerning Antaios two different accounts were current. In one of them,[997] he was king of the city of Irasa in Africa. Like Danaos, he instituted a race for the suitors of his most beautiful daughter, and that was how Alexidamos of Kyrene became his son-in-law. In the other,[998] he was a giant, who used to insist upon wrestling with strangers, like Antagoras, whose name is little altered from his. He was stronger than anyone else, and used to decorate the temple of his father Poseidon with the skulls of those he defeated.

But the source of his strength was that he was also a son of Earth, and as soon as his body touched the ground his mother gave him still greater power.[999] Herakles undertook the struggle with him; he had wrestled in like manner on Kos or at Alkestis' tomb. He did not let Antaios fall to the ground, or if he did, he raised him to his feet again. Thus the giant's strength was exhausted, and he was defeated and killed. But the hero, too, was worn out and lay down to sleep. Then came the Pygmies, the ridiculous dwarfs of the Egyptian territory, who so often play their pranks on Pompeian wall-paintings, and tried, so a quite late version has it,[1000] to avenge their brother Antaios. For they also had come forth from the earth. To them, Herakles was a veritable giant. They prepared an attack upon him with engines of war as against some strong fortress, and furnished the model for a much later tale, told not in Greece, but on a misty island the other side of the northern

Sea of the Dead. As for Herakles, he woke up and with a laugh gathered the dwarfs together in his lion-skin, to bring them to Eurystheus as worthy booty.

It was not only this tale that brought Herakles into connection with Egypt on his travels to Geryoneus; there is also the story of Busiris,[1] king of that city in the Nile delta which had the same name, or of another in the neighbourhood of Memphis. It was called 'House of Osiris' in Egyptian, and the word Busiris reproduces this name more or less. The tellers of the tale have transformed Osiris, god of the dead, into the tyrant Busiris. This king was in the habit of sacrificing strangers to Zeus,[2] and devoured human flesh himself.[3] To make the tale more plausible, it was alleged[4] that Egypt had been visited by nine years of drought, and a diviner from Cyprus had therefore explained an obscure oracle to mean that this horrible sacrifice was to be offered every year. Busiris began by sacrificing the diviner. When Herakles arrived in Memphis, he was made captive; he let it happen. It is also said[5] that he was obliged to wrestle with the king. In wrestling, or, as the vase-painters like to show it, when he was to be sacrificed at the altar, he downed Busiris and made short work of him and all his blacks. But we have still something to say about Herakles and Antaios.

According to the later accounts, it was not in Libya but in Mauretania, on the straits which divide Africa from Europe, that Antaios and Herakles met. There the giant had founded the city of Tingis, the modern Tangiers, and there his grave was shown later, a mound in the shape of a man lying on his back.[6] There the sea opens to the west much more widely than at Pylos, and far off opposite, on the Iberian coast, lies Cadiz. There Herakles erected his pillars with the inscription saying that from Gadeira there was no passage westwards.[7] Further off still, the Guadalquivir runs into the Atlantic. The poet Stesichoros gives us the position of the island of Erytheia: it lay almost exactly opposite the mouth of that stream, the Tartessos of the ancients.[8] The distance to Erytheia was not so long as the way which the Sun had to travel to the eastern Ethiopians, but the direction was the same.

The narrators make the hero take this long journey for nothing; he was no nearer his goal here than he had already been 'at Pylos among the dead', where he had aimed his arrows at gods. He must draw his bow against gods if he would force a passage whose existence his inscription denied, there or here. The story goes on as if it immediately continued the events at Pylos. Herakles now drew his bow against the Sun-god,[9] certainly not because of his great heat;[10] Helios was frightened and lent the hero his great gold cup which he boarded every evening to get to the east across the Ocean.[11] The cup[12] was sent and steered by Erytheia, one of the Hesperides, after whom the Island of the Sunset-glow was named.[13] When the hero was already seated in it, a last attempt to hinder his crossing was made by Okeanos, who roused the waves and showed his threatening countenance.[14] But when Herakles drew his bow against him, he let him through.

On the red island, the hero established himself in the byres on the mountain Abas.[15] The dog Orthos smelled him out at once and attacked him, but Herakles made an end of the beast with his club. Eurytion came to the dog's help and was killed. Another herdsman was pasturing his beasts in the neighbourhood; it was the herd of Hades and its guardian was called Menoites. He told Geryoneus of the robbery. The hero was already driving the cattle along the river Anthemos, the 'stream of flowers', when Geryoneus caught up with him. With three hands he brandished three spears against Herakles, and with three he held three shields to guard against him. He was like unto Ares when he strode to meet him.[16] Herakles fought the triple-bodied monster and shot him down, took the herd with him into the cup and quickly landed at the river Tartessos. The Sun-god stepped into the golden vessel, and the son of Zeus disappeared into the dark thicket of laurels.[17]

There were many stories of his return to Argos along the shores of the Mediterranean with the beautiful herd. Robbers

30 HERAKLES AND THE STYMPHALIAN BIRDS

31 HERAKLES AND THE SEA-MONSTER

32   HERAKLES AND THE AMAZON ANDROMACHE

33   HERAKLES AMONG THE AMAZONS

lay in wait for that rare prize everywhere; and among all the peoples and at every city which he touched and because of which he must make longer and longer detours, from Mauretania[18] to distant Scythia,[19] the genealogists were ready to tell of matings of Herakles from which the ruling families might trace their descent. Not all the stories are to be repeated here, as they have hardly anything to do with the hero-legends of the Greeks. One of them, for example, was that which Prometheus had foretold to the hero;[20] for the journey to the Hesperides, on which allegedly Herakles met the Titan, did not in all accounts happen later than the wanderings with the cattle of Geryoneus. On the Ligurian coast, two sons of Poseidon tried to steal the cattle from Herakles.[21] He killed them, and so had to fight the Ligurian nation. Herakles shot all his arrows at the attackers and then, still kneeling, groped for stones, but the ground was soft and he would no doubt have been overpowered had not Zeus come to his help with a rain of stones.[22] Now he could drive off the Ligurians by pelting them. That spot became the stony Plaine de la Crau.

Herakles drove the cattle on, through the whole of Tyrrhenia, the country of the Etruscans, to that place on the Tiber where Rome was later to arise. In those days a son of Volcanus (that was the name by which the inhabitants of the region called Hephaistos) had his dwelling on the Aventine; this was Cacus, whose shape was only half human.[23] He was a fire-breathing murderer, well worthy of his father, whose power was felt not far from the Aventine in the pyres where corpses were burned. Cacus is said also to have been three-headed,[24] like Geryoneus, and the story goes that he conceived a great desire for the cattle. He stole four bulls and four cows from Herakles and grasping them by the tails, dragged them backwards to his cave. The hero would never even have noticed the theft had not the imprisoned beasts bellowed when the herd, satisfied with pasture, was moving on. Herakles turned angrily back and ran to the Aventine, following the lowing of the cattle. Cacus was terrified and lowered a block of stone on chains before the entrance to the cave. Herakles could not force such a gate, but tore a great rock from the hill, so that the cave was suddenly unroofed. That which was revealed there was like the realm of the departed.[25] Vainly did Cacus spew his fires against the hero, who caught him in his famous wrestler's grip, the 'knot of Herakles',[26] and squeezed him to death. He freed the cattle and dragged the half-bestial corpse out into the daylight. Near by he was given an altar by way of thanks; the Romans called it the Ara Maxima, and his hero-cult long endured there.

At the southernmost tip of Italy a young bull got loose[27] from the herd and swam across to Sicily. That is said to be why the town of Rhegion, now Reggio, was so called, from *rhegnynai*, 'to break loose', and the country was named after the young bull, Vitalia originally (*uitulus* is the native name for a bull-calf), later Italia.[28] Eryx, a son of Poseidon, added the bull to his own herd; this robber had given his name to Mount Eryx. When Herakles thereupon crossed the straits, Skylla also stole bulls from him,[29] but he struck her dead, and challenged Eryx, who was one of the Elymoi, to combat. The conditions were that the land of the Elymoi should belong to Herakles if he won, otherwise Eryx should have the entire herd.[30] Again it was to be a wrestling-match. Herakles defeated Eryx three times in wrestling; the Greeks, when they came from Sparta and took possession of the land, appealed to this.

Finally the hero with his cattle got to the Isthmus of Corinth. There a great enemy was lying in wait for him, the giant Alkyoneus.[31] It has been told among the stories of the gods that two men who were partly mortal must be brought in to the battle between the Olympians and the Giants, since only so could victory be gained over the sons of Earth.[32] These two were Dionysos and Herakles, the heroes among the gods. Herakles fought the giant Alkyoneus and killed him. The later version of this was that[33] the Giants assailed Herakles on his journey through Italy, at the Campi Phlegraei near Cumae, and that it was the gods who hurried to his help. Thus he was victorious there over the Giants, and Alkyoneus among them.[34] According to another version the Phlegraean Fields and Pal- lene, where Herakles fought Alkyoneus, lay on the Chalkidian Peninsula, which extends before Macedonia, and Herakles came there with his followers from Kos. There is yet another variant of the tale which shall likewise be told here.

Alkyoneus was a renowned cattle-owner, like Geryoneus;[35] allegedly his cattle had originally been those of the Sun, which pastured in Erytheia, whence the Giant had stolen them,[36] and that was the occasion of the fight between the Gods and the Giants.[37] But when Herakles and his followers assail the Giants in this version, that is another tale again. Alkyoneus did not let himself be taken by surprise, but shattered twelve war- chariots and their drivers and fighting men by hurling a single stone.[38] The tide turned only when Hypnos at the instigation of Pallas Athene put the Giant to sleep. We know of this only from the vase-painters, who show us the Giant asleep, the winged god of sleep hovering over him, and Herakles with his club and bow, followed by Telamon, approaching him from one side, while the goddess can be seen on the other. On other vase-paintings it is Hermes who is assisting the hero, but any- way it is a miniature gigantomachy, fought out by ruse, which causes the death of Alkyoneus in this telling of the story.

Or yet again, the whole business was enacted on the Isthmus; here the Giant was not a herdsman; his presence there, on the Alkyonian Gulf, the 'fulmars' sea', indicates rather that he was a being resembling Kyknos. Among the many reasons adduced for the crying of fulmars on those still winter days known for that reason as 'halcyon days',[39] one is that it is the lamentation of the daughters of Alkyoneus for their father whom Herakles killed. The stone which the Giant threw at the hero was shown on the Isthmus;[40] Herakles parried it with his club and knocked it back to the thrower. Afterwards he reached Mycenae with the cattle of Geryoneus, and Eurystheus sacrificed them to Hera.[41]

11

THE APPLES OF THE HESPERIDES

Herakles also had to get the golden apples from the Garden of the Hesperides. He had already wandered that far on the track of the Keryneian hind, and he might have got there from Libya[42] or some other point on his journey to Erytheia. But in itself and without divine guidance and allowance, this was clearly impossible. The story was told[43] that to begin with he must seek out the daughters of Zeus and Themis on the Eridanos, presumably in that cave in which this divine stream breaks forth from beyond the world. The narrators call them merely nymphs, but the Moirai also were supposedly daughters of Zeus and Themis,[44] and so were the Hesperides.[45] These enigmatic goddesses were thus the appropriate counsellors. They knew Herakles to be immortal and that the entrance to the Garden of the Hesperides was therefore not debarred him. They advised him to seek out Nereus and use force on him till the Old Man of the Sea showed him the way.

We do not know where Herakles found him, in what bay of the Mediterranean, but it might have been at the mouth of the river Tartessos, since it is said also that Herakles got the gold cup in which to sail to Erytheia from Nereus,[46] even that he started the journey to the Hesperides from Tartessos,[47] and finally, that he used the Sun's cup on this journey, too.[48] Nor do we know why the hero had to wrestle with a younger sea deity, Triton.[49] There were stories of Herakles' wrestling with the Triton or with Nereus, which furnished favourite subjects for early artists, but have since been lost. The Old Man of the Sea knew how to turn into various shapes, serpent, water and fire, but the hero would not let him go and gained the victory. The winner of the wrestling-match between Herakles and Nereus was to be given directions to the Garden of the Hesperides, and the prize of the journey originally was, most likely, to become a god.

Aeschylus, too, in his tragedy 'The Freeing of Prometheus',

provided Herakles with a counsellor and prophet in the person of the suffering Titan, the benefactor of mankind. Zeus had none the less reserved it for his son[50] to release Prometheus from his torments, after Herakles had offered Chiron to suffer eternally on his behalf. The wise Old Man of the Sea apparently had so directed the hero's journey that he began by arriving in the warm lands of the south. It is also said[51] that he passed through Arabia and there killed a son of Eos and Tithonos, Emathion, who tried to stop him gathering the apples of the Hesperides.[52] Thus he perhaps reached the sacred Red Sea with its purple sands, the sea that glitters like bronze and nourishes all, the sea of the Ethiopians on the Okeanos, where the all-seeing Helios bathes his immortal body and his tired horses in the warm flood of its gentle waters.[53]

It was from there that the Titans too came to Prometheus, whose torments began on the Scythian Caucasus.[54] Here, bound to a pillar, said by some to have been driven like a stake through his middle[55] he was exposed to the eagle which by day devoured his immortal liver, an organ destined to grow again each night. One morning, when the eagle was coming, Herakles shot it; an ancient vase-painter depicts the scene,[56] while another old vase-painting shows, over against Prometheus, Atlas with the dragon of the Hesperides behind him.[57] In this version they perhaps were not opposite each other, like the Atlas range and the Caucasus, one at the eastern and the other at the western edge of the world, but one at the south and the other in the north. It is in the north that Atlas carries the axis around which the starry heavens revolve; the pole which the two Bears in the sky keep watch over is there.[58] Thus it seems that there were several approaches to the Garden of the Hesperides. Emathion had guarded one of them in the south. So Prometheus sent the hero to Atlas, the neighbour of the Hesperides, and advised him not to force a way into the Garden himself but to ask Atlas for the golden apples.[59] Herakles could probably never have got back from the Hesperides, according to the generally received account.

So according to this tale Herakles had still a long way to go, towards the north. Prometheus gave him exact directions;[60] it was a straight road on the mainland, as if the hero after all had started from the Caucasus and had first arrived there, as perhaps he also did to the extreme south, on some wonderful vehicle. Apart from that of the Sun's cup, there was a tale, in connection with the journey to Erytheia, of a bronze ship, on which instead of a sail Herakles used his lionskin.[61] But he could also wade across the sea when necessary.[62] In fact a vase painting shows him doing it, in a chariot, with Hermes guiding him.

He would come, the Titan foretold him, first into the realm of the north wind and must be careful lest the everlasting storms whirl him up into the air. Then his way would lead on across the land of the Scythians, who fed on cheese made of mares' milk, and, among them, through the most righteous and hospitable people on earth, the Gabioi, who had no need to work their fields, because the ground bore them everything of its own accord. There he would soon arrive at the Hyper boreans, beyond the Rhipaian Mountains, where the great river Istros (we know it better as the Danube) arises. In the story of the Keryneian hind he also got to the Hyperboreans and from there to the Hesperides, but it was unintentional then.

Certainly not all narrators made the hero take this long, roundabout route. For many, the Garden of the Hesperides lay where the voyage through the red waters by Atlas in the west ends.[63] Zeus had a palace there and Hera her marriagebed, by immortal fountains, where the fruitfulness of the soil beatified even the gods.[64] The tree of the golden apples was Mother Earth's weddingpresent to the Queen of the Gods,[65] and so something had to be said of it, its guardian serpent and the nymphs that guarded it, in the legends of the gods.[66] The former had been posted there by Hera; it was the serpent Ladon, a being which never closed its eyes.[67] The genealogists made out that it was the brother of Echidna, the mother of the deadly hounds Kerberos and Orthos and of the Hydra of

Lerna. Ladon also was many-headed, like the Hydra, and had many voices,[68] horrible no doubt, certainly not the clear tones of the Hesperides, the evening-daughters of Night, for their song rather attracted others to, than repelled them from, what they guarded.

The three Hesperides, or four, or more, were even equated with the death-goddesses who carried off their prey, the Harpies;[69] but they never left the Garden around the tree and they did not, like the Sirens, sing where the seafarers' tracks lay. Anyone who came to them, came as it were to the Island of the Blessed; no mortal ever found the road thither. But if anyone had succeeded in reaching them and if also he dared lay hands on the property of the Queen of the Gods, the golden fruit, that would have been double death for him, or would have meant the disturbance and destruction of a luxuriant, sacred region, so far off that it was not the concern of men.

Atlas, the neighbour of the Hesperides, was thought to be a cunning god, a deceitful, treacherous Titan, who was punished by having to hold up the axis of the sky.[70] He was prepared to get the golden apples, but made it a condition that the hero should carry the heavens in the meantime. Nothing is told us of the ruse by which he got the apples, but something of the trick he played on Herakles.[71] He brought the golden fruit, but not to give it to the hero, who was to continue to hold up the sky in his stead. There was a comical old tale according to which Herakles made a show of agreeing, but asked just one favour of Atlas, that the Titan should take the sky on his shoulders again while Herakles prepared a cushion for his head. And now the cunning Titan proved a stupid Titan, for he laid the apples on the ground and took over the weight of the sky; while Herakles for his part hurried away with his booty to Eurystheus. A carving on a metope at Olympia shows him with the cushion on his neck. There, Pallas Athene is helping the hero, and Atlas, calm and wise, is bringing him the fruit.

But there is another form of the story, namely that Herakles forced his way to the Hesperides, attacked the guardian serpent and finally killed it.[72] On vase-paintings we see him also peacefully in the Hesperides' company; according to this version, he accomplished his task with the agreement and help of the goddesses. This is the latest form of the story, which is told us much more by vase-painters than by poets. True, it is also recorded[73] that Ladon, the never-sleeping snake, also protected the golden apples from the fancies of the Hesperides, who would gladly have plucked what belonged to Hera, or in another tradition, to Aphrodite.[74] They therefore gave their assistance to putting the serpent to sleep. The Attic master-painter Meidias, who introduced a whole company of heroes, like an Argonautic expedition, into the Garden of the Hesperides, makes the sorceress Medeia with her box of magic herbs take part in the journey. Assteas of Paestum portrayed the scene even more elaborately, for he puts Kalypso there, whose island, at the sea's navel,[75] belonged to the same realm beyond the world's end as the Garden of the Hesperides; she is offering the drink to the dragon in a cup, and he merely laps it up, without noticing that on the other side a Hesperid is plucking the fruit, nor that Herakles has already got one apple, and two Hesperides are actually eating others. According to one master, again of Attica, who also painted the Omphalos, the navel of the earth, on the vase,[76] the magic drink was wine. A great mixing-bowl stands there, the serpent is quite tame, the three Hesperides have become maenads, Panes are looking at them from the background, Iolaos is present also, and Herakles in the middle of the picture is garlanded by a flying Nike, for the victory is his. A third Attic master leaves out the dragon; it has been killed. The Hesperides surround Herakles and two younger heroes; behind his shoulder stands Eros and plucks the apples. Love rules. It is quite different from what we find in the poet Apollonios,[77] who brings his Argonauts to the Garden of the Hesperides the day after the serpent was killed. The goddesses are weeping in loud voices and in their grief change themselves into trees, a black poplar, an elm and a willow.

Another scene has not escaped the artists, or rather they alone have recorded it: Herakles giving back the stolen golden fruit to the gods, Zeus and Hera. We are told merely that he simply showed the apples to Eurystheus,[78] but it was stated [79] that the king of Mycenae would not take possession of the booty at all, that he presented it instead to the hero. It would not have been lawful to keep it anywhere, for the apples of the Hesperides constituted the property of the gods, even more sacred than their temple-treasures. If anyone had asked a narrator what became of them, his only possible answer would have been that they came back to their rightful owners.

12

THE HOUND OF HADES

Many narrators followed a sequence in which the bringing up of Kerberos took the last place but one and the tale of the apples of the Hesperides, which amounted to an apotheosis, concluded the list. By no means all did so,[80] however, for the final test of the divinity of the hero, the last attempt to send him to his death, was the task to capture the hound of Hades from the underworld. Eurystheus never contrived a harder labour for him, as the shadow which represented Herakles in the realm of the dead later recognised.[81] Furthermore, this task again involved the violation of a sacred realm. The House of Hades behind its firmly fixed boundaries had been such a realm ever since the division of the universe between the highest gods. Its violation was an unheard-of exploit, which not even a hero could venture upon, least of all an ordinary hero. The heroes were tragically connected with Hades, save only the divine hero, the victorious fighter against death. But even he did not remain quite untouched in this struggle, as we shall hear later.

The Eleusinians told[82] how Herakles, so as not to violate the gods of the underworld, first had himself initiated into the Mysteries; thus he could go to them as one of their own. But he had already killed many and was polluted with the blood of his defeated enemies; he especially needed purification from the killing of the Centaurs. It was also stated[83] that in that age, when Eleusis did not yet belong to Athens, no foreigner might receive initiation. Hence Herakles had to be adopted by an Eleusinian called Pylios, that is to say a 'man from Pylos' or 'from the gate of Hades', and thus became the 'Pylian's' son. This story merely tells in other words what the hero was to attain as an initiate. Eumolpos the hierophant, the high priest of the Mysteries, undertook to purify him; he had received the secret initiation personally from the founder and first initiate of the rite, the great goddess Demeter.[84] The ceremonies of purification which rid Herakles of pollution were by no means a secret; long after this story arose, they were still repre, sented, for instance, on a sarcophagus and a marble urn found in the neighbourhood of Rome. There Herakles is sitting, with his head veiled, on a throne and having performed over him the sacred ceremonies that would give him back purity in the eyes of gods and men. Behind him is visible the foundress and patroness of the Mysteries, sitting on the closed basket which contained the secret objects used in the cult. On one of the two representations Herakles, now purified, is in the costume of an initiate and already making friends with the goddess' serpent. The initiations themselves might not be exposed to profane eyes, much less told to the uninitiate.

On the other hand, it seems as if certain verses of the poet Euphorion[85] referred to Eurystheus accompanying Herakles with his curses all the way from Eleusis across the Isthmus to Tainaron at the southern extremity of the Peloponnesos. He was shudderingly afraid that the hero would return alive once more, even from the underworld. Therefore he would have Artemis, to whom the southernmost tip of the peninsula was sacred—it was there that the entrance to the underworld was—shoot him down and make him carry Askalaphos' stone him, self in the underworld. These ill, wishes no doubt are founded on the Eleusinian tale, but that was assuredly not the oldest.

Originally, Herakles did not make the detour through Eleusis to get from Tiryns to Tainaron. How this story was told in an old 'Descent of Herakles to Hades' is revealed to us only by the few traces which are left in the later narratives and in Vergil's account of Aeneas' visit to the underworld. From Tainaron a cavern led to the realm of the dead; Herakles forced his way in there, not like an initiate but, we may conjecture, sword in hand.[86] Elsewhere in this undertaking he tried again to make use of his sword, but vainly, for it seems that against the gods of the dead and the ghosts only wrestling or stone-throwing was of avail. The rough, evergreen strength of Charon, the old ferryman of the dead, is praised by the Roman poet,[87] but surely not with reference to Aeneas, who drew near him holily, with the golden bough. On the other hand, there might easily have been a wrestling-match between Charon and Herakles; but he must have been so terrified by the hero[88] that he took him aboard his ancient coracle, sewn together from bark.[89] The feeble craft all but sank under the weight of Herakles,[90] seeing that the same thing nearly happened to the Argo, the well-built ship of the Argonauts.[91] Charon later was not pleased that he had taken him aboard,[92] since, so the story goes, he had to spend a year in chains as punishment for it.[93]

Thus the hero got across the waters of Hades. The swampy stream was fundamentally the same as the river Acheron, which forms the Acherusian Mere in north-west Greece, a swampy lake like that at Stymphalos. It was said especially of the Acheron in Epeiros and the Styx in Arkadia that they both ran into the underworld.[94] On the far bank of the swampy region Kerberos was waiting for the newcomers, like a good sheep-dog, knowing which he should include in Hades' flocks and which he should keep away. He even greeted with tail-waggings those whom he was to retain, but if they showed any intention of going back, he devoured them.[95] He was a beast who liked his meat raw,[96] and his barking had a metallic ring. He threatened to swallow everything when he opened his three,[97] or even fifty,[98] mouths.[99] It was not without cause that the Hydra of Lerna was represented as his sister.[100] The artists show us that his body was partly made up of biting snakes, either forming his tail or growing out from him. But when Kerberos caught sight of Herakles, he fled trembling to his master, the king of the underworld, and hid under Hades' throne.[101]

The ghosts also fled before the hero;[102] Meleagros was the only one whose ghost did not. He had died not long before, and having been obliged to leave his sister Deianeira un-wedded in his father's house, entreated Herakles to take her to wife.[103] It is told how he met his future brother-in-law in shining armour and that Herakles bent his bow against him. But Meleagros explained to him that ghosts could not be wounded and also could not wound.[104] Then Herakles was still apprehensive lest it be Hera who had sent this shining hero against him; but when Meleagros told him his sad tale, there came tears into the eyes of the son of Zeus, for the first and only time. He himself asked Meleagros if he had not a sister left in the house of his father Oineus, for if so he would gladly marry her.[105] 'I left Deianeira at home, in the fresh bloom of youth, a stranger still to golden Aphrodite the enchantress,' answered Meleagros. Thus Herakles in the underworld chose a disastrous wife for himself.

Then the Gorgon's head met him. Before that terrible vision Odysseus was later to retreat without having seen it;[106] Herakles, on the other hand, drew his sword.[107] Again he was informed (it was believed that Hermes this time informed him) that the terrifying face in the realm of shadows was nothing but an empty appearance. But he perhaps attacked the image of Medusa. It was not the only time he assailed the ordinances of Hades, that seemed so inflexible. Under a stone, as it were in a tomb in the very underworld, lay Askalaphos, a daimon in the service of Hades, thus punished for having borne testi-mony against Persephone.[108] Herakles lifted the stone and set the daimon free, whereupon Askalaphos was turned by

Demeter, who never forgave him for what he had done, into a screech-owl. Herakles wished to feast all the ghosts on warm blood, and so butchered one of the cattle of Hades. Their herdsman was that same Menoites who had revealed the hero's presence to Geryoneus, Menoites son of Keuthonymos, 'him who conceals his name'.[109] He challenged the hero to wrestle with him, and Herakles gave him such a hug that he broke his ribs, and let him go only to please Persephone.

For now he had made his way to the throne of the King and Queen of the underworld. How the original story continued we are informed by a vase-painter. Herakles lifted a stone against the enthroned pair; Hades leapt up and ran away in one direction, his hound in another, but Persephone stayed where she was, face to face with the hero. Later narrators stated[110] that the queen received the son of Zeus graciously; he was, after all, her brother. This was still more fitting if Herakles had already been initiated at Eleusis when he came to the realm of the dead.[111] And, as the tale continued,[112] the King of the underworld personally gave him permission to take the hound with him, if he could catch him without weapons, equipped only with his corselet and lion-skin. According to this version, then, Herakles went back to the gate of Hades on the Acheron, where Kerberos stood on guard, and choked him until he yielded. The beast still tried to bite him with his tail, but at last let himself be attached to a chain, and so the hero brought up the hound of Hades on the leash.

Near the gate he saw two captives, Theseus and Peirithoos, who were under punishment for trying to carry off the Queen of the underworld.[113] This story also will be told later. Both heroes were sitting on a stone,[114] condemned to sit there for ever.[115] They reached out their hands to him as he went by, the rest of them being paralysed; Herakles was able at least to free Theseus from his rigidity; he took him by the hand and aroused him to life again. He wanted to do as much for Peirithoos, but the earth quaked and he let him be.[116]

Herakles saw the daylight again at Troizen, opposite Athens

on the eastern extremity of Argos,[117] or else at Hermione,[118] on the south side of the same peninsula. From there, still with Kerberos on the lead, he took the road to Tiryns and Mycenae. Drops fell freely from the foaming mouth of the trembling hound.[119] Dragging behind, the snakes hissed under the monster's shaggy belly, right and left. His eyes sparkled with blue lights like the sparks that leap up in a smithy when iron is hammered and the anvil rings under the blows. But he came alive from Hades to Tiryns, the result of the last Labour for the hostile Eurystheus. At the cross-roads near Midea the horrified women and children saw the creature with their own eyes.

An ancient vase-painter has perpetuated the scene of the king of Mycenae fleeing from the chained monster, which was springing at him, into his underground jar, as he had done at sight of the boar of Erymanthos. In one account, Herakles him-self led the hound back to Hades;[120] in another the beast got away from him at the fountain between Mycenae and the temple of Hera, which ever after was known as *eleutheron hýdor*, 'the water of freedom'.[121] But Herakles returned from the realm of the dead so formidably changed that he received an epithet connected with the name of Charon; in Boiotia he was worshipped as Charops.[122]

CHAPTER III

Deeds and Sufferings After the Twelve Labours

I

KALLINIKOS

AFTER HERAKLES HAD RETURNED from the underworld, he justly bore his most famous epithet, Kallinikos,
'glorious victor'. The victory glorious among all victories was
surely that over death, and Herakles, almost alone among all
gods and heroes, was thus called.[123] It became customary
among the most simple folk, certainly before late antiquity, to
write up over the door:[124]

> 'Here dwells the Glorious Victor, Herakles,
> The son of Zeus; let nothing evil enter.'

'Evil' means above all else death, which people preferred not to
mention openly nor write over their own doors. Herakles alone
was able to drive away this evil when it was already in the house
and he came almost too late and by chance. Poor stupid Death
for his part was to believe that the hero had arrived there ahead
of him.

The first altar to Herakles Kallinikos,[125] or Herakles
Alexikakos, another name with much the same meaning as the
lines just quoted, 'Herakles averter of evil',[126] is said to have
been dedicated by Telamon at the capture of Troy, when he
was himself threatened with death by the jealous Herakles; his
appeal to that characteristic of the hero saved him. And the
victory over Troy now leads us to the history of Herakles'
successful campaigns. The Dorians in particular insisted that

the hero had three times helped their oldest king, Aigimios,[127] under whom they had not yet emigrated to the Peloponnesos; first against the Lapithai, next against the Dryopes and lastly against king Amyntor of Ormenion, all inhabitants of Thes-saly and Trachis, in the neighbourhood of the fateful Mount Oita. In Sparta itself, where the Dorians did not yet live, it was Herakles who defeated Hippokoon, brother of Tyndareos, and his twenty sons and brought back the earthly father of the Dioskuroi to his hereditary throne.[128]

He also owed himself another campaign, the punitive expedition against Augeias, who had cheated him out of his payment for the cleansing of the byres. The king of Elis was helped by the twins whom Molionē, the wife of Aktor, had borne to Poseidon. Aktor was Augeias' brother, and the twins were called the Aktorione after their earthly father, the Molione after their mother.[129] These sons of Poseidon, Kteatos and Eurytos,[130] came forth from an egg, like the Spartan Dio-skuroi; it was of silver,[131] and the two brothers formed an even more inseparable unit than Kastor and Polydeukes. If one of them held the reins of the steeds who drew their war-chariot, the other wielded the lash.[132] It was said[133] that they were twins in a special sense, a pair grown together, and they gave Herakles more trouble than the byres of Augeias.

Even Herakles cannot overcome two, so said the old pro-verb,[134] and the marvellous sons of the god defeated his army when he lay in ambush with it in Elis.[135] It is said that his half-brother Iphikles fell in that fight.[136] For, says the tale, during that campaign Herakles was smitten with a disease;[137] we shall hear presently of this ailment, into which his lust for vengeance could grow. On that occasion he had arranged a truce with the Aktorione, but when they heard of Herakles' illness, they broke the truce and the war continued annihilat-ingly, till it had to be interrupted because of the festal season of the Isthmian Games. The twins set out to the Games and were treacherously attacked by Herakles at Kleonai; only so did they suffer defeat and fall by the hand of the hero,[138] and that

34 HELIOS SHOT AT BY HERAKLES

35 HERAKLES AND GERYONEUS

36 HERAKLES IN THE CUP OF THE SUN

success brought him no renown. In this mournful way his struggle against the cunning Augeias and his superhuman allies came to its end. Vainly did Molionē endeavour by her curses to avenge her murdered sons.[139] In Elis, Herakles set Phyleus, Augeias' son who had formerly borne witness on his behalf, upon the throne in place of his father.[140]

He then proceeded to the re-founding of the Olympic Games and became the originator of the finest victories which antiquity knew.[141] The winner at Olympia received the garland of olive twigs that Herakles had brought with him from the land of the Hyperboreans.[142] There was another sacred tree which Herakles had transplanted from Acheron to Olympia, the white poplar;[143] only from its wood might the altar-fire of Zeus at Olympia be lit. Herakles also built the great pyre for hero-offerings to Pelops,[144] erected twelve altars for the twelve gods,[145] and celebrated the Olympic Games in the manner in which they were ever after celebrated. It is added[146] that he won the victory in every contest; who indeed could have seriously wanted to contend with him, the Kallinikos?

2

THE MADMAN

During the time of his service with Eurystheus, Herakles was long absent from the family which he had founded in Thebes. Their destiny belongs properly to the Theban legends and many narrators put it before the Twelve Labours, indeed make out that Herakles took on himself the servitude at Tiryns by way of penance for the fate of his children.[147] However, this tradition of the Boiotians, that Herakles came back from the realm of the dead as Charops—that is to say, grimly altered— seems to justify Euripides, who put this tragic story on the stage and made it take place immediately after the return from the underworld.

The Thebans knew of eight sons whom Megara bore to

Herakles.[148] They did them honour at their graves as young heroes and called them the Chalkoarai, 'those upon whom a curse of bronze fell', but they did not like to tell the story of how these unfortunates met their deaths at their own father's hand. According to Euripides there were but three, but the possibilities of the stage limited him in his representation. In his 'Herakles' he brings on a king Lykos, as in the 'Antiope', this time the son of the other Lykos, who persecutes and wishes to destroy the hero's family, his old stepfather Amphitryon, Megara his wife, and the three sons. They know that Herakles has forced his way into the underworld and that he has not yet returned from it, so now belongs to the dead. Even Amphitryon and Megara can see no way out of their desperate plight than death along with the children. The three little ones are already arrayed as for burial,[149] when Herakles enters, returned from the underworld. He has not gone to Eurystheus, but has left Kerberos in the precinct of the infernal Demeter, Demeter Chthonia, at Hermione,[150] and has hurried to Thebes. He is, however, somewhat confused. He does not at once recognise old Amphitryon, or his name has slipped his memory.[151] He threatens the ungrateful Kadmeians with massacre.[152] Now, with Megara and the children, who are soon joined by Amphitryon also, he finds Lykos and his satellites in the palace. They have no idea of his arrival and are killed in a moment. But madness is already in the house. Euripides makes it also come on to the stage in the person of Lyssa, 'insanity' who is sent by Hera and guided by Iris. Herakles is seized by madness and imagines he is now hurrying to Eurystheus, indeed that he is already in his house and that his own children are the other's. He hunts them down, strikes one dead with his club, dispatches the other two with arrows, shoots down Megara, and would kill Amphitryon as well did not Pallas Athene throw a 'stone of sobriety', *lithos sophronister*,[153] against his breast. At this he collapses, falls into a deep sleep, and wakes heavily, knowing nothing of what he has done.

Euripides himself alludes to the earlier form of the legend, when he makes Herakles speak of purifying fire.[154] In the original story, it seems he kindled such a fire after his return home. The vase-painter Assteas portrays it, showing him bringing up the first child, after having already thrown the furniture and fittings of the house into the flames. Iolaos, Alkmene, and Mania, 'madness', are looking on from the background, as from the upper storey of the palace, and Megara, lamenting, is escaping through the open door. It was indeed told that Herakles threw his sons into the fire.[155] Another account is[156] that when he recovered his senses he married Megara to Iolaos and left Thebes for ever, to found a family elsewhere. For Herakles was no kidnapper of women like Theseus, the son of Poseidon; this did not happen even in the case of Auge, a peculiar story which shall be told in connection with her son Telephos. Even after this misfortune he remained the servant of Hera.

However, the narrators of the tales concerning Herakles' new courtship have but to postpone the time at which the purifying fire, originally intended for himself, into which he threw his sons first, should at the last flame for him. A courtship which after all lapsed into the rape of a girl and involved him in the sin of murdering a guest-friend brought Herakles living to the pyre.

3

THE SINNER

Herakles got no glory from that earlier deed by which he ambushed and killed the two Molione on their way to the Isthmian Games, but it was a result of the deceit which Augeias, the uncle of the divine twins, had committed against the hero. It belonged to the story of the king of Elis' byres and also no doubt to that of his daughter, who had been promised to Herakles. There is a certain resemblance between that tale and the adventure of Herakles with Eurytos, lord of the stronghold of Oichalia, which led him first to murder a guest-friend and later to abduct a girl.

No one knows exactly where Eurytos' town lay. Five Greek cities claimed to have been that Oichalia, one in Messenia, others in Thessaly, Aitolia, on Euboia and in Trachis. Perhaps those are right, though, who heard in the name of Oichalia that of the *oichomenoi*, the departed. Eurytos means 'good archer', one who draws his bow and hits the mark, like Apollo, the *rhytōr toxōn*.[157] He was a son of Melas or Melaneus, 'the black one'.[158] It is also told[159] that he challenged Apollo himself to a contest in archery and was shot down by the god. Apollo in person had given him his bow[160] and instructed him in the use of it;[161] so the narrators express his close relationship to the god, making Eurytos almost appear as a second Apollo. Apollo at any rate is said to have been his grandfather.[162] The bow which he had from him Eurytos left to his son Iphitos,[163] who in turn gave it to Odysseus when he met him on the disastrous search for his father's mares in Messenia.[164] And the suitors of Penelope met their deaths on a feast-day of Apollo by the god's gift,[165] as shall be told later.

Like other cruel kings, who were one and all doubles of the death-god, Eurytos proclaimed that he would give his daughter, the beautiful Iole with her flower-name (its older form is Viola, that is to say Violet) in marriage to anyone who defeated him in his speciality.[166] It was told of him as of Oinomaos that he was in love with his daughter and wanted to keep her for himself,[167] which was why he made victory in a contest of archery the condition. Herakles, after awaking from his madness and parting with Megara, came to Oichalia to compete; a later tale[168] says that he had himself been Eurytos' pupil in archery, while others made out that his teacher was a Scythian,[169] or a Cretan, Rhadamanthys,[170] who by one account[171] came to Boiotia and took Alkmene to wife after Amphitryon's death. No one was so appropriate an opponent as Herakles for the 'invincible bowman'. Or what other name suits Eurytos as well?

37 HERAKLES WITH THE HESPERIDES

38 HERAKLES BEFORE ZEUS WITH THE APPLES
OF THE HESPERIDES

39 HERAKLES CHAINING KERBEROS

40 HERAKLES AND THE KERKOPES

Details of the contest in archery at Oichalia are told us only by vase-painters, and even they are not sufficiently in accord. Once we see four arrows already sticking in the target, but Herakles, who in all accounts won the match, killed two sons of Eurytos as well, one of them being Iphitos. He is now aiming his bow at the girl, as if he would send even the prize of the archery contest into the underworld; Eurytos and a brother of the girl are trying to restrain the hero from shooting. All accounts agree that although he won the contest they refused him the prize; but now they are compelled to give him Iole. The other side of the vase shows him on a couch, while Dionysos enters the house and the bride crowns the victor with a garland. On another vase-painting Iole stands between the recumbent men, Herakles on one side of her, her father and brothers on the other. Other vase-painters again represent an attack on Herakles by the sons of Eurytos, who have taken away his bow and his club at a banquet. We are told only[172] of the insulting speech in which Eurytos and Iole's brothers excuse their promise-breaking. They reproach the hero with the murder of his children which he had committed when mad, and having disarmed him and weakened him with wine, fling him contemptuously out of the house.[173]

That was the cause of the capture of Oichalia, which, like the punitive expedition against Augeias, must inevitably follow on the deceit and shame. Iphitos, the eldest son of Eurytos, had had the ill-luck to fall into the hands of Herakles still earlier. In seeking twelve mares[174] which had their mule-colts still at their udders, Iphitos came to Tiryns, Herakles, seat. Herakles was in possession of the mares, whether he had taken them himself by way of reprisals[175] or Autolykos had stolen them for him from Eurytos;[176] but he was meditating greater schemes of revenge.[177] He received Eurytos' son hospitably, even inviting him in as if nothing had happened.[178] And, reverencing neither the watchful eyes of the gods nor the table which he had set before his guest, he murdered Iphitos.[179] The criminal act is variously described, but all narrators agree[180] that the host took his guest around the tops of the Cyclopean walls of Tiryns and flung him down from a tower.

Herakles, it was said later,[181] had two attacks of insanity, first when he murdered the children and the second time when he murdered his guest. Crime and madness both demanded that the doer should be purified and absolved. Herakles found someone to purify him at Amyklai near Sparta; his name was Deiphobos, son of Hippolytos; no more is told us of this purification,[182] but at least it gave the story-tellers their chance to attach at this point the account of another enmity. This hostility, which made Herakles a still greater sinner, was between him and one who was even greater than the great Eurytos,[183] the deadliest of all archers. The story went that the hero forced his way into the shrine of Apollo at Delphi and sought to pillage the holiest object that was preserved there, the tripod with its cauldron.

Apollo had twice opposed him during the performance of his Twelve Labours. He supported his sister when Herakles had made his way too far into Artemis' realm and was taking the hind of Keryneia. Also he joined the other gods in defending Pylos, the gate through which Herakles broke to get into the other world. But now he had to defend his own temple against Herakles, who broke into the holy of holies to take possession of the most sacred thing his brother owned. This sin would have been Herakles' greatest exploit, all the greater because Apollo was the greater name of the enemy whom he perpetually fought, greater than all others. However, this adventure was but the boundary of his deeds; it was their significant condensation for those who chose to remember that the arrows of the god in his wrath were most potent to bring death to beasts and men.[184]

The robbery of the tripod was later explained[185] by saying that Herakles meant to found an oracle of his own with the holy apparatus, and that he took it as far as Pheneos in Arkadia, wherefore Apollo still held a grudge against the people of that place a thousand years later. A story was told that the quarrel between the two sons of Zeus started for the reason[186] that Herakles wanted to consult the oracle of Delphi on something, and the Pythia gave him answer that the god was not there and would give him no response. Yet another version made the hero come to Delphi for purification and be repulsed.[187] The murder of Iphitos was reason enough for denying Herakles the oracle, if he entered the temple himself, for homicides were debarred from the sanctuary,[188] although they might get advice as to atonement through a third party.

Artists were fond of immortalising the scene of the quarrel at its hottest, for in it they saw nothing but a strife between brothers, a play between gods. They did this in Delphi itself, and the Thebans even stamped their coins with the figure of Herakles hurrying away with the tripod after his sacrilege. Here the sculptors and vase-painters take up the thread of the story. The hero has already left the temple and seems to have got quite a distance with the tripod along a certain road when Apollo overtakes him, in the company of Artemis. Athene participates in the plundering at the hero's side. The goddesses try to hold him back or to separate the pair; the god holds one foot of the sacred object, Herakles raised his club. If the goddesses did not succeed, only Zeus could end the strife of his sons; it was said that he threw his thunderbolt between the combatants.[189] Thereupon they separated and concluded peace. Perhaps this happened as far from Delphi as Gytheion on the coast of Lakonia, for that town is alleged to have been founded by them in common, after their reconciliation.[190]

After this, Herakles had to make atonement—for the sacrilege, according to some,[191] but at all events for the murder of his guest. That was the will of Zeus,[192] and so Apollo advised.[193] He must pay the price of blood, according to one version,[194] not to Iphitos' father but to his brothers; this presupposes that he had already killed Eurytos at the archery contest in Oichalia, and that it was the brothers who would not give him Iole but sent him away with desire for revenge in his heart. And now he must atone further by taking on himself the service of a slave for three years. Hermes conducted him to the slave-market and sold him for three talents;[195] the Lydian queen who bought him was named Omphale.

4

THE SERVANT OF WOMEN

Not all tellers of the story believed that Herakles' servitude to Queen Omphale of the golden sandals[196] needed any particular explanation; the Daktyl-nature of the servant of Hera was enough. Servitude to women in that land of gold where once Tantalos ruled was connected with the other adventures of the hero; he might, for instance, have deserted the Argonauts for the beautiful queen's sake.[197] It was perhaps the Lydians them-selves or the Greeks in their neighbourhood who started the story[198] that the double axe, the cognisance of the Lydian kings before Kandaules, was a present from Herakles to Omphale; he had taken this sacred weapon from Hippolyte queen of the Amazons, and brought it to Sardes. An old legend again was that of the inhabitants of the island of Kos, which lay within sight of the shores of Asia; they worshipped Herakles as their marriage-deity,[199] put women's clothes on their bridegrooms and alleged[200] that Herakles had been the first to do the like in the abode of a Thracian slave-girl. The same is said to have been his lot now with Omphale.

In another tale,[201] the ancestress of the Lydian kings with their double axe, who were descendants of Herakles, was a slave-woman, daughter of Iardanos. Iardanos is the name of a river in Lydia,[202] and Omphale was said to have been his daughter, destined to found a dynasty with Herakles.[203] Her name is the feminine form of *omphalos*, 'navel', and we could believe that slave-women bore that name. But not only does the river-god Iardanos appear as her father, but the mountain-god Tmolos as her first husband,[204] and in all accounts she was the mistress and Herakles the servant. What the Greek narrators were trying to express when they called her a slave-woman or a widow, glossing the matter over or denying it completely, was the most natural thing in the world in Lydia, where the girls did not live as virgins but as courtesans.[205] They did so in order to marry; it was the way they collected their dowry, and so arranged their own weddings as their own mistresses.[206] Also, *omphalos* means not only the navel of the human body but also a stone object of cult, the navel of the earth, with which also was connected the worship of a goddess, Themis at Delphi, Aphrodite at Paphos.

It is true that no account speaks of Omphale as a goddess; the narrators, who are all Greeks, portray her to us rather[207] as a wanton, although Herakles behaves no differently to her than the Koan bridegroom at his wedding. It is often told, and shown by the later artists, how the hero, to please his mistress, put on women's clothes; generally they are portrayed as the clothes and ornaments of Omphale herself. There is still something ceremonial about it when, in a late narrative,[208] Herakles first holds the golden parasol over the queen's head as they go to the festival of Dionysos in the vineyards of Tmolos, and then on the eve of the feast-day, chaste and completely continent, they exchange clothes, he putting on all Omphale's delicate and costly attire and she arrayed in his lion-skin and taking his club in her hand.

It was the late narrators also who elaborated Herakles' service to a woman into woman's work, or into a task set him like those in the service of Eurystheus. A spindle was put in his hand and he was set to prepare wool with the slave-girls.[209] Of the innumerable deeds attributed to Herakles, those were sought out which could appear petty alongside the twelve Great Labours, and represented as tasks set her servant by the Lydian queen.[210] Some told a tale[211] of an all-destroying serpent at the Lydian river Sangarios which Herakles killed as he had the Hydra of Lerna, and gave that as the reason why he came among the constellations as Ophiuchos, the man holding a serpent.

One task which he allegedly performed at Omphale's bidding

was to catch the tailed Kerkopes.[212] 'Tailed' is what their name means, and they might be thought to be Kabeiroi quite as well as monkeys. Old narrators gave them such designations as:[213]

> 'Liars and cheats, doers of naughty deeds,
> Deceivers; as they journeyed far and wide,
> Vagabonds all their days, they choused mankind.'

They comprised a pair of brothers called Olos and Eurybatos. The name Eurybatos actually got the meaning of 'swindler'.[214] It was said of them both that they came from 'Oichalia' (we know what that place could signify), and that they wandered about cross-roads and robbed the Boiotians. They were known by other names also, which reveal that they were in fact the Kabeiric brethren. One of these brothers was named Akmon,[215] that is to say 'anvil', and Akmon and Passalos, 'anvil' and 'peg', were also names of Kerkopes,[216] while their mother was said to be Theia, 'the divine', a daughter of Okeanos,[217] elsewhere a Titaness,[218] and a name of the divine Great Mother.

In Asia Minor the Kerkopes were settled in the neighbourhood of Ephesos;[219] in mainland Greece their haunt was Thermopylai, the narrowest part of the pass through the 'warm gates' (that is what the name means),[220] whose healing springs, according to a later belief, Pallas Athene once caused to arise for Herakles when he was tired.[221] It was a place for robbers, but, because of the hot springs, for the Kabeiroi also. There Herakles fell asleep on one of his many journeys. The mother of the Kerkopes had warned them to beware of the *melampygos*, the 'black-rumped man',[222] but the hero was sleeping on his back with his weapons beside him.[223] These the brothers tried to get hold of, but Herakles was not sleeping deeply enough; he woke up and caught them both in his bare hand, tied the absurd creatures together, hung them by the feet to a carrying-pole, like two buckets, and took them with him. Being head downwards, the fellows laughed aloud behind the back of the hero, although no doubt they were badly frightened at first, for their mother's warning was coming true. Herakles, surprised, asked them what they were laughing at, and then laughed with them. By way of reward, he let them loose from their bonds. Another tale was that Zeus later turned them into monkeys and sent them to populate the Pithekusai, Monkey Island, Ischia.[224] In southern Italy a farce was played and a vase-painting preserves it, in which Herakles brings them, like two monkeys, in a double cage to king Eurystheus, and amuses himself at his expense.

Another task, alleged again to have been by command of Omphale, was to work for Syleus, the robber who owned a vineyard. 'Robber' is too polite a translation of his name, for a *syleus* is one who takes everything, down to the bare body, and then sells that too. In this story Syleus made the stranger work as a slave in his vineyard.[225] But he had a brother named Dikaios, 'the just',[226] and a daughter, by name Xenodike, 'she who is righteous to strangers';[227] Syleus alone appears to have dealt outrageously with passing strangers. Where he did so is a point on which the narrators did not agree, for there was a Plain of Syleus in Macedonia,[228] but those who told the story so as to make Omphale send out the hero to destroy the brigand made Syleus a Lydian.[229]

As Euripides represented the story on the stage in his satyr-play 'Syleus' it was Hermes who sold the hero to the robber. It was not an easy bargain, for Herakles did not look in the least like a slave,[230] and who wanted to buy a master for his house,[231] whose very look induced fear? His flaming eyes were like those of a bull which sees a lion. He did not need even to open his mouth[232] for it to be understood that he was one who gave orders, not took them. Only Syleus was bold enough to buy this slave from the messenger of the gods, and having bought him, he sent him to his vineyard to dig around the vines. That was what Herakles was waiting for, to get a mattock into his hand. Xenodike might run away with the club and lion-skin, which she stole from the hero—a vase-painting shows her doing it, and later narrators make out that she was punished, like her father[233]—but the hero used the mattock as no one else ever did.

He began by digging up all the vines, roots and all,[234] then carried them to Syleus' house and lit a great fire, to bake bread and roast meat. He sacrificed the best bull to Zeus,[235] broke the cellar open and took the cover off the finest wine-jar. He lifted the house door off its hinges and used it as a table, and to put the fire out again he led a river into the garden. Then he began to feast. When Syleus suddenly appeared, furious at the spoiling of his whole property, Herakles invited him to sit down at table too.[236] Whereat, it seems, the ill-advised savage broke out into abuse, and did not escape death. The club some-how awoke in the hero's hand.[237] He bade Xenodike dry her tears and pulled her into the house, but certainly not to punish her.

According to a later version, their love-story played itself out in the house of Dikaios on Mount Pelion.[238] He, after his brother's death, became the girl's foster-father and Herakles' host, and Xenodike became Herakles' wife. When he moved on, she died of longing for him, but he had not left his beloved wife for ever, and came back to her. He found her lying dead on the funeral pyre and wished to choose a fiery death for her sake, but he was restrained, and a shrine of Herakles was built over Xenodike's grave.

The scene of a further deed on the hero's part was the land of Phrygia, which borders on Lydia. But concerning this same deed it is nowhere said that it was performed by order of Om-phale. It does, however, belong to Herakles' Asian adventures quite as much as his servitude to the queen of Lydia. It is the tale of the Phrygian reaper Lityerses, who was also a reaper of men. The song which aroused people to their work at harvest-time was also called Lityerses in Greek districts,[239] after the divine reaper who had sung it for the first time.[240] No doubt the song originally told how he forced harvest work to be done, even if that was forgotten or suppressed by more delicate singers later. Lityerses lived at Kelainai, the 'dark place', and obliged strangers when they passed that way to compete with him in handling the reaping-hook.[241] Those whom he defeated he flagellated, so the gentler form of the story said,

41 THE SHOOTING-MATCH AT OICHALIA

42 THE FIGHT FOR THE TRIPOD

43   NESSOS CARRIES OFF DEIANEIRA

44   HERAKLES LEAVING THE FUNERAL PYRE

which doubtless was heard in the majority of the reapers' songs. But it was also told[242] that he used to mow the heads off those he defeated (and everyone was worsted against a divine reaper), and bind up their trunks with his sheaves. His father was said to be king Midas,[243] but it is no earthly king who brings home such harvests, only the lord of the underworld.

Furthermore, Lityerses was supposed to be a huge eater.[244] He consumed daily three ass-loads of bread alone and called his wine-cup, which held three amphorae, a 'small measure'. That is stated in a satyr-play which told[245] how Daphnis, the tender, beloved shepherd, fell into the clutches of this Phrygian ogre and nearly became his victim. But, we are further assured,[246] Lityerses was not grudging when others ate with him, and entertained his victims. Herakles appeared at the feast, and began by taking up the king's challenge to a mowing-race. They mowed on the fertile banks of the Maean-der, where the corn grew as high as a man. To end it, the hero mowed off Lityerses' head and flung his headless body like a discus into the river.[247]

It is told, moreover,[248] that Herakles was first restored to health by the hot springs of the Lydian rivers Hyllos and Acheles, the latter a tributary of the former. Nymphs, the daughters of Acheles, bathed him in the hot water; and he named one of his sons, whom he begot on Deianeira, Hyllos, and another, whom he had by Omphale, Acheles.

5

THE RESCUER OF
HERA AND OF DEIANEIRA

Herakles was most emphatically a servant of women with Omphale; but he was also a servant of women in his capacity of rescuer—of Hesione from the sea-monster, of Alkestis from Death, of the daughter of Dexamenos from the Centaur. In all these rescues he appeared also as Hera's servant. The story went that he had rescued the Queen of the Gods herself from similar distress.

That must have been a remarkable story-teller to recount this tale to the artists who reproduced and alone preserved it. He would not be misled in the least by the enmity which according to the poets existed between Hera and Herakles. On the metopes of the temple of Hera where the Sele runs into the sea at Paestum, but also on an Attic vase-painting, we see how the attack took place. It was no Centaur but impudent Silens who were the aggressors. In the heavens themselves, in the Greek representations of the Zodiac, a Silen replaces the Centaur-like Bowman. It was Silens who stopped the goddess on her way, when once she was travelling on Earth.[249] Herakles suddenly appeared, to rescue her. The Attic vase-painter added Hermes also as the escort of the Queen of the Gods, but her real rescuer, the one with whom Hera is visibly taking refuge, is the hero who bore her name in his own, and there he stands, with a sword on the metope, with his club on the vase.

In like manner Herakles became the rescuer of Deianeira. This was one of the several names given also to the daughter of Dexamenos who was so nearly the victim of the Centaur. But the real Deianeira was the daughter of Oineus, or as others would have it,[250] of Dionysos himself, who had visited queen Althaia in Kalydon. To judge by her name she should be a virgin hostile to men, not merely warlike.[251] She must have hesitated long before taking a husband, therefore her brother Meleagros implored Herakles in the underworld to take her to wife, since they only seemed worthy of each other.

But when the hero set out on the journey to Aitolia, where Oineus was lord of Pleuron and Kalydon, between the rivers Acheloos and Euenos, a powerful suitor had long been troubling her, and came a-wooing in many forms.[252] He was the river-god Acheloos, and courted her as a bull, a serpent, or as a man with a bull's head, like another Minotaur.[253] The ancient artists showed him as a bull with a horned and bearded head, or even as a Bull-Centaur, except when they wanted to express his likeness to Triton, the Centaur of the sea.[254] That he had more than a little to do with the realm of the dead is made clear by the tales which connect him with the Sirens, both the earlier one,[255] according to which he was their father, and the later,[256] in which they arose from the drops of blood he shed when Herakles broke his horn off.

For that was to be the upshot of it.[257] Deianeira looked on from the high bank of the river,[258] too frightened to watch her two suitors wrestling with one another.[259] It was a real competition, an *agon*, with the bride for prize.[260] Later narrators laid much stress on Herakles winning both the bride and Acheloos' horn, which they equated with the horn of Amaltheia, the inexhaustible vessel of plenty which in many works of art the hero carries instead of his club, or receives from Dionysos.[261] It was also said[262] that Acheloos got his own horn back from Herakles, exchanging it with the hero for that of Amaltheia. So the river-god retired defeated, but not without leaving a valuable gift behind.

With this victory over a god the story of Deianeira's homecoming began, but it did not end there. We have already heard, in the history of Meleagros, of old king Oineus.[263] He was a kindly monarch, hospitable and to judge by his name a double of the wine-god; but as the wicked and lawless Syleus, the owner of the vineyard, had a righteous brother in the worthy Dikaios, so Oineus had a savage one. The parents of this pair of unlike brothers were Portheus,[264] 'the plunderer' and Euryte.[265] Among the sons of Oineus were, besides Meleagros, Toxeus, 'the archer', Thyreus 'the porter', and Klymenos 'the famous'—beings, one and all, with names belonging to Hades. Anyone wishing to leave the kingdom of Oineus in a westerly direction, though the country itself lay to the west, must get across the Acheloos; those who wished to go eastwards must cross the Euenos. On this river, which formerly was known as the Lykormos,[266] Herakles and Deianeira met the Centaur, Nessos, as the young wife was being taken home. The name Nessos was also borne by a river-god, one of the sons of Okeanos.[267] This was the ferryman who took people across the water on his back and demanded payment for it.[268]

Nessos gave out that he had received the office of ferryman from the gods to reward him for his justice,[269] and asked no other payment from Herakles than to take the young wife across the river first. He had hardly got Deianeira on his back when he began to molest her. The vase-paintings show us the hero running after him and, whether the Centaur still has his victim on his back or Herakles has recovered her, running him through with a sword or felling him with his club. Then he had to carry her across the water himself, which he doubtless did, although this form of the story has not come down to us. A variant is that Nessos did not molest Deianeira till they reached the far bank.[270] The poet Archilochos has described how the young wife, when she realised what the Centaur intended, broke out into long wails and called to her husband for help.[271] Now Herakles had to display his skill as an archer; his arrow struck the violator from the other bank and saved his wife.

Sophokles, who put the story of Deianeira on the stage in his tragedy 'The Women of Trachis', makes the heroine herself tell of how the misfortune took place in the Euenos. Herakles appears to have waded safely through the water, as he does in other versions also.[272] Deianeira felt Nessos' presumptuous hand half-way across the river.[273] She screamed, and the son of Zeus, who had just reached the far bank, turned around and sent his arrow through the breast of the Centaur. While dying he still had time to deceive Herakles' wife. He wished, said the liar, to do her a last favour. The blood which ran out of his poisoned wound had great magical powers, and she should collect it. No doubt Deianeira was carrying a little bottle to hold drinking-water, after the usual manner of Greek travellers. Herakles, so said the lying Centaur, would fall in love with no other woman if he wore a shift saturated with Nessos' blood.

Deianeira followed this fatal advice, caught Nessos' blood when he reached the bank at the point of death, and kept it in her house, hidden in a bronze cauldron.[274]

This was Deianeira's homecoming. According to most tellers of the tale, though certainly not all, the whole adventure took place shortly after the return of the hero from the nether world, before he received the insult at Oichalia and became Omphale's slave by way of atonement for his murder of Iphitos. Thus Deianeira became a wife who had long to wait, as Megara had been before her, and she bore her husband Hyllos and other sons also.[275]

6

THE END OF HERAKLES' EARTHLY LIFE

The insult at Oichalia was not yet revenged, so Herakles left Deianeira in the castle of his guest-friend Keyx at Trachis. Thither he had retired with his family after the murder of his guest at Tiryns;[276] it lies in the region around Mount Oita. He led an army[277] against Eurytos' towered city,[278] and Oichalia fell. The lord of the stronghold and his sons were killed and Iole became Herakles' prey. Those who connected her story with that of Deianeira stated[279] that Herakles wanted her as his concubine and preferred her to his wife. But there is no separate tradition of a love-affair between him and Iole. However, the very fact that the servant of women became the kidnapper of a woman led up to his end.

Deianeira thought that the moment was come to use Nessos' gift. The Centaur had given her his blood in order to destroy Herakles; he foresaw that the opportunity would arise. His gift and the deceiving of Deianeira together made up the Centaur's present. We hear also of an oracle[280] which had predicted to the hero that no living being should bring about his death, but only a dweller in the underworld. Now, without suspicion, he accepted the splendid poisoned robe which

Deianeira, also without suspicion, had sent him to wear when he made his thank-offering to Zeus.[281] But when the garment began to scorch his skin and he could not tear away the poisoned material from his body,[282] he soon recognised the sign[283] and had his pyre built on Mount Oita.

It was said later that he came to this decision on the advice of Apollo.[284] In his misery, caused by Nessos' gift, he had sent to Delphi and got the answer that he should go in full equip-ment to Oita and have a great pyre erected there; Zeus would see to the rest. But even in this version, Herakles mounted the pyre by his own decision. Before this decision, we are told in the tragedy, 'The Women of Trachis', came a terrible outburst of anger. The bodily pains which he felt united with that disease of the heroes, their fits of rage, which really is never very far from madness. He flung the messenger who had brought him the deadly garment off Kenaion,[285] the north-western peak of the island of Euboia, into the sea.[286] Carried home to Trachis, the sufferer wished to take vengeance on Deianeira, but she had already taken her life by the sword,[287] when she learned the result of her deed. And now that Herakles was aware also of the cause of his pains, the Centaur's ruse, he communicated his last wishes to Hyllos, his eldest son by Deianeira. The first wish was[288] the construction of the pyre, the second[289] the marriage of Iole to Hyllos, a wedding which he was never to see.

He then had himself carried to the lofty mountain-meadow of Zeus on Oita,[290] where the grass was never mown.[291] Ever since the pyre of Herakles blazed for the first time and, sur-rounded by a stone curb, which has preserved the ashes to our own day, was lit again and again at his festivals, the spot bore the name Phrygia, 'the burned place'.[292] There was a story[293] that the river Dyros, now the Gorgopotamos, sprang forth from the mountain then to put out the huge fire in which the body of Herakles was being consumed. The river came forth in vain, for to burn was Herakles' own will. Hyllos had built the pyre at his wish, but hesitated to light it.[294] The suffering

Herakles sat on the great pile of wood and awaited some friend, some traveller on the road leading over Mount Oita to Delphi. Philoktetes, the son of Poias,[295] came by, he who was one day to cry out the same words in the like pains, 'Light the fire, good man, light the fire!'[296] According to others it was Poias himself,[297] searching for his strayed sheep on the mountain, who lit the pyre. The reward for this was great, nothing less than the bow of Herakles.[298] He himself presented it in return for the act which freed him, either to Philoktetes or to his father Poias, from whom the son inherited it. Only by means of this bow could Troy one day be taken.

But the fire which was kindled there was not a sorrow/ful burning. Whenever Greeks kindled it in memory of Herakles,[299] it was a merry festival, at which the aura of love, the memory of the great Daktyl, bore sway.[300] In the purifying flames his limbs became divine;[301] it was not true that, as many supposed, the mortal body of the god was consumed like the corpse of a mortal.[302] A story was told[303] that he rose from the burning pyre in a cloud, amid peals of thunder, to heaven. When his friends tried to collect his bones from among the ashes, as was usual at a cremation,[304] they found nothing.[305] A master/painter of vases, and probably before him the author of a satyr/play, immortalised the search for Herakles' bones; they represented it as made by satyrs, who leaped back in fright when they found the hero's armour empty on the pyre, which was not completely burned out. Meanwhile Herakles, become young again, almost a child, went with Pallas Athene over the summit of Oita in a four/horse chariot. Astrologers knew[306] that he passed through that gate of heaven which is in Scorpius, close to the Archer, the Centaur that was trans/ported to the skies.

Many artists portrayed Herakles' ascension. A fine picture, on an Attic amphora of early date, stood by the sacred couch which was set in honour of Hera in a little underground temple at Paestum, and walled in. Herakles is mounting the chariot with Athene in the presence of his one/time opponents the brother and sister, Apollo and Artemis. Hermes stands ready to guide the chariot. The vessel could not have stood there with such a design on it if it had not been believed that the Queen of the Gods was well pleased with the ascent of the hero to Olympos. Henceforth he belonged to the company of the gods; in that dazzling assembly the master Sosias shows him crying 'Dear Zeus.' He is then conducted to Zeus by Athene, and Hera, enthroned at Zeus' side, receives him.

Those who believed that there really was enmity between Hera and Herakles told of a reconciliation;[307] Zeus, according to them, actually moved her[308] to go through the ceremony of the second birth of Herakles. In the position of a woman in labour, she took him to her holy body and let him fall through her clothing to the ground. According to one of the tales which were told of Herakles in Italy and cannot all be repeated here (they would have found less credence in Greece), she now offered him her breast as to a suckling. The scene was repre-sented on the reverse of an Etruscan mirror. Thus Herakles became completely the son of Hera.

In her capacity as Hera Teleia, the great marriage-goddess,[309] she herself brought her daughter Hebe to Herakles. The wedding was celebrated by the pair, the stepson of Hera and her young double,[310] among the Olympians on their mountain.[311] Hera's son-in-law rules over his golden palace[312] and of this the poets sang,[313] 'He is now a god, his woes and his toils are over, he lives where the other dwellers on Olympos live, immortal and ageless, and possesses Hebe, daughter of Zeus and Hera.' The phantom of the earthly Herakles—for there was no forgetting even of the wanderer on earth with his toils—his *eidolon*, went to the underworld, and there Odysseus met it. Around him was heard the cry of the dead, like the cry of birds that are fear-driven every way; and he, like unto dark night, held an uncased bow and an arrow on the string, and dreadful was his unquiet gaze, as he seemed ever about to shoot.[314] He was to be seen in a like shape even in the sky, for the constellation Engonasin,[315] the man who kneels on his

45 HERAKLES JOURNEYING TO OLYMPOS

46 DIONYSIAC APOTHEOSIS OF HERAKLES

47 KEKROPS AND PALLAS ATHENE BEFORE
THE SACRED OLIVE

right knee and is always toiling,[316] was thought of as a memorial to the toils of his son which Zeus had put there.

As far as his friends were concerned, his toils here on earth were all in vain. However many kings and peoples traced their origins to him,[317] and however many genealogists racked their brains over him and misled posterity, according to his nature Herakles was neither the founder of a dynasty nor the ancestral hero of a clan. He had sent his sons by Megara, his Theban wife, on the way to death by fire, ahead of himself, and he climbed his pyre from the hospitable stronghold of Keyx, for he had not even a dwelling-place of his own when he left Earth. Of the children whom Deianeira bore him various stories were told, but all agreed that the offspring of Herakles had vanished from the Peloponnesos completely. Only thus could the genealogists speak of the return of his descendants and connect the arrival of the Dorians in Sparta, with that return.[318]

According to all tales, the children of Herakles fled from Eurystheus, who threatened them with death after their father had become a god.[319] Keyx could not protect them against the power of the king of Mycenae, and bade them go further on.[320] They therefore fled from city to city, as far as Thebes according to one account. Those who held that Iolaos did not die in Sardinia, to which he had emigrated with the sons whom Herakles begot on the daughters of Thestios, but lay buried in the tomb of his grandfather Amphitryon, made him, when he was old, set out to meet Eurystheus and cut off his head.[321] Indeed there was one story that Iolaos was then already dead and that he rose from his grave to punish Eurystheus. Then he died again.[322]

According to another version,[323] he remained as the guardian of Herakles' children, which he had been from the beginning, and fled with them from Argos to Attica. The Athenians received the whole band and resisted Eurystheus, who appeared at the head of a great army. Hyllos fought at Iolaos' side and it was he who smote off the head of the king of Mycenae.[324]

In another form of the story,[325] the aged Iolaos prayed to Hebe and Zeus to give him back his youth for but one day. Two stars shone over his war-chariot and the people cried, 'Hebe and Herakles!' They hid him in a cloud, and Iolaos emerged from the mist with his youth renewed, captured the king of Mycenae and brought him alive to Alkmene, who would not pardon him, and so Eurystheus met his death.

But, so the tale ran in Athens,[326] a virgin must die to get the victory; Persephone would have that offering. This account, as we shall see later, was a story that often was heard in Athens. Along with old Alkmene the female descendants of Herakles had come to Athens for refuge, and one of them volunteered to be sacrificed, like a true daughter of Herakles.[327] On the spot where she was offered up a spring arose, which preserved her name for the future;[328] as she was called Makaria, the 'blessed one', so also was the spring at Marathon named, a fountain of blessedness.

BOOK THREE

CHAPTER I

Kekrops, Erechtheus and Theseus

IF THE ATHENIANS wished to be named after their heroic founder, they were called Kekropidai, descendants, or rather kinsfolk, of Kekrops; for although they bore that name, they were of opinion that they did not descend from a male primaeval being but directly from the soft, reddish soil of Attica, which in the beginning brought forth human beings instead of wild beasts.[329] Kekrops, in accordance with the original form of his name, which was Kerkops, that is to say 'the tailed',[330] was half-serpent, half-human:[331] serpent as having sprung from the earth, yet also with a share in human form and therefore *diphyes*, 'of twofold nature'. Being sprung from the earth and the nurseling of the maiden goddess, Pallas Athene, her father's daughter, and formed after her mind, the picture of the primitive Athenian was first present in Kekrops. We are told that he discovered, as it were, the double descent of human beings,[332] that they come not only from a mother but also from a father. He founded the institution of marriage between one man and one woman,[333] which was to be under the protection of the goddess Athene. That allegedly was his act of foundation, worthy of a primaeval father, who was not personally the ancestor of the Athenians, although they had him to thank for their patrilineal descent. Historians,[334] who brought little understanding to the matter of origin from the earth, actually wanted to explain his epithet of *diphyes* by supposing that it expressed the double line of descent which had been in use since the time of Kekrops, when they did not go so far as to conceive of him as a bisexual creature of the beginning.[335]

His reign was portrayed as that of a human king; the Athenians considered the act of foundation, properly so called, to consist in the *synoikisis* or *synoikismos*, in memory of which the festival of *synoikia* was held, i.e. the collection of the people who lived scattered about the coastal district known as Attica into one great community. This achievement was accredited to Kekrops,[336] and it was also said that he named the Athenian citadel, the Akropolis that became so famous, after himself.[337] It is nowhere said, however, that he personally built it; rather is it clear from the legends of his daughters[338] that Pallas Athene was busied in making the Akropolis into an impregnable fortress with her own hands. For that purpose she fetched a still higher rock from Pallene, but in anger at the disobedience of Kekrops' daughters, she dropped it in the place where it stands today and bears the name of Lykabettos. But since Kekrops there is said[339] to have existed one *laos*, one people, instead of a multitude, for he caused everyone, when he instituted the first great assembly, to bring a stone, *laas*, with him and throw it down in the midst of them. Thus he counted every original inhabitant of Attica, and there were twenty thousand of them. Also connected with his name[340] was the custom of burying the dead in the earth, whereby they were, so to say, laid in the bosom of the great Mother. Corn was sown on the burialplaces, which thus were not left as graveyards but given back pure to the living. The funeral repast was eaten with garlands on the head, and songs in praise of the departed were sung; no lies might be told.

Such were the laws ascribed to Kekrops, the primaeval king. Although he was not a human being, but one halfhuman and halfdivine, and for all time the protecting hero and lord of the Athenians,[341] life worthy of human beings is supposed to have begun with him in Attica. Those who emphasised the point that Kekrops instituted marriage were obliged to add[342] that men and women had mated promiscuously before his time. The tradition of another status of women than that in historical Athens, where they were excluded from public life, persisted long. Thus we find it even in the latest form of the story of how Pallas Athene took possession of the land. In this version of that famous tale,[343] the olive grew out of the earth for the first time while Kekrops reigned, and at the same time a spring appeared. The king is said to have inquired thereupon of the Delphic oracle and got the answer that the olive signified the goddess Athene, the water the god Poseidon, and the citizens were to decide after which the city was to be named. Now in those days the woman had still the franchise, and they out-voted the men by one; thus Athene was victorious and the city was named Athenai. Poseidon, as many tales teach us that he did, became angry and flooded the coasts. To pacify him, the women had to renounce their former right, and ever since then the children were not distinguished by the names of their mothers but by those of their fathers.

The original account of the greatest event which took place under the rule of Kekrops ran quite differently. The Athenians, and not only they among the Greeks, were well aware that their gods had not ruled over every Greek district from time immemorial, nor all alike. It was told in Argos[344] that Hera had had a dispute there with Poseidon about the country. The judges of the case were the local primaeval man, Phoroneus, and the river-gods of Argos, and they adjudged the country to the goddess. Undoubtedly, Hera had been the lady of the land from ancient times, and Poseidon was the later arrival. But he then continued to deprive the Argives of water, and to this day the Inachos is generally a quite dry river. Phoroneus is known as an especial devotee and protégé of Hera.[345] The position of Kekrops with regard to Athene was similar, and it is hard to say which story imitated the other, or if both existed side by side even originally.

Pallas Athene and Poseidon, so the ancient story goes, strove with each other for the soil of Attica. In their contest, the goddess caused the first olive-tree to spring up on the rock where her temples were to stand. The god struck the stony ground with his trident at the same spot, and there on the rock there sprang up also a salt spring, which was later known as 'Erechtheus' sea'.[346] The Erechtheion, the shrine of the patroness of the city,

Athene Polias, was to contain both signs of divine power, the olive and the salt spring. But in those primaeval times Kekrops, king of the country (according to this version he was the only being on earth) had to judge which had won. He decided that[347] salt water was to be found everywhere that one looked outwards from the dry land, but the olive which had just sprung up in Attica was unique.[348] So he assigned the land and the city to Athene as the prize of victory. However, some Athenians believed that so great an event as the acquisition of their native place by Athene was not sufficiently glorified if a mere earthly being like Kekrops had decided the matter, and so they made him simply a witness, not the judge. This is how the contest was represented in the middle of the west pediment of the Parthenon by Pheidias. Kekrops was merely looking on from a corner. In the picture of a vase-painter, he actually is represented only by a snake which twines around the olive. In this form of the narrative, the judges were the twelve great gods.[349] Strictly speaking, there can have been but ten of them, since Athene and Poseidon belonged to their number. The narrators again were not in agreement as to whether the contest began in the presence of the gods[350] or they appeared only to decide it. Only in the latter case would they need the witness who, as the only being on earth, could testify that Pallas was the first to create the olive.[351] But it seems that Poseidon originated the dispute;[352] here again he was the later arrival. The votes of the gods were equally divided between the two, and Zeus gave his casting-vote in favour of his daughter.[353] Kekrops was the first to entitle him Hypatos, 'most high';[354] he erected the first altar and set up the first statue of Pallas.[355]

The very intimate relation of Kekrops to the goddess remained for ever. It was a secret relationship of which little, or nothing at all, was said. But we know of his twofold connection with Aglauros, another title of Athene,[356] which she bore at certain gloomy proceedings that were also thought of as mysteries.[357] Originally this name and epithet were probably not Aglauros but Agraulos,[358] 'she whose abode is in the

48 THESEUS MEETS SKIRON, PHAIA AND SINIS

49 THESEUS ON THE TORTOISE

50 THESEUS MEETS KERKYON AND
THE MARATHONIAN BULL

51 THESEUS AND PROKRUSTES

fields'. She was Kekrops' wife,[359] but one of his three daughters also bore that name,[360] and this discloses the double connection. Aglauros, the mother of Kekrops' three daughters,[361] bore him a son also, whose name was Erysichthon, 'protector of the land'. How he protected it we are not told, but only that he died without issue;[362] he seems to have been a similar figure to Sosipolis, the 'saviour of the city' at Olympia.[363] Sosipolis again was no hero, but a divine boy in the form of a serpent, who protected that country. Concerning the daughters of Kekrops we are told[364] that they had entrusted to them by Athene a boy of like shape, shut up in a basket. It was the baby Erichthonios. We know the story; one of them, or even two, were so inquisitive as to look into the basket, and thus showed themselves no worthy guardians of the mysterious child.

Kekrops repeated himself in a way under both names, Erysichthon and Erichthonios. The place which was shown as his grave was not a grave at all, but yet another sign of his very intimate relationship to Athene. It was within the goddess' holiest precinct, where the first olive stood also. When the beautiful building which still stands today, the Erechtheion, was erected over it, statues of girls had to be raised instead of pillars to uphold the roof of the alleged tomb, the Kekropion. No doubt Kekrops was there in the shape of the snake which was tended in the same building and known as the 'goddess' watchman'.[365] But the Attic historians, who tried to give their country a list of kings, made out that in Erichthonios, the second primaeval Athenian with the curious birth-legend, which we know from the stories concerning Athene,[366] a Kekrops reappeared. They put Erichthonios in the third place after the primaeval king and ascribed to him the foundation of the Panathenaia[367] and of other great Athenian festivals. Allegedly also, he built the shrine of Athena Polias, already mentioned,[368] set up the wooden image of the goddess in it,[369] and was buried on the spot. These are not genuine mythological tales, as were those concerning his begetting by Hephaistos and what befell him in the round basket. It seems rather that his significant name, which emphatically signifies a chthonian, a being from the underworld, originally meant not a ruler, not a king of this our world above, but the mysterious child who was worshipped in mysteries and mentioned in seldom-told tales. The earth-born hero of whom we hear more openly (in Homer we read that Athene reared him[370] and chose him as companion in her house,[371] certainly that temple which got its name, Erechtheion, from him)[372]—this hero was called Erechtheus.

The Athenians called themselves Kekropidai after a primaeval being, but Erechtheidai after this their king and hero.[373] The name Erechtheus, in its form Erichtheus,[374] contains the same elements as the other compound Erichthonios, but with the ending of old and genuine proper names. The tradition of a son whom Hephaistos begot on the goddess Earth referred to him as explicitly as it did to Erichthonios,[375] and his connection with Athene was also no less close and intimate. It was not unambiguously told even of Erichthonios that the baby was itself a snake rather than guarded by snakes;[376] when he was enrolled on the list of the Athenian kings, he was given fully human shape. For Erechtheus there is no certain evidence in his history which connects him with serpent-form any longer. On the other hand, a story was told of his tragic conflict with Poseidon, in which he was ultimately worsted; under the blows of the trident he disappeared into the bowels of the earth.[377] This was a different story from the one in which the sea-god's trident merely caused the salt spring to gush out of the rocky surface of the Akropolis. It told how Poseidon, who in the Olympian family was uncle of the daughter of Zeus, did at last intrude into her very own domain and holy place. However, he could be accorded worship in the common temple of the goddess and her house-companion with the many names (Erechtheus was his name as a hero), only by taking that same name, as Poseidon Erechtheus.[378] When the Athenians were already in danger of forgetting the old hero who lived underground beside the mighty god of the sea, an oracle reminded them that they should also make sacrifice to

Erechtheus on the altar of Poseidon in the Erechtheion.[379] The common dwelling and cult was the token of their reconciliation, and recognition of the hero by the god as still equally entitled to reside in that shrine.

But the story was long told of the struggle of Erechtheus with sons of Poseidon at least, who came in from the north and remained in Athenian memory as Thracians. One of them was Immarados,[380] son of Eumolpos, or, by Euripides' account of the strife in his tragedy 'Erechtheus', Eumolpos himself.[381] We shall later hear more about Eumolpos, the 'good singer', the hero of the Eleusinians and ancestor of their hierophants. But connected with that struggle (whether Euripides was the first to connect them we can no longer know) was the memory of Athenian maidens, who, like Demeter's daughter, must die as sacrifices to the god of the underworld, of whose heroism tales were told, and who received cult as heroines in Athens.

The place of this cult was no less holy than the Erechtheion or the Theseion at Athens, and like them was a *heroon*. It was the Leokorion[382] or Leokoreion;[383] that is to say, the shrine of the Leokoroi, the 'people's maidens', in other words the virgins sacrificed on the people's behalf. It was told later how a certain Leos (in Attica his name sounds exactly like *leos*, people) had his three daughters sacrificed to save the Athenians. Their names, Praxithea, Theope and Eubule,[384] might also have been the names of goddesses of the underworld. The same story was told of the Hyakinthides, the four daughters of Hyakinthos, of whom it was later alleged that he was a Spartan;[385] we know that Hyakinthos had a cult at Amyklai near Sparta. The Hyakinthides were allegedly sacrificed on behalf of the Athenians when Minos was threatening the city and the people were suffering from plague and famine also. The simplest name under which all these willing victims were honoured was *Parthenoi*, and there was much discussion as to what 'virgins' were meant. Aglauros was mentioned[386] as the very first to offer herself for her country, she, was the double of Athene in

certain secret and gloomy ceremonies. Besides her, who was a
daughter of Kekrops, there were those of Erechtheus,[387]
especially one, Chthonia, 'she of the underworld'.[388]

Without evidence from non-mythological history we shall
never be able to decide if women in Athens had once really to
die as did their heroines, who are all, in a measure, identical
with Persephone. They are often cited as an example of
patriotism, ever since Euripides brought them on the stage.
When Eumolpos marched against Athens with a great
Thracian army, so the tragedy stated,[389] King Erechtheus consulted the Delphic oracle and received the answer that he must
offer up a daughter for victory. He had three daughters, and
his wife Praxithea, 'she who exacts the sacrifice', herself spoke
in favour of making the offering.[390] The parents did not know
that the three girls had sworn[391] that if one of them died, they
all would. Thus the family of Erechtheus came to an end. One
daughter was sacrificed, the others took their own lives.
Erechtheus was victorious in the battle, killing Eumolpos, as
Euripides describes it,[392] but he too did not remain alive. At
Poseidon's wish, Zeus struck him down with his lightning.[393]
At the end of the tragedy Athene appeared and informed the
spectators that the daughters of Erechtheus had been turned
into the constellation of the Hyades.[394]

The historians who troubled themselves about the list of
Athenian kings gave Erechtheus sons in addition to his
daughters, whose number tradition increased to six. The first
of them was a second Kekrops,[395] whose grandson was
Aigeus, the mortal father of Theseus; the divine father of this
most renowned Athenian hero, whom they honoured as the
true founder of their city, was supposed to be Poseidon. But
Aigeus also, to judge by his name, had something to do with
that sea which was called the Aegean after him, or so it was
said. *Aix*, a goat, was an appellation also of waves,[396] and
perhaps that was why men called Briareos, the older hundred-
armed god of that sea, also Aigaion,[397] and Poseidon's double
in his role as father of Theseus, Aigeus. Now, after the two

52 RECEPTION OF THESEUS IN ATHENS

53 ARRIVAL OF THESEUS IN THE PALACE OF POSEIDON

54 THESEUS BEFORE AMPHITRITE

55 THESEUS AND THE MINOTAUR

sons of Earth, Kekrops and Erechtheus, a son of the sea-god took over the task of a hero-founder in the history of the earliest times of the Athenian State.

Standing on the Akropolis and looking southwards,[398] one may make out in the extreme distance, between the mountains of the Peloponnesian coast, the little town of Troizen. When Aigeus ascended the throne of Athens, the ruler there was Pittheus, a son of Pelops and Hippodameia.[399] His daughter was named Aithra, like the sky when it is cloudless. The hero Bellerophontes had asked for her hand;[400] however, she became, not the wife, but the mother of a hero, and was to be renowned for her son. Even her father Pittheus had nothing against her remaining in his house, as if she were a virgin princess, and there bearing him an heir.

Before Troizen lay a little island, so near the coast[401] that one could wade barefoot over to it. Earlier it had been called Sphairia, 'ball-shaped', but later, after the sacred marriage of Aithra, Hiera, 'the holy'; for sacred this islet was from then on to Athene. Aithra had dedicated the temple which arose there to Athene Apaturia, because the goddess had beguiled her by deceit (*apate*) into visiting the island. The epithet Apaturia, however, rather indicated Athene in her capacity of taking virgins, as future mothers, into the shared life which was ruled by the men. Therefore the Troizenian virgins used to offer their girdles in that temple before their wedding. The story was told[402] that Aithra on that occasion was deceived by Athene in a dream. She dreamed that she must make sacrifice on Sphairia to the ghost of Sphairos, Pelops' charioteer. This charioteer is otherwise known under the name of Myrtilos, but a ball, *sphaira,* likewise signified the union of lovers, as myrtle did. The grave of the charioteer who drove Hippodameia to the wedding was allegedly on the island. When Aithra awoke from her dream, she crossed over and there met her divine bridegroom, Poseidon.

In another version,[403] this meeting took place in the temple of Athene herself, on the same night in which Pittheus caused

Aithra to sleep with Aigeus.[403a] Aigeus had already had two
wives, but his marriages proved unfruitful,[404] and so he made
a pilgrimage to Delphi and there got the oracular response,
'Loose not the foot of the wine-skin till thou come to Athens.'[405]
Aigeus did not understand this saying, and instead of going
straight home went the roundabout way to Pittheus, who had
a reputation as a sage,[406] and thus was all the better able to
understand the god's reply. If Aigeus had gone back to Athens,
he would have begotten the son he had wished for; but
Pittheus wanted his daughter to become the mother of this
long-expected child. Whether he made Aigeus drunk and so
deceived him[407] or merely persuaded him,[408] cannot be decided
now, but before the former left for home, Pittheus contrived
that he should spend a night with Aithra. When the hero
with the name of a sea-god rose from the side of the girl who
bore the name of the light of heaven, he left with her his sword
and his sandals. He rolled a huge stone over these means of
recognition,[409] and gave Aithra the following directions; if she
should bear a son and this son later became so strong that he
could roll away the rock, he was to take the sword and the
sandals and come with them to Athens. Thereby Aigeus
would recognise his son. With these words he left the young
woman in Troizen, which was to be Theseus' first home.

Later there was shown at the little Troizenian harbour of
Kelenderis the spot where he was born, which ever after was
called Genethlion, 'the birthplace'.[410] In an old account,
Pittheus did not play the part of a sage and a protector, for
Aithra actually was instructed by Aigeus not to reveal the
child's father.[411] But the majority of narrators portray the childhood of Theseus as that of a prince in Pittheus' house. When
he was seven years old,[412] Herakles, they say, visited the king
at Troizen and laid off his lion-skin at table. All the sons of
nobles had come to share Pittheus' hospitality, but when they
caught sight of the skin, they ran away again, except only
Theseus. The children believed that a lion was lying there, and
the little hero thought so too; he snatched an axe from a servant

and wanted to kill the beast. Then, when his childhood was over, he went a pilgrimage to Delphi, to offer his hair to Apollo. But he did not have all his boyish hair cut off, only the locks on his forehead, a fashion of wearing the hair which was called Theseis after him.[413] Being now sixteen years old,[413a] he turned over the rock under which the sword and sandals of his father lay, and put them on.

They must have fitted him—that was one meaning of the sign. Not only the sword must fit but the sandals also of Aigeus, with which he now set out upon the road to Athens. In the oldest narratives he certainly was a hero of like growth with Aigeus and Poseidon, and although poets and artists contended with each other to describe his youth, those pictures of him were not quite forgotten which showed him with a beard.[414] On one vase-painting we see the bold, beardless youngster (this remained the normal picture of him) trying to draw the sword, which he may only just have got into his possession, for the first time against Aithra, who is caressing him. Did he come to know of the secret of the rock through Pittheus and not through his mother? Did she try to restrain him from the dangerous journey over the Isthmus from Corinth to Athens? There death threatened in many shapes, like those which Herakles overcame. Later it was alleged that at this time Herakles was with Omphale, and therefore the younger hero must take on his mission in Hellas.

The first dangerous fellow whom he met on the neighbouring soil of Epidauros was Periphetes,[415] 'the widely notorious' —a name which would suit the lord of the underworld also. His nickname was Korynetes, 'club-wielder'.[416] He was a son of Hephaistos and Antikleia, whether that Antikleia who was Sisyphos' daughter and became also Odysseus' mother tradition does not say;[417] his iron club he got from his father, from whom also he probably inherited weak feet. He lay in wait for passers-by and smote them, until he was smitten down by Theseus, who from then on carried the club,[418] with which many pictures show him.

At Kenchreai, one of the two harbours of Corinth,[419] where the road turns off to the Isthmus, a second danger was lying in wait. This was Sinis, 'the robber', a son of Posei‑don,[420] the god to whom that region of pines was sacred, or else of Polypemon, 'the author of much woe'[421] (another possible name of Hades), and Sylea, 'her who plunders'. His nickname was Pityokamptes, 'bender of pine‑trees',[422] because he used to tie wanderers to two pines which he had bent down, and then let the trees fly up again, thus tearing the poor fellows in pieces.[423] They had even to help him by holding one pine while he bent the other. This Theseus did, but he made Sinis himself meet his end after what was his own fashion. Con‑cerning his daughter it was said[424] that she was a remarkably beautiful and tall girl, named Perigune, 'around the garden'. She took flight from Theseus, hid under the asparagus and pimpernels, and conjured the plants in her garden to rescue their mistress. The hero enticed her with sweet words to come to him and Perigune became the ancestress of a family in which those plants were held in honour.

In the territory of Corinth lay the place called Krommyon,[425] named from *krommyon*, an onion. There lived an old woman with a sow which was named, after her mistress,[426] Phaia, 'grey' or 'dark'. The colour of ghosts was assuredly meant by this, and the sow thus shown to be a beast of the underworld, and deadly.[427] Theseus had to fight the sow with spear and sword, or, as the earliest heroes did, by throwing stones. The vase‑paintings show us the old woman (she is once named Krommyo), trying to help her beast by pleading for mercy.

At the most dangerous spot on the road which leads from the Isthmus under the 'Crane Mountain', Geraneios, through the territory of Megara to Athens, sat the death‑dealing lord of this limestone region (*skiron* in Greek), with which his name, Skiron, agreed. In old days the road there became a mule‑track. To the right rises the steep side of the mountain, as it does today; to the left is a precipitous descent to the water, in which, so the story goes,[428] there swam a sea‑turtle, a creature of Hades which seized and devoured men. If the upper path failed, as often happened even in historical times, the wayfarer must climb down to the sea and continue his journey along the narrow beach; or he even had to wade or swim, until he came to the place where he could climb up again to the level of the mule-track. In bad weather there was regularly danger along this strip, and it was always alike a gate of Hades, even without the turtle and even after Theseus had sent Skiron below.

This lier-in-wait sat above on a rock and compelled those who came by to wash his feet;[429] this was ostensibly the payment for leave to pass. If the wayfarer bent down to do this humble service, Skiron sent him into the sea with a kick, to feed the turtle. But Theseus hurled the foot-bath at his head (this is how the vase-painters showed the proceedings, and no doubt the comedians as well)[430] and flung Skiron himself into the sea, so that the murderer was eaten by the turtle.[431] Certain rare works of art show the hero riding on the turtle's back; on a metope at Paestum he is beardless, on an old vase-painting he is a bearded man—as indeed he was often painted —and is being conveyed in this manner from one rock to another. This was in agreement with a once prevalent account which no poet has handed down to us.

In Megara, it is true, they insisted[432] that Skiron did not infest the highway, but was a punisher of robbers and a friend to honest men, the son-in-law of Kychreus and father-in-law of Aiakos. Kychreus was the Kekrops of the inhabitants of Salamis, the island lying opposite; he was born from the earth and was half-man, half-serpent.[433] At the Battle of Salamis he appeared in serpent-form on the Greek ships,[434] a token of their victory and a contributor to it, and in his serpent-shape he was Demeter's temple-servant at Eleusis.[435] Aiakos, Skiron's son-in-law by Megarian tradition, a son of Zeus by the eponym of the island of Aigina,[436] held the keys of the underworld.[437] All the places named—the limestone region of Megara, Eleusis and Aigina—can be seen from Salamis, and it is very fitting for both heroes alike, Kychreus and Aiakos,[438] to have family relationships with a god of the underworld, which Skiron was.

Arrived on the territory of Eleusis, Theseus met a being whose name, in the oldest narratives, indicates that he might have resembled Kekrops or Kychreus in their serpent-forms, for he was called Kerkyon, 'the man with a tail'. According to the well-known versions he was passionately fond of wrestling,⁴³⁹ like so many of the opponents whom Herakles had to overcome. Like them, Kerkyon compelled wayfarers to wrestle with him, and in wrestling he killed them all. The spot was shown on the road between Megara and Eleusis where he played his deadly game.⁴⁴⁰ Theseus lifted him into the air as Herakles did Antaios, and threw him to the ground so hard that he was smashed to pieces.⁴⁴¹ Later it was alleged⁴⁴² that Theseus was the actual inventor of sportsmanlike wrestling and defeated Kerkyon more by his skill than by brute force.

The sixth form in which death encountered Theseus on the way to Athens had several names, but the best known is Prokrustes, 'the stretcher'.⁴⁴³ He stretched with blows, as a smith stretches iron with hammer-strokes. According to others, Prokrustes was merely his nickname,⁴⁴⁴ like its synonym Prokoptas,⁴⁴⁵ and he was really named Damastes, 'the compeller'.⁴⁴⁶ Here there lay an allusion to the hammer, as in the Daktyl-name Damnameneus.⁴⁴⁷ The hammer was allegedly earlier the property of that Polypemon, 'the author of much woe',⁴⁴⁸ of whom it has just been told that he was supposed to be the father of the brigand Sinis, while others make him father to Skiron also,⁴⁴⁹ and to Prokrustes,⁴⁵⁰ if the latter was not himself called Polypemon too.⁴⁵¹ A hammer-bearing god of the underworld, like the one known to us through Etruscan art, was probably in the minds of those who declared⁴⁵² that his abode was by the wild fig-tree (*erineos*) at which, according to the Eleusinian account, Hades had carried off Persephone.

Others again stated⁴⁵³ that this death-dealing smith was on Mount Korydallos, over which ran the Sacred Way from Athens to Eleusis. There Prokrustes worked with his tools,⁴⁵⁴ which however included, not an ordinary anvil, but a bed hewn in the rocks or made by smith's work, in which he laid wayfarers to work on them with his hammer; for the bed was always too big, and he had to stretch those who lay on it. Later it was stated,[455] by those who did not think of the meaning of the names Prokrustes, Prokoptas and Damastes, that he even had two beds, a large and a small one, and that he made small men lie in the large bed, large men in the short one, in which case he cut off the projecting parts of their limbs.[456] Theseus served him in the same manner,[457] and having thus cleared the whole road of deadly dangers,[458] arrived in Athens by the Sacred Way.

His reputation had preceded him. At the spot where the Sacred Way crossed the river Kephisos, the clan of the hero Phytalos received him.[459] Here Phytalos, 'the planter', had once shown hospitality to the goddess Demeter and received as her gift the first fig-tree.[460] His descendants, the Phytalidai, caused Theseus to pass through a ceremony of purification, of which he stood in need after his many necessary man-slayings.[461] They brought the sacrifice of purification to the altar of Zeus Meilichios, the Zeus of the underworld, to whom the fig tree was sacred. Thus Theseus for the first time rose out of the sphere of death, though only to be immediately threatened again. It was the eighth day of the month of Kronos, which the Athenians later named Hekatombaion;[462] it corresponded roughly to our July. Now the eighth day of the month belonged to Poseidon,[463] and thus Theseus' arrival fell upon a day sacred to his father. But the threat to him came from the sorceress Medeia, according to those narrators who make the hero's earthly father, king Aigeus, already married to her.

She knew in advance that the approaching guest was heir to the throne,[464] and it was her doing that made Aigeus, after all that was told him of Theseus, conceive a great fear of him,[465] and let himself be over-persuaded by his wife to offer the guest a poisoned cup. At Athens, that was the method of execution; was it supposed to have been introduced then by Medeia? The

reception of the guest took place in the temple of Apollo
Delphinios, of which it was said⁴⁶⁶ that Aigeus' palace had
stood there. A later version states⁴⁶⁷ that Apollo's temple was
still under construction, the workmen were standing on the
walls, which were complete, and the roof was being fetched
on an ox-cart. According to this account, Theseus was still
beardless, and had on the long Ionian robe which resembled
women's clothing, and his hair braided. The men called to
him from above, 'What, a girl husband-high, straying alone
like that with no company?' Thereat Theseus unyoked the
oxen, took the cart with its load of roofing materials, and
hurled it up to the workmen. Other tellers of the story, including vase-painters, had this account to give: that the young man
was first sent out against the bull of Marathon, and that his
reception with the poisoned cup took place only after he had
returned victorious.⁴⁶⁸

The rumour that had preceded Theseus spoke of him as a
boy in the first bloom of youth, accompanied by two ser-
vants.⁴⁶⁹ A cap like that which Spartans wore sat on his
auburn hair, on his body he wore a purple tunic and a soft
woollen cloak. His eyes glowed with a fire like that of the
divine smith on Lemnos, and his mind was set on battle. In
this way he had sought the road to Athens, in this way he
entered and found a sacrificial banquet going on, at which the
poisoned cup awaited him. His father handed him the goblet,⁴⁷⁰
but he drew his ivory-hilted sword from its sheath, as if he
meant to cut off a piece of the victim's flesh,⁴⁷¹ yet in reality so
that Aigeus should recognise him. He even handed the sword
to the old man as he himself took the cup.⁴⁷² 'Stop, my son!'
cried Aigeus,⁴⁷³ as now his eyes lighted upon the sandals,⁴⁷⁴
'do not drink!' And he knocked the cup from the youth's
hand.⁴⁷⁵ The spot where the poison spilled upon the floor was
fenced around in the Delphinion, and Medeia was banished
from the country.⁴⁷⁶ Her own story, to which this invention
did not originally belong, will be told soon in detail.

Tradition knows also of native enemies of Theseus in

Attica.[477] They were Pallas and his fifty sons, who hoped to rule the whole country after Aigeus' death. Their home was in Pallene, on the southern declivity of Pentelikon, and they were a savage giant-people.[478] Their father Pallas was supposed to be a son of Pandion and brother of Aigeus. His sons went to war against Theseus, and divided themselves into two parties. One made as if it would attack the hero from Sphettos, while the other lay in ambush at Gargettos. But a man from Agnus, that same Leos whose daughters were famed for their sacrificial death, betrayed their strategem to Theseus. He was the herald of the Pallantidai at Gargettos; these the hero killed, and the rest scattered. Ever since there was enmity between the inhabitants of Pallene and those of Agnus (all these are names of villages in Attica, whose locality is seldom known and then only by accident). It was told that Theseus killed Pallas[479] and all his sons,[480] or that he killed but one of them, when they were hunting a wild boar,[481] and had to atone even for that with voluntary exile.[482] This he did by retiring to Troizen for a year; but that must have happened much later.

Perhaps the narrators supposed that the Pallantidai lay in wait for Theseus when he was on his way to Marathon to overcome the bull, for the road there leads under the northern slopes of Hymettos to the Plain of Marathon, which the wild beast was ravaging. According to the most famous account,[483] Aigeus, having so unexpectedly got his son back, tried to keep him as it were shut up, so that he should not expose himself to the danger of a new adventure. The series of deeds which one might compare with those of Herakles, had already been completed by the hero; now follow those which rather display his own character: three bold attempts, after the capture of the Marathonian bull, to carry off women, and the war against the Amazons. Of the bull it was indeed alleged later that it was the same one which Herakles brought from Crete to Argos and let loose,[484] but it may be that this adventure, like the struggle against the Amazons, was told earlier of Theseus and only later of Herakles. One detail, that the bull spewed out fire, is entirely to be attributed to the latest tellers of the story.[485] To fight a bull demanded special skill, exactly that skill which the young people of Crete showed in the time of Minos. For Theseus, it was a preparation for his expedition against a far more dangerous bull, the dweller in the Labyrinth at Knossos.

It would be still early morning when he secretly left Aigeus' palace. The sky was crystal-clear,[486] as only the sky over Attica can be. In the afternoon the clouds gathered over Mount Parnes and lightnings flashed over Hymettos, which Theseus had left behind him. On the spot where he was over-taken by the thunderstorm, a little shrine stood in later times, resembling the tomb of a heroine. The country folk worshipped there with deep affection an inhabitant of the underworld whom they named Hekale, or even more tenderly Hekaline.[487] She must once have been a great goddess and particularly friendly to the king of the heavens, just as Hekate was;[488] so the name is better known. But it was told[489] that she had been a hospitable old woman, whose cottage was shut against no wayfarers. On that night of storm her guest was the young Theseus, who next morning went merrily on and met the bull. He caught it by the horns,[490] held one horn in his right hand, grasped the nostrils of the snorting beast with his left, and so forced it to the ground.[491] It must needs follow him,[492] and the hero led the famous creature to Athens on a rope. Many men came and stood by the road, and he cried out to the people.[493] 'Remain, be of good cheer, but let him that is the swiftest-footed among you go to the city to my father Aigeus with the message, "Theseus is here, nigh at hand, bringing the bull alive from well-watered Marathon."' They all remained and sang the paean, while they pelted the young man with leaves from the trees. Thus his victory was celebrated on all hands. But Theseus hurried back to Hekale, and arrived just as they were getting the old woman ready for burial.[494] He interred her with great honour and founded the deme Hekale[495] and the cult of Zeus Hekaleios, or at least these foundations were ascribed to him later. The bull he sacrificed to Apollo Delphinios.

If Androgeos, son of Minos, fell a victim to the bull, as many others had before him, this had already happened before Theseus arrived.[496] It was alleged[497] that this did not occur without the fault of the Athenians, for Aigeus had sent out the foreign prince against the savage creature.[498] Other accounts declared that he was murdered in Attica on his way to Thebes to take part in Laios' funeral games.[499] But here one might well suppose that the Cretan prince was anxious to try his skill against the famous bull. Minos was staying on Paros[500] and making sacrifice to the Charites when he got word of his son's misfortune. He tore the garland from his brows and bade the flutes stop; ever since then the Parians made sacrifice to the Charites without garlands or flute-music. The death of Androgeos was to bring misfortune to the Athenians.

We know Minos' own misfortune from the stories of the gods,[501] and also from the narrative of Herakles' Cretan adventure, the love of Queen Pasiphae for the beautiful bull and the birth of the bull-headed Minotaur, which Daidalos' marvellous construction, the Labyrinth, a prison of wandering paths, concealed within it. Minos was then lord of the sea,[502] and he set out with his navy against Athens, to avenge his son and to demand sacrifices for Pasiphae's son. He first captured Megara. The ruler there was Nisos, another brother of Aigeus. To this son of Pandion immortality was ensured by a purple lock of hair.[503] Had not his daughter Skylla fallen in love with the foreign monarch and cut off that lock, he could not have been defeated. Minos was not grateful to her; he had her tied to his ship and dragged through the sea, and while Nisos became a sea-eagle,[504] Skylla was also transformed into the bird called *ciris*. The inhabitants of those coasts knew which sea-bird they meant, but all we hear is that the one bird ever after has pursued the other. Minos moved on against Athens.

Either his power was sufficient, or it was the strokes of deity,[505] plague and famine, for the sin against Androgeos, which subdued the Athenians; they undertook to pay a terrible tribute. Every ninth year they were henceforward to send to

Crete seven young men and seven virgins, who were to disappear into the Labyrinth as victims for the Minotaur. When
Theseus overcame the Marathonian bull, eighteen years had
passed and the third group of victims had to be picked to set
out on the voyage to Knossos. The rest were chosen by lot,
but Theseus went with them of his own free will,[506] either as
one of the fourteen or as a fifteenth.[507] There were some indeed
who said that he too was simply chosen by lot.[508] The oldest
version, however, suggests that he sailed on his own ship or
one belonging to his father Aigeus, to Crete as to an adventure;
that story is assuredly one of the later ones which makes Minos
come in person to Athens and choose the victims, including
Theseus, and take them on his own ship to Knossos.[509]

Those who told the tale or painted it on vases believed they
could even give the names of the seven youths and the seven
maids.[510] The first of the latter was that Eriboia, remembered
also under the name Periboia,[511] who later, as the wife of
Telamon, became the mother of Aias of Salamis.[512] In the
version according to which the king of Crete himself collected
his piteous tribute, Minos during the voyage fell in love with
the beautiful girl,[513] and touched her white cheek with his
hand, as if she were his slave. Eriboia screamed and called to
Theseus, who saw what was happening, wildly rolled his
dark eyes beneath his brows, and cruel pain pricked his heart
as he spoke: 'O son of peerless Zeus, the spirit in your breast
no longer obeys righteous control; withhold, hero, your
presumptuous force. Whatever the resistless doom given by
the gods has decreed for us, and the scale of Justice inclines
to ordain, that appointed fate we will fulfil when it comes. But
do you forbear your grievous purpose. If the noble daughter of
Phoinix, the maiden of gracious fame, taken to the bed of
Zeus beneath the brow of Ida, bare you, peerless among men;
yet I, too, was borne by the daughter of wealthy Pittheus, in
wedlock with the sea-god Poseidon, and the violet-crowned
Nereids gave her a golden veil. Therefore, O war-lord of
Knossos, I bid you restrain your wantonness, fraught with

woe; for I should not care to look on the fair light of divine Eos, after you have done violence to one of this youthful company: before that we will come to a trial of strength, and Destiny shall decide the sequel.'

Thus far the hero. The seafarers were amazed at the youth's lofty boldness; and he whose bride was daughter of the Sun-god felt anger in his heart; he wove a new device in his mind. He prayed to Zeus, if he was really his father, to confirm it with a lightning flash. As a sign from Poseidon, he demanded that the youth should bring back the ring which he then threw into the sea; then they should know whom his father would listen to. Zeus heard the unmeasured prayer, and ordained a surpassing honour for Minos; he sent the lightning. Now it was the turn of Poseidon and Theseus. And the spirit of Theseus recoiled not; he took his place on the well-built stern, and sprang thence, and the domain of the deep received him in kindness. The son of Zeus felt a secret awe in his heart but let the ship drive on quickly before the north wind. All the Athenian youths and maidens shuddered when the hero sprang into the deep; and tears fell from their bright young eyes, in prospect of their grievous doom.

According to Bakchylides, the poet whose narrative we have listened to almost word for word, it was dolphins that carried Theseus into his father's house. Vase-painters, who probably followed some famous picture, showed Triton, son of Poseidon and Amphitrite, receiving his younger brother. With gentle hands he accompanied the young man into the palace in the depths of the sea. The king of the sea received him on his couch, the queen on her throne, and there[514] he was awe-struck; for a splendour as of fire shone from the Nereids' radiant forms. Amphitrite clad him in gleaming purple and set on his thick hair a choice wreath, dark with roses, given her at her marriage by the love-goddess. How the boys and girls shouted for joy when Theseus rose near the ship, in royal attire, not even wet with the water, and handed Minos the golden ring;[515] and how startled Minos was!

But, as already said, another way of telling the tale was that the hero undertook the journey to Knossos in his father's ship. It put to sea with black sails, this version had it,[516] but the king had provided it also with a white or even purple set,[517] to be hoisted if Theseus returned victorious. And in all accounts, not only in the one already told, it was a tender womanly figure, if it was not actually a goddess, like Amphitrite, who received the young hero at Knossos. The reception by Amphi-trite was no more than the prelude, or possibly the late echo, of his reception by Ariadne. She, a granddaughter of Helios and Zeus, whom Pasiphae, daughter of the Sun-god, had borne to Minos, had pity on Theseus, so it is told in so many words,[518] when he volunteered to be the first to enter the darkness of the Labyrinth. She was famous under that name only, which in Cretan Greek signified 'exceedingly pure', *ari-hagne*, but she also was called Aridela there, i.e. 'exceedingly bright'.[519] Under these two names she had originally been a great goddess, 'pure' as queen of the underworld, 'bright' as queen of the sky.

She had her place then, too, in the stories of the gods when she had to be counted among their unfaithful sweethearts on account of her too-famous passion for Theseus.[520] For love of the Athenian youth she betrayed her own brother,[521] the Minotaur, the monster with the body of a man and the head of a bull, who had also the name of a starry being, Asterios[522] or Asterion.[523] For that reason if for no other she could be reckoned among the great sinners,[524] and placed beside another granddaughter of the Sun, Medeia, who also murdered her own brother. But properly speaking she was untrue to Dionysos, otherwise the god would not have called in Artemis against her.[525] That seems to have been a story better known to the older tellers of it than to the later ones, who have por-trayed rather the faithlessness of Theseus. The hero allegedly swore to Ariadne that he would bring her home as his wife, and thus persuaded her to aid him.[526] But the tale of how Theseus won the love of the princess is not handed down to us.

It is only a very late version which makes her see him contend-
ing with someone named Tauros, that is to say Bull, a human
rival of Minos with Pasiphae. But even here there is still
preserved from very early times the information that Cretan
women looked on at the men's games.[527]

We are not told how Theseus managed to have a quite
private interview with Ariadne and got from her the simple
gift that was to guarantee him safety on his return from the
Labyrinth. She was occupied in spinning, so a very old representation shows us, when the young man entreatingly and
caressingly stretched out a hand to her. It was no doubt her
own cleverness which made her give him her spindle with the
yarn on it; or was it a ball into which the yarn had already been
wound, as we see on an old vase-painting? She did not have
to wait to be taught her device by the master-craftsman
Daidalos, as late narrators inform us she did.[528] The hero was
advised by the clever maid to fasten the end of the clew high
up on the door of the Labyrinth and never let it out of his hand.
The Labyrinth was not a maze in the sense that an intruder
could not find the innermost recess of it, but he must come
back from there by the same road, and that was the difficulty.
Later, when its constructor, Daidalos of Athens himself, was
shut up in it with his son Ikaros, his only way of escape was to
prepare wings of feathers and wax and discover the art of
flying. We all know the sad story of how Ikaros flew too near
the sun, his wings melted, and he fell into the sea which
allegedly was named Ikarian after him.[529] Only the old artist
saved himself.

In the innermost recess of the Labyrinth the Minotaur slept.
Theseus was to catch him by the hair of his brow and sacrifice
him to Poseidon. It was told[530] by artists as well as narrators
that the loving Ariadne accompanied the hero and lightened
the darkness for him with her crown. Or had she given
Theseus her diadem instead of the clew? That would then be
an unpardonable act of infidelity, for by one account she had
got the garland as the price of her virginity.[531] The narrators

and the vase-painters seem, however, not to have thought of a sin in this connection, but only that the garland was Ariadne's ornament, known from of old, no matter from which bride-groom it came, Dionysos or Theseus. Theseus might have brought her that one which he had got from Amphitrite, but in that case also Ariadne's garland, set among the constella-tions by the god, ended by shining in the heavens. Theseus stabbed the Minotaur to death in the Labyrinth; an old vase-painting shows the outcome of the duel with the bull-headed monster, which there is given the name of Taurominion. With one hand each grasps his opponent; with the other, the hero holds his sword, the half-bestial creature a stone. Another account said[532] that Theseus was not in possession of any weapon, but strangled his opponent with his bare hands while wrestling and boxing with him. But he often carries a club or staff. Thus he appeared victorious at the gate of that building of the underworld, if he did not also drag the dead bull-man after him. The Athenian boys welcome him, and one of them kisses his saving hand.

With Ariadne, he embarked. He took the lads and maids with him also, and it is said that he had previously scuttled the Cretan ships.[533] It was night when they began their voyage homeward,[534] and if it was that same night when they reached the island of Dia, which witnessed the parting from Ariadne and her reunion with Dionysos, that could not have been Naxos, which is said to have been called Dia in those days,[535] but the Dia which lies before the Gulf of Amnisos, the little island near Crete. There is an old account[536] according to which Artemis killed the unfaithful daughter of Minos here with her arrows on the evidence of Dionysos. The Cypriots, on the other hand, believed[537] that Ariadne died on their island in childbed, while others again held[538] that she was left behind in Crete by the faithless Theseus and hanged herself. Those were stories invented because, on the spots where sacrifices were made to her as to a goddess of the underworld who had returned thither, her grave was shown; for instance, at Argos[539]

56 THESEUS AND ARIADNE ON NAXOS

57 THESEUS CARRIES OFF KORONE

58 THESEUS FIGHTING THE AMAZONS

59 THESEUS AND HERAKLES

in the temple of the Cretan Dionysos, next to that of the Celestial Aphrodite, or on Cyprus, where she was herself adored
in her heavenly aspect, as Ariadne Aphrodite.[540] But this very
fact that she did not remain a merely chthonian goddess nor a
mortal princess, for whom the master-craftsman Daidalos
built a beautiful dancing-place,[541] and who was then considered the Lady of the Labyrinth,[542] was something which
Ariadne had Dionysos to thank for. Whether her ascension to
heaven with the god took place on the Cretan Dia or, as the
Naxians would have it, on theirs, and whether it happened after
Theseus had proved his faithlessness or before things could come
to that pass, this story was the only authorised one for later times.

In the night on Dia, so ran one form of the story of the
ascension of Ariadne,[543] Dionysos appeared and took the
beautiful bride from the hero. On a Tarentine vase-painting
we see Theseus, sword in hand as if to defend himself, retiring
to his ship, while the god touches the sleeping Ariadne's
breast. In another variant,[544] also paralleled by a vase-painting,[545] two deities, Dionysos and Pallas Athene, appeared on
Dia. They jointly moved Theseus to journey on without
Ariadne. The third form of the story[546] was, that the god
appeared in a dream to the hero and threatened him if he would
not yield Ariadne. Theseus awoke in terror and left her, pro-
foundly asleep as the scene is generally described.[547] That
same night she was conducted by Dionysos to Mount Drios
on Naxos;[548] there he first disappeared and she after him. In
the later accounts the god comes with his whole following,
awakes the sleeping girl and takes her with him in a Dionysiac
marriage procession. It was he,[549] says another version, who
sent forgetfulness upon Theseus, so that he was completely
oblivious of his bride on that lonesome rocky island[550] and
sailed on without her. She too did not remain there quite
alone, but with her nurse Koryne, the 'tree-bud' whose grave
was shown on Naxos.[551] In that case Dia was the little island
lying before the present Naxos, where people cross by a mole
to admire the imposing marble frame of a temple-gate.

Theseus travelled on with the lads and the maidens to Delos, where he danced with them the Crane Dance, an evolution which imitated the windings of the Labyrinth,[552] made sacrifice to Apollo, and set up the statue of Aphrodite which Ariadne had brought with her as her *alter ego* and presented to him. She was then venerated on Delos as Hagne Aphrodite. According to the representation of an ancient vase-painter, at this festival it was not the statue which was present at the rejoicings over the deliverance, but still Ariadne with her nurse. Theseus led the dance and played on the lyre. The Athenians afterwards,[553] in memory of the arrival of their sons and daughters at Phaleron on the coast (it was at the time of the wine-harvest), worshipped the divine pair, Dionysos and Ariadne. But at that feast a sad event was also remembered. Theseus or his pilot forgot in their joy,[554] or else in their sorrow for the loss of Ariadne,[555] to change their sails. Aigeus from the Akropolis saw the black sails which the ship had carried on her departure, and flung himself down from the rock. Thus Theseus became king of Athens, and ever after that sea over which the figure of Ariadne, goddess and heroine, broods has been called the Aegean.

If the stories of Theseus' faithlessness were able to hold water, it was simply because the son of Poseidon was reputed to be in any case a great abductor of women.[556] Allegedly,[557] he deserted Ariadne because he was devoured by passion for Aigle, daughter of Panopeus. Aigle, 'brightness', is the name for a maid of light, like Phaidra, 'the shining', Ariadne's sister, whom Theseus got as his wife from Deukalion, son of Minos, after he had made an alliance with him,[558] if indeed he had not, in some forgotten tale, carried her off along with Ariadne. Such names corresponded to the expression of the light-side of Ariadne, as Aridela. One might almost say that in that instance Ariadne was deserted for Aridela. Perhaps the daughter of Panopeus was a goddess in earlier times, and identical with that Aigle who was reputed in Orchomenos, which is near the walled city of Panopeus, to be the mother of the Charites and wife of Helios,[559] but also bore the nickname Koronis, 'crow-girl'. The faithless love of Apollo, who bore him Asklepios, was also named Aigle and nicknamed Koronis.[560] In like manner, Aigle[561] and Koronis[562] were reckoned among the nurses of Dionysos, like Ariadne herself.[563] And finally, a vase-painting shows us Theseus carrying off Korone (the name is written alongside the girl in that form), while two other famous loves of the hero, Helen and the Amazon Antiope, try to prevent him. He had hardly caught sight of her when he ran off with her, the artist's caption tells us.

No narrator has ever found it possible to fix the order of all these abductions of young women so firmly as to make it canonical. There seems to have been an old tradition which stated that Theseus carried off Helen before he did Ariadne.[564] Against this, it was later calculated[565] that he must have been fifty years old when he became the first abductor and husband of the beautiful daughter of Zeus. His friend Peirithoos bore a part in this adventure, the carrying away of Helen; it was at his marriage in Thessaly that the struggle between Lapithai and Centaurs began. If the two tales, that of the marriage and that concerning the abduction, were not mutually independent but told alongside each other as part of the life-history of a pair of heroes, and if there was added the maddest adventure of the two champions—their attempt to carry off the queen of the underworld—then certainly their greatest ventures, the objects of which were the two daughters of Zeus, Helen and Persephone, must have taken place when the friends were already well on in years. In time they became the Kastor and Polydeukes of the Athenians, as if they had from time immemorial been connected with Helen, and not famous as her abductors; as if they had not had to get her from Sparta to Aphidna, but the island of Helene which lies before Cape Sunion on its eastward side had got its name from a less-known story of the birth of Nemesis' daughter. Perhaps this Attic version of the birth-legend said that the goddess Nemesis, who was worshipped on the same coast at Rhamnus, had borne her daughter Helen on the island of Helene. As the tradition lies before us, we must now insert the Thessalian tale of Peirithoos, king of the Lapithai.

Peirithoos had his place in the catalogue of the sons of Zeus.[566] Dia, wife of Ixion, a heroine whose name connects her with heaven,[567] bore him to the King of Heaven.[568] Therefore in later times[569] he was supposed to be a son of Ixion and brother to the Centaurs, who descended from that sinner.[570] Zeus allegedly begot him in the shape of a stallion,[571] as Kronos did Chiron. This tribe of the Lapithai was a strong, almost a Titanic race, and Peirithoos was their king. Kaineus son of Elatos belonged to the same stock, Elatos the 'spruce-man',[572] which was the name also of that Centaur whom Herakles killed. But to begin with, Kaineus was Elatos' daughter and named Kainis, 'the new'. From Poseidon, who was her lover, she got the favour of turning into a man and being invulnerable.[573] So the Centaurs hammered him into the ground alive with trunks of pine-trees.[574] He did not even bend his knees under their blows,[575] and in the under-world he recovered his earlier, female sex.[576]

This happened after the savage, bestial creatures had tasted wine at the wedding of Peirithoos and Hippodameia;[577] we know this characteristic of the Centaurs from the history of Herakles. Hippodameia is also known as Deidameia[578] or Ischomache,[579] 'she who fights with strength', while in her other names the idea of taming is expressed. She seems to be the same august figure as Pelops' Pisan bride, of whom there was not much more to discover than that she, too, was a 'tamer of steeds', to judge by her name. According to the oldest story, which is set before us with much reticence, the Centaur Eurytion entered Peirithoos' palace alone, where the Lapithai were celebrating the wedding, and behaved scandalously, being maddened by wine. His ears and nose were cut off and he was thrown out; this occasioned the war between the Centaurs and the Lapithai.[580] Later we have plentiful accounts[581] of how the Centaurs who had been invited to the feast assaulted the women, Eurytos (another form of his name) attacking the bride, and how the slaughter began, at first with wine-vessels, resulting in the deaths of many on both sides. Theseus too had a share in it, being the first to come to the bridegroom's aid,[582] or else during the war which followed.[583] This war is said to have ended with the expulsion of the Centaurs from the region of Pelion, on the day on which Hippodameia bore her son Polypoites.[584]

The story of the friendship between Theseus and Peirithoos, however, did not have Thessaly for its scene, but the region of Attica, except when the two left the country on their joint ventures. The inhabitants of Attica, especially those of the deme Perithoidai, honoured Peirithoos as their own hero. There is no fixed tradition of how he came there before becoming acquainted with Theseus; he may have been what his name implies, a 'runner around'. The fame of Theseus' strength and valour is said to have reached him,[585] and incited him to make trial of them. One of Theseus' herds of kine was then pasturing at Marathon; Peirithoos came and drove them away. Theseus caught up his weapons and went after the robber. When the latter saw that, he stood still and turned to face him. They gazed at each other admiringly, each observing the beauty and courage of the other, and refrained from fighting. Peirithoos was the first to offer his hand, and asked Theseus to act as judge concerning the cattle-raid, promising to pay whatever fine he fixed. The other remitted the fine and offered him friendship and alliance. They confirmed their compact with an oath at Kolonos. Later the hollow in the rock was shown which had served them as a mixing-bowl when they drank to their alliance.[586] Then, according to one account,[587] Peirithoos invited Theseus to come to Thessaly for his wedding, and it was not till much later that they troubled themselves about the marriage with Helen. According to another,[588] they decided, since they were sons of Zeus and Poseidon, to get daughters of Zeus for their wives.

Helen was then but twelve years old,[589] or even younger,[590]

whether it was Leda who had borne her to Zeus in Lakonia
or the goddess Nemesis in Attica. From Theseus' city Aphidna
one could see down into the valley of Rhamnus, in which the
daughter of Night, Helen's divine mother, had her sanctuary.
The tale was told later[591] that Theseus had asked for the girl's
hand from Tyndareos and would gladly have had the Spartan
Dioskuroi for his brothers-in-law.[592] It was only when he
could not get Helen peaceably that he carried her off from the
dance at the temple of Artemis Orthia,[593] unless it was at
Rhamnus or the neighbouring temple of Artemis at Brauron
that it happened. Nothing is told us, it is true, about this, only
of the abduction from Sparta. The abductors were followed
by the Dioskuroi as far as Tegea; they then cast lots to see which
of them should have Helen for his wife, and Theseus won the
lot-casting.[594] He took the maid home to Aphidna, to his
mother Aithra. Helen was rescued from Aphidna by Kastor
and Polydeukes, and Aithra became their prisoner.[595]
Theseus' mother was still serving Helen in Troy,[596] where she,
thus twice abducted, waited in vain for her brothers to appear
and set her free again.[597] She bore a girl-child to Theseus, that
Iphigeneia who then passed for the daughter of Agamemnon
and Klytaimnestra,[598] since Helen, after being delivered of her
in Argos, handed her over to her sister. By one account,[599] the
destiny of this girl had a further connection with Attica, for it
was not at Aulis but at Brauron that she was apparently
sacrificed.

Aphidna was defended against the Dioskuroi, not by
Theseus but by the eponym of the place, Aphidnos, who even
wounded Kastor in the right thigh.[600] Theseus himself had
been obliged to leave his young wife, whom he kept imprisoned
and hidden in Aphidna, and in his turn to follow Peirithoos
on a much more perilous journey—to carry off a daughter of
Zeus for him also.[601] Or was it originally his own venture,
appropriate to the seducer of Ariadne, and only later ascribed
to Peirithoos on account of its wickedness? For the journey
led to the other world, for which later accounts substituted

the country of the Thesprotians[602] or the Molossians[603] in Epeiros, and the intended bride was Persephone. The mad adventurers wished to take the Queen of Hades with them[604] from the bedroom which she shared with the King of the underworld. They made their way through the hell-mouth at Tainaron[605] (a Roman poet makes Theseus describe it),[606] the very place by which Herakles was later to force his entrance, not long after them.

It was said[607] that they did not find Charon with his boat at his usual harbour on the Acheron. We have lost the continuation of the story, and can no longer say how they managed to induce the ferryman of the dead to come to them, and while still alive to board the ship of souls.[608] Probably it was not done by force, for that was reserved for Herakles, but by guile, since it was by guile also that the lord of the underworld subsequently caught them. He bade them sit on thrones[609] hewn out of the rock[610] beside the gate of his palace.[611] They were to sit there while he fetched them his gifts. But these were the seats of forgetfulness, of Lethe.[612] They sat there as if they were fettered;[613] forgetfulness of self had paralysed them. They could only stretch out their hands to Herakles when he passed.[614] The fetters of Lethe are described as if they were snakes,[615] or hundreds of chains,[616] or as if both men had grown into the seats.[617] There was a comic account[618] of how Theseus left part of his back-side sticking when Herakles dragged him up; the lithe outlines of his descendants, the Athenian youths, were due to this. We know from the stories of Herakles that only Theseus could be awakened and return. In the old accounts he probably was still young then, and it was even alleged that Peirithoos returned with him.[619] But after his death, Theseus' punishment had to continue; he then had to sit for ever on his rocky seat,[620] while a like penalty was reserved for his friend as for the sinner Ixion,[621] who wished to seduce the Queen of Heaven, or for Tantalos before them.

It seems that a long life still awaited Theseus, although it is explicitly said only of the abduction of Helen that it preceded the Cretan adventure, but not also of the invasion of Hades. A tale that he won his way there once again in his lifetime and perhaps (though later generations would not believe this)[622] delivered Peirithoos, has not come down to us, and there were even some[623] who denied his own deliverance from the underworld. His famous return was from the Labyrinth, although he could no more claim its lady as his own for ever than he could Persephone. The Dioskuroi had taken Helen from him, as Dionysos had Ariadne; nothing was left him but the sovranty of Athens, ever since Aigeus at sight of the black sails had flung himself from the Akropolis, or, as some who claimed more accurate knowledge declared,[624] into the sea which bears his name. Theseus' famous act as founder was the uniting of the village-communities of Attica into the city of the Athenians; it was allegedly his doing that a single common *politeia*, a communal life in one State, came into being.[625] This was a deed the scene of which was the whole land of Attica and which was perpetually celebrated at the festival of the Synoikia. It was not as a union of village-communities already in existence but as the assembling of primaeval dwellers in the land that a similar action was accredited to Kekrops. Theseus is said to have been the first[626] to give the city its plural name, *Athenai*, and make the Panathenaia, of which it was otherwise stated that it had been instituted by Erichthonios, into the festival of 'all Athenians', not of the inhabitants of the city only but also of those of the countryside. The narrators made him take part in nearly all the common undertakings of the heroes of his day, and a proverb sprang up, 'Not without Theseus',[627] or, since he himself needed no one to help him, 'A second Herakles is come.'[628]

Thus he became Herakles' follower in the campaign against the Amazons. From this adventure he brought back the warlike consort who bore him Hippolytos. But the undertaking was worthier of Theseus than of Herakles. The Amazonian queen whom Herakles had to deal with was named Hippolyte, as the mother of Hippolytos often is, a name which perhaps originally connected her with him as her son. The report that it was Theseus who made the girdle of Hippolyte his booty and presented it to the older and greater hero was even preserved in the legends concerning Herakles. The narrators had some trouble to distinguish between Herakles' Amazons and those of Theseus. Those who held that Theseus got his Amazon from the son of Zeus as a meed of honour spoke of her as a sister of the queen of the Amazons and gave her the lunar name Antiopeia or Antiope, which was borne also by the mother of the Theban Dioskuroi. In the stories concerning Theseus the figure of the Amazon was associated with those of Helen, Persephone and Ariadne, who all resembled each other, and it was apparently this figure which the narrators had in their mind's eye under the different names.

Indeed, she appears to us as an Asian Helen, carried off from east to west and then fought over on Greek soil, as the daughter of Leda was on eastern, at Troy. The tale of the Danaids was one of the arrival of Amazonian maidens from the Orient to Greece. But the Athenians alone had the story that the real Amazons came from Asia Minor with their whole army and besieged the Akropolis. Curious graves were shown to strangers and ascribed to the Amazons, in Athens the grave of Antiope,[629] in Megara that of Hippolyte.[630] The latter tomb, it was thought, could be known by having the shape of the half-moon Amazonian shield. The war against the Amazons in which Theseus had to defend his own city was preceded by the abduction of the Amazon, and here again the original tale was surely that not Herakles but Theseus carried her off.

There was a story[631] that Herakles vainly besieged the Amazons' city of Themiskyra and could not take it until Antiope fell in love with Theseus and betrayed her own people. A more famous account, however,[632] was one in which Theseus had Peirithoos with him when he set out to abduct the Amazon, much as when they went out to steal Helen. A vase-painting shows Antiope in the arms of Theseus, while his friend stands beside him to protect him. In Athens, the Amazon bore him a son. According to most accounts this son was Hippolytos; according to an older one it was that Demophon, who was later to go on the expedition to Troy and rescue his grandmother Aithra from the burning city.[633] Other-wise, Demophon and his brother Akamâs are accounted the sons of Phaidra, Theseus' wife after he concluded a peace with the Cretans. Antiope, or whatever the name of the Amazonian queen was, lived until that time with her abductor, as Helen did with Paris in Troy.

To free their queen,[634] or to wipe out the disgrace inflicted on them by Theseus taking a second wife,[635] the Amazon host appeared. It came from a northerly direction, making wide detours, from the coasts of the Black Sea, since the Amazons were no seafarers but a people of riders.[636] Or it could have been merely a rebellion of the female warriors, which the injured Antiope herself commanded. The left wing of their army[637] rested on the Areopagos at the point where the Amazoneion, the hero-shrine in honour of the Amazons, was to stand, and their right wing on the Pnyx. From there they drove forwards against the Akropolis. But an Athenian army fell upon their rear from the Hill of the Muses, and thus they were compelled, in the fourth month of the siege, to make peace. For the Athenians, all this was real history. Two great wall-paintings showed them the battle with the Amazons, one in the Theseion, the shrine of Theseus (not the one which was so called in later times),[638] the other in the Stoa Poikile, the 'many-coloured hall'.[639] The vase-painters also were fond of representing individual scenes, not to speak of the sculptors who decorated so many buildings, and not in Athens alone, with reliefs of the fighting and dying Amazons.

It is true that another story said[640] Herakles hurried to the assistance of his friend, and that the other famous Amazon, who later went to Troy and fell at the hands of Achilles, Penthesileia, already took part in this struggle. It is said that she accidentally killed her lady,[641] but others held that it was

Theseus himself, or perhaps his followers, at the moment when the Amazons' revolt flared up and the queen was threatening the guests in the palace at Phaidra's wedding.[642] Finally, there was also the following tale of the death of Antiope:[643] she was fighting at the side of Theseus against her countrywomen, who wanted to get her back by force, when she fell to the arrow of the Amazon Molpadie, 'the singer', and was immediately revenged by the hero. The Athenians put up a sepulchral monument to Molpadie as they did for Antiope, or at least they believed that two old gravestones in the city belonged to the two Amazons.

The hero was now left with only the second Cretan princess, Phaidra, and the son of the Amazon, the beautiful and strange youth Hippolytos. The great deity whom the Amazons served above all others was Artemis, although they made the cruelty of the goddess worshipped on the Black Sea their model, rather than the purity of the Greek Artemis. If we go by his name, Hippolytos must have been the wild stallion let loose, as the Amazons resembled uncontrolled mares and therefore bore names such as Hippolyte, or that Hippo who according to one tradition founded the temple of Artemis at Ephesos,[644] but was afterwards punished by the goddess because she ceased to take part in the dances of the virgins before her altar. Hippolytos as a young hunter in Troizen served none but the virginal Artemis; it was there that he grew up, in the country of his great-grandfather Pittheus, and it was there[645] that Phaidra fell in love with her sublime, maiden-like stepson.

Euripides put the story of this unfortunate love twice on the stage, and one of the two tragedies has come down to us. The Athenians had, high up on the south slope of the Akropolis,[646] a little shrine of Aphrodite 'for Hippolytos', and said[647] that Phaidra had founded it when she looked out from there with lovelorn gaze to the coast of Troizen. According to this version,[648] she saw the youth for the first time when he, being devoted to all initiatory rites, including those of Orpheus,[649] came to Athens to take part in the Eleusinian Mysteries. She restrained herself for a long time before Hippolytos, who guessed nothing of her secret, until she was obliged to go to Troizen with Theseus. The Troizenians for their part[650] possessed in their shrine of Hippolytos a temple of the 'spying Aphrodite', and told how from that spot the amorous Phaidra used to look across to the stadium where Hippolytos exercised naked, and which was later known by his name. There also stood the myrtle whose leaves she used to prick through with her hairpin in the outbursts of her passion. Aphrodite went mightily to work, but only the beautiful queen was overcome by her, not the youth as well. He would know only of Artemis, not of Aphrodite also.[651] However, Phaidra's love was made known to him, and he repulsed the proud woman.

And thus the story of Bellerophontes was repeated, a story which was told not only among the Greeks. The despised love of the royal lady, who had offered herself in her passion, turned to hate and fear. Phaidra complained to Theseus that Hippolytos had tried to seduce her. In the simplest form of the narrative,[652] she showed him the door of her bedchamber broken open and her clothing torn. Her husband believed her, cursed his son and banished him from the kingdom; and, as his father Poseidon had granted him fulfilment of three wishes,[653] he wished death for Hippolytos. As the youth was driving his noble steeds along the coast of the Saronic Gulf to Epidauros, intending to go on from there to Argos,[654] there came an earthquake and a disturbance of the sea. A wave arose which hid the Isthmus, a bull emerged from it and made Hippolytos' horses wild with fright; they broke loose, tore the chariot from the driver's control and dragged him to death. But the Troizenians denied that Hippolytos came to his end in that manner. Also, they did not display his grave,[655] as the Athenians did,[656] although they knew where it was; but they showed the wild olive near the temple of Artemis Saronia and told[657] how Hippolytos had entangled himself in the reins of his horses there and been hanged somehow on the crooked tree. That was a kind of death which often took place in Artemis' sphere. Phaidra too hanged herself, and it was said[658] that in the underworld she swung to and fro on a swing, in mockery of her end.

The virgins of Troizen used to mourn for Hippolytos in the beautiful shrine which Diomedes founded in his honour;[659] they did so on the day before their own marriage,[660] and offered up to him the sacrifice of woman's devouring love, a lock of their hair. For all that, he was not dead. He was not one of those heroes who die once and for all, for Artemis delivered her darling from death. For her sake,[661] Asklepios, whose home was close at hand in Epidauros, recalled him[662] with his simples to life again. The Troizenians recognised him in the sky in the constellation of the Charioteer,[663] but the inhabitants of the Alban Hills in Italy, near Rome, knew that the god Virbius, who hid himself in the grove of Diana near Aricia, in the dark woods about the Lago di Nemi, was no other than Hippolytos, whom Artemis had carried away thither.[664] That was why no horses might be brought into the sacred precincts, being the beasts which reminded men of the death of the re-awakened god.

As to the death of Theseus, there is no unambiguous tradition. He, who had received Oidipus, so that the Theban hero should find his rest in the soil of Attica, and who had helped the Herakleidai to get free for good and all from Eurystheus, their father's enemy and their persecutor, must leave Attica and lie in a distant grave, on the island of Skyros, until his bones were found again many centuries later.[665] And there were some who claimed that he never came back again from the underworld, whither he had gone with Peirithoos to carry off Persephone. Others again, who also put his journey to Hades towards the end of his career, had a tale[666] of a great-grandson of Erechtheus, the first demagogue, who made the people rebellious against him while he was in the realm of the dead. That allegedly was why he voyaged to Skyros and there was cast by king Lykomedes from a high rock into the sea;[667] a death which he suffered in a far country without cause, and after which there cannot originally have been a grave, assuredly no site for hero-worship, remaining; it was more like a rape from the earth. His shrine, the Theseion near the ascent to the Akropolis, became his tomb only when his supposed bones were brought there from Skyros in the year 473 B.C.

CHAPTER II

Jason and Medeia

THE HERO WHO WENT FORTH to get the Golden
Fleece was born into that family to which Phrixos, son of
Athamas, belonged. The golden ram had brought him to
Kolchis on the Caucasus. Besides Athamas, father of Phrixos,
Salmoneus and Kretheus were also sons of Aiolos, from whom
this great line was descended. The ancestress of the branch of
which we have now to speak, Tyro daughter of Salmoneus,
bore to Poseidon the twins Nelus and Pelias, and afterwards
several sons to her uncle Kretheus, the eldest being Aison, who
founded the city of Aison in Thessaly. His son Jason (properly
Iason or Ieson) was the hero of the Golden Fleece. After
Phrixos, his father's cousin, died in Kolchis as son-in-law of
Aietes, the Fleece remained in the possession of the son of
Helios, this same Aietes. From him it was to be recovered for
the family.

The cities of Aison and Iolkos, the latter a foundation of
Kretheus, lay close to each other on that great Thessalian bay,
the Gulf of Pagasai, now known as the Gulf of Volo. In
Iolkos the stepson of Kretheus, Pelias son of Poseidon, was
king; Aison was his half-brother, and their common mother
was Tyro, as already said. All the brothers had had sons born
to them, Akastos to Pelias, and as many as twelve sons to
Neleus, who ruled at Pylos on the south-western extremity of
the Peloponnesos; one of his sons was Nestor. Their half-
brothers Aison, Pheres and Amythaon had sons too; Amythaon, the seer, Melampus, who healed the daughters of Proitos;
Pheres, Admetos, the beloved of Apollo and husband of
Alkestis, Aison, as already said, Jason. The mother of this,
the most famous figure of the entire stock, is known, or rather
hidden, under a variety of names, Polymede,[668] said to be[669]
a daughter of Autolykos, Alkimede, a Minyad,[670] to mention

no others. Jason was brought up by the wise Centaur Chiron,[671] whose habitat, Mount Pelion, rises above both towns, Aison and Iolkos. The divine forest creature is said to have been the first to name the boy *Iason*,[672] and the name was felt to signify something healing or health-bringing.[673]

So far as his name goes, indeed, Jason might have had some-thing in common with Iasios or Iasion, the beloved of Demeter.[674] He, however, was a favourite of Hera, not of the mother of Persephone.[675] It is told of the two great sister-goddesses that they wandered about on Earth, Demeter in search of her daughter, Hera when in anger she had withdrawn from Zeus, or was returning to him. On that occasion also she was assailed by impudent Silens, as we know from the history of Herakles. Jason met her when he was hunting, as no doubt the Cretan hunter Iasios or Iasion met Demeter, but this meeting happened by a river which was in spate, whether it was the Thessalian Anauros,[676] or Enipeus,[677] or some other stream.[678] Jason did not recognise the goddess in the old woman whose shape Hera had assumed, but he took her on his back and carried her across the water. It is said[679] that in doing this he lost a sandal, and consequently presented himself with but one shoe at the sacrifice[680] which Pelias was making in Iolkos to his father Poseidon and the other gods, but not to their Queen.[681] As we know from the story of Tyro, he was no worshipper of Hera. For this, too, he was to be punished.

Jason lost a sandal in all of the stories, and the arrival of the *monosandalos*, the man with one shoe, was ominous, and not only in the history of this hero. The person in question, even if he was a god, like Dionysos, always gave the impression that he came from another world, possibly from the underworld, and had left the other shoe there as a token and pledge that he had one foot in it. Moreover, Pelias had received an oracle that he should die at the hands of a man with one sandal.[682] Now, when he had invited the whole town of Iolkos to his sacrifice, the hero was in the fields on the other side of the Anauros.

60 PHINEUS ON HIS COUCH

61 THE SONS OF BOREAS AND THE HARPIES

62 JASON SPEWED UP BY THE DRAGON

Those who represented him as a ploughman, not a hunter,[683] alleged that he had left his plough by the Anauros, waded barefoot through the river and forgotten to fasten on his left sandal again. Otherwise, he lost it in the river.[684] When, therefore, he appeared before Pelias, the latter at once thought of the oracle. He said nothing that day, but the next day he sent for Jason again and asked him what he would do if it were foretold him that he should be murdered by a certain fellow-citizen. 'I would send that man to fetch the Golden Fleece', replied Jason and Pelias answered, 'Go and fetch it.'

There is another version,[685] in which Pelias had actually had two oracles. One threatened him with death from a descendant of Aiolos, but according to the other, he was to take the greatest heed of 'him who came from lofty pastures down to Iolkos, wearing but one sandal'. And in the fullness of time, there came the man, arousing terror and astonishment. He carried two spears and was clad after the fashion of Magnesia, the neighbouring peninsula. Also, a panther-skin covered his shoulders to protect him from rain. He had never cut his hair, and it hung gleaming down his back. As if he would test his own self-possession, he stood on the market place of Iolkos amid the thronging people. No one knew him, and all tried to guess who he was; they thought of Apollo, of Ares, of the Aloadai and Tityos, and then rejected these thoughts. While the people were thus talking to one another, Pelias the king came up on his mule-carriage. His eyes were riveted on the sandal which the youth strangely wore on his right foot only. He concealed his terror and asked the stranger where his home was and who his parents were.

And he was of good cheer and replied in courteous words: 'I bring with me the teaching of Chiron, for I come from his cave, from Chariklo and Philyra, his wife and mother, where the Centaur's virgin daughters reared me. Twenty years have I spent and never done a deed or spoken a word to them that was out of season, and now am I come home to get the ancient honour of my sire, now governed against justice, the honour which Zeus formerly gave to prince Aiolos and to his offspring.'

This and more he said with great frankness, not guessing before whom he stood. By this account Pelias had usurped the sovranty which belonged to Jason's parents, and therefore, in fear for their child's life, they had made a show of mourning him as if he had died immediately after birth, but secretly sent him to Chiron. Now the young man asked the way to the house of his father Aison and named the name which the wise Centaur had given him.

The presupposition, therefore, of this story was that Aison, the eldest son of Kretheus, should have been ruler of Iolkos, not Pelias, whom Tyro had borne to Poseidon before her marriage to Kretheus. Aison, the tale goes on, received his son with tears in his eyes.[686] His brothers and their sons arrived to greet their nephew and cousin, Pheres and Admetos from Pherai in Thessaly, Amythaon and Melampus from Messenia. For five days and nights Jason feasted them in his father's house, but on the sixth day he laid before them his intention to demand the kingship back from Pelias. They arose at once and accom, panied him to Pelias' palace, where he spoke gently and wisely to the king. He appealed to their common ancestry on the distaff side and proposed a peaceful partition; Pelias might keep the herds and lands which he had taken from Aison, but must give back the sceptre and throne which were the due of a son of Kretheus. And Pelias answered him quietly; he would do this, but a demand from the powers below troubled him. He was too old to satisfy it, but Jason was in the prime of his young strength. Phrixos, said Pelias, had appeared to him in a dream and desired that someone should go to the house of Aietes and thence bring his soul and the Golden Fleece. Pelias had thereupon consulted the oracle at Delphi, and it agreed that a ship should be sent. That should be Jason's price for the kingship; this he confirmed with an oath.

In the golden chambers of Aietes, an old narrative stated,[687] the rays of the sun rested at night. It was assuredly not thought

of as a place for mankind, this dwelling of Aietes on the banks
of the Phasis, which according to the accounts of seafarers ran
from the Caucasus into the Black Sea. Aia was the name of the
city, and from Aia Aietes derived his name; Aia was also the
name of the country which was equated with Kolchis on the
Caucasus, but probably meant the Land of Morning, of Eos.
For a royal soul on its way to becoming a god (for Pelias
certainly lied with his story of his dream, or expressed the ideas
of a later age), this far-off land of dawn was the proper place.
It must be a place for immortal, divine beings. We know[688]
that Aietes was a son of Helios and the Sun's consort, Perse[689]
or Perseis,[690] a brother of the Cretan queen Pasiphae and of
Kirke, whose island of Aiaia belonged to Aia, whether it lay
east or west of that land in which the sun's rays slept and woke
again. As the house of the Sun, but at the same time a house of
invisibility, of Hades—thus we must think of the mansion of
Aietes. It sheltered the Golden Fleece, well guarded in the care
of a huge serpent. Jason had to undertake an adventure like
that of Perseus, and like Kadmos, to fight a dragon. And also,
as Kadmos found Harmonia and Perseus Andromeda, he was
to find a bride whom he had not gone out to seek and in whom
he should have a helper as Theseus had in Ariadne; a second
granddaughter of the Sun, who should accompany him to the
world of men, but not to his lasting happiness.

According to all accounts, Jason took upon himself no
more than what he had in some measure invited, the task of
winning back the Golden Fleece from that house outside the
mortal world. It was said that this task had lain like a curse
upon the race of Aiolos, ever since Athamas had wished to
sacrifice his son Phrixos and forced him to take flight to that
other-worldly realm of Aietes.[691] The sacrifice of the king's
'curly-headed' son was in a way accomplished thereby, the
wrath of Zeus aroused against the sacrificer and atonement
made necessary. A consequence of this was the gathering of the
company that was to go with Jason. He needed, if he was to
be able to get to Aietes and come back again, an extraordinarily

fast ship and a crew of companions who were ready to die. This ship, which was as much admired[692] as if she had been the first ever constructed,[693] was built him with the help of the goddess Athene,[694] if not actually by her.[695] She was called 'Swift', *Argó*,[696] and her earthly constructor Argos. Pines were felled on Pelion,[697] and descended to the bight of Pagasai.[698] The ship which was made from them had, in the oldest accounts, the gift of speech,[699] because, as was averred later,[700] wood from the oaks of Dodona was built into her. The first crew was composed of Minyans,[701] the inhabitants of many a town in the regions over which Athamas (a son of Minyas in one tradition)[702] had ruled. Such towns were Orchomenos in Boiotia and Minya in Thessaly. In Orchomenos the Minyans worshipped Zeus Laphystios, to whom Phrixos was to have been sacrificed. They boarded the Argo with Jason and rowed her, when she was not speeding under sail, towards distant Aia.

The Argo had to be particularly fast because of the return journey. The very little which we can tell of the oldest tales concerning the sailors on the Argo, the Argonauts, as they were always called then, is told by Kirke to Odysseus,[703] though not quite exactly, as she did not want to expose the whole secret of the route. Odysseus was then staying on the island of Aiaia, on the return journey from the realm of the dead, and in the oldest account of the Argonauts probably the rocky gate which led to the other world was dangerous only to those returning. Kirke revealed the name by which it was known among men; she called it the Planktai, the 'moving rocks'. She further told that the doves which brought ambrosia to Father Zeus flew by these rocks, but even they invariably lost one of their number, and the Father had always to make it up again. He did this, it is not hard to guess, so that the flock of doves in the sky should ever remain as we see them, in the Pleiades. The land from which the doves came with the ambrosia assuredly can be compared only with the Garden of the Hesperides. But the hindmost dove always fell a victim to the moving rocks when they clashed together. Therefore these were known more accurately as Plegades[704] or Symplegades,[705] less correctly as Planktai.[706] Apart from the doves, the Argo, beloved of all and guided by Hera, was the one thing to get past them safely on the return journey from Aietes. So the sorceress declared;[707] the Argonauts had reached her on that return journey.

As the journey is described to us by later poets, and especially by Apollonios of Rhodes, not only Minyans but heroes from all over Greece took part in it, as in the Kalydonian hunt. Jason, it is said,[708] after king Pelias had set him this toilsome task, which was equal to a whole series of difficult exploits,[709] and after Argos (whoever his father was)[710] had completed the Argo under Athene's guidance, sent out heralds to enlist them. The Argo, according to the received tradition,[711] was built for fifty oarsmen, so at least that number of men must assemble for the undertaking. Let us begin by naming Tiphys, the Boiotian helmsman, who was connected with the Argo most probably even in the time when she carried only Minyans. He was doomed to death, although it was Athene herself who induced him to join the voyage;[712] Jason lost him on the journey, as Aeneas did his Palinurus.[713] Of the sons of gods, those of Zeus were the very first to arrive in Iolkos:[714] Herakles, Kastor and Polydeukes. Next came the sons of Poseidon: Euphemos of Tainaron and Periklymenos of Pylos, who was otherwise accounted a son of Neleus, Nauplios son of Amy׳mone,[715] and the Messenian twins Idas and Lynkeus.[716] From Apollo's stock came Orpheus,[717] with whom also the singer Philammon,[718] a son of Apollo,[719] took part in the voyage. Sons of Hermes were Echion and Erytos the twins,[720] and Authalides the Argonauts' herald.[721] Following them came Augeias king of Elis, who as we know from the history of Herakles was a son of Helios,[722] and the sons of Boreas, Zetes and Kalais; furthermore, two prophets, Idmon, another son of Apollo,[723] and Mopsos, whom Apollo had taught,[724] Peleus and Telamon,[725] sons of Aiakos and grandsons of Zeus, Admetos,[726] Jason's cousin, and even Akastos, son of Pelias, of whom it was said that he came against the will of his father.[727]

So far, we have gone through the list of sons of gods, and yet not all have been named who could lay claim to divine descent. Lastly even Meleagros and Atalante[728] were added to that brilliant company, Theseus and Peirithoos too;[729] this assembly of heroes which now replaced the nameless or forgotten Minyans was the greatest before the Trojan War. Therefore in the later tales of the journey, attention is paid to many famous names. The separate adventures of each hero, however, did not make up the destiny of Jason; only the events affecting the Argo and the company of Argonauts belong to it. Risks were indeed run, but they did not, in the known versions of the story, go beyond the world of mortals; they did not pass over into a world beyond ours, but made up a voyage from Iolkos to the shores of the Black Sea. The voyage was begun with the building of an altar to Apollo Embasios, the god of embarkation, however, and a sacrifice to him,[730] and its prelude was furnished by Orpheus,[731] who of all mortals should best know the way to the underworld and back again to the land of the living. He sang, the night before the start, of the beginning of things and of the gods. It was the preparation for a specially sacred journey.

Indeed the enterprise took, on the first island where the Argonauts landed, a peculiar, though not unambiguously Apolline trend. There was a curse on that island, the Lemnian evil, the greatest that Greece knew even in later times.[732] The women of the great island of Lemnos had apparently the same feelings of hostility towards men as the daughters of Danaos and the Amazons; they did not pay the proper honours to Aphrodite,[733] and were punished by the goddess with an un-aphrodisiac stench. Their men would have no more to do with them, adopted the manners of the Thracian coast,[734] carried off Thracian girls and lived with them. Thereupon the Amazonian fury of the Lemnian women against the men and their concubines broke out. They conspired among themselves and made an end not only of the offenders but of the whole male sex in the island, fathers, husbands and sons. Hypsipyle, who now became queen of Lemnos, saved a solitary male, her father, king Thoas, 'the quick-moving', a son of Dionysos. She put him into a chest on the sea, as happened to Perseus and, according to the legend told by the inhabitants of Pra-siai,[735] to Dionysos himself. With him the Kabeiroi, the male deities of the island, forsook Lemnos.[736] The women ruled there alone, but they could get no more husbands.

That was the first great evil in Lemnos, the massacre of the men and its consequences. Later yet another was recounted,[737] the slaughter of the Lemnians' Attic concubines, but that no longer forms part of this story. In this matter Jason and his Argonauts brought a remedy, and that is where the Apolline trait appears. Two great tragedians, Aeschylus and Sophokles, dramatized the story of their coming.[738] A storm is said to have forced them to land; the Lemnian women ran armed to the coast[739] and made to drive the men off, until an agreement was reached between Jason and Hypsipyle, as to which should pacify Aphrodite. The agreement was not due to Herakles, for he would have nothing to do with the Lemnian women,[740] but to the hero who set out after the Golden Fleece and already found the love of a royal maiden here. For it he had to thank the women's yearning for love. Games were instituted; the victors among the Argonauts were given handsome garments and thus celebrated their union.[741] Erginos was prematurely grey, and the women laughed at him when he took part in the race in full armour, but he won and thus showed that youth and white hair can go together.[742] At the great wedding-feast the Kabeiroi reappeared on the island and filled the wine-jars.[743] The festival lasted several days[744]— according to later narrators it was months or years[745]—on Lemnos. Aphrodite was reconciled[746] and Hypsipyle, who was to become a tragic heroine, thanks to Euripides, when she was deserted, did not complain of Jason when he was obliged to sail on.[747] She bore him two sons, Euenos[748] and little

Thoas.[749] The other Lemnians also bore children again and the island was repopulated with the two sexes.

Samothrace lies not far from Lemnos, and the Samothracians later told[750] that Jason and the Dioskuroi, Herakles and Orpheus, were initiated into their mysteries and shared in the epiphany of the Great Gods. That was why these heroes always had good fortune on their voyages and campaigns. They also showed the goblets which the Argonauts dedicated[751] after they had landed and received initiation.[752] This too was to sanctify the voyage.

An older account of how the Argonauts sailed through the Hellespont and met an adventure at the Bear's Fountain, Artakia, perhaps at the very place where Odysseus and his followers were supposed to have been attacked with stone-throwing by the gigantic Laistrygones,[753] has not been preserved to us. The citizens of the city of Kyzikos, which afterwards stood at the same spot on the Propontis (the Sea of Marmora, as it was named later), had a tale that six-armed sons of Earth lived in their neighbourhood, on Bear Island, or rather Bear Peninsula, where Mount Dindymon rose.[754] They themselves, the Doliones, did not suffer at their hands, being descended from Poseidon. Their king, Kyzikos, a young man of Jason's age, had once received a warning to meet in friendly wise a company of heroes if one should visit him. He was in the middle of his honeymoon with Kleite, 'the famous', daughter of the king of Perkote, when the Argonauts landed. But he hurried to meet them and showed them lavish hospitality. Only when the heroes wished to climb Mount Dindymon was the Argo attacked by the native giants. However, Herakles was there; he killed most of them and the returning Argonauts the rest. Here began the misfortune which the heroes were to bring upon the Doliones.

They left their harbour with the Argo at once and did not notice that during the night they were driven back by the wind to a spot on the coast which was later to be known as the Sacred Rock, but in the darker sense of the word 'sacred'. In the darkness they did not recognise the Doliones nor the Doliones them, but supposed that enemies were trying to attack them, and so met the arrivals in hostile fashion. Again king Kyzikos left his young wife, and never returned to her. He fell, and many of his men with him, at the hands of the Argonauts. When day dawned and the supposed enemies recognised each other, the Argonauts were the first to raise the lament for the fallen, and their wailing lasted three days. The nymphs wailed for the young wife, who hanged herself on receiving news of her husband's death. From their many tears arose the spring, Kleite. After this, contrary winds blew for twelve days and prevented the Argonauts from going further. On the twelfth day the diviner Mopsos noticed the cry of the fulmar and understood it. He advised Jason to appease the Great Mother of the gods. The heroes climbed Dindymon again and found in the woods an extraordinarily thick grape⁄vine growing wild. The woodworker Argos, who built the Argo, carved it into a statue of Rhea, the goddess to whom of all goddesses the grape⁄vine surely was sacred.[755] She was called Dindymene from this mountain and others of the same name.

As they journeyed on, in the country of Mysia, the Argo⁄nauts lost the beautiful Hylas to the water⁄nymphs,[756] and with him Herakles, who went back to his Labours[757] after long and vain search for the beloved lad. In the country of the Bebrykes, later known as Bithynia, on the Sea of Marmora, Polydeukes showed that he was the best of boxers. He over⁄came the local potentate and owner of the spring from which the heroes wanted to draw water. His name was Amykos, a son of Poseidon and the Bithynian Nymph Melia.[758] Perhaps Polydeukes did not even kill him,[759] but merely bade him swear by his father that he would no longer molest strangers who came that way. According to this story the Argonauts by that time had already put the Bosporus behind them, but in the better⁄known version of the tale they landed once again before reaching this last strait, on the European coast opposite Bithynia, among the Thynians in Thrace.

The narrators transferred to this people the palace of Phineus, which originally was stationed where the realm of darkness begins. For that reason Perseus had already met a Phineus, who wanted to take his niece Andromeda to wife, as Hades did Persephone. The genealogists counted him among the descendants of Agenor[760] in about the same degree as Kadmos, either as son or as grandson, when they did not actually make him out a brother of Agenor and a son of Belos,[761] or simply a son of Poseidon.[762] The oldest narrators probably gave him Erichtho as his wife, as an ancient vase-painter does; her name marks Phineus as at once the husband of the queen of the underworld and of a daughter of Boreas, for both one and the other were known by the name Chthonia, the more transparent form of Erichtho. However, in the stories that have come down to us, Phineus is rather the victim than the lord of the underworld, which torments him in a variety of shapes, that of blindness and of the Harpies. But blind though he was, he knew, since he must endure the horrors of the realm of the dead more than anyone else, being in its neighbourhood, how one could force a way into it so as to have perhaps some chance of return. The men who were capable of this should also bring him release from his torments.

Thus he is represented as a prophet, who, being in possession of the gift of seeing everything, had himself chosen length of days with blindness of his eyes;[763] this blindness was allegedly his punishment for this overweening choice, or else for having previously shown Phrixos the way to the other world. For other narrators (since they all wanted somehow to account for Phineus' combination of blindness with sharp sight into the darkness of the realm of the dead), his prophetic gift was a present to him from Apollo, while Zeus had inflicted loss of sight and the weariness of old age upon him.[764] The King of the Gods was ill-pleased that he revealed the future to men, even to its uttermost end. Helios is said to have sent the Harpies against him because[765] he presumptuously renounced the sight of the sun's beams. They always came when Phineus' meal was served and snatched it from his hand and mouth. What they left was infected with a stench that no one could bear at close quarters.[766]

On the famous vase-painting which once also showed the name of the woman who sits at the head of his couch as Erichtho, he appears like a corpse, blind and with sunken cheeks; and that also is how the narrators describe him.[767] The Harpies were with him again, robbing him of his food, but he heard the heroes drawing near, and of them he knew by what Zeus had told him that they would give him back the enjoyment of eating. Like a lifeless shadow he arose from his couch, and felt his way along the wall, supported on his staff, on shrivelled feet to the door. His limbs trembled as he walked, from weakness and age. Dirt lay like a stiff crust on his dried-up body, where only the skin held the bones together. He left the hall, but his knees could take him no further; a dark red cloud of faintness shrouded him and the ground seemed to slip from under his feet. He collapsed in a swoon. The Argonauts gathered around him astonished. The old man could hardly recover breath to greet the heroes, of whom he knew every-thing, and to tell them of his own lot. His two brothers-in-law, the sons of Boreas, Kalais and Zetes, who had come with the Argonauts, were to rid him of the Harpies.

This the twins did, after Phineus had sworn to them that they would anger no god thereby, a proof that the Harpies had not been sent by any deity to Phineus' abode on the edge of the other world, which began there for the Argonauts. The young heroes set food before the corpse-like ancient for the Harpies' last prey. These swooped screeching upon it, and the men cried out, but the two winged sons of Boreas stood ready with drawn swords and flew after the birds of prey, who had swallowed everything in an instant and left only their foul odour behind. The pursuit was over the sea, as we know from the stories of the gods,[768] as far as those islands that were known from this incident as the Strophades, the Islands of Turning. There pursuers and pursued turned back, when Iris, the winged messenger of Zeus, stopped the brothers and swore to them that the Harpies should never molest Phineus again. They could not die, for they too belonged to the natural order, but for their dwelling they chose the depths of the earth under Crete, Minos' island.[769]

All that night, until Kalais and Zetes returned, the Argo-nauts feasted with Phineus, and he now instructed them, as Kirke had Odysseus, concerning the road by which one may pass from one world to the other. Originally, no doubt, the Argonauts learned from Phineus how they were to return, not how they were to make their way thither. For, by the counsel of the blind prophet, they were to imitate the doves of Zeus who brought ambrosia from the other world to the gods of our world on Olympos. At the 'dark blue rocks', which were at the Bosporus, but originally at the borders of the world beyond this one, they were to let a dove fly through the gap; as it came through, so should they. The rocks clashed together to kill the bird as it flew, then opened again—and lo and behold, as they never could catch any but the last of the doves of Zeus, so now they had but cut off a few feathers from the tail of the dove which the Argonauts, by Phineus' advice, had brought with them. And between the rocks, which had just drawn back again, the Argo flew like a feathered arrow. Only the extremity of her stern was torn off, otherwise she was undamaged. From that time on, the rocks have stood as close together as was later reported of the Bosporus with some exaggeration; actually the strait widens towards the Black Sea. Originally this road to the other world closed, most likely for good and all, after some human hero had succeeded in getting back through it. But as the story was then told, the rocks separated for ever after Jason with Medeia had passed them.[770] Even a later narrator of the story, the poet Apollonios, makes the heroes, when the Argo has happily won through, tell each other that they are saved from Hades.[771]

But according to Phineus' revelation, after they had escaped from the 'dark blue rocks' they were to come to a 'black rock', and from the 'black rock' to a 'promontory of Acheron',[772] where a steep path leads to Hades and the river Acheron flows into the sea. Phineus did not mention the name of king Lykos, the 'wolf', who received the Argonauts hospitably;[773] but although this country appeared so friendly, they lost two of their number there, who were overtaken by death—Idmon the prophet and Tiphys the pilot. And on the desert island of Thynias,[774] the 'island of tunnies', which stands before the coast of Asia Minor just where Bithynia borders on the land of the Maryandynoi, Lykos' people, they met Apollo.

Tradition also has it[775] that the goddess Athene forced back the 'dark blue rocks' with her left hand while she pushed on the Argo with her right. However, when the Argonauts arrived at the little bay on that desolate island, it was the hour of dawn, the time when the god of night changes to the god of day, and at that moment he appears completely. The son of Leto was coming from Lykia, and hastening to the Hyper-boreans, or so it was told.[776] His golden locks swung like grapes hanging on the vine on either side of the god's cheeks as he strode along. In his left hand he held his silver bow, and the quiver hung down his back from his right shoulder. Under his feet the whole island shook and the waves rose high on the beach. Helpless astonishment seized on the Argonauts, and none of them dared look the god in his beautiful eyes. They could only stand with their eyes on the ground, but he passed over the sea through the air. Not till much later did Orpheus find his voice, and he said to the heroes: 'Come now, let us name this island holy to Apollo of the Dawn, since at dawn he passed and was revealed to us all; and let us make sacrifice to him of what comes to hand, erecting an altar on the seashore. If he grant us safe return, then will we offer up thigh-pieces of horned goats. Now let us but seek his favour with burnt sacrifice and with libations. And do thou, O Lord, be gracious, be gracious, thou who hast appeared to us.'

Apollo sent the heroes good fortune in hunting and thus they could make him an abundant offering. They called upon

him as Heoos, Apollo of the Dawn, and they sang the paean
to him and danced before him. Orpheus began their singing
with a hymn to the divine child who had shot the dragon on
Parnassos, and to end the feast, they swore fidelity to each other,
with their hands on the offering, and dedicated a sanctuary to
Homonoia, Concord, a sanctuary which in later times still
stood there. On the third day the Argonauts left the island of
Thynias.

Phineus had foretold them which coasts and which peoples,
beginning with the Mariandynoi, they were to visit and which
they were to pass by before they rowed up the broad river
Phasis in the land of Kolchis to Aia, the seat of king Aietes.
At the tomb of Sthenelos,[777] who had fought against the
Amazons with Herakles and fallen on the shore, no great
way from the Acheron and the Dionysiac river Kallichoros,[778]
the Argonauts offered sacrifice. For Persephone allowed the
ghost of that hero to appear on his grave-mound in full armour
and to see the men with whom he had lived. At Sinope,[779]
three more companions of Herakles, who had remained there,
encountered the Argonauts. In the country of the Amazons,
at the mouth of the Thermodon, Jason also pitched camp, but
it did not come to a fight with the inhabitants, as Zeus sent
them a timely favourable wind.[780] The land of the wretched
Chalybes, who work at iron, shrouded in smoke,[781] the heroes
merely passed by; as also they did those of the Tibarenians and
the Mossynoikoi, two peoples who live perversely, for among
the Tibarenians the men lie in bed while the women are
in childbirth,[782] and among the Mossynoikoi everything is
done openly which is done privately elsewhere, even the act
of love, and that is done privately which elsewhere is done
openly.[783]

Following Phineus' advice, however, the Argonauts landed
on the island of Ares, where the birds of Lake Stymphalos had
settled when they were driven out of Greece by Herakles. They
endangered the heroes with their sharp feathers, which they
dropped on them. This the Argonauts were able to detect as

they approached the island,[784] and the heroes divided themselves, only half remaining at the oars, while the other half
roofed over the ship with their shields and made a noise with
their weapons, which scared the death-dealing birds away.
Thus the four sons of Phrixos—Argos, Kytissoros, Phrontis
and Melas—were able to land on the island of Ares at the same
time, clinging to planks, for they had been saved from a shipwreck. It was the wish of their deceased father that they should
undertake the journey to Orchomenos in Boiotia to get
possession of the treasures of their grandfather Athamas. And
since Athamas and Kretheus, the grandfather of Jason, had
been brothers, they could now be useful to their kinsman; they
returned to Aia with the Argonauts to introduce the heroes
there to their maternal grandfather, Aietes.

The island which the Argonauts passed after this adventure[785]
was called the Island of Philyra, not after the lime-tree, which
has the same name, but after Kronos' love,[786] a daughter of
Okeanos, who bore him the wisest of the Centaurs, Chiron.
There Rhea, mother of the gods, surprised the two lovers, and
the father of the gods leaped away like a stallion from the
nymph's embrace.[787] She, too, fled in shame, to Mount Pelion
in Thessaly, and there the Centaur was born. This happened
in the days of the Titans, when Zeus was still a baby and lay
hidden in a cave on Crete. But from this island of Kronos, as
it once was, the Argonauts soon came within view of the
Caucasus. They caught sight of the eagle of the King of the
Gods, making his way with a stronger wing-beat than common birds have to the highest peak, and ere long they heard also
the lamentation of the tortured Titan, whose liver the eagle
was devouring. The deliverer of Prometheus had not yet
appeared when the Argo turned up the stream of the Phasis at
the foot of the Caucasus.

In the oldest accounts, the sons of Phrixos play hardly any
part in the history of the Argonauts; indeed, they had gone back
to their father's country earlier. Even according to the poet
Apollonios, whom we have followed thus far, when they

introduced Jason with two of his company into the palace of
Aietes, they rather irritated that son of Helios than soothed
him. He is said to have learned from his father[788] that danger
threatened him from his own kin, but he harboured no suspicion of either his own son Apsyrtos, whom the Kolchians
called also by the solar name Phaethon,[789] nor his daughter
Medeia, but only against the sons of Phrixos and Chalkiope,
who now arrived with the strange warriors. Also, it is probable
that in the older accounts Aietes had not two daughters,
Chalkiope, 'bronze-face', and Medeia, 'well-counselled', but
only the latter, whom his wife Eidyia, 'the knowing one'[790]
—or, to give her another lunar name, Neaira, 'the new'[791]—
had borne him. In all accounts, the lord of Aia was suspicious
and ill-tempered, while his daughter Medeia, full of helpful
and harmful magic, yet herself enchanted by the love for
Jason, had a beautiful countenance though quick to darken.

In the oldest account, Jason came without an intermediary
before the king of the land of Aia, and claimed the return of
the Golden Fleece for his kin. Probably also the Argo did not
remain hidden in the reeds of the Phasis as she does in
Apollonios. The youth, so the well-known account tells us,[792]
who shone like Sirius, glimpsed the princess through the silver
veil which covered her.[793] The king's reply was to send the
hero into the jaws of the gigantic serpent which watched the
Golden Fleece. We also hear that the Fleece hung, in a thicket,
from the mouth of the dragon, which could easily swallow
such a ship as the Argo whole, with all her fifty oarsmen.[794]
This dense thicket was called the Grove of Ares, and that, in
all stories, exactly as in the Theban tale of Kadmos and
Harmonia, means a place of death, a precinct of Hades. And
the Fleece, if it did not hang from the mouth of the monster,
was hung, spread out on the branches, from the top of an
oak[795] that was guarded by the serpent, or, as vase-paintings
show it, it lay on a rock around which the dragon was coiled.

It is from a vase-painter again that we learn how Jason
returned from the jaws of the gigantic snake. He was in the

63 MEDEIA'S REJUVENATING MAGIC

64 ORPHEUS AMONG THE THRACIANS

65 THE DEATH OF ORPHEUS

same state as Herakles when he emerged from the Nemean lion's den, as indeed it was natural for a mortal to be whenever the underworld gave one back to the world of the living. He hung fainting from the dragon's mouth. The Fleece can be seen on the tree, and the presence of the goddess Athene with her owl testifies that the hero after all is not dead. Lifeless from exhaustion he came back from the belly of the monster and needed a rescuer who should awaken him from the drunken swoon of death. In this painting it is Athene who does this; elsewhere it is Medeia, who is seen on vase-paintings following the hero with her magic herbs. The hardest point for the later narrators was the death apparently, and in a sense really, undergone by Jason, through which he won the Golden Fleece.

They preferred to say that Jason had three trials assigned him by Aietes,[796] and that with the help of Medeia he succeeded in all three.[797] Even in this later form of the story, the slaying of the dragon must originally have taken the first place. The second test was a contest in ploughing with Aietes, and this finally was actually moved up to the first place. Hephaistos had presented to the son of Helios two bulls with bronze hooves and bronze mouths, from which they snorted fire, and a plough of steel, all made in one piece.[798] With this Aietes was able to plough a deep furrow, and Jason was now required to do the same. He threw off his clothing;[799] his limbs were protected against the fire by an ointment which Medeia had given him. Thus he forced the marvellous beasts under the yoke and ploughed the furrow assigned to him.

To this test yet another was added.[800] After the ploughing-match, the hero must undertake to sow the teeth of the slain dragon and kill the gigantic warriors who sprang up from them. Those who relegated Jason's killing of the dragon to the third place declared[801] that Pallas Athene had kept back half the teeth from Kadmos' sowing in Thebes and given them to Aietes for this purpose. Thus there was nothing left for Jason too, but to imitate Kadmos further[802] by throwing a great stone among the earth-born men, who thereupon began to slaughter one another. The rest he did himself with the Argonauts.

But in all these accounts—in the old ones, which are full of meaning, and where Jason won the Golden Fleece from the darkness of death, from the belly of the serpent, and in the later, idle inventions which told of the trials—the exploits would have been in vain if the heroes had not succeeded in escaping the vigilance of Aietes, who wished to annihilate them. The dark son of Helios and his dwelling were like Hades and his house. In one of the older versions it is stated[803] that the Golden Fleece lay in the house of Aietes. After Jason had succeeded in the trial (in this case it was probably only the ploughing-match), the king invited the Argonauts to a banquet. He intended to set the Argo on fire as the heroes were feasting. But when it had nearly come to that, Aphrodite aroused in Aietes a longing for the love of his wife Eurylyte.[804] The king lay at the queen's side, the prophet Idmon called to the Argonauts to flee, and the trample of their feet was the signal for Medeia, who also rose and fled with Jason.

The poet Apollonios describes this otherwise.[805] Medeia rose while Aietes, after the two trials which Jason had passed —the ploughing-match and the killing of the giants who grew out of the ground—was taking counsel with his men how they might destroy the Argonauts. The Titaness of night,[806] the moon-goddess, saw the princess hurrying through the night as though it were herself; her double, Medeia,[807] called Jason to her from the Argo, and they entered the holy Grove of Ares, where the gigantic snake guarded the Fleece. With the branch of a freshly cut juniper, which she had previously dipped in a magical preparation, Medeia, singing, sprinkled the eyes of the dragon. The monster fell asleep and Jason took the Fleece from the oak. According to this version he did not kill the serpent but merely departed, looking behind him, till the maid rejoined him. As a virgin in her bower tries to catch the light of the rising full moon in her thin night-attire and is pleased with it, so Jason now was joyous as he lifted the great Golden

Fleece on high, the sheen of which was reflected from his head.[808] According to an older account,[809] they made love to each other at once, on the bank of the Phasis, but in the well-known later poetry Medeia followed the Argonauts for some time time yet as the virgin bride of Jason, until their wedding was celebrated on the island of the Phaiakians.

More than once Apollonios portrays for us Medeia's visit to Hekate. She was the expert priestess of the nocturnal goddess, who ruled over the entrance to the underworld; nay more, who in her secret identity with Persephone, under the name of night-wandering Brimo, the infernal, the lady of the dead,[810] governed the realm of the dead itself. Some genealogists[811] declared that Hekate was the mother of both the sorceresses: Kirke, who was supposedly the sister of Aietes, and Medeia. The latter had spoken to Jason for the first time in the temple of Hekate,[812] where she took the ointment from her breast-band[813] and handed it to the hero, so that he should be pro-tected against the fire of the bulls. It was the 'Promethean ointment',[814] the juice of the flower which sprang up in the glens of the Caucasus from the blood of the tormented Titan; a cubit high, in hue like the Corycian saffron, but with a flesh-coloured root. The earth roared and shook when it was cut from the ground. The second time[815] that Medeia made sacrifice to Hekate was at the mouth of the Halys in Paphla-gonia, on the third day of her flight with Jason. The poet does not venture to describe the gruesome rite.

Others have described the horrible act[816] which Medeia committed to check Aietes and the Kolchians from pursuit. This terrible deed was comparable to the action of Tantalos, or the rending of the infant Dionysos, son of Persephone, by the Titans,[817] save that here the intention was not that the limbs should serve as food but that they should be collected. It has already been said that Medeia had a brother by the name of Apsyrtos or Phaethon.[818] His mother was called Astero-deia,[819] 'she of the starry path', a name for the moon-goddess.[820] According to the older narrators,[821] Apsyrtos was a small child, perhaps like the stars which are always fading away in the sky. Medeia lifted him from his cradle and took him on board the Argo with her. It was also alleged[822] that she murdered her brother before leaving home, in the palace of Aietes, and did not wait till they were under way and the pursuit had begun. For that was the purpose here of the sacrifice of the child; he was cut in pieces and his limbs strewn before the feet of the pursuers, or cast into the Phasis. By the time Aietes had picked them up and fitted them together, the Argonauts were out of reach.

To Apollonios, Apsyrtos was the full-grown son of Aietes. As the Argo was crossing the Black Sea from the mouth of the Halys and running into the mouth of the Istros (the Danube, of which it was believed that it had an additional mouth, leading into the Adriatic), Apsyrtos is represented as getting ahead of the heroes by another branch of the river. A tale was told of an island of the Istros in the Ionian Sea, the extension of the Adriatic, which had a temple of Artemis.[823] By this was meant probably that sanctuary of the goddess in Istria which Herakles allegedly reached in pursuit of the hind of Keryneia. Here the Argonauts found themselves surrounded by an army of Kolchians, whose commander was Apsyrtos. Another Kolchian fleet was rounding Greece and coming up from the other side of the Ionian Sea. Medeia was to be left to her fate in the temple of Artemis and the company of heroes to proceed unmolested with the Golden Fleece; that was the compact with which Medeia cajoled her brother into the ambush. Jason slaughtered him like a bull close by the temple.[824] The Kol-chian army dispersed, and the Argo again ran into a Greek sea, the Ionian, from the Adriatic, laden not only with the Golden Fleece, but with a blood-polluted pair. She was passing 'Black Kerkyra', the island now known as Korčula, seriously endangered by carrying the two sinners,[825] when the ship herself raised her voice,[826] and warned the heroes to make for the dwelling of the sorceress Kirke, who could purify Jason and Medeia from the murder of Apsyrtos.

The Argonauts therefore chose a course northwards around the Apennine peninsula, which was believed to be an island, bounded to the north by two mighty rivers, Eridanos, the Po, and Rhodanos, the Rhone. The heroes sailed up one stream until they got into the other, of which it was told that besides the Eridanos it had two further arms, running one of them into Okeanos and the other into the Tyrrhenian Sea.[827] They nearly missed the Tyrrhenian arm, but in Apollonios' narrative Hera stood by them at that moment. Kirke, in this tale, did not live in the east, but in the west; to be precise, where Monte Circeo rises, nowadays no longer on an island but on a peninsula of the Tyrrhenian coast. She knew her niece by the golden sheen of her eyes, a peculiarity of all children and grandchildren of the Sun-god,[828] and she cleansed the pair,[829] holding a new-born pig over them both and praying to Zeus the god who purifies, her hands dripping with the beast's blood. But then Kirke bade Medeia depart from her house, because she had betrayed her father.[830]

The Argonauts, except Jason, had not entered Kirke's dwelling, and they were able to pass the Sirens' rocks because Orpheus drowned their baleful singing with a cheerful strain. Between Skylla and Charybdis and between the Planktai, which this version distinguishes from the Symplegades, the 'Dark-blue Rocks' on the Bosporus, Thetis with the Nereids helped the Argo to pass.[831] The heroes saw the cattle of Helios and heard their lowing on Trinakria,[832] and, quickly leaving Sicily behind them, soon landed on the island of the Phaia-kians.[833] Its name Makris or Drepane, 'the reaping-hook', denotes Corfu. Immediately after the Argonauts, the Kol-chians' other force also arrived there and demanded of King Alkinoos the surrender of Medeia, who had begged protection of Queen Arete; that is how the story in this late form is fitted on to the adventures of Odysseus, which were to take place there later in the sequence of the stories of the heroes.

It is said that then[834] Alkinoos had decided to give the Kolchian princess back to her father only if she was not yet

Jason's wife. Arete learned of this decision in a conversation with the king at night, and secretly passed it on to the Argo-nauts. In that same night they celebrated the wedding, in the cave of Makris, the nymph of the island. There the bed was made ready and the great Fleece spread out upon it.[835] Hera, who loved Jason, willed the marriage and as marriage-goddess was in future to protect Medeia; she sent a whole choir of nymphs to the wedding, with bright-coloured flowers in their white bosoms. The sheen of the Golden Fleece, which shone about them also, inflamed the fire of longing in their eyes, but they were ashamed to let their hands touch it. The heroes, garlanded, sang the nuptial song to the tones of Orpheus' lyre. Medeia and Jason must imagine that their marriage was being consummated not in a cave but at home in Iolkos in Aison's palace, as indeed it should have been.

But they were still far from arriving in Jason's native land. Storms drove the Argo from Drepane in nine days and nights[836] to Libya, to the shallow, dangerous Syrtis, where there was nothing left for them but to disembark and travel through the desert. There, in the heat of noonday, three ghost-like divine women,[837] the daughters of Libye,[838] appeared to Jason and advised him to recompense the benefit of their mother, who had borne their heavy weight in her own body, by doing her a like service. Thus it happened[839] that the heroes took the Argo on their shoulders and carried the ship for twelve days and nights through the desert. During this time they suffered terribly from the torments of thirst, and when at last they laid down their burden on the surface of Lake Tritonis, they hurried to find a spring. Thus the Argonauts reached the holy ground[840] where, up to the previous day, the serpent Ladon had guarded the apples of the Hesperides; for Herakles had come there and killed the dragon but one day earlier. He had taken the apples with him. Before the eyes of the heroes, the mourning Hesperides were transformed into three trees, but they could also change back again, and they showed them the spring,[841] which Herakles had caused to rise from the ground with a blow of his foot.[842] The men were too late to catch up with the son of Zeus; only Lynkeus fancied that he could catch a glimpse of him in the extreme distance, striding through the country.[843]

They would also have failed to find the way out from lake Tritonis to the open sea if the Triton had not met them, first in human shape,[844] then as a god with the tail of a sea-creature. In his human form he presented the Argonauts with a clod of earth, which the hero Euphemos, son of Poseidon, thankfully accepted. In his own shape he then guided and pushed the Argo into the sea. The heroes were able to land in Crete only after Medeia had with her magic overthrown Talos, the man of bronze,[845] who walked around the great island three times a day. With a hostile gaze she bewitched the eyes of the giant;[846] he accidentally grazed his ankle on a sharp stone at the spot where his vulnerable vein lay concealed, and fell bleeding with a great crash to the ground. Then the Argonauts, as they had previously built altars to Poseidon and to his son Triton,[847] now erected a shrine to the Minoan Athene.[848]

Finally, in the dead of night, they reached the Greek islands, which they once had quitted by the Hades gate of the 'Dark-blue Rocks' on their way through the Hellespont and the Bosporus. That night was so dark, so ugly and black, that the Argonauts no longer knew if they were sailing through Hades or over the waters.[849] Jason extended his arms and called with a loud voice on Phoibos; then the god appeared again on a lonely island, as he had done before when the heroes had forced their way through the 'Dark-blue Rocks'. At his former epiphany, on the island of Thyias, Apollo's silver bow had shone in his left hand;[850] now he held the golden bow on high in his right[851] and stood on one of the two Melantian Rocks, which allegedly were not so named until later, after a man called Melas, 'the black'.[852] In the splendour of the god the Argonauts caught sight of a tiny islet, and as they were landing on it, the light of dawn arose. They built an altar in a shady grove on the island and forthwith gave Apollo the

added name of Aigletes after the splendour, *aigle*, in which he
had appeared; they called the island itself Anaphe, a name
which for Greek ears contained the word for lighting a fire,
anapto. A festival of Apollo Aigletes was straightway held.[853]

When the heroes were leaving Anaphe after the festival,
Euphemos remembered a dream he had had that same night,
and told it to Jason. He had dreamed of the clod[854] which he
still kept as the Triton's gift. In the dream, he was holding it
to his breast and it appeared to him that the clod was quite
saturated in his milk; but then it turned into a maiden and he
had union with her. He was sorry for what he had done, since
he had himself suckled the girl, but the young woman com-
forted him and introduced herself as a daughter of the Triton
and the goddess Libye. He was to make her the companion of
the Nereids, so that she could live in the sea near Anaphe and
soon after rise into the sunlight again as a dwelling-place for
his descendants. By Jason's advice, Euphemos threw the clod
into the sea, and then there arose from the depths the island
Kalliste, 'most beautiful', which was later known as Thera,
'the hunting-ground', and inhabited by a clan which descended
from Euphemos.

That was the tale told by the inhabitants of Thera, the
modern Santorin. The Aiginetans also had a story of the
landing of the Argonauts on their island;[855] so as not to miss a
favourable wind, they had made a race of carrying water to the
Argo and thus founded the festival of the Hydrophoria.[856] But
the great tale of Jason and Medeia, which was no longer also
the story of the Argonauts, for that ended with the arrival of the
Argo in the Gulf of Pagasai, was to take a new turn in Iolkos.
We now see the common element and the difference between
the fortunes of Jason and those of Theseus. Both heroes forced
their way into a region of the underworld, Jason into the jaws
of the serpent of Aia, Theseus into the Labyrinth; each found
a gracious helper in a divine maiden of that region, Theseus in
Ariadne, the 'Lady of the Labyrinth', who betrayed her father
for his sake and gave over her brother to death, Jason in Medeia

who did the like. Ariadne too entered upon the road to the hero's native world, but she was brought back. Medeia, who like her was at home yonder in the world beyond ours, and belonged to the family of Helios, made her entrance with Jason into his home, and the people now were soon able to discover the power of a lady of the other world.

It was told of her that she could bring about rebirth and rejuvenation by killing and cutting in pieces, the sort of thing that it was alleged Dionysos had undergone at the hands of the Titans.[857] It was a gloomy performance, belonging to the underworld, which was undertaken in cult with a sacrificial victim, probably openly in early days, secretly later. Medeia had already sacrificed her brother in this fashion, but it must have appeared even more gruesome when the pieces of the butchered victim, who represented the god, were boiled in a cauldron according to an elaborate ritual.[858] Still, there was no doubt consolation in being told that the Sun himself entered a cauldron every evening (the poets sometimes called it a golden goblet), travelled in it over Okeanos in the night and emerged from it rejuvenated in the morning.[859] We know the story of how Helios let Herakles have the use of his cauldron for the journey to Geryoneus. The tales of Medeia's magic cauldron connect with the series of reminiscences of such a vessel, a sacrificial one in cult, but for the narrators a wonderful vessel, out of which Pelops once leaped alive, and before him assuredly some divine child.[860]

When Jason and the Argonauts arrived in Iolkos, his father Aison was grown so old that he could not even take part in the great feast with which the people and the other fathers and mothers welcomed the heroes.[861] That, they say, was the first time that Medeia showed her art, with which, according to poets and other narrators, she later rejuvenated Jason also.[862] It is possible that Pelias was already dead by the time the heroes arrived, and his son Akastos, who had made the journey with Jason, came just in time to institute the funeral games which were such a favourite subject for art[863] and for song;[864] the

Argonauts too took part in them then, before they dispersed. But it was also said that Pelias was still alive, though now an old man, in need of rejuvenation. Towards him Medeia showed a different countenance, for it was out of the question for Pelias, after having driven Aison, his wife and a younger brother of Jason to death, as this version had it,[865] now to get the Golden Fleece. Also, according to the oracle concerning the man with the one sandal, it was bound to transpire that Jason and Medeia were bringing destruction for Pelias.[866] The foreign woman hoodwinked the king's daughters into undertaking the sorcery which should make their father young again. Of Pelias' daughters (they numbered five in one account),[867] only Alkestis refused any credence to Medeia, and according to artmonuments also she alone turned away from the deed. But the other four, or perhaps there were only two,[868] let themselves be deceived into doing it, after the sorceress had first cut up an old ram, boiled the pieces in a cauldron, and made a lamb leap out of the vessel. They cut their father in pieces and boiled him, but he never came to life again.

After this act of vengeance Jason left the kingship of Iolkos to Akastos and set off with his wife to the place where the Sun's granddaughter herself had an ancestral home in Greece, where she was queen and could share her throne with her husband.[869] Corinth, of all the cities of the mainland, was part of Helios' possessions. The Corinthians honoured him, the Sungod, as the highest among all gods. His sacred place was the towering summit of the Akrokorinthos,[870] which the god handed over to the goddess Aphrodite.[871] His wife bore the name of Antiope, like the mother of the Theban Dioskuroi who elsewhere is the reputed bride of Zeus. She had borne Aietes to Helios,[872] also Aloeus, who was hardly to be distinguished from the father of the Aloadai[873] and received the land below on the river Asopos as the Sungod's gift. Aietes got Corinth as his share of the division; his governor was named Bunos after an elevation on the Akrokorinthos. On that height, but not so high as the temple of Aphrodite Urania,

stood the temple of Hera Akraia,[874] or, to give her her Corinthian title, Bunia.[875] Thither the Corinthians used to send
for the service of the temple as many children as the Athenians
sent to the Labyrinth at Knossos, seven boys and seven girls,[876]
who must spend a whole year in the shrine, as if they were in
banishment or death. They were mourned for and offerings
were made them as if they were wrathful chthonian gods.

It was indeed said of Medeia that she founded the temple of
Aphrodite on the highest point.[877] But her temple there was
the temple of Hera, as in Aia it was that of Hekate. It was
alleged[878] that Zeus desired to be her husband, but as she
remained faithful to Hera, the goddess promised her children
immortality. In this immortality the sons and daughters of the
Corinthians participated in the shrine of Hera. If, according
to the wellknown tale, the children of Medeia must nevertheless die and the seven boys and seven girls had to undergo
death in their stead in a modified form, the responsibility for
that probably rested simply on the course of the lunar month,
of which fourteen days were consecrated to the waxing and
then to the waning. As soon as Medeia bore a child—so ran a
version which allotted part of the blame to her—she sent
it to the shrine of Hera, and she kept them all hidden, in hopes
that they would become immortal.[879] What she did with the
children there we are not told, but only that she made a fatal
error and Jason caught her at her unnamed procedure—a thing
which happened also to Demeter when she wished to make
Demophoon immortal at Eleusis,[880] and to Thetis, when she
tried the same experiment on the child Achilles.[881] Jason did
not understand Medeia's exculpation, would not forgive her,
and went back to Iolkos. Medeia, too, thereupon left Corinth,
and according to other, later, stories Sisyphos, whom she loved,
received the kingdom from her.[882]

It was also alleged[883] that it was the Corinthians who could
not bear the rule of the foreign sorceress and murdered her
seven sons and seven daughters. Or it was the relatives of King
Kreon, the second in succession from Bellerophontes,[884] who

did this by way of revenge, because Medeia had killed the king. They also put about the rumour that she was the murderess of her own children. That must have been an old form of the tale of the apparent death of the fourteen. It was a trait belonging to that other face of Medeia which she had already shown, in the course of these stories, to Aietes and Apsyrtos, Pelias and his daughters, and which Euripides made known to all the world in his tragedy 'Medeia'. In his hands, Medeia, wronged in her love and in her dignity as queen and wife, Medeia the representative of Hera the goddess, appeared on the stage as a mortal woman,[885] bearer of the common lot of womankind,[886] and of the greatest injustice and ingratitude that ever fell to the share of any deliverer.[887]

The Corinthians had a legend concerning the fountain Glauke, which springs from an immense cube of rock, not far from the market place of their city. According to it the nymph of this name was once a princess who had cast herself into that water to be rid of the torments that Medeia's gift had brought her; for it was for her that Jason deserted the daughter of Aietes in Corinth. Thereupon the sorceress in her anger sent to his new wife the gift which destroyed her. The carriers of it were the two sons whom she had borne to Jason, Mermeros and Pheres. In this tale they were stoned to death by the Corinthians. There were monuments to them near the fountain. But Euripides insists that they died at their mother's hands, and tells us also of greater insults than the choice of a second wife and the repudiating of Medeia.[888]

According to him, Kreon, the bride's father—this royal name, 'ruler', was always and everywhere at the service of poets and other narrators—banished the Kolchian woman from the country. With this, the cup of her humiliation was full.[889] Jason appeared beside her, not as a co-regent alongside a queen of the blood of the Sun, but as a truckling refugee, who wished to turn to advantage his marriage to the king's daughter.[890] At this point there appeared suddenly a real king, Aigeus of Athens, still childless and on his way from Delphi to Pittheus at Troizen.[891] And with him also appeared the promise of a new home,[892] the earthly land of gods, Attica,[893] for Medeia. Nothing now could contain the savagery of the royal lady from Aia, land of a Titaness.[894] Jason should become childless. She guilefully besought him for permission to send gifts to the bride by her children.[895] The two fair-haired boys[896] presented the bewitched robe and golden diadem, by which the princess and her father were burned, and they were afterwards butchered by their own mother, so that their father Jason might, as he deserved, be also smitten by the annihilating doom.

The murderess appeared with the corpses of the boys on the chariot which Father Helios gave her:[897] a car drawn by dragons, like that of Triptolemos, who rose from the realm of Persephone on it. But Medeia's chariot, as vase-paintings show us, was drawn by yet more formidable serpents. On one painting a daimon from the underworld, named Oistros, 'rage of madness' conducts it; he has serpents in his hair. Medeia took the dead children with her into the sacred precinct of Hera Akraia, and buried them there with her own hands, so that in the future they should share in the mystic worship.[898] To Jason she foretold the death which was to overtake him in the place where he had dedicated the Argo to the goddess. This is said to have occurred on the Isthmus, in the sanctuary of Poseidon.[899] There the hero lay down in the shadow of the decaying ship and was struck by a plank from her;[900] or he was struck down in the temple of Hera, where the Argo's figurehead had been dedicated to the goddess.

Medeia was immortal.[901] She lived with Aigeus until Theseus came and took over the power of the king of Athens. This she could not prevent. To Aigeus she bore Medos,[902] and, it is said, fled with this her son to the Orient, where she became through him the eponym of the Medes. These and similar tales, which would take us far from Greece, were readily attached to the older tales, which told of another and final arrival of the Sun's granddaughter. In Elysion,[903] or, if we prefer to use the other name of the place where Kadmos and Harmonia also lived forever, on the Islands of the Blessed,[904] Medeia was married for ever to Achilles. Sanctuaries were erected to Jason in places which it was supposed the Argonauts had reached, even in Armenia and Media.[905] But in Greece his fame had to give way to that of the younger hero, just named, who at that time was still being nurtured in Chiron's cave by the nymphs.[906]

CHAPTER III

Orpheus and Eurydike

WITHOUT ORPHEUS, the wonderful singer and lyre-player, we could not now imagine the Argo. Ancient artists already show him as one of the Argonauts. He, if anyone, could be useful to their company, which wished to make its way into the other world. The very thing for which Orpheus was famous was that he had been capable of undertaking the dangerous journey into the underworld quite alone. He was not the first of whom it was said, in the tales of gods and heroes, that he had performed miracles with his singing and lyre-playing (the two made up but one art). We know that Hermes invented the lyre and was the first to sing to its strains.[907] Among the gods, he presented the lyre to his brother Apollo; among the heroes, to another brother, who later quarrelled with Apollo, Amphion. When we are told concerning Orpheus that the endless flocks of birds flew about over his head as he sang, and the fish leaped high from the dark-blue sea to meet him, we know that this was the effect of his song.[908] We see him, lyre in hand, travelling on the Argo. But when we also are told that his song set stones and trees in motion,[909] we remember the walls of Thebes, which Amphion's lyre raised. The deed which only Orpheus accomplished was that he subdued everything wild, even the savage powers of the under-world, by his song, and made his way to Persephone. That puts him alongside of Perseus and Herakles, Theseus and Jason in the ranks of the Greek heroes.

His worship was maintained by a great community which believed itself to be in possession of books containing revela-tions of Orpheus, accounts of his journey to the underworld and all that he had learned there and afterwards taught and originated. In the popular mind he was more closely linked to the community of his disciples and adherents than with any particular race or family. Apart from them, his legends, and also the sites of his worship, connected him especially with the region of Olympos and not till later with districts which lay further north. By all accounts he was the son of a Muse, and according to most,[910] of Kalliope. To his son[911] and disciple[912] was given the name Musaios; or a certain Musaios, 'the Muses' man' was made out to be the son of him who had been entitled to the same name. And being 'musical', he surely was originally Apolline.[913] Apollo could be regarded as his divine father,[914] whereby his fundamental Apolline nature was doubly emphasised, through his mother and through his father. But those who claimed to know more of his descent and birth called his father Oiagros.[915] Whether a river north of Olympos had that name,[916] as, for instance, Marsyas was the name of a river and also of a wild inhabitant of the woods who competed with Apollo, need not concern us. Oiagros means 'lonely hunter', 'one who hunts all alone'. Orpheus grew up in Pieria,[917] the country of the Olympian Muses. Apollo is said to have been his teacher;[918] the god gave him lessons on that lyre which Hermes had given him and he presented to Orpheus. In the wooded glens of Olympos[919] the young man first gathered about him by the music of his lyre and his song the trees and the wild beasts. The son of Kalliope showed him-self there as a double of Apollo, the god to whose music wild creatures, lynx and lion and stag, yielded as he guarded the herds of Admetos.[920] If the name of the singer were not expressly named or written alongside the pictures which show Orpheus playing his lyre, we should not always know which of the two is meant by the scene depicted.

For most narrators the savage land of Thrace began there, on the slopes of Olympos, although Pieria was still on the Macedonian side of the border. They sang[921] of a Thracian Pieria and made Orpheus a king there, alleging that the trees had followed him thither from the real Pieria; they dubbed him a Thracian. The later vase-painters believed them, where-as the earlier ones still held to the true account, without which the legends of Orpheus and the hero himself would lack all meaning. He is represented as a Hellene among the Thracians, and his name is not at all foreign. 'Orpheus' would be pronounced differently on Thracian lips. True, it is not so readily intelligible as Oiagros, which also cannot be the name of a Thracian in his own tongue. But perhaps it was not out of place and not without object when a late disciple of the singer described the sombre garment in which Orpheus made sacrifice to Hekate on behalf of the Argonauts with a word[922] derived from *orphne*, 'darkness'. Orpheus was connected with darkness, both in his journey to the underworld and also later, when he communicated his initiations at night, as was proper.

Longing for Eurydike led the Muse's son into the other world. In this he was different from Theseus and Jason, not to speak of Perseus and Herakles, who made their journeys for love of no woman, mortal or divine. Orpheus, however, shared the fate of Theseus to this extent, that Eurydike might not, any more than Ariadne, become the lasting possession of her beloved nor follow him to his home. It is indeed said of her that she had been the singer's wife, but Orpheus, like Theseus in Dionysos, had had a divine rival, and to that rival was due Eurydike's early association with the realm of the dead.

To go by her names—for the heroine of this famous tale has two names given her by tradition, even as Ariadne was also known as Aridela—she might even have been the queen of the other world. 'Eurydike' means 'wide-ruling', a name which originally belonged to the queen of the underworld only, however many distinguished women bore it later among mortals. We can no longer be sure of her other name; it may have been either Agriope, 'wild-faced',[923] or Argiope 'bright-faced', like the mother of the singer Thamyris.[924] In favour of Argiope, later disciples of Orpheus,[925] who otherwise held that Musaios was the son of their master, made Selene the moon-goddess his mother. It seems that the beloved wife of Orpheus resembled the moon in the opinion of the narrators, even when they knew

her as a victim, not as the queen, of the underworld. Persephone, it is true, was victim and queen in one, having been
abducted by Hades, and to her Orpheus descended, into the
house of her husband, impelled by love of Eurydike.

The tale as it is told us[926] began in Thessaly, where a faithful
wife, Alkestis, king Admetos' queen, had already been rescued
from the claws of Death. We know of Herakles' adventure on
his way to Diomedes the Thracian. As Apollo had done
earlier in Admetos' household,[927] so Aristaios was living the
life of a herdsman in the beautiful valley of Tempe under
Olympos; the nymph Kyrene had borne him to the son of
Leto, to be a little Zeus, a second holy Apollo.[928] Aristaios'
greatest pride was notoriously his bees. His name signified
that he was 'the best' that the world has to show. The 'honeyed'
Zeus of the dead, Zeus Meilichios, who was accustomed to
receive the worship of the living in serpent-form, was of course
no other than Aristaios, although no legend specifically
mentions his bees. This divine bee-keeper lay in wait for the
newly-married[929] Eurydike; she fled from him and in that
flight she met her end, for a snake had bitten her on the
ankle.[930] Her companions the Dryads mourned her in the
mountains, far into Thrace.[931] When Orpheus ran up, his
young wife had already been carried off by Hades. He
journeyed after her with doleful singing, all through Greece
to the southernmost point of the Peloponnesos, Tainaron.

Putting his trust in his lyre,[932] he entered upon the gloomy
road to the realm of the dead,[933] on which but few living men
had preceded him—the two friends Theseus and Peirithoos, and
Herakles when he brought Kerberos up. Charon remembered
them only too well,[934] but the lyre had its way even with him.
It is said[935] that he quitted his boat and followed Orpheus as
he sang, to listen to the wonderful song which he gave before
the lord and lady of the lower regions. While Orpheus sang,
Kerberos did not bark, Ixion's wheel stood still, Tityos' liver
was not torn, the daughters of Danaos ceased their fruitless
water-carrying, Sisyphos sat down on his stone, Tantalos

forgot hunger and thirst, the Erinyes were awe-struck and the judges of the dead wept.[936] The numberless throng of the ghosts which had gathered about Orpheus wept also; but Eurydike was not yet there, for she was still one of the newly arrived phantoms, and came slowly up with her bitten ankle.[937] The painting of a master from Magna Graecia, where the vases in graves often have scenes from the underworld, shows her brought by love in the form of a flying Eros. Persephone also is to be seen, softened by the singing and summoning Eurydike with a gracious gesture. The singer stands between the two; he already holds the hand of his beloved, but in none of these pictures is he looking at anyone.

That was the law of the infernal powers; no one must look at them. Sacrifice to the deities of the dead was made with averted face; no looking, only the voice, was allowed in the realm of the departed. That could work miracles, but had no power to undo death, to effect release from the gods of that other realm. The law of those below was the law of Persephone,[938] and was only confirmed when the living strove against it. Only when it was violated did the law take its course. Eurydike might follow her loving husband; that much Orpheus had accomplished with his singing, but on the hard road which led from death into life, he must not look upon her. Then why did the singer do so? What was the reason, except the great and final separation between the living and the dead? Was it madness?[939] Did he wish to kiss her?[940] Or was he only anxious to make sure she was following him?[941] The scene is represented on a much admired Attic relief on which there are now not two figures but three; Orpheus is turning around and looking at Eurydike, whose left hand lightly touches his shoulder in loving farewell, but her right is already caught by Hermes the Guide of Souls. As it was told that Zeus thundered on the disappearance of Oidipus at·the threshold of the under-world, so it was said there came also a peal of thunder thrice repeated, the sound of inexorable destiny, when Eurydike was recalled to the realm of the dead.[942]

In vain did Orpheus try to run after her when she disappeared to return to the underworld. Charon would no
longer ferry him over.[943] The analogies drawn in antiquity[944]
between Orpheus and Dionysus were over-presumptuous. The
god brought up his mother Semele from Hades, but what he
could do, Orpheus could not. Yet the shadow which from
then on fell over his Apolline nature was Dionysiac. Orpheus
did not belong to the one god more than to the other. Nevertheless he did not become the opponent or the victim of
Dionysos, but the opponent and victim of the Thracian
women's wild excesses, the exaggerated outcome of their
worship of the wine-god. Seven months long, it is said, he
lived in a cave under a huge rock at the mouth of the Macedonian river Strymon,[945] having first, as others add,[946] endured
for seven days by the river of the underworld without tasting
a morsel. He kept away from women and would enter
upon no second marriage.[947] At this time the wild dwellers
in the woods came to him,[948] men of Thrace, as vase-paintings
show us; or satyrs, older and younger boys, as a later bas-relief
records. They were not the very young boys, not yet old enough
for the higher initiations, but adolescents. Orpheus refrained
from the eating of flesh, according to the 'Orphic way of life',
sang to them of the beginning of things and of the gods, and
caused them to take part in the initiations which he had
brought back from his visit to the queen of the underworld.
Later it was told[949] that Zeus smote him with his thunderbolt
because he taught men through the Mysteries.

But the older account ran thus: it was the women of Thrace
who took it ill that Orpheus had kept away from the love of
women for three whole years.[950] He was accustomed to seek
the company only of youths, and it was said of him[951] that he
had introduced homoerotic passion into Thrace. He was all
the more like Apollo for that very reason, that it was young
men who surrounded him and not women, as they did
Dionysos. In his tragedy 'The Bassarai', the Thracian name of
the Bacchantes, Aeschylus made him wake up in the night and

climb Mount Pangaion to adore Apollo in the rising sun.[952] Thither also the Thracian maenads were driven by their god[953] at their nocturnal festivals of Dionysos in hurrying throngs. They could hardly have known the secret which Aeschylus seems to have revealed in another tragedy of the same trilogy, the 'Young Men', in which he made his chorus invoke Apollo himself as Kisseus and Bakcheus, that is 'ivy-garlanded' and 'Bacchant'.[954] And perhaps in the poet's opinion Orpheus went too far in a one-sided worship after his return from the realm of the dead and the beginning of his grudge against the gods of the underworld, among whom Dionysos held sway as Hades and subterranean Zeus. As he wandered over Mount Pangaion, the singer fell in with the secret ceremony of the Thracian Bacchantes.[955] They recognised him indeed—it was no fit of madness as with the women of Thebes who mistook Pentheus for a lion—and they tore the son of the Muse limb from limb.

One narrator,[956] on the other hand, knew of a great hall of initiation instituted for secret ritual in the city of Libethra in Macedonia, probably like that one which has been excavated on Samothrace. Thither on a certain day the men of Thrace and Macedonia came to Orpheus. They were accustomed to lay down their arms before the doors. The angry women snatched up the weapons, killed the men who fell into their hands, and flung the dismembered body of the priest of the initiation, Orpheus, limb by limb into the sea. According to this version Orpheus' head floated into the mouth of the river Meles at Smyrna, where subsequently Homer the poet of the Trojan War was said to have been born, being a son of the river-god. There the head was picked up and a hero-shrine of Orpheus, later a temple, built, which no woman was allowed to enter.

According to another tale,[957] Orpheus journeyed all over Thrace, as the Orphic initiators later did in Greece, and the men joined him. At first the women dared not attack him, but then they drew courage from wine, and ever after the Thracians used to go drunken into battle. Vase-paintings show us the drunken women of Thrace attacking the gentle singer with spears, large stones, or anything they could lay their hands on. He has only his lyre, with which, as he falls to the ground, he vainly defends himself. The fragments of his body were strewn in all directions;[958] the Muses are said to have collected them and buried their darling in Libethra. His lyre, which could find no worthy owner after Apollo and Orpheus, was set by Zeus among the constellations as Lyra.

There was a separate story about his head and his lyre.[959] The murderesses cut off Orpheus' head, nailed it to the lyre, and so threw it into the sea, or rather into the Thracian Hebros,[960] in which it floated singing while the lyre went on playing.[961] The current brought the singing head to the sea and the drift of the sea to Lesbos, the island which later was to be the richest in song and in the sweet strains of the lyre. The head was buried in the Bakcheion, the shrine of Dionysos, and the lyre was preserved in the temple of Apollo.[962] That was as it should be, and well-becoming to the Dionysiac fate and the Apolline nature of Orpheus. Much later a tale was told[963] of his oracle on Lesbos, and beautiful vase-paintings and gems testify that young men received revelations from the head of the singer until Apollo himself bade it be silent.[964]

Wherever Orpheus lay buried, nightingales nested on his tomb and sang there, more sweetly and full-throated than they sing elsewhere.[965] There were two graves of Orpheus in Macedonia, at the foot of Olympos: one at Libethra[966] and another at Dion,[967] the City of Zeus, to which the bones must have been transported after the other tomb was laid open by the collapse of its pillars. The pillars and the urn were accidentally knocked over by a great crowd which had come together to hear the marvel with their own ears; a shepherd had gone to sleep at noonday on the tomb and in a dream he sang sweetly and loudly the songs of Orpheus, as if it were his immortal voice sounding from the realm of the dead.[968]

Tereus, Eumolpos and Kephalos

TEREUS, IN THE LEGENDS and on the Attic stage, appears as a genuine Thracian. He was connected to the royal family of the Athenians through his two wives, Prokne and Philomela, just as Eumolpos, another Thracian, was through his mother Chione, or Kephalos through his faithless wife Prokris, beloved of Eos. The stories of these three heroes and their wives bring us back to Attica or its neighbourhood, before we take up the thread of the great events in Thebes and Mycenae once more.

For Tereus allegedly reigned not far from the border of Attica, in Daulis,[969] at the foot of Parnassos. He too, therefore, can hardly have been at home in Thrace itself. Only in a late version[970] do we hear that he came by sea to visit his father-in-law, king Pandion, in Athens. He belonged rather to those Thracians who, like their modern kinsfolk the Albanians, were settled in wild mountainous regions in the middle of Greece, and of whom the Athenians had something to tell in their earliest history. Later, the grave of Tereus was actually shown in Megara,[971] and the story there was that he turned not, as in the usual version, into a hoopoe but into a falcon. It was merely stated that the hoopoe was first seen in that region. The metamorphosis by which the tragical story of the hero was transformed into one of the many tales of birds was perhaps not told everywhere even of him. It was narrated especially of his wives and even before them of the wife of Zethos, a daughter of Pandareos called Aedon, which as we know signifies a nightingale. There is also an ancient picture in which the wives of Tereus too are called, not Prokne and Philomela, but Nightingale and Swallow, Aedon and Chelidon.

Tereus, king of Thrace and son of Ares[972] was given Prokne's hand by Pandion. She was one of the two daughters of the king of Athens, a granddaughter of Erichthonios. Tereus was thus rewarded for the help which he had given in the war against Labdakos king of Thebes. Prokne bore him one son, Itys, who was soon and for ever to be mourned. For not long after, the Thracian came back to Athens to get Prokne's sister Philomela, 'the lover of flocks'—a name which fits a swallow, since it is fond of nesting in byres, but also Hekate the infernal goddess, who is no less fond of byres and cattle.[973]

Indeed, the story of Philomela reminds us of the under-world. Tereus brought to Athens a false report of the death of Prokne,[974] so as to get the other princess as well for his wife. And when he had possession of her, he brought word of her death to Prokne.[975] It was quite untrue; but that was how the fate of Persephone, too, appeared to ill-informed mortals, who did not know that she had become the queen of the under-world. The same thing might have been said of her as of Philomela, that she had suffered violence and was become as dumb as a corpse. Exactly that was told in Italy of a goddess of the lower world,[976] but the other way about; namely, of Lara, who used to chatter like any swallow, but became dumb for ever and had to follow Mercurius, as the Romans called Hermes, into the subterranean grove of the dead. On the way, against her will, she was made mother of the Lares by the Guide of Souls.

Philomela became the victim of the dark king, her sister's husband, in a byre hidden away in the depths of a wood.[977] There Tereus secretly conveyed his sister-in-law, and to prevent her telling of his deed of violence, the barbarian cut out her tongue. In that byre in the primaeval forest she was thenceforth kept prisoner, and Prokne was to suppose her sister dead. But Philomela was skilled in weaving, and in her forest prison she embroidered a garment with pictures of her unhappy story and sent it to Prokne. The queen realised the crime Tereus had committed. It was the time of the nocturnal festival of the wine-god; she ranged through the woods with the Bacchantes and caught up Philomela into the hurrying throng. Now the two sisters treated the child Itys as the daughters of Minyas, when Dionysos brought madness upon them, did a little son;[978] they did not tear but cut the boy in pieces. This they did knowingly and of set purpose, and boiled the pieces in a cauldron. Thus it happened also in the history of Dionysos,[979] not to mention the terrible deeds of Medeia. Prokne invited her husband as to a secret sacral banquet,[980] but it was that banquet of Titans to which Zeus was beguiled into coming,[981] the banquet of Tantalos to which the gods were invited. Tereus ate, and realised what he had devoured only when Philomela threw his son's head at him. Then he drew his sword and pursued both women, and would have killed them but that Zeus turned all three into birds. However, it did not result in an unambiguous tale of metamorphosis, for there was no agreement as to whether Tereus took the form of a falcon or a hoopoe, or whether Philomela, who in the older versions is a swallow, does not mourn for Itys in the shape of a nightingale,[982] as Prokne does according to most accounts.

The Thracian Eumolpos has been named in connection with Erechtheus, Pandion's successor in the list of kings. The leading family of the Eleusinians traced their descent from him; it was that family which on every occasion gave them the chief priest of the Mysteries, the hierophant, or 'revealer of the holy things'. They were the Eumolpidai, originally no doubt all *eumolpoi*, good singers, for they all needed to be able to sing well, seeing that they led the secret ceremonies on the holy nights. *Eumolpos* was not a personal name, but a ceremonial title which the priest of the Mysteries adopted along with his office, during which he had no name,[983] for he cast his old name into the sea,[984] to whose depths the original Eumolpos of Thrace stood in a special relationship, as will appear from his story.

This is almost the same as the history of Tereus, only we do not hear of a tragical outcome, nor have the narrators anything to say of a transformation of Eumolpos into the shape of a bird. However, on a vase-painting of classical date, where he appears as a pendant to his father Poseidon, there is shown at his feet a swan, a singing bird in the belief of the ancients, and to the Athenians a Thracian fowl, whose habitat was the mouth of the Strymon. It is, of course, possible that those who called Eumolpos a Thracian were not thinking of the northern region any more than in the case of Tereus, but of the district of Megara, which borders Eleusis to the south. Stories were told of a Lake Eschatiotis,[985] the 'lake of the uttermost end', which lay beyond the Isthmus, and where many of Eumolpos' Thracian host, with which he helped the Eleusinians against the Athenians, disappeared while bathing.

Eumolpos' mother Chione, 'snow-white', may have originated from this Lake Eschatiotis and the sea between the Isthmus, Salamis and Megara, just as well as from the Thracian Sea in the far north. Through her, the priestly singer was connected with the royal family of Athens. Boreas, the god who reveals himself in the north wind,[986] had carried off Oreithyia, daughter of Erechtheus and niece of Prokne and Philomela, from the Ilissos.[987] Oreithyia, 'she who rages on the hills', a Bacchante like her aunts to judge by her name, bore the wind-god his winged sons Kalais and Zetes, who took part in the voyage of the Argo, and Chione, with whom Poseidon celebrated one of his innumerable marriages.[988] In secret, she bore Eumolpos to the god of the sea, and into the sea she cast her child. It was told how his father took him up and brought him to Ethiopia. Where the baby was reared is revealed by the name of his foster-mother, Benthesikyme, 'she who dwells in the depths of the waves'. There, in the realm of waters, much the same history as that of Tereus took place. Grown to manhood, the boy took to wife a daughter of Benthesikyme, and to her his son Ismaros or Immarados (both names are Thracian) was born, who was to die in the battle against Erechtheus on the side of the Eleusinians.[989] But Eumolpos is said to have ventured to force his attentions upon his wife's sister.[990] Nothing is said of what came of this instance of the marriage of one husband to two wives, of the union of one hero with two heroines, probably two goddesses originally. These events took place in the depths of the sea, in an underworld, which Eumolpos was obliged to leave with his son on account of his audacity. But by the grace of Demeter he was one of the first to be admitted to the Mysteries,[991] which he and his descendants at Eleusis were to make accessible to the initiated.

Prokris, 'the chosen above all', was the name of a daughter of Erechtheus, a sister of Oreithyia, and therefore again a niece of Prokne and Philomela. Of all the women of her royal house she most resembled the moon-goddess. Selene also not only loved Endymion but let herself be seduced by Pan; change is characteristic of the moon. The husband with whom Prokris played tit-for-tat at loving and deceiving was the 'handsome head', Kephalos, from *kephale*, head; an Attic community also had that name. The name and the appearance of the young man we know from the history of the gods.[992] He was even reckoned among the kings of Athens.[993] Thorikos, where he ruled according to most accounts, lay on the east coast of the country, near the southern extremity of the peninsula, and of all harbour-towns in Attica was most directly opposite Crete; more so than even Prasiai, from which they used to voyage to Delos and Naxos and only from there on to Crete. In the mountains inland from it stretched the hunting-grounds of Kephalos and Prokris.

For not only was Kephalos passionately fond of hunting,[994] but Prokris too was a great huntress. She possessed a spear which never missed,[995] also the swift, immortal hound, the story of which has already been told in connection with the fox of Teumessos, in the history of Herakles. The story of her first infidelity is connected with her golden headband. It is said that the hero Pteleon, founder of Ptelea, 'Elmsby', in Attica, seduced her with the gift of this headband. Kephalos caught her making love to the stranger. In another account, Kephalos concealed himself by assuming the shape of the stranger. He left his young wife, making a pretext of his love of hunting,[996] or of pollution from homicide which obliged

him to make her wait untouched for eight years.[997] According
to this version he himself came with the golden ornament in so
beautiful a shape that Prokris no longer recognised him and let
him seduce her. Or he came at night,[998] after sending on
ahead a pandering messenger with much gold, and moved her
to the adventure. Only on the bed of love did he reveal himself
to his deluded wife. Prokris leapt up, ashamed and offended,
and fled to Minos on his great island.

   Thence she came back, after she had helaed the king of
Crete and got from him as her fee the spear and the hound.
The form Minos' sickness took, at least as it is indicated and
described in late accounts, was that he could approach no
woman, for in the embrace creatures poured forth from his
body: snakes, scorpions and millepedes. These late narrators
do not agree either as to whether Pasiphae wished with such
evil magic[999] to prevent her husband's love-affairs or the illness
had some other cause, nor yet as to what remedies Prokris
applied to it. Pasiphae was by no means thought of merely as
an unhappy queen, but also as an immortal goddess. We know
of course what a monster she had borne. Here a mysterious old
Cretan legend survived, associated for better or for worse with
the absence of Prokris from Attica and with sundry magical
arts, such as are proper to moon-like women.

   When Prokris returned to Attica, she was still in love with
Kephalos and jealous of the love-affairs which he might have
had during his long absences, ostensibly at the chase. It was
told[2000] that she now wished to test her husband in her turn,
and under the disguise of a stranger she led the handsome
young man into temptation. According to this story Prokris
did not reveal herself to Kephalos until he yielded to the
temptation. Thus he was put to shame, but afterwards his
loving wife presented him with the spear and the hound.
According to other narrators,[1] Kephalos' hunting-spear, when
Prokris ran after him and hid in some bushes, struck the
jealous huntress accidentally. He thought that his throw was
killing a beast in the thicket. Whether she now died or lived

on—a lunar being could combine both in her own person—
Kephalos was torn from her. We heard in the history of the
gods how Eos, goddess of the dawn, whose jealousy late tellers
of the tale made responsible for the folly of Kephalos,[2] fell in
love with his beauty and carried him off.

CHAPTER V

Amphiaraos and the Heroes of the Theban War

IN THEBES the curse of Oidipus fulfilled itself on both his sons—on Eteokles, 'the man of true renown' and on Poly-neikes, 'him of much strife'. The first name many kings and other outstanding persons bore in old times, but not all narrators and dramatists always kept in mind that originally only Eteokles could be the worthy brother and Polyneikes the bad one. Sophokles understood[3] that at first the brothers wished to leave the sovránty entirely to their uncle Kreon, because they both feared the curse—the curse which weighed upon the family of Oidipus. Then longing for mastery and strife became too much for them both. To begin with Poly-neikes, the elder, was king, apparently together with Kreon, since Oidipus accuses them both of having driven him into banishment.[4] But then it appears that Polyneikes was sole monarch and that Eteokles, the younger, drove him out.[5]

Euripides understood it differently.[6] According to him, the brothers agreed to rule by turns, each for a year, while the other went into voluntary exile. Eteokles, who was the elder, was the first to rule and Polyneikes, the younger, to be exiled. But at the expiration of the year Eteokles had no desire to quit his throne, and he banished Polyneikes permanently. Polyneikes there-fore sought help against his brother in Argos. But the oldest version seems to be that which perhaps Aeschylus also followed in his tragedy 'Seven against Thebes', for he made Polyneikes, who justified his name as being quarrelsome from his birth and childhood, the very opposite of Eteokles.[7] In this ancient version the bridal gifts which Kadmos received from the goddesses and with which he adorned Harmonia—the garment of Athene and the necklace of Aphrodite—played their fatal role.

For Polyneikes, so the story ran, was given his choice between the kingdom of Thebes and the treasures from the inheritance of Kadmos, if he wished to rule in some other city.[8] But he wished to have both, or rather, to destroy his brother at all costs. Therefore he chose the treasures and went with them to Argos, where Adrastos, 'he who flees from nothing', was king. Let us now say a few words as to how the kingship came to Adrastos.

After Perseus had unwittingly killed his grandfather Akrisios, he left Argos to his great-uncle Proitos and took Tiryns in exchange for it. We know the history of Proitos' two, or three, daughters from the legends of Dionysos;[9] as they would not accept the secret rites of the god, madness overtook them. It was the prophet Melampus, a son of Amythaon and cousin of Jason, who cured them, at the price of two-thirds of the kingdom of Argos. One-third remained for Megapenthes, Proitos' son, one-third Melampus kept and one-third he ceded to his brother Bias. Melampus in all accounts was the helper of his brother. We shall hear presently how he got him the beautiful daughter of Neleus, Pero, for his wife. He was himself more a prophet and an apostle of the worship of Dionysos, whose phallic rites he introduced, it is said, among the Greeks,[10] than ruler of any city. His closest connections were with the harbour of Aigosthena at the southern foot of Kithairon, where his grave was shown in later times and a yearly festival held in his honour.[11] In Argos, Bias and his descendants bore rule; his son Talaos and then Adrastos, son of Talaos. Before Polyneikes came to Argos, Adrastos received a strange oracle; he was to marry his daughters to a lion and a boar.

In the same night as Polyneikes, another banished man arrived in Argos, Tydeus, a half-brother of the unfortunate Meleagros of Aitolia. By the will of Zeus, Gorge, daughter of Oineus, had borne him to her own father.[12] This sinister hero with such an unholy origin had made a massacre of his cousins at home, for allegedly plotting against the life of Oineus.[13] He was the most savage of all the warriors of old days. Adrastos was lying sleepless on his bed, pondering over the meaning of the strange oracle,[14] when the clash of arms reached his ears from the forecourt of his palace. The two exiles were fighting before his gate for a sheltered place to pass the night. Adrastos came out by the gate and suddenly understood the oracle; the two were like a boar and a lion.[15] Late narrators wished to make it easier for him, and declared[16] that the com/ batants carried a boar and a lion as devices on their shields, or even[17] that Polyneikes was clad in the hide of a lion, Tydeus in that of a boar. Surely Adrastos did not need this; he knew already what lay before him when he caught sight of the two heroes, and he gave his daughter Deipyle in marriage to Tydeus (from that marriage Diomedes, the terrible champion of the Trojan War, was born), his other daughter, whose name was Argeia, to Polyneikes. He promised to restore them both to their native lands, and the Theban first.

Had Polyneikes brought Harmonia's treasures as a bridal gift for the 'Maiden of Argos', Argeia? He now made use of the necklace at the gathering of the army against his father's and mother's city. Seven leaders were needed against the seven gates of Thebes, and Amphiaraos, Adrastos' brother/in/law and once his most powerful enemy, who had even driven him out of Argos for a while, must not be missing.[18] For his sufferings, Adrastos was to receive in Sikyon similar honours to those which Dionysos enjoyed elsewhere.[19] Amphiaraos, son of Oikles, was descended from Melampus as Adrastos was from Bias. It was said also[20] that Adrastos' father Talaos, 'the endurer', was killed by Amphiaraos, 'the twice Ares/like', when the latter drove out Adrastos. But Adrastos remained the stronger; he won Argos back, and the former enemies were reconciled. They bowed to the decision of a woman, for they chose as arbitress Eriphyle the wife of Amphiaraos, a daughter of Talaos by most accounts.[21] We recognise the old triad, one woman and two men. Now the two heroes be/ came connections by marriage through her. However great the quarrel between them may have been,[22] they promised

Eriphyle to accept her decision. The quarrel consisted in this, that Amphiaraos would not go to the war which Adrastos was preparing against Thebes. He advised against it,[23] for although a great warrior, he also had that trait of beings connected with the underworld (perhaps this was why he was called 'the twice Ares-like'), that he could see the future. He knew that he would meet his end in the war against Thebes.

But now Eriphyle too was to display her infernal nature, for which she was famous.[24] Amphiaraos had not only refused to set out against Thebes, but, so late narrators tell us,[25] had hidden himself, and only his wife knew where he was concealed. So Polyneikes resorted to her. A famous vase-painting shows him coming as a wanderer before the beautiful Eriphyle, while a crane, the swan's kinsman, stands between the pair, and bringing the young wife into temptation by taking the necklace of Harmonia out of the jewel-box. She betrayed her husband and bade him obey Adrastos. Amphiaraos, prophet as he was, knew also of the bribery; he went to the war, but he ordered his sons to kill their mother if he did not come back from the war.

Amphiaraos had foreseen not only his own end but that of the rest of the seven commanders who were assembling. He also threatened Adrastos with it,[26] but Adrastos did not, in all accounts, appear in person before the gates of Thebes. In one version he escaped death, with his garments torn,[27] saved by the horse Areion, a present from Herakles.[28] His sufferings, of which we are not told, still awaited him. There was one story[29] in which he and his son Hipponoos, following the advice of Apollo, threw themselves, like Herakles, willingly on the funeral pyre. But this tale is lost, like the epics which described the campaign against Thebes in detail. However, we can see that the expedition of the Seven was the most useless and most tragical campaign that ever yet was undertaken. Its only result was that Polyneikes and Eteokles were able to destroy each other and the seven gates beat off every attack.

After Polyneikes, Tydeus was the most vigorous instigator

of this war.[30] According to an old account,[31] he went as an ambassador to Thebes in advance of the great army. The message which he had to deliver to Eteokles and the Kad-meians is easy to guess; they were to hand over the sovranty to Polyneikes. Zeus protected the ambassador and Pallas Athene guarded Tydeus with especial affection.[32] He was of small stature, but he had challenged the young warriors of Thebes one after another to contests and easily defeated them all. Then the Kadmeians sent fifty men to lie in wait for him as he took the road back. With one exception he killed them all, and that one was allowed to escape because the gods delivered him by a sign.

All the omens of the gods gave warning when the whole army moved.[33] Among them was reckoned the fate of a child, whose sufferings at Nemea gave rise to the founding of famous festal games, much as those of the child Palaimon did on the Isthmus.[34] Only epithets and not real personal names of this child have come down to us; he was styled Opheltes, 'the helpful'[35] or Archemoros, 'the first-in-death', which is what Amphiaraos is said to have called him because his death was but the beginning of the disaster. He is said to have been the son of a king and tended by a nurse of famous name, Hypsi-pyle, 'her of the high gate', whom Euripides identified with the queen of Lemnos, daughter of Thoas the son of Dionysos, alleging that she was carried as a slave from that distant island to Nemea, and the later narrators followed the tragic poet.[36]

Her name was also worthy of the queen of the underworld, this Hypsipyle, to whom the child of the king of Nemea was entrusted. A tale was told of an oracle which forbade the baby to be put on the ground before he could walk.[37] The army of the Seven was marching through the valley of Nemea; the men were looking for a spring and asked the nurse, who happened to meet them with her charge, to show them one. In her confusion she laid the child on the ground, where a flourishing plant grew in abundance; it was wild celery, with which the dead used to be garlanded, assuredly not without an allusion to a flourishing condition after death. Hypsipyle ran on before the heroes to show them the spring, which was thereafter to be called Adrasteia[38] and meanwhile the baby was almost entirely devoured by a great serpent who guarded the place.[39] The heroes killed the dragon, buried the child, and originated in his honour the funeral games which thenceforth were repeated in every second year as the Nemean Games.

At last the Seven leaders arrived before the seven gates; according to Aeschylus[40] they were Tydeus, Kapaneus, Eteoklos, Hippomedon, Parthenopaios, Amphiaraos and Polyneikes, and in Euripides they are the same, with the exception of Eteoklos, for according to him Adrastos, the sole survivor, also took part.[41] In Aeschylus' tragedy, the 'Seven against Thebes', the Theban heroes whom Eteokles selected and opposed to the assailants are also named, but the Seven who stood without were more famous, and of them, those who met a remarkable death during the attack were especially so. Kapaneus, a grandson of Megapenthes son of Proitos, thought he could storm the wall with a scalingladder,[42] being the first and only hero among the Greeks who climbed up one and in his foolhardiness he challenged Zeus, crying[43] that the lightning would be merely like hot sunbeams to him. With a single flash Zeus hurled him down from his ladder.

The death of Tydeus was also a dreadful example. Melanippos, 'he of the black steed', son of Astakos, 'the lobster', said to have been one of the race of the Spartoi,[44] though perhaps rather a Poseidonian hero, thrust his lance into the belly of Athene's terrible favourite.[45] It is not clearly told by tradition whether he was then himself mortally wounded by Tydeus or by Amphiaraos, who hurried to the rescue. His enemy was already lying in the deathagony, and Athene was approaching to bring her protégé the drink of immortality, when Tydeus, bleeding and raging from his wound, called to Amphiaraos to throw him the head of his opponent.[46] The prophet knew what the result would be, but he abominated the instigator of the war and threw him the severed head of Melanippos.[47] Like a beast of prey, Tydeus with his last breath sucked his enemy's brain.[48] Athene turned away and left him to die.

Amphiaraos now saw Periklymenos, 'the very famous' coming against him; he was a son of Poseidon and had a name which would fit Hades also. It was he who had already killed Parthenopaios, son of Atalante, with a stone hurled from the battlement of the gate.[49] The prophet took to flight on his chariot before him, and the son of Poseidon pursued him. How far the pursuit went, narrators did not agree, for there were many spots in the neighbourhood of Thebes, and even rather further off, which claimed Amphiaraos for themselves as a hero dwelling in the depths of the earth. To spare him the disgrace of an enemy's spear wounding his back, Zeus split the ground with his thunderbolt, and it swallowed up the prophet, chariot and all.[50] But where did this happen? The inhabitants of Oropos, a little harbour town on the north coast of Attica and on the border of Boiotia, declared that it occurred in their territory, in a mild valley, shut off like a ravine, where a sanctuary of Amphiaraos, an Amphiareion, stood later. There, henceforth, the great warrior-prophet had his oracular seat, and there likewise he was worshipped as a chthonian god of healing, a second Asklepios.

In him the saying was already justified which we shall encounter in the history of Telephos, 'he that wounds shall also heal'. Thus it was also with his son, who bore the warlike name of Amphilochos, 'he of the twofold ambush'. He too became a healing hero after his death.[51] The other son, Alk- maion, revenged his father's death on his mother. According to a late account, Eriphyle let herself be corrupted again, by Thersandros, son of Polyneikes, who bribed her with the garment of Harmonia, and drove her son into the war of the Epigonoi, the sons of the Seven, who again set out against Thebes. Alkmaion killed Eriphyle, but the fatal gifts remained in his family, and he too was in the end murdered for them.[52]

We know from the history of Oidipus that the brothers Eteokles and Polyneikes fell in a duel, each by the other's hand, and from Sophokles' tragedy which bears the name of Oidipus' elder daughter, the august virgin Antigone, that she, against Kreon's edict, buried her banished brother and had to die for it. There was also a story concerning the burial of the Seven—or rather of the six only who were to be buried, for at any rate Amphiaraos' pyre remained vacant[53]—which said[54] that the Thebans would not yield the bodies of the fallen at all for their mothers to bury, and that it was Theseus who at the entreaty of Adrastos and the mothers brought the dead by force of arms to Eleusis and Kithairon; Euripides put it on the stage in his tragedy 'Hiketides', 'The Suppliants'.[55] It was believed in antiquity concerning six imposing tombs of early date in the neighbourhood of Eleusis that they concealed the bones of the greatest heroes of the Theban War.[56] Concerning those same tombs it is believed today that they have been rediscovered.

What the fathers failed to do, the sons, the Epigonoi, accomplished. Ten years later they set out against Thebes, where Laodamas, the 'master-of-folk', son of Eteokles, was then on the throne.[57] In this war Thebes was taken for the first time, and (as some even ventured to declare) destroyed. Of the seven new commanders only Aigialeus, son of Adrastos, fell, in contrast to his father, who was the only one who did not meet his end in the first Theban War.[58] Many of them were soon to fight under the walls of Troy, where also the son of Tydeus, Diomedes, was to win his renown.

CHAPTER VI

Atreus and his Dynasty

TWO SONS OF PELOPS, Atreus and Thyestes, were closely associated with their mother Hippodameia. After the murder of Chrysippos, all three found refuge in the lofty citadel of Midea in the realm of the descendants of Perseus under king Sthenelos.[59] This was certainly a flight of the three after the horrible deed perpetrated upon the youngest brother. In Mycenae, the House of Perseus came to an end with Eurystheus, when he was slain by Hyllos in punishment for the sufferings of Herakles and his descendants. But the Herakleidai were not allowed to return at once to the Peloponnesos. Omens from the gods stopped them.[60] Atreus then took over the kingdom of Mycenae [61] and led an army of Peloponnesians, including men of Tegea, against the Herakleidai. Hyllos, Herakles' son, fell in a duel with Echemos king of Tegea. The Herakleidai retired to Trikorythos in Attica, and it was not till fifty years later that they might return home.[62] It was in vain that Polyneikes and Tydeus had visited Mycenae to seek assistance for the war against Thebes, in which Argos was to be bled white; Zeus stopped the Mycenaeans from taking part by terrifying signs.[63] Therefore the last fifty years of Greek hero-mythology before the return of the Herakleidai were reserved for the House of Atreus and its deeds, the greatest of which was the Trojan War.

The sceptre of an empire over Greece, corresponding here on earth to the kingdom of Zeus on Olympos, had not been held by Perseus, nor by any sovran of Thebes, nor by Herakles, who in one place and the other, in Thebes and in Mycenae, was the subordinate of the king. Pelops, who emerged from the sacrificial cauldron of Tantalos his father, was the first to receive the sceptre; we hear in Homer[64] that Hephaistos fashioned it and gave it to Zeus; the King of the Gods handed it on to Hermes,

Hermes to Pelops, and Pelops bestowed it on Atreus. After that, the kings of Mycenae inherited it; Thyestes had it from Atreus, Agamemnon from Thyestes. But the two brothers inherited something else also from their father,[65] the curse of Pelops, because they had murdered his favourite child Chry-sippos, a murder the story of which has been lost, but which forms a kind of link between the butchering of Pelops and that of the sons of Thyestes. And there was also another fateful possession in the house, the golden ram,[66] upon which, not less than upon the sceptre of Zeus, the sovranty depended. Jason's Golden Fleece appears to be an allusion to, and abbreviation of, this marvellous beast, in another cycle of tales.

In the history of Pelops, Oinomaos offered up a light-coloured ram, a vicarious sacrifice, while the future ruler escaped death. The sacrifice took place before a statue of the goddess whom the Greeks called Artemis and who was accustomed to receive human sacrifices on the Black Sea. After the death of the hero, at least his bones were laid away in a sanctuary of Artemis. In the history of Phrixos, the ram which rescued him from death at the altar bore the Golden Fleece, which Jason must bring back from the Black Sea in order to win the throne of Iolkos. How Phrixos was to have been sacrificed we are not told, but we know from the history of the gods[67] that his stepmother Ino threw two sons of Athamas, her own children, into the cauldron of sacrifice. From Medeia's cauldron at Iolkos a rejuvenated ram emerged. Probably there was an old Eastern tale in which a young ram, replacing the future ruler, experienced the sufferings of a god cut in pieces and cooked in the cauldron, or a golden lamb did so, the fore-runner of the symbol of Christ, the Son of the King of Heaven. In Mycenae the possession of the ram was the sure mark of the rightful king.

When the story of the kingship of Atreus and his brother Thyestes begins for us,[68] they were residing in Midea, but no longer with their mother Hippodameia to make a third. Another, ominous, female figure united them, as Eriphyle did

Adrastos with Amphiaraos. She bore the name Aerope, 'she with a face of white mist', and is said to have been a grand-daughter of Minos and wife of Atreus, but she deceived her husband with Thyestes. She kept the golden lamb shut up in a chest, undoubtedly in the shape of its fleece, and passed it secretly to her lover. The narrators knew that the lamb belonged to Artemis as a sacrificial victim, and coloured the narrative thus: Atreus once vowed to offer to the goddess the finest head of his cattle, and failed to do so when he saw its golden fleece. Wishing to keep it for himself, he hid the treasure in a chest. Others claimed to know[69] that Hermes, the father of that unfortunate Myrtilos, the charioteer to whom Pelops owed his victory over Oinomaos, put the marvellous creature among the flocks of Atreus in order to avenge the death of his son upon the family of the victor. A shepherd brought the lamb to Atreus, and so, thanks to Aerope's infidelity, it finally made its way to Thyestes. All this took place while they were still in Midea.

Now when the Mycenaeans received an oracle[70] bidding them choose a son of Pelops for their king, they sent for Atreus and Thyestes. A quarrel began as to which of the two should be king, and Thyestes slyly proposed that they should choose the one who possessed the golden lamb. Atreus, who imagined that he was in possession of it, agreed, and now Thyestes produced the fleece and became king of Mycenae; Atreus had to go into exile.[71] But Zeus could not allow this. He altered the motion of the heavenly bodies, making the sun rise in the west and set in the east.[72] At this the Mycenaeans realised that they had made the wrong choice, and thereupon Atreus drove his brother out,[73] and Thyestes wandered here and there as a banished man. But the other also was not in sure possession of the kingship, for Thyestes, who had obtained the golden lamb by grace of Aerope, seems after all to have had a better claim to it than his brother. The meaning of his name is 'the man of the sacrifice', however little later narrators still knew of any such sacrifice. By virtue of it he had been consecrated king, and this consecration must now be reversed. Thereupon Atreus contrived his most horrible deed.

The later narrators had great difficulty in finding a reason for this horror. They alleged[74] that it was not till then that Atreus discovered his wife's infidelity, and that he summoned Thyestes back under colour of a reconciliation, in order to take vengeance upon him. In the older versions, however, perhaps Thyestes had not gone into banishment at all, but it was immediately after Atreus ascended the throne that he set that horrible meal before his brother. As a result, the world governed from Mycenae under this dynasty fell into complete disorder. Atreus did what was told of his grandfather Tantalos, but he did not butcher his own son. He slew the children of Thyestes, and invited his brother, quite alone, to eat[75] of the roasted viscera and the boiled flesh.[76] Prokne and Philomela had issued a similar invitation to Tereus. In the East, this was a horrible punishment,[77] the unholy carrying-out of a sacred act, which in Greece was preserved in the form of the boiling and roasting of a kid, the vicarious victim in the mysteries of Dionysos.[78] This offering had already been profaned by Tantalos, and it was now profaned still more by Atreus, so that Thyestes, on eating of it, should himself become unholy and be totally destroyed. When Thyestes realised what he had eaten,[79] he fell backwards, vomited up his meal, dashed the table over with his foot and put a curse upon his family that it should be overthrown in like manner. It was also said[80] that the Sun on that occasion turned back his chariot.

Atreus had two sons by Aerope, Agamemnon and Menelaos. Thyestes, after the butchering of his sons, had left only a daughter. So most narrators have it; only those who wished to avoid relating the story of the birth of Aigisthos[81] made out that the avenger was then already born and was taken with him into exile as a baby by Thyestes. As to how the avenger came to be born, there were two versions of a tradition undoubtedly old. Manifestly that tradition would have it that the avenger was sprung from a union not of this world, the union of the father of the murdered children with his own daughter, like the legendary wedding of Zeus with Persephone.[82] In one account Thyestes received from the oracle at Delphi the direction to raise up the avenger in this manner.[83] He had taken refuge with king Thesprotos on the borders of the under-world.[84] There he had relations with his daughter Pelopia, who showed herself most pious towards her father, in that she conceived the avenger by him.[85] In the other version, much the same thing happened to her as did to Auge, Athene's priestess at Tegea,[86] who conceived Telephos by Herakles, a tale which shall shortly be told. Pelopia was living at Sikyon; Thyestes came there during the night in which a sacrifice was made to Athene.[87] His daughter was leading the virgins' dance at the festival; while dancing she slipped and stained her dress with the blood of the victim. She then left the maidens and went down to the river, to wash her clothes clean of the marks of blood. When she was unclothed, Thyestes, who had hidden in some bushes, veiled his head and assaulted her. Thus she bore a son whom she abandoned. A she-goat nourished the boy, and therefore he was named Aigisthos.[88] On reaching manhood, he learned who his father was, murdered Atreus and put Thyestes on the throne of Mycenae again.[89]

In later times, the tomb of Atreus was shown in Mycenae,[90] and that of Thyestes by the road which led to Argos. It was crowned with a stone ram.[91] Many old graves have similar decorations, but if it was told that this particular grave belonged to Thyestes, it must also have been believed that he and not Atreus was the king marked out by the possession of the golden lamb. In another story,[92] Thyestes was driven away by Agamemnon and Menelaos to the Island of Kythera. Not all narrators agree that these were the sons of Atreus, for some make them his grandsons and the sons of Pleisthenes,[93] whom the genealogists introduced into the family tree of the Pelopidai with no agreement as to his place. The brothers who were to continue the dynasty grew up in exile. Tyndareos king of Sparta later brought them home to Mycenae. Thyestes took refuge from them at the altar of Hera,[94] and so saved his life. Agamemnon became the Great King of Mycenae, Menelaos inherited the kingship of Sparta from Tyndareos. That king-ship was not to prove happy, but the heavier curse lay upon the elder brother, who bore the sceptre of Pelops after Thyestes.

CHAPTER VII

The Prelude to the Trojan War

NEITHER DID THE ELDER HEROES OF GREECE lack the protecting and gracious power of great goddesses. Pallas Athene, daughter of Zeus, stood by the sons of Zeus. It was she who had brought about the begetting of Theseus by Poseidon; Hera in her fashion aided Herakles and Jason to win fame. As mother of divine twins, a celestial goddess under various names (Antiope, Melanippe, Tyro and Leda are the most famous) took upon herself the part of the primaeval woman, not to speak of divine maidens such as Harmonia, Ariadne or Medeia, in whose shape she contracted relations with mortals. But only at the beginning of that Heroic Age with which the history of the world began in mythological fashion, in the days when the earth was already suffering under the weight of all too numerous mankind[95] were great goddesses condemned likewise to bear sons to mortal men. Through these the human race was to reach its ultimate peak. We may say that the history of the heroes in 'time', in our sense, opens here; everything earlier was either 'primaeval time' or 'time' still blended with the 'primaeval'.

On the Asian side of the Greek sea the goddess of love mated with the Trojan herdsman Anchises,[96] nephew of that Laomedon who was punished by Herakles, and bore him Aineias, who she did not rear herself but entrusted to the nymphs on Mount Ida.[97] Aphrodite's son is said to have become like the gods in appearance,[98] and he alone in Troy was so protected by the Celestial Ones[99] that he was saved for the future history of mankind. In him the Romans honoured the founder of their nation, the originator of their power, which was to include all the coasts of the Mediterranean and more as well. His mother and Phoibos Apollo saved him from his fight with Diomedes,[100] Poseidon from the defeat which he

308

nearly underwent at the hands of Achilles.[101] On the Greek side, Achilles was the son of a goddess. The story of Aineias' birth we know already from the tales of the gods. How the birth of Achilles came about shall now be told.

We know from the stories of the gods[102] that besides Tethys, Eurynome and Amphitrite, Thetis also was one of the great goddesses of the Greek sea. Before she became Achilles' mother, Zeus and Poseidon had striven for her. Had she borne a son to one of the two great gods, that son would have become still mightier than his father, and instead of the wars at Thebes and Troy in which mankind weakened itself in and around Greece, the age of a new divine sovranty under a new king of the gods would have dawned. Themis, the mother of the Horai, who neither befool nor deceive but bring the times to their ripeness in due season, knew of the threatened change in the rulership of the world. She warned the rival brothers,[103] and on her advice[104] Zeus decided to force the sea-goddess into marriage with a mortal.[105] Other ancient narrators add that Hera had chosen for her a husband especially dear to the gods, for Hera had brought her up[106] and for Hera's sake she had herself fled from marriage with Zeus,[107] assuredly into her own element, the sea. There the King of the Gods suddenly found himself confronted with Poseidon and the struggle between the brothers would then and there have come about if the saying of Themis had not sobered them both.

The chosen bridegroom of the sea-goddess lived in Thessaly, on Pelion, with the Centaur Chiron.[108] We can no longer say if his name connected him with that great mountain or with clayey soil, *pelós*, or if 'Peleus' meant something else, which is hidden from us. Aiakos, son of Zeus and of the island-goddess Aigina, for love of whom the King of the Gods made men, the Myrmidones, come forth from ants,[109] begot Peleus on Endeis, 'her who lives at enmity', the daughter of the infernal Skiron whom Theseus killed. Others, who insisted that the Myrmidones, said to have composed Achilles' following at Troy, were a people settled in Thessaly and not immigrants

to the country with Peleus,[110] declared[111] that Chiron was
Endeis' father, and Zeus had brought his son from Aigina
to Thessaly and established him on Pelion as king.[112] Otherwise, the piety of Aiakos was famous.[113] He is said to have
freed all Greece from the unfruitfulness under which it suffered
on account of Pelops, who, making hypocritical pretence of
friendship, had killed king Stymphalos and scattered his limbs
all over the land—yet another tale of a sacrifice made unholily,
such as we have already had to mention so often. Aiakos was
honoured not only by Zeus but by the King of the underworld; we know that he received the keys of Hades.

Allegedly, Peleus was not his only son. It was told of
Telamon, the 'bearer' or 'endurer', the father of Aias of Salamis, that he was not only the friend but also the brother of
Peleus.[114] The two had also a half-brother in the person of
Phokos, the 'seal-man', whom Aiakos begot upon Psamathe,
the 'sand-girl', a daughter of Nereus, who tried to hide from
him by taking the shape of a seal.[115] This Phokos was killed,
accidentally or of set purpose, by the brothers.[116] His grave was
shown on Aigina near the shrine of his father, the keeper of the
keys of Hades.[117] Telamon thereupon, the story continues,
emigrated to the island of Salamis, Peleus to Thessaly. He
found a refuge with the king of Phthia, who bore the Centaur-
name of Eurytion. By him he was purified and had a third of
the country given him as the king's son-in-law.[118] But Peleus
was then, as it were, in deep shadow and brought misfortune
with him. He went to the Kalydonian hunt with Eurytion,
and, as we know from the story of that luckless undertaking,
accidentally killed his father-in-law.[119] Instead of returning to
Phthia, he had to flee to Iolkos, and there he was purified by
Akastos, son of Pelias. As a wrestler, Peleus took part in that
favourite theme of poets, the funeral games of Pelias.[120]
Artists were fond of portraying his wrestling, especially his
bout with the beautiful Atalante, an exciting spectacle, in
which all precautions were taken to prevent the wrestling
becoming a lovers' encounter. For Peleus also was handsome,

and it is not to be wondered at that his beauty was as harmful to him as that of Bellerophontes and of Hippolytos. Akastos' wife fell in love with the wrestler, and as the hero would not comply with her, she tried to ruin him. According to the late narrators, who have put together all these tales about Peleus, the first victim of her slander was Eurytion's daughter in Phthia, who felt deserted by her husband and hanged herself.[121]

Akastos believed his wife, as the husbands always do in this old tale, and acted accordingly. As his host, he would not himself murder the guest whom he had just purified, but sent him out to hunt the wild beasts on Pelion, at first not alone but in competition with other hunters. This too appears to be an ancient tale, by which originally the custom of bringing only the tongues of the game as offerings to the deities of hunting, Artemis Agrotera and Apollo Agraios, was explained;[122] for the story was told that[123] the other hunters brought back the beasts which Peleus had killed and claimed the prize of victory for themselves. Meanwhile the hero was probably asleep on Pelion, and came in last, with the tongues in his wallet, thus proving his superiority.[124] Akastos tried to destroy the hero, as he slept in a byre, by first taking possession of his knife.[125] The details are not preserved to us; all we can discover is that Peleus got the knife, a masterpiece of Daidalos, from the gods as a reward for his virtue,[126] and that Akastos, when he had the marvellous object in his hand, found nothing better to do with it[127] than to pray, and hide it under some cow-dung,[128] so that at least the hero should not be able to defend himself against the Centaurs who prowled about. It seems that it was a magic knife, and that the reason why it was called a product of the arts of Daidalos was that it would not let itself be used against its master. Chiron sought it out again from under the cow-dung, and gave it back to the hero. In his cave,[129] the message of the gods reached Peleus, that he, as the most pious mortal in all the country, was to celebrate his marriage with Thetis.

Next to the marriages of Zeus and the union of Kadmos

with Harmonia, this wedding-feast was the most important of
all those told in the stories of the gods and heroes. But it
was not made so easy as later poets give us to understand[130]
for Peleus to bring the sea-goddess out of Nereus' palace
first into Chiron's cave[131] and finally to Phthia on the fertile
mainland where Eurytion had once ruled.[132] A night of
full moon must first be awaited,[133] a wedding-night.[134] At the
full moon, Thetis used to visit the cuttle-fishes' shore, the
beach by the steep slope of Pelion, and to dance with her
sisters about the altar on which they, the daughters of Nereus,
received their offerings. The silver-footed goddess[135] emerged
from the waves even as at the beginning of time Phoibe came
forth from her own lake on the western side of the same
mountain.[136] It was for the hero to get her in an enduring grip
and hold her fast in his arms.[137] This was no mere wrestling-
match like that with Atalante, but a struggle for love. The
resisting bride displayed all the old sea-deities' arts of transformation. She changed herself into fire and into water,[138]
bared the teeth of a lion,[139] and tried in the form of a snake to
defend herself against his embrace.[140] At last she surrendered
in the form of the most delicate of all fish, that after which that
coast is known, the *Sepias Akte*.[141] Not a sound escaped the
mouths of the wrestlers.[142]

In the morning the gods came to the wedding-feast. It was
an ancient Greek custom, which is merely confirmed by this
story, for the relatives on the day after the marriage-night to
bring their gifts to the young couple, a continuation of the
festival. This was known as *Epaulia*,[143] because in very early
days the bride and bridegroom probably had slept together for
the first time in an *aulion*, a hut in the fields. It seems that the
ancient vase-painter Klitias meant to show Thetis in such a
lodging on that morning: in a round mud-hut, which, however, the artist decked in his picture with columns and a gable,
to ennoble it. Before it stood the hero, to receive the procession
of gods. The first was Chiron, who greeted him. Beside him
Iris, the messenger, strode in and led the goddesses and gods.

66 POLYNEIKES AND ERIPHYLE

67 VISIT OF THE GODS TO PELEUS AND THETIS

68 THE THREE GODDESSES BEFORE PARIS

Hestia, Demeter and Chiron's wife Chariklo came first, Dionysos and the three Horai at their heels, then Zeus and Hera with the Muses, of whom we hear elsewhere[144] that they sang at the feast. Other pairs of gods followed, Poseidon and Amphitrite, Aphrodite and Ares, Apollo and Artemis, Nereus and Doris, Hermes and his mother Maia, and before these two the Moirai, four in number, who perhaps intended, like the Muses, to sing at the banquet[145] and foretell the birth of the great son. Okeanos also was present, and with him certainly Tethys arrived; they constituted the great pair of grandparents, while Zeus also may have appeared as grandfather of Peleus. It is certain that the Charites came, for without them it would have been no real wedding.[146] As his gift, Dionysos brought the wine along, in an amphora on his back; the artist and the spectators of his picture knew that it was to have a tragic significance. The story went[147] that on that occasion Poseidon presented Peleus with the immortal horses, Balios and Xanthos—Dapple and Chestnut—which accompanied Achilles to Troy and proved themselves prophets of tragedy. It was then that Chiron presented the ash spear which in the hands of Peleus' son, whose birth this wedding indirectly solemnised, was likewise to have a tragical renown;[148] unless indeed it was Peleus himself who cut it and with it in his hand went forth alone against Iolkos and captured the city.[149]

But that happened rather later. The gods came not only to greet and to bestow but also to feast,[150] for in those days immortals and mortals often sat and ate together.[151] At Thetis' wedding with the mortal Peleus this occurred for the last time. All the gods were there together, for Zeus had invited them all, except self-evidently (or so it might seem), the goddess Eris, Strife.[152] But previously he had taken counsel, we may suppose, with Themis the wise goddess,[153] by whom he had been prevented from celebrating a marriage himself with Thetis to his own ruin; or did perhaps a great sea-goddess come and advise him? According to another tradition[154] it was Momos, Blame, who counselled him then. When, at the complaint of

the overladen Earth, he was for destroying mankind by lightning and flood, it is said that Momos found fault with Zeus,
and advised him instead to beget Helen and arrange the marriage
of Thetis and Peleus, with all the consequences which would
result from these two events, including the final one, which
consisted in the disappearance of the race of heroes.[155] However, Eris was to appear at the marriage-feast, and not being
admitted, she threw an apple into the midst of the company,[156]
which was to become almost as famous to posterity as that of
which the Hebrews had to tell.

Now, whether Eris' apple came from the Garden of the
Hesperides, as one very late poet would have it,[157] or was
simply made of gold[158] because nothing else would be suitable
among goddesses, it had added to it a word which, whether
scratched on it[159] or spoken with it[160] or not mentioned at all
was yet understood by everyone: 'To the Fairest'. Now 'Fairest',
Kalliste, was in human mouths a divine name, which Artemis
bore above all other goddesses.[161] Then the three most powerful, Hera, Athene and Aphrodite, grasped at that harm-laden
dedication. A dispute broke out, which was to lead, through
the decision of a mortal, to the weakening of the human race,
the annihilation of Troy and the dissolution of the empire of
Mycenae. The King of the Gods himself nominated the young
man with whom the decision rested.[162] To him Hermes must
bring the apple and lead the three goddesses across the sea,
while Peleus with his spear and his immortal horses first set
out against Iolkos to punish Akastos and his wife, and then
made his entry into Phthia with Thetis and his booty.[163]
According to the later narrators,[164] it was in the cities of
Pharsalos and Thetideion—'shrine of Thetis'—that he lived.[165]
There he ruled, the mortal husband of a goddess, who, as we
shall presently hear, did not in all traditions remain with him.

Across the Hellespont rose Mount Ida, and under that
mountain of the gods, on a hill on the banks of the river
Skamandros (in the language of the gods it was Xanthos, 'the
fair-haired'),[166] stood the strong city of Troy. Poseidon and

Apollo had built it for Laomedon, and Herakles and Tela⁄
mon, Peleus' brother or friend, had destroyed it for the first
time; we have heard the story of it. Now Priam was ruling
there, the only son of Laomedon whom Herakles had
spared.[167] Originally he had been named Podarkes, 'Swift⁄
foot', but we know the tale of how he allegedly got his famous
name. His sister Hesione had ransomed him from Herakles
with her gold⁄embroidered veil. She herself had followed
Telamon to Salamis and borne him Teukros, who later took
part in the Trojan War with his half⁄brother Aias.[168] For her
hope, that Troy should arise again under the rule of her
youngest brother,[169] had been fulfilled. In the newly built city
Priam founded the most numerous royal family of which the
legends of the heroes tell. His wife and his concubines bore him
fifty sons, not to speak of his daughters; he mentions that
number to Achilles[170] after most of them were fallen. Really,
Priamos means much the same as *perramos*; that is, 'king'.[171] On
the other hand, his queen Hekabe bore a divine name, for that
is how the name of the goddess whom Attic peasants called
Hekale must have been pronounced in Phrygian. Behind
both old ladies of heroic legend rises the uncanny figure of the
great goddess Hekate. Hekabe's father was said to have been
the river Sangarios, or, if he was a mortal, a certain Kisseus,
'the ivy⁄bearer'.[172] Also, she was not to die as women die, but
turn into a bitch—a ghostly bitch with fiery eyes[173]—and cast
herself into the sea,[174] in a manner worthy of the 'strong
goddess' of whom the sea⁄bitch Skylla was one name.[175]

Soon after the birth of her first son, Hektor, 'the supporter',
who was to have the most success in keeping the Greeks away
from Troy, Hekabe,[176] pregnant for the second time,[177]
dreamed that she had brought forth a burning brand, the fire
of which spread all over the city. A fire⁄bearing Erinys with a
hundred arms tore down Troy in her dream, so says a poet.[178]
Among the interpreters who had to explain the dream we hear
of Herophile, 'beloved of Hera', the first and oldest of the
Sibyls, priestess of Apollo Smintheus.[179] But Kassandra also

was a prophetess, a daughter of Priam who likewise had Apollo to thank for her prophetic gift, although, since she rejected the love of the god, she never was believed.[180] Kassandra demanded that the child that Hekabe was to bear should be killed;[181] thereupon Priam had the boy taken to Mount Ida and exposed there.[182] It was the realm of the Lady of Wild Things, of whom we know[183] that she favoured the form of a bear. The child had the same experience as Atalante, for a she-bear suckled him for five days.[184] The shepherds who found him[185] at first named the child Paris,[186] but later Alexandros, 'repeller of men',[187] both names apparently befitting a king's son from the very beginning. Was Oinone, the nymph with the Dionysiac name, daughter of a river-god, whom the late narrators know[188] only as Paris' wife while he was a shepherd, originally his nurse? Whatever her form and whatever her name, a divine inhabitant of Mount Ida had preserved the child alive.

To this Trojan prince and herdsman Hermes, by command of Zeus, conveyed the three goddesses, so that he should decide to which the apple belonged. He was to say which was the most beautiful—so it is expressed by the old poets and other narrators, who by no means meant mere erotic charm, but the highest of all good things that the world contains. For it needed neither a king's son nor a herd-boy to decide that Aphrodite possessed the most erotic attractiveness of all in Heaven, on Earth and in the Sea. That philosopher was right who stated[189] that Paris had to choose between warlike discipline, a life devoted to love, and sovranty; the first was Athene's gift, the last Hera's. He was confronted by three forms of beauty all of which were divine; the representatives of its forms wore beauty's splendour. All three were beautiful, but to enhance their beauty they washed in the abundant springs of Ida.[190] In the old accounts, however, not even Aphrodite disrobed, for in those versions it was not the glory of a beautiful body that was in question. The goddess of love caused the Charites and the Horai to clothe her in a splendid dress having all the colours of spring, crown her with fragrant flowers and lead her with song to Paris.[191] But for all that, when the goddesses appeared the shepherd's hair stood on end,[192] as if he were seeing ghosts. He would dearly have liked to run away. Then the goddesses offered him their gifts:[193] Athene victory and heroism, Hera empire over Asia and Europe, Aphrodite the possession of Helen, daughter of Zeus.

When Paris realised what choice he might make, he abused the other two goddesses.[194] In his folly, he harmed himself unnecessarily and yielded to his love-madness, without ever having seen the beautiful sister of the Dioskuroi. The renown of her beauty had at that time filled the whole world. Theseus had already carried her off, but her brothers had brought her back from Aphidna and she was living in Lakonia. Thither Paris was to voyage. Ships must be built for him,[195] whence no doubt the scene arose which a vase-painter apparently gives us. Aphrodite first conducted the prince back to the home of his parents. It was also told that Paris himself was busy felling pines on Ida to make the ship that was to create incomparably more woe than that other which of old came down to the sea from Mount Pelion.[196]

There in Thessaly Thetis had borne Peleus a son and afterwards, according to most accounts, went back to the depths of the sea,[197] though perhaps not for ever; she may have divided her divine existence between the house of Peleus and the palace of Nereus. True, there were some narrators who would have it that she was united but once to the hero,[198] as Aphrodite was to Anchises in the well-known tale of the gods.[199] Perhaps according to this story Achilles was born in the depths of the sea and placed by his mother on the shore, to which he so often resorted later to invoke her.[200] The name Achilles, properly Achilleus, is most nearly connected with those of river-gods, beings who live in the deeps, such as Acheloos and Acheles. There was also a tale concerning him[201] that his name had been changed, he having been earlier known as Ligyron, 'clear-voiced'. Various reasons were invented to account for

Thetis' natural preference for her own element over the fruitful soil of Phthia. Peleus allegedly insulted her,[202] or she tried to test her children (she bore several according to these late narrators) to see if they were immortal, by throwing them into a cauldron full of water;[203] or she wanted to make them immortal by laying them on the fire, as Demeter did with Demophoon.[204] They all died of it, excepting Achilles who was rescued by Peleus. But Thetis was angered, like Medeia, when she was disturbed in her secret activity.[205] All these are the merest repetitions of well-known tales which originally were all quite foreign to Achilles. It seems to be an older story, although not very old, that the goddess dipped her son in the infernal river Styx,[206] and so Achilles became invulnerable, except for the heel by which his mother held him. But then, too, she left even the son she had nearly made immortal. Peleus brought the lad to Chiron, and the Centaur nurtured him in his cave with the entrails of lions and boars and the marrow of bears.[207] At six years of age he began to hunt wild beasts;[208] he had Chiron to thank for his simple ways,[209] and from him he learned the art of healing.[210] That Achilles was taught by Chiron to play a stringed instrument was later readily believed and portrayed.[211]

CHAPTER VIII

The Heroes of the Trojan War

THE OLD NARRATORS never succeeded in fitting to-gether the separate tales belonging to the mythology of the heroes into a single long narrative without any contradictions. Especially did uncertainty always remain as to what happened simultaneously, or later, or earlier. Everybody knew that the two sons of Atreus, Agamemnon and Menelaos, chose as their wives the two most dangerous daughters of the house of Tyndareos, who had brought the brothers home—Klytaim-nestra and Helen. But when did that happen? As Helen had already been ravished once before Menelaos married her, so too Klytaimnestra had had a husband before Agamemnon. Allegedly he was a son of Thyestes,[212] named Tantalos after his great-grandfather. Agamemnon must have been con-sumed by strong passion for his cousin's wife, and that was when his royal nature, which never knew any bounds, his character of a Zeus on earth, with even the Titanic traits of his youth, displayed itself for the first time. He struck Tantalos dead, tore his child from its mother's breast, dashed it on the ground, and carried off the young wife by force.[213] His early passionate union with Klytaimnestra, who was not thought to be a daughter of Zeus, explains why Agamemnon, after the Dioskuroi had set Helen free, came a-wooing to her on behalf of his brother Menelaos; for the great king of Mycenae must not be absent from that wooing, but must emerge victorious.

The wooing of Helen, then, came as early as the time when Agamemnon was on the throne in place of Thyestes. But the statement[214] that the only reason why Achilles did not outdo Menelaos on that occasion was that he was still a child under Chiron's guardianship, or Helen's gossip in Euripides[215] about the son of Thetis having been one of her suitors, will not fit the chronology. If Helen, when Paris carried her off, left behind

her little daughter,[216] who was perhaps nine years old,[217] then
her marriage must have taken place earlier than the wedding
of Peleus and Thetis. The meaning of the custom of letting a
princess be wooed by claimants from the whole country all at
once was not so much to give the girl an opportunity to choose
as to furnish the suitors with the possibility of displaying all the
splendour and power of which they were capable. They could
do so even if they did not appear in person.

It was now a sort of competition for the famous and beautiful
daughter, the likeness of golden Aphrodite,[218] whom Leda, a
daughter of Okeanos at least—for such by one account she
was[219]—had borne to Zeus and Tyndareos. Besides her
earthly father,[220] her brothers the Dioskuroi could take on
themselves the post of judge.[221] It was told[222] that all the heroes
who were to fight at Troy for Helen's sake took part one way
or another in the wooing; that is, those who were not merely
petty kings or their retainers, 'heroes' only in the sense of gentlefolk, but destined to have their history and especial honour
after their death, figures upon whom rested the shadow of a
fate which could be interchanged with no other. Anyone who
would know them must look forward to that destiny.

It has already been said that Agamemnon joined the suitors,
not on his own behalf but for his younger brother. For
Menelaos he was also to lead the army of the Greeks against Troy,
and after nine years of warfare nearly become the cause of a
complete setback, simply because he was what he always
showed himself to be, a king through and through,[223] with
head and eyes like those of Zeus, with loins like those of Ares,
a breast like Poseidon's, handsome and majestic;[224] yet always
connected dangerously with a woman—before Troy it was
with Chryseis, daughter of Chryses, priest of Apollo, his concubine, on whose account he insulted the god.[225] He was then
more passionately attached to this woman than to Klytaimnestra,[226] who meantime[227] was associating herself in Mycenae
with the avenger, the son of Thyestes by his 'underworldly'
connection with Pelopia. It was a story fit for the tragic stage,

the great king slaughtered like a bull[228] by the lover of his wife. The image of the bull and the cow which the prophetess Kassandra, brought by Agamemnon to Argos, saw in the royal couple,[229] was indeed in old days not unworthy of even a divine pair such as Zeus and Hera. In Sparta, the kingdom of his surviving brother Menelaos, there stood an altar of Zeus Agamemnon,[230] as if the hero after his death was actually identified with the King of the Gods. The sheltering earth has preserved to us the place of his worship, on the outskirts of Mycenae, where Perseus also had a cult, near an ancient bridge on the road leading to the city.

Odysseus is named to us as the first,[231] or one of the first,[232] of the suitors. He did not come himself and also sent no gifts, since he knew very well that Menelaos would be the successful one; a king of little Ithake could not compete with the brother of the Great King of Argos and Mycenae. He only advised the Dioskuroi from a distance by his messengers.[233] It is said that he was the author of the counsel[234] that Tyndareos should take an oath of the suitors to acquiesce in Helen's choice and afterwards to help the man she chose if anyone tried to dispute the possession of his wife. For when they came to woo, they were full of murderous feelings against each other.[235] So all of them took the oath, standing on a sacrificed horse.[236] That was one of the reasons—the other was the leading power in the hands of Agamemnon—why the former suitors took part in the expedition against Troy as helpers of Menelaos.

Odysseus preferred wedding Penelope to marrying Helen; she was the daughter of Ikarios, a brother of Tyndareos, and was to become the emblem of fidelity for all time.[237] Her name contained the word *penelops*, 'duck',[238] a bird whose image on old vases found in graves so often signifies a protecting, kindly goddess. The human form of Odysseus' wife, however, belongs to heroic poetry, the borders of which must continually be touched here, but not passed unless it is unavoidable for the setting forth of heroic mythology.

We see that Odysseus showed himself the cleverest of all

men, though not so clever—as we shall shortly hear—that he could escape the dolorous and painful war which was to separate him from Penelope and end, for him, in his famous and adventurous journey. But even so, he was worthy of his grandfather, the master-thief Autolykos, who according to an old tale that we have already told brought his daughter Antikleia and the arch-rogue Sisyphos together in order that between them they might produce him just such a grandson. When Odysseus was born in the house of Laertes, for whose son he passed among the heroes of the Trojan War, Auto-lykos was staying there as the guest of his son-in-law and his daughter. They set the baby on his grandfather's knee and asked him to find a name for the new arrival.[239] The old robber then is said to have replied, 'As the hate of so many people attended me here, he shall be called Odysseus.' The Greek for 'hated' is *odyssómenos*, and that is how the poet of the 'Odyssey' explained the name of his hero, although there he is portrayed as by no means so hateful a figure as in other tales which do not come from Homer. Here we learn that in those days names must have a meaning, among the Greeks as among other peoples.

Through Autolykos, son of Hermes, Odysseus was descended from that god. But at the same time he was one of those heroes who were under the especial protection of the goddess Athene.[240] He was born, so it is said,[241] within the precincts of the temple of Athene Alalkomene in Boiotia, and that, so the story goes on, is why a town in Ithake was also called Alalkomenai. Be it from one or the other holy place of the Alalkomene, the goddess took him under her charge from his birth. In the Trojan War he was most closely associated with another protégé of Pallas Athene, Diomedes, who was named immediately after him among the suitors of Helen.[242] With him he undertook bloody deeds, and not only those which were essential for the capture of Troy. They made him hated by many people, not to speak of the hate of Aias against Odysseus. We shall hear of all this by and by.

Among the Seven who marched against Thebes, the father

of Diomedes, Tydeus, was Athene's favourite, but, as will be remembered, a horrible and unworthy favourite. The goddess transferred her maternal affection to his son. He, as already mentioned, took part in the destruction of Thebes by the Epigonoi and ruled in Argos as Adrastos' son-in-law. He was of a character not much gentler than his father's, more like a second Ares, associated with Athene. Under the walls of Troy he was to be the mightiest warrior next to Achilles and to show himself actually superior when opposed to Ares. Supported by Athene, he struck the war-god with his spear, so that he fell and screamed like the shout of nine or ten thousand fighting men.[243] Before that he had wounded Aphrodite, who had rescued her son Aineias from him.[244] Among all those who fought, Athene took away the mist from his eyes above, so that he might recognise the gods in the turmoil of battle.[245]

But the punishment of the passionate warrior, who left his beautiful wife for his gory work, was already prepared. Aigialeia, the clever daughter of Adrastos, was not for long to sob by night in a lonely bed, so that the whole house was awakened.[246] She soon sought consolation among the youths of Argos.[247] Whether Diomedes ever came home[248] and was driven out by his wife's lovers,[249] or avoided Argos[250] and made at once for southern Italy, it is said[251] that the fair-haired goddess with the owl's eyes made him an immortal god who received worship in Magna Graecia,[252] especially on one of the little islands, now known as Le Tremiti, opposite Monte Gargano. It was to bear his name while his followers turned into shearwaters, 'birds of Diomedes', in the marshes under Garganus.[253] Up on the mountain, where the Archangel Michael has his cult now, Kalchas, the diviner of the Greeks before Troy, supposedly had his oracle.[254]

The future enemy of Odysseus, Aias son of Telamon, was also one of Helen's suitors.[255] From his little island of Salamis he could not promise much, but he offered, and that seemed to him a large offer,[256] to make spoil of all the herds of Troizen, Epidauros, Aigina, Megara, Corinth, Hermione, Mases and

Asine. And with his long spear he would have been capable of doing it. Without the protecting presence of the goddess Athene he strode like Ares into battle.[257] In his appearance and his warlike exploits he was inferior only to Achilles.[258] Of gigantic stature,[259] with his tower-like shield,[260] which could completely cover his half-brother Teukros as well as himself,[261] unique in that he wore no corslet, he stood out above the fights at Troy like one from the olden days. Stone-throwing, like that of the ancient heroes, was still part of his art of war.[262] Later narrators made him out invulnerable, as they did Achilles.[263] and alleged that Herakles was the author of his name.[264] The son of Zeus visited Telamon, to summon him to his expedition against Troy, just as he and his followers were sitting at table. Holding the golden goblet in his hand, Herakles prayed to his father and asked a bold son for his guest-friend, the husband of fair Eriboia, a son whose body should be as impervious to wounds as his own lion-skin and whose courage should accord therewith. Zeus caused his eagle to fly to them in confirmation of these words, and thereupon Herakles, like a prophet, cried, 'A son shall be born to thee, Telamon, the son thou wouldst have. From the eagle [*aietos*] do thou name him Aias.'

According to another version,[265] Herakles made the little Aias invulnerable by wrapping him in his lion-skin, all except his armpit, where the child was not touched by the skin. For Aias was very vulnerable in his unrestrained nature, which knew no bounds either in its itch for plunder or in its munificence. At the funeral games in honour of Achilles matters came to a head. Thetis had made her son's armour, which had been fashioned by Hephaistos, the prize of honour for that hero who had deserved best in the war against Troy.[266] It was a difficult decision that had to be made between Odysseus and Aias.[267] When finally, by the will of Pallas Athene,[268] it was made in favour of the subtle and not the strong claimant, Aias went mad and killed himself.[269] It was a gruesome example of the punishment which the gods inflict on a lack of restraint which seems to us rather childish than sinful and is characteristic of none of the heroes so much as of this giant with his long spear and his towering shield.[270] In the underworld, he still was angry with Odysseus and would not answer his conciliatory words.[271] But the people of Salamis built him a shrine in their market place and erected there his statue in ebony, and the Athenians joined in their worship.[272] Before the battle of Salamis, all the Greeks prayed to Aias and his father.[273]

Allegedly, another hero of the same name, Aias son of Oileus, from East Lokris, north of Boiotia, was one of Helen's suitors, too.[274] The Salaminian was so friendly with him before Troy that, although the second was a man of far smaller stature,[275] they appeared almost as a pair of heroes, the two Aiantes, like two lions who make their prey of the same kid,[276] or two oxen who draw the same plough;[277] both were insatiable for battle.[278] Being smaller, the son of Oileus had swift feet to pursue the enemy,[279] and he was a real sinner against the gods. When Troy fell and Kassandra took refuge with the statue in which the Trojan women honoured Athene, Aias dragged her away by force. She clung to the image of the goddess so that it was overthrown.[280] But the savage Aias paid no heed to this. Even if it is not true[281] that he violated the unhappy prophetess and that the idol at sight of that sin raised its eyes to heaven,[282] that was only because the Greeks themselves prevented it and would have stoned him.[283]

Aias, who cared nothing for the gods, denied it upon oath,[284] and Kassandra had to follow Agamemnon, but the wrath of Athene pursued them both, Aias especially.[285] The fleet with which both sinners intended to return home, Agamemnon taking Kassandra, was caught in a storm off Cape Kaphareus, the southernmost extremity of the island of Euboia.[286] Aias' ship was sunk, but Poseidon let him get himself to the near-by rocks by swimming.[287] He held fast to them and cried that he had saved himself against the will of the gods. The sea-god shattered the rock and Aias was drowned.

However, the inhabitants of Opus in Lokris honoured the hero,[288] probably in the form of a great serpent which, as a late narrator told, used to follow him like a dog while he lived.[289] But to atone for his sin the Lokrians[290] had for a thousand years,[291] or even more,[292] to send a constant supply of their daughters to do the hardest service for Athene at Ilion, once in the country of Priam.[293]

It is said[294] that the two physician-heroes of the Trojan War, Machaon and Podaleirios, the sons of Asklepios, also wooed Helen. When Machaon, the wonderful physician, was wounded by Paris' arrow, it was the worst moment of the war for the Greeks.[295] Of Idomeneus, grandson of Minos, it is said in so many words that he came in person to press his suit and did not send messengers, or the like.[296] But he, too, was not destined to become famous as Helen's husband, but only through his warlike exploits before Troy and by the fate which overtook him after his return. He also met with a great storm on his voyage home. In fear, he vowed to sacrifice to Poseidon the first living thing he encountered;[297] but the first to meet him on land was his own son. Or, according to another version of the story, it was his daughter.[298] The late narrators do not say if he did actually sacrifice his child; perhaps he refused. He was driven out by his people and so had to emigrate to Magna Graecia, where he took possession of the farthest extremity of the land, south of Otranto.

Helen handed to Menelaos the crown that was reserved for the son-in-law of Zeus.[299] Agamemnon's brother's place in the great story would have been merely that of yet another king from Asia Minor, crowned by the grace of a goddess, if the deity, in the shape of Helen and by the will of Zeus and of her mother Nemesis, had not chosen him as her consort. Opposite Sparta, on the east bank of the Eurotas, stood in old days the shrine of the goddess Helen, who, as the tale went, also appeared there in person when it was a question of making an ugly baby into a beautiful girl.[300] But Menelaos was destined, after being promoted to a godhead by Helen,[301] to be carried off while yet in the body to Elysion,[302] although both of them were worshipped in Therapne at so-called tombs.[303] He was to be named as not the least of the heroes at Troy,[304] and also renowned for all time by virtue of his gentleness,[305] as befitted the companion, rather serving than commanding, of his divine consort. If the name Menelaos, 'he who awaits the people', suits a god of the underworld, yet this was a gentle god of the dead. He was fair-haired, with blue eyes, the down of youth on his cheeks, and with shapely feet.[306] Helen bore him one daughter, as it were her younger double, as Hebe was of Hera and she herself of Leda or Nemesis. The gods, so says the old tradition,[307] manifested no offspring again to Helen when once she had brought forth her lovely child Hermione.

The marriage were best compared with that of Thetis and Peleus, if, once more by the will of Zeus and this time of Aphrodite also, Paris, the new chosen one, had not made his appearance. This happened apparently in the tenth year after the wooing of Helen. We remember from the history of the Spartan Dioskuroi that the Trojan prince, who came to Lakonia in company with Aineias, the son of the love-goddess, was received by Kastor and Polydeukes. This happened not in Sparta itself but at Amyklai.[308] Furthermore, we know already that the Dioskuroi were soon drawn away by their quarrel with their cousins of Messenia. In Sparta Menelaos received the strangers. On the tenth day[309] (ten is the significant number in this story), he was obliged to journey to Crete, for he had often had Idomeneus, the grandson of Minos, for his guest.[310] Helen yielded to the power of Aphrodite like any mortal queen, as which she is represented by the great Homer.[311] She followed Paris in the night, taking with her many treasures from the royal house.[312] The pair were united on a 'Rocky Island', Kranae,[313] whichever one of the innumerable little islands of the Aegean that may have been. It was like a repetition of the story of Ariadne, save that Paris played the parts of both Theseus and Dionysos. The wedding-feast was celebrated in Troy.[314]

Iris, the messenger of the gods, brought the news to Menelaos in Crete.[315] He betook himself to his brother at Mycenae,[316] and also sought advice from king Nestor at Pylos,[317] the one surviving son of Neleus, for Herakles had killed the rest; it seems that the gist of the counsel of that already old and wise man was this, to go with Odysseus to Peleus and induce him to send his son Achilles to Troy.[318] The fate of Thetis' son was bound up with Troy; of that the Moirai must have sung with lofty yet obscure words at the wedding of his parents. All Greece seems to have known of this destiny, though not so well as his divine mother. But Achilles was not bound by the oath of the suitors to take part in the campaign. To the erstwhile suitors Agamemnon sent messengers,[319] reminding them of their oath and also that from then on no king in all Greece could be sure of his wife if they did not punish the seducer. Even so it needed ten years[320] to move them all to assemble their men and ships at Aulis and then to sail away towards Troy.

Odysseus was cunning enough—he alone[321] with the excep⁄tion of Peleus, who knew from Thetis of his son's destiny and therefore did not wish to send him[322]—to avoid the call. It was said[323] that an oracle had warned him that he should return alone to his people only after twenty years. And in fact the Trojan War was to last ten years and the wanderings of Odysseus another ten. So, when Agamemnon, with a great following which included not only Menelaos but also Pala⁄medes, son of Nauplios and the Danaid Amymone,[324] arrived in Ithake, the ingenious Odysseus behaved like a mad⁄man. Not long before, he had married Penelope. They had a little son, whom they were soon, with good reason, to name Telemachos, for then it was decided that his father should become 'a fighter far away'. As if he were completely out of his wits, Odysseus yoked a horse and an ox to his plough and wore a cap on his head[325] which was quite unworthy of a king but made him look like a comic Kabeiros, or Hephaistos.

Palamedes, the hero of 'skill of hand and feats of skill', *palamai*, saw through him. He put little Telemachos on the

69 PARIS COMING HOME FROM IDA

70 PELEUS BRINGS ACHILLES TO CHIRON

71 ORESTES AND IPHIGENEIA BEFORE
THE TAURIAN TEMPLE

ground in front of the insane ploughman, and said to him, 'Come and join us.'[326] Odysseus had no choice, unless he wanted to drive the furrow through his own son. But he soon showed his hateful side to Palamedes. The latter was to be known to posterity not only as a great inventor, the originator of letters,[327] numbered dice and counting,[328] but also as the first man to be unjustly condemned. The Greeks stoned him under the walls of Troy after Odysseus had smuggled gold and a forged letter from Priam into his tent.[329]

In Homer we hear nothing of all this, nor is the tale told of how Achilles, before Nestor and Odysseus could bring him, was placed in safety by Thetis.[330] She sent the lad, then nine years old,[331] to king Lykomedes on the island of Skyros, where Theseus met his undeserved death; according to his name, the king had the 'thoughts of a wolf'. Achilles, in Homer, calls the king of Skyros Enyeus,[332] a name which means a good warrior, but elsewhere we learn of this Enyeus that he was a son of Dionysos and Ariadne.[333] Achilles fared on Skyros as the child Dionysos had in the house of Athamas;[334] he was brought up there as a girl. He lived with the king's daughters and was known as Pyrrha, 'red-head', from the colour of his hair.[335]

Word got abroad that Achilles was hidden in Lykomedes' house. The king of Skyros was sure that the boy would not be found, and sent a message to the kings gathered about Agamemnon, 'Come and look for him.' Odysseus made his appearance in Lykomedes' palace and brought women's clothes with him, which he wished to offer to the king's daughters. Thus he was admitted to the *parthenon*, the girls' quarters.[336] Under the clothing were hidden a shield and a spear. While Odysseus was showing the girls all the finery, he had a trumpet-call sounded as if to battle. Achilles snatched at the weapons and was thus discovered. But by that time the princess Deidameia, 'compeller of enemies', was pregnant by the hero.[337] She bore him the future warrior with the double name, Pyrrhos, 'red-head', or Neoptolemos, 'renewer of war', and Achilles was proud of his son.[338] Later, Odysseus was to fetch him also from Skyros,[339] so that the Greeks could take Troy.

As Homer tells the story,[340] Achilles ran out from his father's house to meet Odysseus and Nestor, admiringly led the two heroic warriors in by hand, and Peleus could not bear to hold him back. He gave his son his immortal horses, the gift of Poseidon, to which Hera was to lend human speech,[341] to warn their young master or to foretell his early end, and his mighty spear, the shaft of which had been cut at his wedding.

CHAPTER IX

Iphigeneia and her Brother and Sisters

WHEN AGAMEMNON WENT TO AULIS to the assembly of the allied kings, in order to lead the army of the Greeks against Troy, he left three daughters and one promising son,[342] the little Orestes, behind in his city with his unhallowed wife Klytaimnestra. The names of the daughters were, according to Homer, Chrysothemis, Laodike and Iphianassa,[343] but the two who were to be renowned especially through the tragedians are known to us by different names, Elektra instead of Laodike and Iphigeneia instead of Iphianassa.[344] True, not all poets took Iphigeneia and Iphianassa to be two names for the same heroine,[345] though it is certain that to begin with they served indifferently to address the same divine being, who had not belonged from all time to the family of Agamemnon. Iphianassa signifies 'she who governs mightily', and Iphigeneia 'she who governs births mightily', perhaps, and Iphigeneia was a title of Artemis.[346] In her person there appeared alongside of Helen another and much sterner manifestation of the Moon-goddess in her many forms, resembling Artemis and not Aphrodite, in the closest connection with the House of Atreus

We know from the stories of Theseus that Iphigeneia was actually thought to be a daughter of Helen, who bore her after being rescued from Aphidna and handed her over to her sister to be reared. According to the story which now follows, Iphigeneia was the first-born and most beautiful daughter of Agamemnon and Klytaimnestra. While the army and the fleet which was to take it across were assembling at Aulis— indeed were assembling for the second time, according to the Cyprian poet who told of the prelude to the War of Troy and the events of it up to those in the 'Iliad', interpolating the tale of Telephos before that of Iphigeneia—the great king and commander of the Greeks sinned against Artemis.[347] The great bay where the ships were waiting lay, it seems, between Hyria and Aulis—the two places which Homer names first[348]— opposite Euboia, in Boiotia, in a region where now there are no woods to be seen any more; but it then had, besides the temple of the goddess,[349] a sacred grove of Artemis.[350] There Agamemnon's sin was committed, and there it must be atoned for.

The story of Agamemnon's offence is not easy to repeat, since the late narrators of it shorten and simplify it very much,[351] if they do not corrupt it,[352] and the tragedians do no more than allude to it. It would appear that on that occasion unfavourable weather for the sea-voyage was lasting unusually long. Thereupon Agamemnon promised to offer to the goddess the fairest thing that the year had yielded.[353] This, it seems, Artemis accepted; but it happened that the king accidentally[354] caught sight of a fawn in the goddess's grove, with its antlers sprouting and a dappled hide.[355] Did the goddess desire this beautiful creature as a sacrifice to herself? A careless word escaped the king's mouth,[356] 'Not even Artemis herself...'.[357] He probably meant[358] 'Not even Artemis, if she wished, could save the beast now', for he killed the fawn immediately[359] with sure aim, in the sacred grove. If only his too great self-confidence had not called the power of the goddess in question!

So the favourable weather ceased again, be it that a gale rose[360] or that the wind failed altogether.[361] Kalchas, the diviner of the army, was consulted, and he revealed[362] that Agamemnon's eldest daughter must be sacrificed to calm the wrath of the offended goddess; she was the only equivalent for the misconducted sacrifice.[363] But how would Klytaimnestra yield up her daughter to be a victim? Odysseus is said to have thought of the lie:[364] Iphigeneia was to come to Aulis to marry Achilles. Marriage and death, as in the famous lament of Oidipus' daughter,[365] were always associated ideas, ever since

Hades carried off Persephone. An embassy was sent to Klytaimnestra, with Odysseus for its spokesman,[366] and she herself
accompanied her daughter to the wedding.[367]

But Iphigeneia was not dragged by her fair hair to the
sacrifice.[368] A wall-painting at Pompeii shows us Odysseus
and Diomedes lifting her up in their arms[369] and carrying her
to the altar. The saffron-dyed dress[370] which the girls who
served Artemis at Brauron used to wear[371] slipped off her, her
bosom lay bare to the knife.[372] Agamemnon turned away and
covered his face. She stretched out her arms to her goddess.
Kalchas, the sacrificial priest, however, now saw what was
coming. Artemis watched over the scene and showed her
power to save, which Agamemnon had doubted. At the very
moment of the killing[373] she substituted a hind for the girl and
carried off Iphigeneia through the air to the Tauric Peninsula
—we call it the Crimea now—to serve her as priestess among
the barbarians. Human beings were sacrificed to her there,
namely such Greeks as were cast ashore. These the priestess had
to take possession of for the goddess,[374] who there was named
Parthenos—that is, Maiden—or actually Iphigeneia,[375] and who
enjoyed such inhuman worship. Yet Iphigeneia was to find
her Greek home again on Attic soil, at Brauron, as a heroine
in the service of Artemis and her *alter ego*.[376]

The Greeks were of opinion that they had sacrificed Iphigeneia,[377] and it was in vain that Klytaimnestra knew better, if
indeed she did. Her maternal pride was injured by the deceit
and the loss of her daughter, and her savage nature showed
itself to the uttermost against her husband. So there were deeds
of blood in Agamemnon's house after his return from the
war, which his eldest daughter was to learn of much later.
Agamemnon was butchered like an ox, says the account in
the 'Odyssey', not in his own palace but in the house of Aigisthos, who had received him hospitably on his arrival.[378] He
never guessed that his wife had long since followed the avenger
who had seduced her to his home.[379] The only person who
could have warned him, Kassandra, fell a victim to the hand of

Klytaimnestra, whose first murder was that of her husband's
concubine.[380] The merciless woman[381] raged in the fulfilment of
her long-planned revenge (it occurred, according to Aeschylus,
in the palace of Agamemnon), and struck home twice, even
a third time, with her axe[382] when the Great King, stepping
out of his bath and entangled in the bath-robe, could not
defend himself. Thus she herself describes it[383] in the tragedy
which bears the name of Agamemnon for its title. It might
have been part of the plan of revenge to murder also the future
avenger, her own son, Orestes.

Him Elektra had protected, the sister with the name of a
great goddess whom we know from the history of Kadmos,
like a second Pallas Athene; she had brought him out of range
of Aigisthos' power into safety.[384] Orestes was worthy of his
name, 'man of the mountain', during the time when he was
growing up in Phokis and later, when after the murder of his
mother he wandered about pursued by the Erinyes. Phokis
includes the high mountainous country about Delphi. There
the boy was received at the foot of Parnassos, probably in the
town of Krisa, by old Strophios, his father's guest-friend[385] and
relative,[386] and found in his son Pylades the true friend who
was to accompany him in his wanderings. They grew up
together, two young men, certainly dear to and under the protection of Apollo, the god of the oracle in whose neighbourhood
they lived. When Orestes inquired of the oracle[387] if he should
avenge his father's murder, that was even more fitting than the
inquiries by other heroes of the god of Delphi. As his father's
adult son he would no doubt have set out to revenge him even
of his own design; but might the son take vengeance for his
father's death on his own mother? Who would take the
responsibility for that? Apollo, by one account, presented the
youth with a bow with which to defend himself against the
Erinyes, the avenging spirits of his mother.[388] The god's
directions left no room for doubt.

For seven years Aigisthos ruled over the kingdom of Argos
and Mycenae. In the eighth year Orestes returned from Phokis

by way of Athens.[389] He came, it would seem, under the protection of Pallas Athene, a true daughter of her father, who was represented as it were in the family of Agamemnon by Elektra, to the royal city of his fathers. Homer refrains from details and avoids describing the revenge of the son on his mother and her paramour. We will follow his example rather than that of the great tragedians, who act out the scene of the murder each in his own fashion; Aeschylus in the 'Choephoroi', that is 'The Libation-bearers', Sophokles and Euripides in the tragedies which are both entitled 'Elektra'. They may be taken as guides on this field of blood. On the day on which Orestes organised the funeral feast over his horrible mother and the cowardly Aigisthos, Menelaos too arrived at Argos with Helen from their wanderings after the Trojan War, and went on further overland to Sparta.[390] Orestes was still very far from finding his rest in a hero's grave in Arkadia.[391]

Two of the great tragedians picture to us his pursuit by the Erinyes, Aeschylus in his 'Eumenides' and Euripides in the 'Orestes'. The bow which Apollo gave him, indeed the very arrows of the god, which he aimed in his Delphian temple against the primaeval goddesses who avenged matricide,[392] did the victim of their pursuit little good. Even the supreme Athenian court, before which Apollo took the responsibility on himself and Athene cast her vote for Orestes,[393] did not by universal tradition free the matricide by its equally divided verdict. The wanderings of Orestes were not to end yet. Not all the Erinyes set him free; many followed him further.[394] Then he prostrated himself on the ground before the altar of the god at Delphi and begged for a final counsel, since otherwise he could not remain alive.[395]

Thus Orestes received the direction to bring from the land of the Taurians the image of Artemis which fell from heaven.[396] Iphigeneia served before that image, and to her the god, without saying so, had sent Orestes and Pylades. When they arrived, the two young Greeks were to be consecrated for sacrifice by her. Then followed the recognition and the rescue of them all, the theft of the image and the bringing home of the priestess, a tale for poets, old and new, to relate. Of the ancients, Euripides made it his subject, and after him a modern, in a manner still more worthy, as it must seem to us today, of the hardly veiled divine figure of Iphigeneia.

CHAPTER X

Telephos

I T W A S N O T only the Trojan War which started from Aulis. The sequel of the sacrifice of Iphigeneia takes us far be-yond it into the future. The first expedition of the Greeks turned into an involuntary campaign, the description of which must lead us back to earlier events. The tale went that the Greek fleet which assembled at Aulis put to sea as early as the second year after the abduction of Helen,[397] but that by mistake it landed, not in Phrygia, Priam's kingdom, but somewhat further south, in the coastal district of Mysia which was called Teuthrania after king Teuthras.[398] There the Greeks found kinsfolk to oppose them, who strove to check their advance, and as their principal opponent a hero who according to the tellers of the tale had been driven there from Arkadia, but whose worship, both on the Arkadian mountain Parthenion and in Asia Minor, seems to rest on very old legends. He was repre-sented as not only a son of Herakles, but as that son whom his mother bore to resemble his father most closely.[399] His name was Telephos, or more accurately—so it seems to have been understood and used again—Telephanes, 'he who shines afar'.

In most versions his mother is called Auge, a word ordinarily used to mean 'light'. No doubt that is what she was called in that old tale also,[400] in which Herakles met her on his way to Laomedon, assuredly in the house of king Teuthras, who in all accounts had received the mother of Telephos. According to this legend, Telephos, son of Herakles, was begotten in Asia Minor and did not merely emigrate there from Arkadia.[401] In Arkadia itself there was a sacred story, connected with the temple of Athena Alea and the holy precinct of Telephos on Parthenion, which was told of the conception and birth of the hero. Alea, the epithet of Athena at Tegea, signifies the cherishing warmth which is eagerly sought in the south during the cold and damp of certain seasons of the year. After it also the father of Auge[402] and founder of the temple[403] was called Aleos. Auge was supposed to be a priestess of Athena at Tegea;[404] she was rather her *alter ego*, save for this difference— that she underwent childbirth and consequently had her image in Tegea as 'Auge on the knees', in the attitude of a woman in labour in old times.[405]

How she conceived her child was a sacred story, because it was connected with a temple. But it was none the less a gloomy one; it resembled the story of the violation of Pelopia by her own father. It can hardly have happened at the full moon in a night when the nuptials were celebrated and Achilles was conceived, although the narrators know of a nocturnal choral dance.[406] These were held for Athene at new moon. It was also the time at which girls used to wash their clothes, blood-spotted clothes according to the story of Pelopia, and we are told in so many words that Auge was surprised at the spring by the temple of Athena Alea by Herakles.[407] Pompeian wall-paintings show her just in the act of washing her garments. By way of excuse for Herakles it is alleged that he was drunk.[408] He was then coming from Sparta,[409] where he had put Tyndareos back on the throne,[410] and what happened was rare in the career of that servant of women; as the tool of the divine power which willed this birth he became a violator.

According to one account, Auge hid her secretly born child at first in the sacred precinct of Athena;[411] but the goddess would have none of this and sent warning signs. Aleos discovered the secret, exposed Telephos on Parthenion, and sent Auge oversea by Nauplios, son of Poseidon.[412] Thus, or even in a chest, as the coins of the harbour town of Eleia in Teuthrania show us, she came to king Teuthras. Telephos was suckled by a hind on Parthenion, which by another account was his birthplace.[413] She wore antlers,[414] like the wonderful hind of Artemis. The great goddess, who presumably was called Parthenos on those heights and Alea below on the plain of Tegea, protected the child and perhaps had willed his birth.

Herakles also returned and was amazed at the marvellous child, who found a companion on Mount Parthenion in the person of Parthenopaios, Atalante's son.[415]

That is the more cheerful tale of the birth which followed upon the gloomier one of the conception, as decked out by poets and painters. The boy nurtured by the doe, a son of Herakles who resembled his father, had to become a wanderer. Not very different in his lot from other errant heroes, he grew up among king Korythos' herdsmen[416] in Arkadia and was adopted by the king himself as his son.[417] Korythos was an epithet also of Apollo, as a god of healing,[418] whom Telephos later sorely needed. As a young man he became the slayer of his uncles, the brothers of Auge, and so was struck dumb,[419] for it was the law for homicides that they must lose their voice.[420] The oracle bade the speechless Telephos[421] depart to 'the farthest Mysians'.[422] Without uttering a word, he journeyed across the sea to Teuthrania. It was also said that Parthenopaios accompanied him.[423] King Teuthras was hard pressed by an enemy, and the two heroes, especially Telephos, rescued him. Certainly Teuthras purified him from blood-guilt, but did he recover his voice? Was he dumb by design or in reality? There almost the same thing happened to him as to Oidipus;[424] Teuthras gave him Auge, whom he had adopted as his daughter, to wife, and they were already lying together when a huge snake appeared between them. At that moment —if not, indeed, earlier—Telephos got his voice back, and the mother recognised her son.

By all accounts, Telephos succeeded Teuthras on the throne. His wife is variously named Argiope, 'white-faced', or[425] Hiera, 'holy', an imposing Amazonian figure, who was to fall in the great battle with the Greeks on the plain of Kaikos.[426] His son was Eurypylos, 'he of the wide gate', leader of the Keteioi,[427] a people whom the later Greeks almost completely forgot,[428] but they probably were survivors from the empire of the Hittites. Among the sons of Telephos were also reckoned Tarchon and Tyrsenos, two founder-heroes of the Etruscans who made a home in Italy,[429] and finally Kyparissos,[430] Apollo's beloved who was turned into a cypress.[431] Telephos, the Arkadian hero with Asian connections, perhaps a hero of that distant time in which Greeks still belonged to the Hittite empire, joined battle with the Greeks who, imagining that they were in the Troad, were laying Teuthrania waste.

The battle-field was the plain at the mouth of the river Kaikos.[432] Telephos drove the new arrivals back to their ships,[433] only Achilles and Patroklos resisting him still.[434] Patroklos had been sent by Peleus as an older[435] follower to serve Achilles.[436] But from then on, as that follower showed his courage, the younger hero never again allowed himself to be separated from him on the battle-field. For Patroklos, who should have attended to Achilles, was already heedless; he was wounded by Telephos. The vase-painting of the master Sosias shows us how he who had learned to treat wounds from Achilles,[437] was himself bandaged by him. Telephos was driven back by Achilles and took to flight; in his flight he was entangled in the vines which covered the plain of the Kaikos,[438] and thus received from Achilles a deep wound in the upper thigh, which would not heal.

However, he had not driven off the Greeks in vain. They sailed back to Argos[439] and were slow in reassembling at Aulis; but for Telephos there now began the most painful journey to the man who had wounded him. From the oracle of Apollo at Patara in Lykia[440] he received by way of advice the saying, 'He who wounded shall also heal.'[441] He must seek out Achilles and obtain healing from him, a story which the tragedians fastened upon still more than they did upon the earlier fortunes of Telephos. Euripides put him on the stage in the guise of a beggar, wearing the Mysian felt cap,[442] in the circle of the Greek kings.[443] His eloquence and the means which he employed to attain his end do not belong to the old tale. Achilles, who had cured Patroklos, healed him; it was also told, however, that the cure must be brought about not by the hero who had dealt the wound but by the weapon which had done so.[444] The remedy was scraped off the point of the famous spear[445] and sprinkled on the wound. Cured and become a friend of the Greeks, Telephos was able to return home, if he did not himself actually lead them to Troy.[446]

It was not to him but to his son Eurypylos, who succeeded him on the throne,[447] that Priam sent an embassy and begged help. At first Eurypylos did not venture, for his mother's sake, to respond to the call; then Priam sent him a golden vine,[448] presumably to atone for the wound which Telephos had once got when entangled in the vines, and so the son set out for the war. His mother was surely not that Hiera who had fallen in battle against the Greeks. Heroic offerings were later made to Telephos at Pergamon. No one coming from these offerings was to enter the temple of Asklepios until he had bathed.[449] In the hymns which were sung to the healing god in the Askle pieion, however, Telephos was celebrated first.[450] But it was forbidden for Eurypylos to be mentioned by anyone in the holy place because under the walls of Troy he had killed the physician-hero Machaon.

CHAPTER XI

Protesilaos and Laodameia

EIGHT YEARS ELAPSED after the first sortie of the Greeks before they reassembled in Aulis[451] and were ready to start. They knew that at least nine years of war awaited them, for they had been gathered in Aulis but two or three days when the portent took place which Homer relates in the 'Iliad'.[452] They were busied about the making of an offering of the finest cows at altars close to a freely flowing spring, which, like so many in Greece, poured forth under a great plane-tree. Many centuries later a piece of wood from that tree was shown in the temple of Artemis.[453] During the sacrifice there appeared a snake with a blood-red back. From the altar, out from under which it had crept, it hurled itself at the plane, on the topmost branch of which was the nest of a swallow with her brood. The snake devoured the eight nestlings at once, then finally, their mother. The monster itself was turned to stone by Zeus. Thus it was seen that this was no natural happening, and Kalchas the prophet interpreted it: the war was to last nine years, and Troy would not fall till the tenth.

Troy, also known as Ilios or Ilion, already showed itself by this sign to be a place of death for the Greeks, where so many years of each one of their lives and so many lives themselves should be completely devoured. Apollo of the silver bow[454] in his deadliest form defended the city. Troy stood under the protection of the bow, whether the god himself or a mortal hand guided by him directed the arrows of death. Spears and swords, nay even shields and corslets, were of little use there. Only one bow could have opposed it. It will not have been forgotten that Herakles on his pyre presented his bow, with which he had so often fought death, to a passer-by who had taken the way over Mount Oita; whether it was Poias or Philoktetes, the father or the son, the recipient was a native of

Thessaly, in the neighbourhood of Phthia, where Eurytion had once been ruler, and Peleus after him. With this bow Philoktetes now appeared in Aulis, for the 'lover of the possession' (that is what his name means) never would be separated from this possession. He was soon to be separated from his followers, who accompanied him on seven ships and were all good bowmen,[455] and the bow was to be of no use to the Greeks, now heading for Troy, for a long time yet.

There lay a little island some considerable distance from Troy, close to Lemnos.[456] It was long known;[457] the altar which had become famous through Philoktetes, the hero's weapons and a bronze figure of a snake were shown on it. The islet was also called Nea, that is 'new',[458] a very proper name for a volcanic island which could easily disappear again, as it is said this one ultimately did.[459] For the old narrators its name was Chryse, 'the golden', after the golden cult-partner of the god with the silver bow, who could also manifest himself with one of gold.[460] Apollo stood over the island as its protector and lord;[461] he had his altar there, to which nine years later the Greeks were to send a hecatomb by way of sin-offering.[462] On that occasion, when they landed on Chryse for the first time and so passed the border by which the larger circuit of Troy might be bounded, it is said that Philoktetes guided them there, to bring an offering to the goddess, which was a prerequisite for the taking of Ilios.[463] Jason had built the altar[464] (in late accounts Philoktetes was one of the Argonauts),[465] or else it was Herakles on his journey to Laomedon.[466]

Now, whether it was Philoktetes who led them to the altar or the Greeks of their own design wished to visit the sanctuary, the goddess brought to pass something compared to which the portent at Aulis was at best but a pale imitation. Her sacred serpent, the guardian of the temple,[467] attacked, of all those that approached, him who carried the bow of Herakles. It bit him in the foot,[468] and from the bite was left a festering wound which repelled all the Greeks.[469] His retainers carried the wounded man over to Lemnos and left him and his bow lying there. Philoktetes was the first victim, but the second, who actually died, followed when the Greeks trod Trojan soil for the first time. This second victim was perhaps a cousin of Philoktetes, being a son of Iphiklos, who according to one tradition[470] was a brother of Poias.

Iphiklos belonged to Phylake, again in the neighbourhood of Phthia, and was a son of Phylakos, who was renowned for his herds; his name means 'watcher'.[471] Iphiklos himself, whose name signifies 'renowned for strength', had no children, for he was unable to beget any. Then the prophet Melampus— he whom we know as Proitos' heir and the healer of his daughters[472]—came to Phylake to steal Phylakos' cows, with which he meant to woo the beautiful Pero, Neleus' daughter, for his brother Bias; but he was caught before he could do so. Yet, since he actually understood the speech of the wood-worms in the beams, he succeeded, to the great amazement of Phylakos and his men, in saving himself from his prison, which was about to collapse. The price of his liberty and of the cows was, however, the healing of Iphiklos. Melampus had two bulls slaughtered and with their meat attracted the birds of prey, among whom an old vulture came flying down, and from him Melampus learned the reason for Iphiklos' weakness. As a child he had seen his father geld rams and afterwards throw down the knife close to him. The boy ran away, his father was furious and drove the knife deep into a sacred oak. In time the bark grew over it. The prophet had the knife taken out of the tree, scraped it and gave the rust to Iphiklos to drink.

Thus Iphiklos was cured. He first begot Podarkes, 'swift-foot', to whom he gave that name because he could himself run so quickly over the cornfields that he never bent a stalk.[473] His second, and better, child was Protesilaos,[474] whose name expressed the claim to be foremost, 'the first who looses the warriors'. He was the first to jump ashore when the ships were beached at Troy. An unknown Trojan killed him, and he left behind a young wife and a half-finished house.[475] But in those days a consummation, the carrying out to the end of a sacrifice

72 ACHILLES AND TROILOS

73 ACHILLES AND PENTHESILEIA

or taking part in an initiation which brought the initiates into close association with the underworld powers, a *telete*, was war too.[476] Later it was told[477] that Protesilaos had given Ilios its first initiation, and the Greeks raised him a particularly high barrow at Elaius across the Hellespont. From its summit Troy could be seen,[478] and inside it the hero was honoured as in a temple.[479] It was believed[480] that the elms which stood about this hero-shrine[481] withered, and then grew again, when they were so tall that their tops could see the hostile city.

But a great favour of the gods of the underworld was reserved for Protesilaos. His young wife was left unsatisfied by the scarcely begun marriage; nor could the highest honours which a fallen hero could receive compensate her for the loss of her husband. She had been really the wife of Protesilaos for but a single day,[482] this Polydora, daughter of Meleagros,[483] or, to use the name which poets both early and late have made famous,[484] Laodameia, daughter of Akastos. As Laodameia, she herself bore a name of the queen of the underworld, 'she who masters the people'. As Polydora, 'rich-in-gifts', she had rather a Dionysiac name. What she undertook was worthy also of the house of her grandfather Oineus, who was once visited by Dionysos. For from the half-finished house of Protesilaos she returned thither, rather than, as others would have it,[485] to that of Akastos, and was to be married a second time.[486] But she preferred the nocturnal rites of Dionysos, secret ceremonies which representations on late sarcophagi hint at to us. Thus it fell to her lot that not Dionysos but her own husband appeared from the underworld and she united herself to him in everlasting companionship.

The gods of the underworld showed Protesilaos this favour; they let him go for one day,[487] or perhaps but three hours,[488] to his wife, not as a shade but in his living vigour, as if he had not died.[489] Tales were told of an image of her husband which she contrived and to which she was actually talking when Hermes brought Protesilaos to her.[490] The representation on a sarcophagus shows the head in a shrine for Dionysiac sacred objects. She was bringing the portrait an offering of fruits,[491] in the winnowing-basket, as we can see on another sarco- phagus. Now she belonged again to her husband, and after Protesilaos disappeared, she too was dead. She died in his embrace,[492] or took her own life.[493] She was burned with the image and the Dionysiac apparatus.[494] In his native town of Phylake there were also races in honour of Protesilaos.[495] On the Hellespont he received offerings of grapes and other fruits and in spring, of milk.[496]

CHAPTER XII

Achilles and the Aftermath of the Trojan War

HIS MOTHER had been loth to let Achilles go against Ilios. Agamemnon and his allies had done everything possible to induce him to join in the war and to move Peleus to send his son with them. They knew of Achilles' origin and that he was the only son of a goddess among them. Thetis on the other hand clearly foresaw her son's fate, that he could not with impunity overthrow Hektor, the bulwark of the city which Apollo protected. And who would be capable of holding him back from an achievement which his great soul drove him to? His was a different destiny from that of the 'god-hero' Herakles. Achilles, the most beautiful of the heroes who gathered before Troy,[497] and so much 'born for a short time'[498] that he above all others must be called the 'mortal hero', maintained in the face of death, and taking death upon himself, his half-divine form with the dark shadow which it bore.

The Judgement of Paris and his unnecessarily insulting words put two goddesses on the side of the assailants from the outset, even if they had not been already the protectresses of Greek heroes: Athene and Hera. It was not mortals delivered over entirely to the arrows of Apollo, but heroes with destinies of their own, who wished to take Troy. They had free play in the struggle with the warriors who came against them; the god did not guide the hand of every one of them. According to the old narrators, even the Kyknos who tried to hinder the Greeks in the strait between the mainland and Tenedos,[499] or on the shore afterwards,[500] was no son of Apollo, any more than that other Kyknos whom Herakles killed on his way back from Diomedes of Thrace. It is only of a third Kyknos that we are told in late narratives[501] that he was Apollo's son, and of a fourth, a king of the Ligurians and a relative of Phaethon, that he turned into a swan[502] in his mourning for the son of Helios, which of course does not prevent there having been some lost and very old tale of a single Kyknos, a son of Apollo whose name was Swan, and who probably was always a Thracian.

The Kyknos who was the first to attack the Greeks may have been a Thracian ally of Priam; allegedly he was the off-spring of Poseidon and Kalyke, 'flower-calix', a nymph. The child was surrounded by swans when fishermen found him on the beach.[503] When he met Achilles, the next after Protesilaos to land, he was not like a man but like a figure of terror, all white[504] and invulnerable.[505] He threatened the son of Thetis[506] with blows from a leather thong, and Achilles struck down this primaeval figure with a stone,[507] a deed long cele-brated by the poets.[508] Kyknos let out a cry[509] like the swans in the hour of their death; but the Trojans, when they saw him fall, retired behind their walls, and the siege began.[510] The women from the city came out only to a certain fountain in front of the oft-mentioned Skaian Gates, near the temple of Apollo Thymbraios, named from the fragrant savory, *thymbra*.[511] They fetched water, accompanied by a young man on horseback; and this led to a terrible deed of Achilles, which the poets of later times hardly recounted any more, though the older artists were all the fonder of putting it on vases intended for graves, on the pediments of temples, and on weapons or on the walls of sepulchres. The character of the sacrifice to a horrible deity preserved this deed for ever.

How else could it be understood that Achilles lurked behind the well-house,[512] not for the purpose of capturing the women, but to slay the young man at the near-by altar of the god? In Greece, young men belonged to Apollo, although not as blood-sacrifices. They were accustomed to bring rams for themselves. But we know that handsome youths such as Hyakinthos[513] or Kyparissos[514] often enough had the god's impetuosity to thank for their deaths. It seems as if Achilles wanted to mollify the Trojans' deadly Apollo by this human sacrifice. He let the women and girls run away—one of them was a daughter of Priam and Hekabe, Polyxena—and dashed at the fleeing youth, who was little more than a boy; it was Troilos, a brother of Polyxena and perhaps actually a son of Apollo, whom Hekabe had conceived by the god.[515] Tradition tells us[516] that his death was a necessary preliminary to the taking of Ilion. Then it was seen how thoroughly Achilles deserved his epithet of Swift foot.[517] He caught the lad as he galloped away on his great horse, pulled him down by his hair and dragged him to the altar of Apollo Thymbraios, on which, according to the testimony of an ancient art-monument, it was customary to offer cocks. By this time Troilos' brothers, led by Hektor, were hurrying to his help, but they were not able to prevent the butchery; vase-paintings show us the boy's trunk lying on the altar while Achilles flings the victim's head to the Trojans. Troilos' delight in riding[518] was all too premature and Achilles' cruel approach to Thymbraian Apollo was of no avail.

The predicted nine years went on with the pillage of the country around Troy and the capture of many cities by the hand of Achilles. He even led plundering raids on the great island of Lesbos and brought back women of skill by way of booty. He gave them nearly all to Agamemnon,[519] yet kept for himself the beautiful Diomede,[520] though she could hold but second place, after Briseis, daughter of Briseus.[521] Briseis' father had a name which was an epithet of Dionysos on Lemnos and probably also in Mysia, where Briseus was his priest.[522] And Briseis was like golden Aphrodite;[523] Achilles had made her his prey at Lyrnessos in Mysia,[524] the city of her husband Mynes, whom he killed in battle along with her three brothers.[525] She would gladly have accompanied him to Phthia as his wife.[526]

In the same raid,[527] at the taking of Thebe, the strong city under wooded Plakos, Chryseis, daughter of Chryses, fell into Greek hands.[528] This Thebe was the home of Eetion, father of Andromache, Hektor's wife with her Amazonian name, 'she

of the battle against men'. Eetion was killed in battle by
Achilles and buried with heroic honours.[529] Andromache's
seven brothers also fell, all on the same day and by the hand of
Achilles.[530] Andromache's mother, who ruled as queen in
Thebe,[531] became his prisoner, but he let her go for ransom.
The daughter of Chryses, priest of Apollo at Chryse, was
assigned to Agamemnon when the booty was divided.[532] She
was the only one who could be thought equal to Briseis as a
concubine. It was in vain that Chryses came later (it doubtless
needed time for him to get word of his daughter's capture on
his out-of-the-way island), in his priestly costume,[533] to the
king, to ask for her return at the price of a large ransom. We
know already that Agamemnon was not the man to part
easily from a woman. He rudely repulsed the priest,[534] and so
the anger of the god broke out over the Greek host, as it were
from that ominous island Chryse.

The arrows from his silver bow[535] sent plague, first among
the mules and dogs of the Greeks, then among themselves. This
led to the quarrel between Agamemnon, who was now obliged
to send Chryses' daughter back, and Achilles, from whom the
great king took Briseis as compensation. Thetis' son withdrew
in high dudgeon from the fighting (we know the story of all
those gloomy days and sorrowful nights in the tenth year of the
war, from the 'Iliad') and would have voyaged home with his
Myrmidones, had not the inconsiderate Patroklos, to whom in
a moment of weakness he gave the use of his own armour,
been so bold as to try to mount the walls of Troy, where
Apollo stood on guard.[536] Three times Patroklos gained the
battlements, and three times the god thrust him back. And
when he proceeded to attack three times more and killed thrice
nine Trojans,[537] Apollo struck him with his bare hand, so
that Achilles' armour fell off him. Of the human beings,
Eurphorbos, son of Panthus, the priest of Apollo at Troy,[538]
hurled a spear at him, and Hektor came third and adminis-
tered the *coup de grace* with a lance-thrust.[539]

Achilles had entrusted his armour to his friend on condition that he should not allow himself to be tempted into attacking Ilion without him, for Apollo loved the Trojans too much.[540] But what took place was what Thetis had foretold to her son.[541] And now again, when, forgetting his wrath, he was for charging out at once against Hektor to avenge Patroklos, she gave him another prophecy, 'When Hektor falls, straightway your death is dight.'[542] He replied,[543] 'Then let me die straightway.' Thus he took death upon himself. It meant nothing to him that he recovered Briseus' fair daughter with a great oath from Agamemnon that he had not touched her.[544] Homer gives us a sufficient description of the beautiful armour which Hephaistos forged for Achilles at Thetis' wish;[545] but the recipient's thoughts were at once engaged again by the corpse of his friend and he wished his mother to protect it against the flies.[546]

It would be impossible for Hektor to withstand his attack, and nothing was more natural than that he began by fleeing from the raging Achilles, whom not even the gods could have stayed.[547] Pallas Athene, the enemy of the Trojans and protectress of Achilles, watched over the duel which had become so unequal. Apollo appeared to Hektor for the last time,[548] but his dying eyes saw the god return[549] to avenge him in days to come. Achilles would not be deterred by any prophecy, and was about to lead the attack upon Troy at once over Hektor's body, when he stopped in the middle of his fiery speech.[550] The thought of his friend's still unburied corpse held him back. He had yet to perform the most grisly offering to the dead, the slaughter of twelve young Trojans on Patroklos' funeral pyre,[551] and to be softened by old Priam, who ventured to make his way to the slayer of so many of his sons in the Greek camp by night. Achilles gave up the ill-used body of his enemy Hektor to be buried with heroic honours.[552]

There were also battles awaiting him, which Homer no longer sang, with allies of the Trojans, famous opponents who came against him after the fall of Hektor and undertook the defence of Troy. There came Penthesileia the Amazon. She is said to have accidentally killed the mother of Hippolytos, Hippolyte or whatever the queen of the Amazons was called. This has been told in connection with Theseus. Priam was to purify Ares' daughter from this homicide,[553] though in his youth the old king had had to fight the Amazons himself on the river Sangarios;[554] it was a battle in which large armies were engaged on both sides. It was alleged[555] that these warlike women had to distinguish themselves in battle against men before they might choose a lover, and therefore the virgin Penthesileia now hastened with her followers to the walls of Troy. She appeared during Hektor's funeral with an army of Amazons.[556] Achilles had granted Priam eleven days' truce in which to bury his son.[557] So this was the twelfth day, and the hero had scarcely recovered yet from his profound grief. Then the beautiful Penthesileia, whose name contained the element *penthos*, 'mourner's grief', assailed him like an incarnation of the queen of the underworld. How lovely she was and how worthy to replace the daughter of Briseus (although she was more like Artemis than like Aphrodite)[558] Achilles did not realise until his spear had already pierced her breast[559] and she could scarcely raise herself from the ground;[560] her equipment then fell off her, and the helmet left her noble head bare.[561] In the picture by a great vase-painter, who has been named after Penthesileia, Achilles is driving his sword into the Amazon's heart as if she were an unarmed boy.

Achilles returned the body of Penthesileia to the Trojans for burial. As unexpected as she had been, the handsome Memnon,[562] son of the goddess Eos, came hurrying up from the land of the Ethiopians in his armour, the work of Hephaistos, to set free Ilion.[563] And like the Amazon, the young hero from the east fell, being overcome in a famous duel by Achilles.[564] There, two sons of goddesses opposed one another. So now it needs must be that Zeus took his golden scales in his hand,[565] as he had done before,[566] when the fates of Achilles and Hektor were in the balance. Vase-painters put a winged creature in either pan, the death, the *ker*, of the two heroes.[567] But it was at the same time a *psychostasia*,[568] a weighing of the souls the possession of which signified life.[569] In Aeschylus' tragedy of that title, probably two figures of young men were weighed, of whom one was shortly to 'quit youth and manly vigour, wailing'.[570] Memnon's *ker* pulled his scale-pan down, and the goddess of the dawn had to mourn for her dead son.[571]

In Aeschylus' 'Weighing of Souls' she, who was so fond of carrying off young men,[572] now carried off his fair body, for Zeus in the end did allow her to make her son immortal.[573] Nevertheless, at the mouth of the Aisepos on the Sea of Marmora[574] the grave-mound of Memnon was shown, which was yearly visited by the 'birds of Memnon', ruffs or whatever they may have been, who engaged in bloody fights in honour of the hero.[575] And one of the two colossi at Thebes in Egypt, which allegedly emitted sounds when the dawn appeared, was supposed to be his statue.

'Thou shall'st sound, Leto's son; for Memnon's here,
A part of thee, touched by dawn's radiance clear.'

So run the verses of a late poet, written on its gigantic leg.[576] This might make it hard to decide who exactly is to 'sound', Apollo or Memnon, who is regarded as a part of the god, and who, no doubt, originally appeared like a young sun-god before Troy.

Still more exalted by this victory of the son of a goddess than the fall of Hektor had already exalted him, Achilles irresistibly drove the Trojans back into the city,[577] and forced his own way in through the Skaian Gate at the back of the fleeing enemy. There he was struck from behind in the heel[578] by the arrow which Paris discharged with a sure hand, for Apollo guided it.[579] Was Paris, even in this old account, lying in wait in the precinct of Thymbraian Apollo, quite close to the city gate, as Odysseus on other occasions did?[580] Is that the very foundation of the late tale[581] which puts the slaying of Achilles wholly on that spot? Achilles fell in the Skaian Gate, as the dying Hektor saw and foretold.[582] Struck in the right heel, the hero turned around once more, and then a second arrow struck him in the breast. This is how an ancient vase-painting shows it. Aias of Salamis took the corpse on his back and carried it under a rain of missiles out of the fight,[583] while Odysseus protected him against the attacks of the Trojans.[584] The dead Achilles very nearly fell into the hands of the enemy. Glaukos the Lykian, Bellerophontes' grandson, had already passed a thong through his heel when he was killed by Aias.[585] The fight over the body lasted all day, until Zeus put an end to it with his thunderstorm.[586]

Thetis came to her son as he lay on his bier, accompanied by all the goddesses of the sea.[587] The voices of the wailing Nereids could be heard while they were still far off, and the Greeks would all have fled in terror if Nestor had not restrained them and explained what the sounds meant. The Muses came with the daughters of Nereus, and sang the lament.[588] Seventeen days the lamentations of immortals and mortals continued over the corpse, but on the eighteenth, Achilles, dressed like a god and with ointment and honey poured over him, was laid on the pyre. Sheep and cattle were killed and the warriors were in continual movement on foot and in their chariots, with great clashing of weapons as they passed around the huge fire. In the morning, when the flames had died down, the bones were gathered up, and put into the golden amphora, Dionysos' gift at the wedding of Peleus and Thetis, with wine and ointment, united to the bones of Patroklos, as the two friends had wished.[589] The entire consecrated army[590] raised the barrow over the grave on a prominent cape on the coast at the entrance to the Hellespont, towering high, so that seafarers saw it from a great distance ever after. There the gigantic monument stood, on Cape Sigeion, and was still honoured with funeral offerings by posterity,[591] and garlanded by Alexander the Great.[592]

Such was the death which Achilles took upon himself. Hardly any ancient poet had anything to say of the slaughter of

Polyxena on his tomb after the conquest of Troy.[593] She had escaped him when he was hunting Troilos; it was told later that the hero appeared on his tomb and demanded as his share in the booty the sacrifice of the daughter of Priam and Hekabe.[594] The poets prefer to tell us that Thetis snatched her son from the pyre, as Eos had the corpse of hers, and brought him to Leuke, the 'White Island'.[595] This was a kind of immortality, although not that of the gods or of Herakles on Olympos. The distant island with its white sheen was looked for in the Pontos Euxeinos, the Black Sea,[596] and some believed they had found it in a little islet lying before the estuaries of the Danube, or in the island of Borysthenitis off the estuary of the Dnieper, where the Greek settlers built a temple[597] to Achilles as Pontarches, 'Lord of the Pontos',[598] and also, as was appropriate to the cult of a hero, showed his grave.[599]

Here it is said he was united to a great lady of the Pontos, Medeia.[600] Or, as another tale ran,[601] Iphigeneia did not go home with Orestes, but came to Achilles as his wife under the name of the goddess Orsoloche[602] or Orsolocheia, 'she who incites to attack', which was also a name of the Taurian Parthenos. Finally, some held[603] that Helen was married to Achilles on Leuke. While he was still under the walls of Ilion, they said, Thetis had brought her to him with the help of Aphrodite, because he wished at least to see that fairest of women, for whose sake he was fighting.[604] True to his character, however, he dwelt, a shade among the shades, in the under-world.[605] He did not let Odysseus comfort him concerning death. 'Liefer would I be in the fields, the serf of another, of a portionless man with little wealth, than be king of all the perished dead.' Those were his words, as he passed with great strides through the asphodels, and was glad only at what Odysseus told him of his son: that in the Trojan War he had followed in his father's footsteps.

For, after all, Troy the holy city must sometime fall. Hektor knew it,[606] and the Greeks endeavoured also to learn from diviners and oracles how they might at last conquer it. It was even said that they were to bring the bones of Pelops from Olympia to Troy,[607] but more serious conditions, not yet ful/ filled, were to fetch Philoktetes with Herakles' bow from Lemnos,[608] and Neoptolemos, Achilles' son, from Skyros.[609] The second condition was the easier to fulfil. Odysseus sailed over to Skyros,[610] and whether it was his powers of persuasion which produced the result, or those of old Phoinix, who accompanied him and had been Achilles' fatherly friend,[611] or the appearance in a dream of Achilles himself[612] that furnished the impetus, Neoptolemos was soon wearing his father's armour in the struggles for Troy, for Odysseus, who had formerly won it against Aias, handed it over to him.[613] It was more difficult in the case of Philoktetes, who could not forgive the Greeks for leaving him on Lemnos with his festering wound. It needed all the cunning and violence of the man of Ithake, the son of Sisyphos. As an assistant, Diomedes came with him,[614] but in the 'Philoktetes' of Sophokles it is Neoptolemos. What torments of the ailing and betrayed hero fill that tragedy! But after the appearance of Herakles[615] had moved Philoktetes to accompany them and the arts of the sons of Asklepios had healed him,[616] a shot from the fated bow struck Paris in a duel.[617] So fell the fate/laden prince, the possessor of Zeus' daughter Helen by grace of Aphrodite, and with his fall the ruin of Troy set in.

Ilion possessed a divine image which had fallen from heaven. Ilios, father of Laomedon, found it one morning in front of his tent, cast there by Zeus as a sign of his approval of the founding of the city.[618] The figure was a Palladion, a representation of Pallas; not the goddess herself, according to a legend of Pallas Athene's youth,[619] but Pallas her companion, who had been killed in a sham/fight with the goddess. This archaic statue measured three cubits in height; its feet were not separated, and it held a spear in its right hand, a distaff and spindle in its left, like a goddess of death and fate.[620] After the pattern of this image a number of replicas of different sizes were fashioned,[621] so that no one should know which was the genuine one. For the continuance of the city depended on the possession of the Palladion; if it fell into the hands of the enemy, Ilion fell. Odysseus and Diomedes undertook to fulfil the condition and steal the Palladion.

First Odysseus, disguised as a beggar and disfigured with stripes, stole into the city alone.[622] His business was to find the way through the streets and the many apartments of the royal palace to the hidden shrine where the figure and its replicas were stored. Unrecognised and almost without trying he found his way to Helen. After the death of Paris she had been given in marriage to another son of Priam, Deiphobos, who bore the warlike name of 'router of the enemy', but had soon to pay dearly for his brief happiness. Helen recognised the beggar[623] and longed for her home, her daughter and the husband she had left.[624] She swore to Odysseus that she would not betray him, and it was her advice[625] which made possible the theft of the genuine Palladion, the smallest of all.[626] In the night Odysseus returned with Diomedes.[627] They had to climb over the city walls,[628] get into the palace by the drain,[629] and kill the guards.[630] The story was told that they returned with the Palladion to the Greek camp, but no longer as friends.[631]

Even before this condition was fulfilled, the building of the gigantic horse allegedly began;[632] it was a ruse of Odysseus',[633] inspired by Pallas Athene,[634] and at the same time a gift for her, to replace the Palladion. She bore the epithet Hippia, that is to say 'horse-goddess',[635] and took pleasure in exercising her horses.[636] We know that Bellerophontes had her to thank for the gift of the bridle and the taming of Pegasos.[637] The wooden horse which was now being built is said to have borne the inscription 'From the Greeks, a thank-offering to Athene.'[638] It was so constructed that the Trojans, if they would draw the votive offering into the city,[639] must break down the lintel of the Skaian Gate itself. This, too, allegedly was a condition of the taking of the city,[640] the removal of the gigantic stone beam which the ancient narrators probably pictured to themselves as being like those which we still admire today above the gates of Mycenae. Odysseus with a chosen band of warriors climbed into the belly of the steed;[641] the rest of the army burned its tents[642] and disappeared with the fleet behind the island of Tenedos.

Except Kassandra, to whom no one would listen,[643] only one person tried to prevent the Trojans, doomed as they were to destruction, from doing in their joy and folly what was expected of them. This was Laokoon, at that time chosen by lot to be priest of Poseidon,[644] but, as later experts in the antiquities of Troy still knew,[645] a priest of Apollo Thymbraios, who hated him because he had made love to his wife in the shrine of the death-dealing god and begotten sons there.[646] He hurled his spear at the planking of the horse. When he was then about to bring, with his two sons, the offering of a bull to the sea-god, two enormous snakes appeared from the direction of the islands[647]—one of which was Chryse—devoured the two youths, then killed the father and afterwards retired to the feet of the statue of Athene which was worshipped in the citadel.[648] It thus became manifest that the two deities, the god who guarded Ilios and the goddess who was the Trojans' enemy, had united to overthrow the city. According to one tradition,[649] it was then that Aineias retired to Mount Ida with his people, without waiting until the city was on fire. Laokoon's fate, however, as an example of futile opposition to divine ordinances, was to be immortalised by great sculptors and stand among the dedications in a temple of Athene.

The Trojans were blind; they gave themselves up to revelry,[650] and were overcome by sleep.[651] The great warriors in the belly of the horse wept and trembled all this while,[652] for Helen put them to one more terrible test.[653] It is not told us whether this happened while the Wooden Horse still stood outside the city or after it had been brought with great difficulty up to the citadel. Helen of course knew of this stratagem through Odysseus. Three times, accompanied by Deiphobos, she walked around the war-engine and called the names of the leading Greeks in the voices of their wives. Menelaos, Diomedes and the younger men would have rushed out if Odysseus had not held them back by main force. But Neoptolemos was not one of these, nor of those who trembled.[654] Odysseus had to restrain him also, but only because he could hardly wait for the agreed signals which announced the return of the fleet and beginning of the attack.

He was the hero of that bloody night, a *heros* indeed, because under the name of Pyrrhos he was to become the ancestor of the kings of the Epeirote tribe of the Molossians,[655] and receive a hero's tomb at Delphi;[656] but it was a questionable fame, for he paid the penalty of death in the very shrine of the purifying god for what he had done at Troy.[657] In that last night of Troy he had murdered the aged king Priam, whom Achilles had spared, at the altar of Zeus in his palace.[658] He did as much for the son of Hektor, whom Hektor himself had named Skamandrios, as if the child were a gift of the river-god Skamandros, but the Trojans called Astyanax, 'lord of the city', since his father guarded their city.[659] Pyrrhos tore the child from his nurse's breast and flung him down from the city walls, while he was driving his booty of slave-women, including Andromache, as being the most valuable, before him to the ships.[660] Thus were fulfilled the gloomy prophecies both of Hektor himself[661] and of the unhappy mother of his son.[662] The House of Priam was extinct.

In the midst of such cruelties, Helen was awaiting her deserted husband. Odysseus led Menelaos to her in Deiphobos' quarters, no doubt in the great royal palace,[663] near the shrine of the Palladion, the way to which he already knew. Menelaos threw himself upon her, the cause of the long war and of that terrible night, with drawn sword. Did she need to take refuge in the sanctuary, as artists and poets afterwards elaborated the scene, introducing Aphrodite as her rescuer or even transferring the encounter to her temple?[664] Helen uncovered her breasts as if she would receive the blow, but the sword fell to the ground.[665] The two kissed one another.[666] Did Deiphobos fall, slain by Menelaos, before this or not till after? They hurried to the ships,[667] and thenceforth it remained for Helen's husband only to set about his homeward journey as soon as might be with the divine bride he had recovered.[668]

The return of the heroes of the Trojan War now began. We know that for Agamemnon it ended at the hands of mur-derers, for Aias the Lokrian in shipwreck and death, for Diomedes and Idomeneus in exile to the southern coasts of Italy. Only a few, like old Nestor of Pylos, achieved a fortunate homecoming. Helen and Menelaos in the end reached their palace in Sparta, where in the tenth year after their reunion they entertained Telemachos, the son of Odysseus, who had set out to search for his still absent father.[669] But they too had not long arrived, after eight years of wanderings.[670] After being wrecked at Phaistos[671] on the south coast of Crete, where they had lost fifty-five of their sixty ships,[672] their journey took them against their will to Cyprus, Phoenicia, Egypt and Libya.[673] From the little sandy island of Pharos, where Menelaos was so fortunate—we know the story from the history of the gods[674]— as to hold the old man of the sea fast and get advice from him, Proteus sent them back to the Nile, there to repeat the neglected sacrifice to Zeus and all the gods.[675] Later, a story was told that Menelaos took his real wife home with him from Pharos and Egypt, the veritable daughter of Zeus, who ever since she was carried off had been waiting there for him.[676] The insulted Hera had put a living image of Helen into the arms of Paris and had Helen herself taken by Hermes to Proteus.[677] It was for an idle appearance on account of an idle choice that all that blood flowed at Troy.

Of many an adventure experienced by Odysseus on his way home we know from the history of the gods.[678] For this un-fortunate man, most ill-rewarded for his ruses in wartime, continually hovered over gulfs and precipices, always close to death, which often displayed itself to him in the frightening shapes of primaeval divine beings. He underwent much the same things as Herakles, and at last returned home from the underworld in the tenth year of his wanderings, after dangerous

74 ODYSSEUS AND NEOPTOLEMOS

75 THE BATTLE OVER THE CORPSE
OF ACHILLES

76 MENELAOS BRINGING HELEN
HOME AGAIN

encounters with Death in his many forms. But he escaped that great enemy only with sore pain and trouble, not as a victorious hero but as an old, ship-wrecked beggar-man. An aged body hid the hero within it, and only the goddess Athene could restore his glory to him.[679] He had left his powerful bow at home, and no one except himself could now bend it. At the new moon,[680] the festival of Apollo,[681] him of the silver bow, he stood once more in his palace and might handle his bow, as men did on that day in honour of the god.[682] Odysseus hit his mark, then shot down the haughty suitors who were oppressing his wife, and became once more the lord of his house and his island.

Death came for him out of the sea, by the hand of the son whom Kirke had borne him, Telegonos, 'the one born far off'. He landed on Ithake[683] in quest of his father, when Odysseus imagined that he had escaped all danger. Word was brought him of a robber who had come to steal his herds. He ran to the coast to punish him, and fell to the spear of Telegonos, a weapon whose point was formed by the sting of a ray.[684] Too late the son recognised his father, but was not too late in recognising his brother Telemachos. The two sons carried the dead Odysseus and the ever-young Penelope with them to Kirke.[2685] There they lived as two couples, Telegonos with Penelope and Telemachos with Kirke, on Aiaia, the magic island, which, as we know from the story of the Argonauts, can very well signify a promontory which rises up from the Tyrrhenian Sea, the worthy abode of a daughter of the Sun, Monte Circeo.

GENEALOGIES

Concordance

☐ around the name of a hero or heroine signifies that
he or she is dealt with in more detail in the text
~ marriage or other sexual union

BOOK I	*genealogy*	BOOK II	*genealogy*
I	A		H
II	B		
III	A	BOOK III	
IV	A	I	IL
V	B	II	C
VI	B	IV	I
VII	C	V	C
VIII	C	VI	K
IX	C	VII	E
X	D	VIII	E G,K
XI	F	IX	K
XII	G	XII	E

A

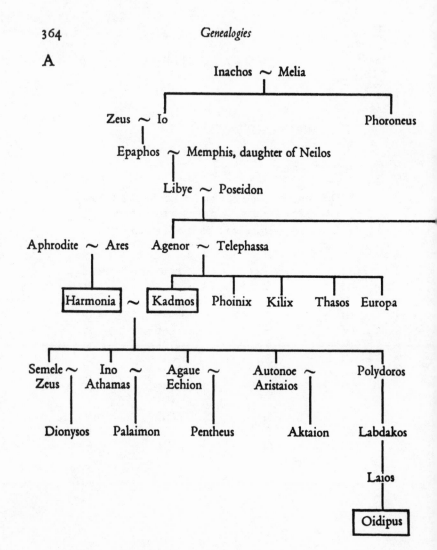

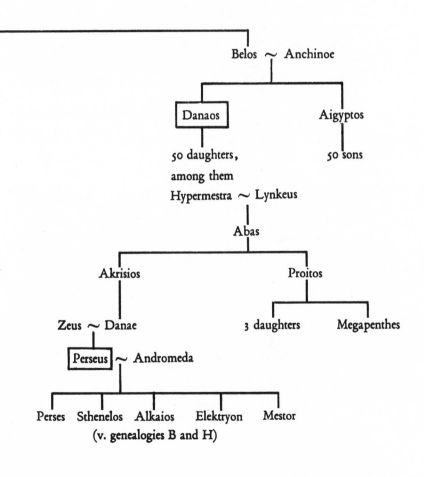

B

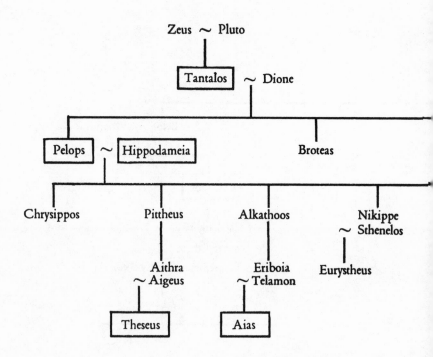

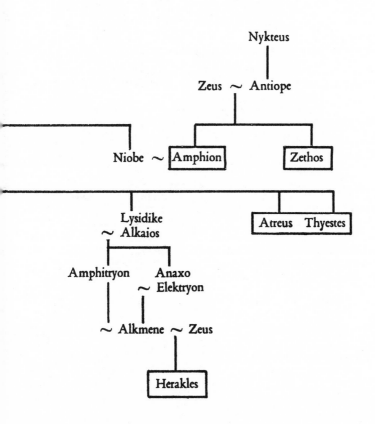

C

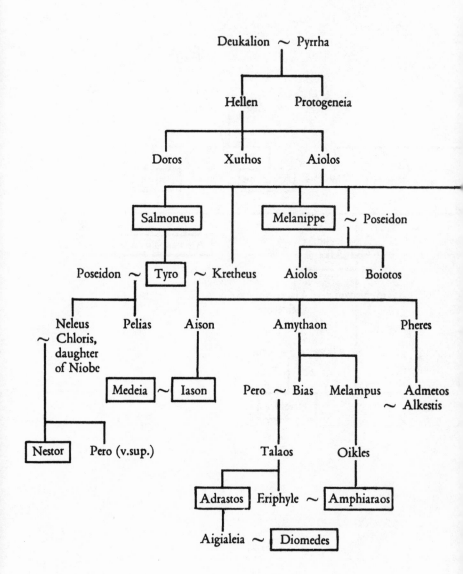

TO BOOK ONE, VII, VIII, IX
BOOK THREE, II, V

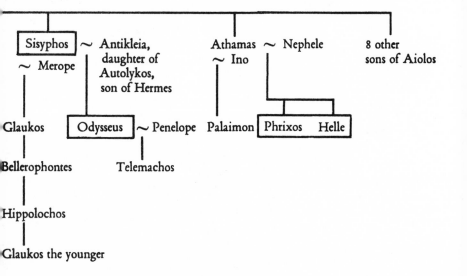

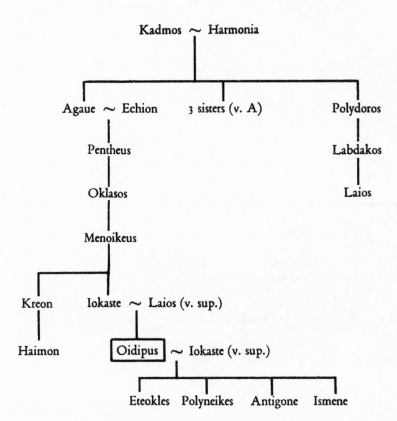

TO BOOK THREE, VII, VIII, XII

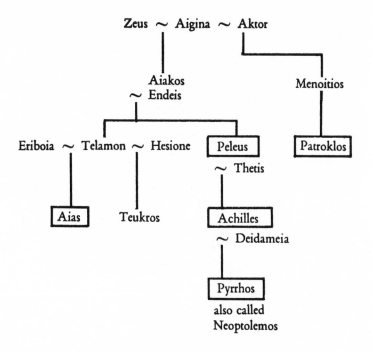

F

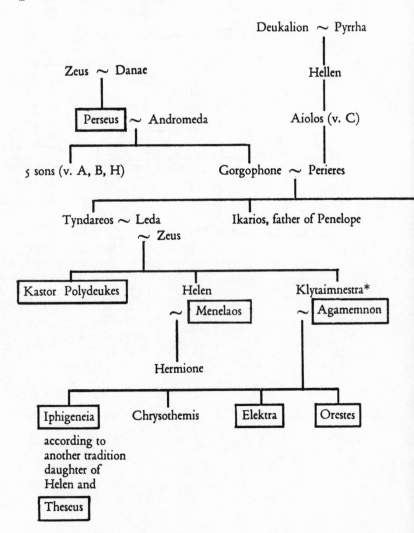

* Klytaimnestra is treated as a daughter of Tyndareos, not of Zeus

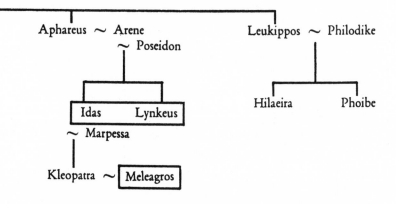

G

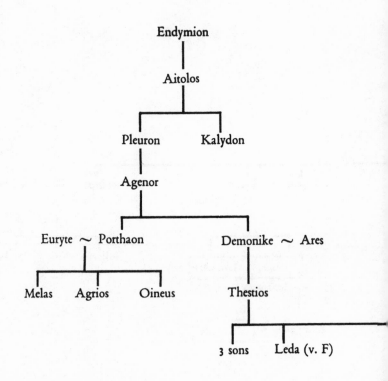

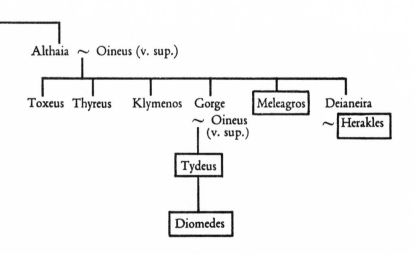

H

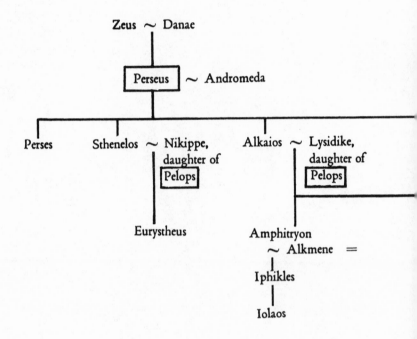

Zeus ∼ Danae

Perseus ∼ Andromeda

Perses   Sthenelos ∼ Nikippe,
daughter of
Pelops

Alkaios ∼ Lysidike,
daughter of
Pelops

Eurystheus

Amphitryon
∼ Alkmene =

Iphikles

Iolaos

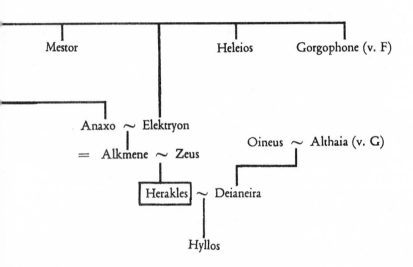

I

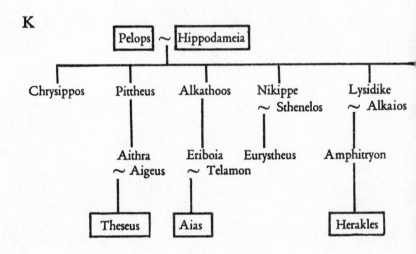

Erichthonios ∼ Praxithea

Pandion ∼ Zeuxippe

Erechtheus ∼ Praxithea Butes Prokne ∼ Tereus ∼ Philomela

Kekrops II Protogeneia Pandora Chthonia

Pandion II

Aigeus ∼ Aithra (v. inf.)

Theseus

K

Pelops ∼ Hippodameia

Chrysippos Pittheus Alkathoos Nikippe Lysidike
∼ Sthenelos ∼ Alkaios

Aithra Eriboia Eurystheus Amphitryon
∼ Aigeus ∼ Telamon

Theseus Aias Herakles

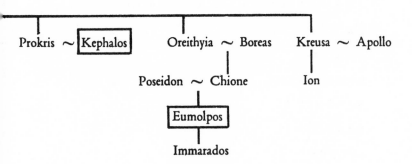

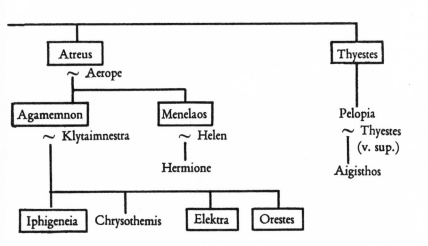

L   LIST OF KINGS OF ATHENS UP TO THE TROJAN WAR

KEKROPS

KRANAOS ('STONY')

AMPHIKTYON ('DWELLER AROUND')

ERICHTHONIOS

PANDION

ERECHTHEUS

KEKROPS II

PANDION II

AIGEUS

THESEUS

MENESTHEUS, LEADER OF ATHENIANS
IN TROJAN WAR

SOURCES FOR INTRODUCTION

1: In accordance with the principles set forth in my book *Umgang mit Göttlichem*, Göttingen 1955.

2: W. F. Otto, *Die Götter Griechenlands*, Frankfurt a/M. 1947, p. 183.

3: *See* André Jolles, *Einfache Formen*, Halle-Saale 1930, p. 238.

4: *Op. cit.*, p. 82.

5: Plutarch, *de genio Socratis*, 557e.

6: Kerényi, *Apollon*, Düsseldorf 1953, p. 162; Spengler in the periodical *Die Welt als Geschichte*, Stuttgart 1935, p. 197.

7: *See* Kerényi, *Griechische Miniaturen*, Zürich 1957, p. 109; T. B. L. Webster in the periodical *Classica et Mediaevalia*, Copenhagen 1956, p. 149.

8: *cf.* G. E. Mylonas in *Studies Robinson*, 1951, p. 64.

8a: *See* Kerényi in A. Randa, *Handbuch der Weltgeschichte* I, Olten and Freiburg i. Br. 1954, 64.

9: Carlyle, *On Heroes and Hero-Worship*, Lecture I.

10: Plutarch, *Quaest. Graec.*, 36.

11: *The Gods of the Greeks*, p. 257. For Asklepios, *see* my *Asklepios* New York and London 1959, p. xix.

12: Plutarch, *op. cit.*, 12.

13: *The Gods of the Greeks*, p. 259.

14: Schol. Townl. on *Iliad*, 14, 319.

15: Plutarch, *de Iside et Osiride*, 364f.

16: Fgts. 15, 60 and 61 Diels.

17: *The Gods of the Greeks*, p. 253, with illustration there.

18: *See* Todd-Wace, *A Catalogue of the Sparta Museum*, Oxford 1906, p. 102 and Plates 1–3 and 10.

19: Publication by Ch. A. Christu in preparation.

20: Aristophanes, *Eccles.* 1031; *Athenische Mitteilungen*, 1893, pp. 165, 184.

21: *cf. Dramatische Gottesgeburt in der griechischen Religion*, *Eranos Jahrbuch*, Zürich 1951, p. 13.

22: *See* the periodical *Maia,* Florence 1951, p. 12.

23: W. F. Otto, *Dionysos,* Frankfurt a/M. 1939, p. 62.

24: Schol. on Apollonios Rhodios, 1, 916.

25: *cf.* Hesychios *s.v.* κέρσαι. κόψαι, τεμεῖν, κεῖραι, γαμῆσαι, first taken into consideration by N. Fréret in 1761. For the form, *cf.* E. Schwyzer, *Griechische Grammatik,* i, p. 516, n. 6, and for the meaning, V. Magnien in *Mélanges Cumont,* p. 319.

26: Pausanias 9, 12, 4, according to the MS. text.

A.: *Aeschylus*
  A.: *Agamemnon*
  Ch.: *Choephori*
  Eu.: *Eumenides*
  Pe.: *Persae*
  Pr.: *Prometheus*
  Se.: *Septem contra Thebas*
  Su.: *Supplices*
AAmbr.: *Anonymus Ambrosianus in Studemundi Analectis I p. 224*
Acc.: *Accius Tragicus*
  M.: *Medea*
Ach. Intr.: *Achillis Introductio in Aratum*
Ae.: *Aelianus*
  NA: *De Natura Animalium*
  VH: *Varia Historia*
Al.: *Alcaeus*
ALib.: *Antoninus Liberalis Mythographus*
Alcid.: *Alcidamantis Ulisses*
Am. M.: *Ammianus Marcellinus Historicus*
Ant.: *Antigonus Carystius Paradoxographus*
Ap.: *Apollodorus Mythographus*
APal.: *Anthologia Palatina*
Apost.: *Apostolius Paroemiographus*
App.: *Appianus Historicus*
  M.: *Bellum Mithridaticum*
Ar.: *Aristophanes*
  Ach.: *Acharnenses*
  Av.: *Aves*
  Eq.: *Equites*
  Ly.: *Lysistrata*

N.: *Nubes*
Pax
Th.: *Tesmophorizusae*
Ve.: *Vespae*
Arat.: *Aratus Epicus*
Archil.: *Archilochus Lyricus*
ARh.: *Apollonios Rhodios*
Ari.: *Aristoteles*
  EN.: *Ethica Nicomachea*
  HA.: *Historia Animalium*
  MA.: *De Motione Animalium*
  Po.: *Poetica*
  Pr. an.: *Problemata anecdota*
Aristid.: *Aristides Rhetor*
Arn. AN.: *Arnobius Adversus Nationes*
Arr. A.: *Arriani Anabasis*
Art.: *Artemidori Onirocriticus*
Athenag.: *Athenagoras Apologeta*
Aug. CD: *Augustinus De Civitate Dei*

B.: *Bacchylides*
Batr.: *Batrachomyomachia*
Bion *Bucolicus*
BKT.: *Berliner Klassikertexte*

c.: *cum*
Ca.: *Callimachus*
  Ap.: *Hymnus in Apollinem*
  Ce.: *Hymnus in Cererem*
  De.: *Hymnus in Delum*
  Di.: *Hymnus in Dianam*
  Die.: *Diegemata*
  He.: *Hecale*

Ca.: *Callimachus—contd.*
  Io.: *Hymnus in Iovem*
  LP: *Lavacrum Palladis*
Cat.: *Catullus*
CG.: *Kaibel, Comicorum Graecorum*
  Fragmenta
Chr.: *Chrysippus Stoicus*
Ci.: *Cicero*
  Le.: *De Legibus*
  ND: *De Natura Deorum*
  TD: *Tusculanae Disputationes*
CIA: *Corpus Inscriptionum*
  Atticarum
CIG: *Corpus Inscriptionum*
  Graecarum
Cl.: *Clemens Alexandrinus*
  Pr.: *Protrepticus*
  Str.: *Stromateis*
Cla. RP: *Claudianus De Raptu*
  Proserpinae
Co.: *Coluthus Epicus*
c. s.: *cum scholiis*

D. Chr.: *Dio Chrysostomus*
Diog. Ep.: *Diogenes Cynicus in*
  Epistolographis Graecis
D. H.: *Dionysius Halicarnassenis*
  AR: *Antiquitates Romanae*
  Op.: *Opuscula*
DM.: *Ventris, Chadwick, Documents*
  in Mycenaean Greek
D. P.: *Dionysius Periegeta*
D. S.: *Diodorus Siculus*

E.: *Euripides*
  Al.: *Alcestis*
  An.: *Andromache*
  B.: *Bacchae*
  Cy.: *Cyclops*
  E.: *Electra*

He.: *Hecuba*
Hel.: *Helena*
Her.: *Heraclidae*
HF: *Hercules Furens*
Hi.: *Hippolytus*
IA: *Iphigenia Aulidensis*
Ion
IT: *Iphigenia Taurica*
Me.: *Medea*
Or.: *Orestes*
Ph.: *Phoenissae*
Rh.: *Rhesus*
Su.: *Supplices*
Tr.: *Troades*
EGr.: *Kaibel, Epigrammata Graeca*
  ex lapidibus collecta
Enn.: *Ennius*
Ep.: *Epimenides Philosophus*
ep.: *epitoma*
Er. C.: *Eratosthenis Catasterismi*
Et. Gen.: *Etymologicum Genuinum*
Et. Gud.: *Etymologicum Gudianum*
Et. M.: *Etymologicum Magnum*
Eud.: *Eudoxiae Violarium*
Eu. Il.: *Eusthatius ad Iliadem*
Eu. Od.: *Eusthatius ad Odysseam*
Euph.: *Euphorio Epicus*
Eus.: *Eusebius Caesariensis*
  Chr.: *Chronica*
  PE: *Praeparatio Evangelica*

Fe.: *Festus Grammaticus*
FGH: *Jacoby, Fragmente der grie-*
  chischen Historiker
fr.: *fragmentum*

GArat.: *Germanici Aratus*
GG: *Kerényi, The Gods of the Greeks*
  The figures in brackets refer
  to the Penguin edition

Gra. Cy.: *Grattii Cynegetica*
h. Ap.: *Homeri hymnus in Apollinem*
h. C.: *Homeri hymnus in Cererem*
h. Ho.: *Homeri Hymni*
h. M.: *Homeri hymnus in Mercurium*
h. Ve.: *Homeri hymnus in Venerem*
Harp.: *Harpocratio Grammaticus*
Hdt.: *Herodotus*
He.: *Hesiodus*
   Sc.: *Scutum Herculis*
Her.: *Herodas Mimographus*
Him.: *Himerii Orationes*
Him. E.: *Himerii Eclogae*
Hi. RH: *Hippolyti Refutatio Omn-*
   ium Heresium
Hor.: *Horatius*
   AP: *Ars Poetica*
   C.: *Carmina*
   Epi.: *Epistulae*
Hsch.: *Hesychius Lexicographus*
Hy.: *Hygini Fabulae*
Hy. A.: *Astronomica*
Hyp.: *Hyperides*
hyp.: *hypothesis*

Ib.: *Ibycus*
ICo.: *Inscriptions of Cos*
IG.: *Inscriptiones Graecae*
Il.: *Homeri Ilias*
Io.: *Iosephus Historicus*
   BI: *Bellum Iudaicum*
Is.: *Isocrates Orator*
Iust.: *Iustinus Historicus*

La. Inst.: *Lactantii Institutiones*
Li.: *Libanii Orationes*
Li. N.: *Libanii Narrationes*
Li. Pr.: *Libanii Progymnasmata*
Lic.: *Licymnius Lyricus*

Lu.: *Lucianus*
   Am.: *Amores*
   Ba.: *Bacchus*
   Charid.: *Charidemus*
   Cy.: *Cynicus*
   DD.: *Dialogi Deorum*
   DMar.: *Dialogi Marini*
   DMo.: *Dialogi Mortuorum*
   Ind.: *Adversus Indoctum*
   ITr.: *Iuppiter Tragoedus*
   Lex.: *Lexiphanes*
   Ph.: *Philopseudes*
   Sa.: *De Saltatione*
   SyrD.: *De Syria Dea*
Ly.: *Lycophron*
Lycurg.: *Lycurgus Orator*

Ma.: *Macrobius*
   S.: *Saturnalia*
   So.: *Somnium Scipionis*
Mal. Chr.: *Malalas Chronographus*
Me.: *Menander Comicus*
Mi.: *Mimnermus*
Mo.: *Moschus Bucolicus*
Mo. Chor. Pr.: *Mosis Chorenensis*
   Progymnasmata in Eusebii
   Chronica ed. Mai
MVat.: *Mythographus Vaticanus*

N. Al.: *Nicandri Alexipharmaca*
N. D.: *Nonni Dionysiaca*
N. N.: *Nonnus commentator*
   Gregorii Nazianzeni
N. Pr.: *Nicolai Progymnasmata*
N. Th.: *Nicandri Theriaca*

Od.: *Homeri Odyssea*
Op.: *Hesiodi Opera et Dies*
Opp.: *Oppiani Halieutica*
Or.: *Kern, Orphicorum Fragmenta*

Or. A.: *Orphei Argonautica*
Or. H.: *Orphei Hymni*
Ori. C.: *Origenes contra Celsum*
Ov.: *Ovidius*
  AA: *Ars Amatoria*
  Am.: *Amores*
  F.: *Fasti*
  Ib.: *Ibis*
  M.: *Metamorphoses*

Pa.: *Pausanias Periegeta*
Pac.: *Pacuvius Tragicus*
Par.: *Parthenius Mythographus*
Ph.: *Philostratus Sophista*
  Her.: *Heroicus*
  Im.: *Imagines*
  VA: *Vita Apollonii*
Pha.: *Phanocles Elegiacus*
Phi.: *Philemo Comicus*
Philo: *Philo Iudaeus*
Ph. iun.: *Philostratus iunior*
Phot.: *Photii Lexicon*
Phot. B.: *Photii Bibliotheca*
Phr.: *Phrynichus Tragicus*
Pi.: *Pindarus*
  I.: *Isthmia*
  N.: *Nemea*
  O.: *Olympia*
  P.: *Pythia*
Pl.: *Plato*
  Ax.: *Axiochus*
  Epi.: *Epinomis*
  Ethd.: *Euthydemus*
  Ethph.: *Euthyphron*
  Le.: *Leges*
  Mx.: *Menexenos*
  Phd.: *Phaedo*
  Phdr.: *Phaedrus*
  Pr.: *Protagoras*

Sy.: *Symposium*
Ti.: *Timaeus*
Pla. *Plautus Comicus*
  Am.: *Amphitruo*
  B.: *Bacchides*
  Ru.: *Rudens*
Pli. NH: *Plinii Naturalis Historia*
Plu.: *Plutarchi Moralia*
Plu. Ro.: *Plutarchi Romulus*
Plu. Ser.: *Plutarchi Sertorius*
Plu. Ti.: *Plutarchi Timoleon*
Plu. Th.: *Plutarchi Theseus*
PMag.: *Preisendanz, Papyri Magici Graeci*
PO.: *Oxyrhynchus Papyri*
Pol.: *Pollux Grammaticus*
Po. M.: *Pomponius Mela Geographus*
Pr. Chr.: *Procli Chrestomathia; quae ad Homerum pertinent ed. Allen, caetera ed. Bekker*
Prop.: *Propertius*
PSI: *Papiri della Società Italiana*

Q. S.: *Quintus Smyrnaeus*

Rh. Gr.: *Spengel, Rhetores Graeci*

s.: *scholium in (Servius vel Probus in Vergilium)*
S.: *Sophocles*
  Ai.: *Aiax*
  An.: *Antigone*
  E.: *Electra*
  OC: *Oedipus Coloneus*
  OT: *Oedipus Tyrannus*
  Ph.: *Philoctetes*
  Tr.: *Trachiniae*
Sa.: *Sappho*
Scy.: *Scythinus Lyricus*

Se.: *Seneca Tragicus*
  HF: *Hercules Furens*
  HOe: *Hercules Oetaeus*
  Thy.: *Thyestes*
  Tr.: *Troades*
SEmp.: *Sextus Empiricus Philo-*
  sophus
Si.: *Simonides Lyricus*
Sol.: *Solinus Historicus*
Sosi.: *Sositheus Tragicus*
St. By.: *Stephanus Byzantinus*
  Lexicographus
Ste.: *Stesichorus Lyricus*
Str.: *Strabo Geographus*
St. Th.: *Statii Thebais*
Su.: *Suidas Lexicographus*
Sup. E.: *Supplementum Euripideum*
  ed. Arnim
Syll.: *Dittenberger, Sylloge*
  Inscriptionum Graecarum ed. 3.

Terp.: *Terpander Lyricus*

Tert. Val.: *Tertullianus contra*
  Valerianos
Th.: *Hesiodi Theogonia*
The.: *Theocritus*
Thgn.: *Theognis*
Thu.: *Thucydides*
Tz.: *Tzetzes*
  Chil: *Chiliades*
  Co.: *de Comoedia*
  Ly.: *ad Lycophronem*
  Posthom.: *Posthomerica*

Va. LL: *Varro De Lingua Latina*
Ve.: *Vergilius*
  A.: *Aeneis*
  Cu.: *Culex*
  E.: *Eclogae*
  G.: *Georgica*
V. Fl.: *Valerii Flacci Argonautica*

Zen.: *Zenobius Paroemiographus*

27: GG 112 (99)
28: s. Pi. P. 3. 153
29: GG 254 (228)
30: GG 28 (24)
31: Hdt. 2. 51. 2
32: Lu. Charid. 9
33: Ap. 3. 1. 1
34: Il. 14. 321
35: s. E. Rh. 29
36: Ap. 3. 1. 1
37: D. S. 5. 48. 2
    s. E. Ph. 7
    s. A. Rh. 1. 916
38: D. S. 5. 49. 1
39: s. E. Ph. 7
40: D. S. 5. 49. 1
41: s. Il. 2. 494
    Ov. M. 2. 8
42: Ap. 3. 4. 1
43: Hdt. 4. 147. 5
    s. Ly. 1206
44: s. E. Ph. 638
45: s. Ca. Io. 3
46: Pa. 9. 12. 2
47: s. Il. 2. 494
48: Ov. M. 3. 26
49: s. S. An. 126
50: Phot. B. 2 277. 6
51: Pa. 9. 5. 1
52: s. A. Rh. 3. 1178
53: E. Ph. 663
54: s. E. Ph. 662
55: E. Ph. 667
56: s. E. Ph. 670
57: s. A. Rh. 3. 1178

58: E. Ph. 939
59: Ari. Po. 16
    Hy. 72
60: Ap. 3. 4. 2
61: s. A. Rh. 1. 916
62: N. D. 3–4
63: GG 72 (63)
64: Pa. 9. 16. 4
65: Ap. 3. 4. 2
66: Pi. P. 3. 90
    Ap. 1. 4. 2
    s. Il. 2.494
67: N. D. 5. 120
68: Ap. 1. 9. 15
69: Thgn. 15
    E. B. 881; 901
70: Pi. P. 3. 91
    Ca. fr. 11. 4
71: s. Il. 2. 494
    Pa. 3. 18. 12
72: Ap. 3. 4. 2
73: s. Pi. P. 3. 167
    Ap. 3. 4. 2
74: GG 109 (96)
75: GG 257 (226)
76: GG 262 (230)
77: GG 146 (124)
78: GG 264 (233)
79: Pa. 9. 5. 3
80: E. B. 1333
81: E. B. 1330; 1334
82: St. B.
83: s. V. Ae. 1. 243
84: Ca. fr. 11. 4
85: E. B. 1338

86: Pi. O. 2. 77
87: Ap. 3. 5. 4
88: E. Ph. 822
89: GG 153 (135)
90: GG 204 (184)
91: Ca. De. 80
92: s. Ly. 1211
93: PO. 1241. IV. 6
94: s. Pi. P. 9. 5
95: Pa. 9. 10. 5
96: Od. 11. 260–5
97: Pa. 2. 6. 1
98: s. Pi. O. 13. 74
99: s. A. Rh. 4. 1090
100: Pa. 2. 6. 2
101: St. B.
102: Hsch.
103: E. HF 29
104: Pa. 1. 38. 9
105: Sup. E. p. 11
106: E. fr. 1023
    Ph. Im. 1. 10
107: Hor. Epi. 1. 18.
    41
108: Pac. fr. XIII
109: Pa. 9. 17. 6
110: Pa. 9. 5. 7
111: GG 222 (196)
112: s. E. Ph. 159
113: Hy. 9
114: Pa. 9. 17. 4
115: Pa. 9. 17. 6
116: Pa. 10. 31. 10
117: GG 222 (196)
118: Ap. 2. 1. 4

119: s. A. Rh. 3. 1186
120: s. E. He. 886
121: Ap. 2. 1. 4
122: s. Il. 1. 42
123: Ath. 651 f
124: Cl. Str. 4. 19.
　　120. 4
125: A. Su. 250
126: Pa. 2. 19. 3
127: Ap. 2. 1. 5
128: Pa. 2. 19. 6
129: A. fr. 44
130: Pa. 2. 25. 4
131: Ap. 2. 1. 5
132: Pi. P. 9. 112
133: s. E. He. 886
134: Pl. Ax. 371 e
135: Hy. 169
136: Pa. 2. 15. 5
137: Ap. 2. 1. 4
138: Pa. 2. 38. 2
139: Str. 8. 6. 8
140: Ap. 2. 2. 1
141: Pa. 2. 25. 7
142: Pa. 2. 16. 2
143: Ap. 2. 2. 1
144: Str. 8. 6. 11
145: GG 253
146: s. Il. 14. 319
147: s. A. Rh. 4. 1091
148: S. An. 944
149: Si. 27
150: PSI. 1209
151: PO. 2161. I. 23
152: s. A. Rh. 4. 1091
153: s. A. Rh. 4. 1515
154: h. C. 9 et 17
155: Pi. P. 12. 15
156: Hy. 63

157: GG 129 (114)
158: Ap. 2. 4. 2
159: s. A. Rh. 4. 1515
160: GG 185 (164)
161: s. A. Rh. 4. 1515
162: Art. 4. 63
163: Er. C. 22
164: N. D. 25. 32
165: Et. Gud. 462
166: Th. 275
167: GG 45 (40)
168: A. Pr. 796
169: Ov. M. 4. 778
170: A. Pr. 791
171: Hy. A. 1. 12
172: N. D. 31. 17
173: Er. C. 22
174: A. fr. 261
175: GG 49 (43)
176: s. A. Rh. 4. 1515
177: Ap. 2. 4. 2
178: Lu. DMo. 14. 2
179: Ap. 2. 4. 3
180: Ov. Am 3. 11.
　　24
181: He. Sc. 220
182: Pi. P. 10. 31
183: Pa. 4. 35. 9
　　Str. 16. 2. 28
　　Io. BI. 3. 9. 3
184: Ar. R. 52
185: E. fr. 125
186: E. fr. 132
187: Ap. 2. 4. 3
188: Ov. M. 5. 180
189: Er. C. 15–17; 22
190: Ap. 2. 4. 3
191: s. Pi. P. 72
192: s. A. Rh. 4. 1515

193: Ap. 2. 4. 4
194: s. A. Rh. 4. 1091
195: Hy. 244
196: Ap. 2. 4. 4
197: Pa. 2. 16. 4
198: Od. 2. 120
　　s, N. Al. 103
199: s. Il. 15. 302
200: Pa. 2. 16. 3
201: A. Pe. 79
202: s. Il. 14. 319
203: Pa. 2. 20. 4
204: Pa. 2. 22. 1
205: N. D. 47. 666
206: Pa. 2. 23. 7
　　N. D. 47. 714
207: Pa. 2. 23. 8
208: s. Il. 14. 319
209: Plu. 364 f
210: GG 259 (228)
211: Pa. 2. 18. 1
212: GG 222 (196)
213: Pa. 3. 22. 4
　　s. E. Or. 5
214: Pa. 5. 13. 7
　　8. 17. 3
215: Pa. 7. 24. 13
216: Pa. 2. 22. 3
217: Pa. 2. 22. 2
218: St. By.
219: Aristid. 15
220: E. Or. 5
221: s. E. Or. 5
222: s. Pi. O. 41
223: N. D. 48. 730
224: Hy. 83
225: A. fr. 158
226: St. By.
227: Him. E. 3. 11

228: Pl. Ethph. 11e

229: Apost. 16. 16

230: GG 159 (141)

231: E. Or. 9

232: E. Or. 8

233: Plu. 607f

234: Pi. O. 1. 38

235: E. IT 386

236: Se. Th. 144

237: GG 254 (224)

238: s. Ly. 152

239: E. Hel. 389

240: Pi. O. 1. 48

241: s. Ve. G. 3–7

242: Or. 36

243: B. fr. 42

244: s. Pi. O. 1. 40

245: Pi. O. 1. 26

246: Ap. ep. 2. 3

247: Pi. O. 1. 27

248: s. Ly. 152

249: s. Ly. 152

250: Ari. Po. 16

251: Pi. O. 1. 43

252: Pi. O. 1. 47

253: Pi. O. 1. 65

254: E. Or. 10

255: Ov. AA 2. 606

256: D. S. 4. 74. 2

257: Pi. O. 1. 60

258: GG 109 (96)

259: GG 210 (186)

260: ALib. 36

261: Eus. Chr. 2 p. 40

262: s. Il. 20. 234

263: Ath. 281b

264: s. Od. 11. 582

265: s. E. Or. 982

266: E. Or. 7 cum s.

267: N. D. 18. 32; 35. 295

268: E. Or. 982 cum s.

269: GG 159 (141)

270: GG 135 (119)

271: Od. 11. 582

272: Pa. 10. 31. 12

273: Il. 2. 101

274: s. Il. 2. 104

275: GG 202 (178)

276: s. A. Rh. 1. 752

277: Pi. O. 10. 49

278: Ap. ep. 2. 4

279: Hy. 253

280: Pa. 5. 22. 6

281: Ly. 166

282: s. A. Rh. 1. 752

283: Ap. ep. 2. 5

284: D. S. 4. 73. 5

285: Pi. O. 1. 79

286: s. Pi. O. 1. 127

287: Pi. O. 1. 67

288: Pi. O. 1. 71

289: Ci. TD 2. 27. 67

290: Pa. 5. 13. 7

291: Pa. 8. 14. 10

292: Pa. 8. 14. 11

293: s. Ve. G. 3. 7

294: Hy. 84

295: GG 173 (153)

296: s. S. E. 504

297: S. fr. 433

298: Hy. 84

299: D. S. 4. 73. 4

300: s. A. Rh. 1. 752

301: Ap. ep. 9. 2. 7

302: E. IT 823

303: S. E. 504
E. Or. 987; 1547

304: Ap. ep. 9. 2. 8

305: Pa. 8. 14. 12

306: Pa. 5. 20. 6

307: GG 84 (74)

308: Pa. 5. 7. 10

309: Pi. O. 1. 94

310: B. 7. 53

311: Pi. O. 1. 93

212: Pa. 6. 22. 1

313: Pa. 5. 13. 2

314: Pa. 5. 13. 3

315: s. Pi. O. 1. 149

316: Pa. 5. 10. 6

317: Pa. 5. 16. 4

318: Pi. O. 1. 89

319: s. E. Or. 4

320: s. Il. 2. 105

321: Pa. 6. 20. 7

322: GG 228 (201)

323: Ap. 1. 7. 2

324: Od. 10. 2

325: GG 206 (182)

326: Er. C. 1. 18

327: Ov. M. 2. 639

328: GG 144 (127)

329: GG 221 (196)

330: E. fr. 481. 15

331: Hy. A. 1. 18

332: GG 185 (163)

333: Rh. Gr. 7. 1313. 6

334: GG 16 (14)

335: D. H. Op. p. 346. 19

336: Hor. C. 1. 2. 17

337: s. Ly. 722

338: Od. 11. 238

339: s. Ar. Ly. 139

340: s. Il. 10. 334

341: Ae. VH 12. 42
432: Ap. 1. 9. 8
343: S. fr. 648 Pearson
344: D. S. 6. 6. 5
345: Pi. P. 4. 136
346: Pol. 4. 141
347: S. fr. 598
348: s. E. Or. 1691
349: Ap. 1. 9. 8
350: Od. 19. 109
351: Pi. I. 5. 14
352: Ap. 1. 9. 7
353: Ve. A. 6. 586
      E. fr. 14
354: Hy. 61
      D. S. 4. 68. 2
355: V. Fl. 1. 665
356: s. Ve. A. 6. 585
357: Ap. 1. 9. 7
358: Od. 10. 608
359: Ap. 1. 9. 9
360: Ap. 1. 9. 9
361: GG 138 (122)
362: GG 261 (230)
363: Il. 6. 146
264: Hy. 60
365: Il. 6. 153
366: GG 163 (145)
367: Ap. 1. 9. 3
368: s. Ly. 174
369: GG 210 (186)
370: Pa. 2. 5. 1
371: s. Il. 6. 153
372: Thgn. 703
373: GG 250 (220)
374: A. fr. 220
375: Hy. 200
      s. Od. 19. 432
376: Od. 19. 396

377: He. fr. 136
378: Hy. 201
379: Tz. Ly. 344
380: Polyae. 6. 52
381: s. S. Ai. 190
382: A. fr. 175
      S. Ai. 189
      S. Ph. 417
      S. fr. 142
      E. Cy. 104
      IA 524
      Ly. 344; 1030
383: s. Ve. G. 3. 267
384: A. fr. 39
385: s. Il. 6. 153
386: Pa. 2. 2. 2
387: Pa. 2. 1. 3
388: GG 265 (234)
389: Od. 11. 593
390: Hy. 157
391: GG 42 (37)
392: GG 44
393: Ap. 1. 9. 3
394: GG 50 (44)
395: GG 112 (98)
396: s. Il. 155
397: St. By. Mylasa
398: Str. 8. 6. 21
399: GG 105 (42)
400: St. Th. 4. 61
401: s. Il. 155
402: Pi. O. 13. 63
403: GG 111 (98)
404: Pa. 2. 4. 1
405: Pi. O. 13. 86
406: GG 138 (122)
407: Ap. 2. 3. 1
408: Pa. 10. 30. 5
      s. Od. 11. 326

409: Il. 6. 160
410: s. Il. 6. 170
411: Il. 16. 328
412: GG 111 (98)
413: s. Il. 16. 328
414: Il. 6. 181
      Th. 319
415: Ap. 2. 3. 2
416: s. Il. 6. 200
417: GG 110 (97)
418: E. fr. 664
419: s. Ar. Pax 141
420: Pi. I. 7. 45
421: E. fr. 285
422: E. fr. 286
423: E. fr. 306–8
424: Pi. I. 7. 44
425: Il. 6. 201
426: Th. 286
427: s. Il. 6. 155
428: Pi. O. 13. 92
429: GG 264 (233)
430: Str. 9. 5. 8
431: Ap. 1. 9. 1
432: s. Ar. N. 357
433: GG 159 (141)
434: GG 264 (233)
435: Hy. 2
436: s. Pi. P. 4. 288
437: Hdt. 7. 197. 2
      s. A. Rh. 2. 654
438: GG 183 (162)
439: Pa. 9. 34. 5
440: s. A. Pe. 71
441: s. Ly. 22
442: s. A. Rh. 1. 256
443: A. Rh. 2. 1151
444: Pa. 9. 16. 5
445: GG 257 (226)

446: Pa. 9. 12. 4

447: E. B. 11

448: E. Ph. 651 c. s.

449: s. E. Ph. 8

450: Ap. 3. 5. 5

451: GG 105 (92)

452: Od. 19. 518

453: GG 62 (55)

454: Od. 19. 522

455: s. Od. 19. 518

456: Pa. 9. 5. 9

457: Ap. 3. 5. 5

458: Th. 1. 9. 2

459: Ath. 603 a

460: Ae. NA 6. 15;
     V. H. 13. 5

461: Ap. 3. 5. 5

462: Hy. 85

463: Plu. 750 b
     D. S. 4. 64. 2

464: hyp. E. Ph.

465: s. E. Ph. 1760

466: Plu. 313 e

467: s. Il. 2. 105

468: s. E. Ph. 1760

469: s. E. Ph. 1010

470: A. Se. 745

471: A. Se. 750; 802;
     842

472: A. Se. 756

473: A. fr. 122

474: A. Se. 691

475: s. E. Ph. 1760

476: s. E. Ph. 1760

477: A. fr. 173

478: E. Ph. 14

479: E. Ph. 18

480: E. Ph. 22

481: E. Ph. 38

482: S. OT 713

483: hyp. S. OT III

484: DM. PY 40
     Palmer

485: Ar. R. 1190

486: s. E. Ph. 1760

487: hyp. E. Ph. I
     104

488: E. Ph. 26

489: E. Ph. 32

490: s. E. Ph. 26

491: GG 263 (232)

492: s. E. Ph. 26; 28
     Hy. 66

493: s. E. Ph. 26

494: Pa. 2. 6. 6
     FGH 90. 8

495: Ath. 296 b

496: Hy. 66

497: s. E. Ph. 1760
     S. OT 775

498: E. Ph. 24

499: S. OT 1157

500: S. OT 1022

501: S. OT 774

502: E. Ph. 40

503: E. Ph. 41

504: E. Ph. 42

505: S. OT 809

506: Hy. 67

507: S. OT 811

508: E. Ph. 44

509: S. OT 806

510: Et. Gen.

511: FGH 90. 8

512: Od. 11. 271

513: Pa. 9. 5. 11
     s. E. Ph. 1760

514: s. E. Ph. 53

515: Il. 23. 675

516: FGH 90. 8

517: s. E. Ph. 934;
     1031

518: E. Ph. 810

519: Th. 326

520: GG 52 (46)

521: Pa. 5. 11. 2

522: s. E. Ph. 1760

523: s. E. Ph. 45

524: Ap. 3. 5. 8

525: E. Ph. 48

526: s. E. Ph. 50

527: s. E. Ph. 50

528: D. S. 4. 64. 4

529: Ap. 3. 5. 8

530: S. OT 60

531: Ap. 3. 6. 7

532: Ca. LP 70

533: Ap. 3. 6. 7

534: Hy. 75

535: ALib. 17

536: s. Ly. 683

537: Ap. 3. 6. 7

538: s. Od. 10. 494

539: Ov. M. 326

540: s. Od. 10. 494

541: s. Ly. 372

542: Od. 10. 493

543: Od. 11. 91

544: S. OT 372

545: A. Se. 783
     Se. OT 1270

546: s. E. Ph. 61

547: E. Ph. 303

548: E. Ph. 1457

549: S. OT 1426

550: S. OT 1429

551: E. Ph. 63

552: A. Se. 709; 725; 781

553: Ath. 465 e

554: A. Se. 727; 788; 815

E. Ph. 66

555: s. S. OC 1375

556: E. Ph. 1543

557: MVat. 2. 230

558: E. Ph. 1693

559: S. OT 420

560: E. Ph. 1705

561: S. OC 3

562: S. OC 88

563: S. OC 95

564: S. OC 1456

565: S. OC 1548

566: S. OC 1590

567: S. OC 1621

568: S. OC 1644

569: s. Ari. EN 1111 a 7

570: S. OT 421

571: s. S. OC 91

572: EGr. 1135

573: GG 107 (94)

574: Pa. 4. 2. 4

575: Pa. 2. 21. 7

576: Pa. 3. 1. 4

577: Ap. 3. 10. 4

578: Ap. 3. 10. 5

579: Mal Chr. IV O 100

580: Pa. 3. 1. 4

581: s. A. Rh. 1. 146

582: h. Ho. 33. 4

583: GG Pl. IVa

584: s. Ly. 506

585: Pa. 3. 26. 2

586: Pa. 3. 26. 3

587: Pa. 4. 2. 4; 7

588: s. Il. 9. 557

589: Ap. 3. 10. 3

590: Il. 9. 558

591: s. Il. 9. 557

592: Il. 9. 564

593: Ap. 1. 7. 9

594: Il. 9. 559

595: MVat. 1. 77

596: s. Il. 9. 557

597: Ap. 1. 7. 9

598: Il. 9. 562

599: Pa. 3. 16. 1

600: Hy. 80. 1

601: Pa. 3. 16. 1–3

602: The. 22. 137

603: Ap. 3. 11. 2

604: Od. 11. 300

605: Pr. Chr. 103. 13

Ly. 535–52

s. Ly. 536–52

Pi. N. 10. 55

s. Pi. N. 10. 114

Ap. 3. 11. 2

606: Pi. N. 10. 79

607: Od. 11. 301

608: E. Hel. 140

609: Er. C. 10

610: SEmp. 9. 37

611: h. Ho. 33. 8

612: Ap. 1. 8. 1

613: GG 202 (178)

614: He. fr. 120

615: N. D. 43. 60

616: Hy. 175

617: Ap. 1. 7. 7

618: Ap. 1. 7. 6

619: Ath. 35 ab

620: Ap. 1. 8. 1

621: MVat. 1. 87

622: s. Ve. G. 1. 9

623: Ve. G. 1. 9

624: Hy. 129

625: He. fr. 135

626: Hy. 171

627: Hy. 171

628: Ap. 1. 8. 2

629: Il. 9. 533

630: Il. 9. 544

631: Il. 9. 547

632: GG 84 (73)

633: Ap. 1. 8. 2

634: Ap. 2. 6. 3

635: s. A. Rh. 1. 188

s. Ly. 488

636: A. Rh. 1. 169

E. fr. 530. 5

637: Pa. 8. 45. 7

638: Ari. fr. 640. 44

639: Il. 21. 482

640: Thgn. 1288

641: Ae. VH 13. 1

642: GG 113 (99)

643: He. fr. 20; 21

644: Pa. 8. 35. 10

645: Ap. 3. 9. 2

646: Ae. VH 13. 1

647: GG 146 (129)

648: Thgn. 1291

649: GG 153 (136)

650: Ca. Di. 221

651: GG 204 (180)

652: Thgn. 1291

653: Ov. M. 10. 560

654: Hy. 185

655: Ov. M. 10. 578

656: s. The. 2. 120

657: The. 2. 120
658: The. 3. 42
659: Ov. M. 10. 687
660: Gra. Cy. 490
661: Ov. M. 10. 686
662: GG 89 (78)
663: s. Ve. A. 3. 113
664: Ap. 3. 9. 2
665: Ap. 3. 9. 2
666: Ar. Ly. 781
667: Pa. 5. 19. 2
668: Prop. 1. 1. 9
669: Xe. Cyn. 1. 7
670: Ov. AA 3. 775
671: Ap. 3. 9. 2
672: Ap. 1. 8. 2
673: E. fr. 520
674: Ap. 1. 8. 2
675: B. 5. 113
676: Il. 9. 548
677: Ap. 1. 8. 2
678: Ap. 1. 8. 2
679: Il. 9. 549
     Pa. 10. 31. 3
680: Il. 9. 566
681: Il. 9. 553
682: Il. 9. 571
683: Pa. 10. 31. 3
684: Pa. 10. 31. 4
685: ALib. 2
686: Ap. 1. 8. 3
687: Ae. NA 4. 42
688: B. 5. 89
689: GG 272 (240)
690: Syll. 1027
691: Hdt. 2. 44. 3–5
692: Pa. 2. 10. 1
693: Pa. 2. 6. 6–7
694: Pa. 6. 21. 6

695: Pa. 5. 7. 7
696: Pa. 9. 27. 8
697: Ci. ND 3. 42
698: Plu. 304 c–e
699: Pa. 8. 31. 3
700: Pi. N. 3. 22
701: Is. 5. 32
702: D. S. 4. 10. 1
703: Pi. fr. 301
704: Ae. VH 2. 32
705: The. 24. 1
706: s. St. Th. 4.
     147
707: D. S. 4. 10. 2
708: E. HF 388
709: E. Al. 481; 491
710: s. Ly. 932
711: s. A. Rh. 1.
     747
712: He. Sc. 12
713: Ap. 2. 4. 6
714: Pa. 19. 1. 1
715: Ap. 2. 4. 7
716: GG 109 (96)
717: ALib. 41
718: s. Ly. 932
719: GG 109 (96)
720: s. Od. 11. 266
     Pa. 5. 18. 2
     Pla. Am. 760
721: Ath. 498 c
722: Ap. 2. 4. 8
723: GG 164 (146)
724: APal. 9. 441
725: s. Od. 11. 266
726: Ap. 2. 4. 8
727: Hy. 29
728: Ap. 2. 4. 8
729: Il. 19. 100

730: s. Il. 19. 119
     ALib. 19
     Ov. M. 9. 397
731: Ae. NA 12. 5
732: Pa. 9. 11. 3
733: Hsch. tetradi
734: The. 24. 2
735: He. Sc. 89
736: Pi. I. 5. 32
737: D. S. 4. 9. 5
738: D. S. 4. 9. 6
739: Hy. A. 2. 43
     Er. C. 44
     Ach. Intr. 24
740: Pi. N. 1. 33
741: The. 24. 1
742: Ap. 2. 4. 9
743: Pa. 1. 43. 7
744: Su.
745: s. Il. 18. 570
746: Zen. 4. 45
747: Ap. 2. 4. 9
     D. S. 3. 67. 2
748: Ap. 2. 4. 9
749: The. 24. 37
750: Plu. 271 b
751: Pa. 9. 10. 4
752: IG. 14. 1293 B
753: Pa. 9. 27. 8
754: Ap. 2. 4. 9
755: s. The. 13. 6
756: The. 25. 207
757: Pa. 2. 31. 10
     Ap. 2. 4. 11
758: Ap. 2. 4. 10
759: Pa. 9. 27. 7
760: D. S. 4. 29. 3
761: Pa. 9. 27. 6
762: Ap. 2. 4. 10

763: Pi. I. 6. 47
764: Ap. 2. 4. 9
765: Ap. 2. 4. 11
766: Pa. 9. 37 .1
767: D. S. 4. 10. 4
768: E. HF 220
769: Ap. 2. 4. 11
770: Od. 11. 269
771: E. HF 11
772: D. S. 4. 10. 6
773: Ap. 2. 4. 11
774: E. HF 1
775: Pi. P. 9. 81
776: Pa. 9. 11. 1
777: Plu. 577f
778: GG 138 (122)
779: D. S. 4. 10. 6
780: E. HF 16
781: Pa. 2. 15. 3
782: D. S. 4. 11. 3
783: The. 25. 200
784: Th. 326
785: GG 51 (45)
786: Ep. fr. 2 Diels
787: Pa. 9. 17. 2
788: Il. 21. 483
789: GG 209 (177)
790: Ca. fr. 54–59
791: Ap. 2. 5. 1
792: St. B.
793: The. 25. 256
794: D. S. 4. 11. 4
795: s. Ve. G. 3. 19 Keil
796: Plu. Ti. 26
797: Plu. 676f
798: Ca. fr. 59. 18
799: Ap. 2. 5. 1
800: The. 25. 277

801: Er. C. 12
802: Pa. 2. 36. 8
803: Th. 313
804: E. HF 420
805: Th. 311
806: Hy. 30
807: Pa. 2. 37. 4
808: Ap. 2. 5. 2
809: GG 51 (45)
810: Al. fr. 118 Bergk
811: S. fr. 203 Bergk
812: E. HF 1190
813: Ap. 2. 6. 2
814: Ap. 2. 5. 2
815: Er. C. 11
816: Ma. So. 1. 12. 2
817: Ap. 2. 4. 12
818: GG 138 (122)
819: Ap. 2. 5. 11
820: Ap. 2. 5. 3
821: Ap. 2. 5. 5
822: Ca. Di. 109
823: E. HF 377
824: E. Hel. 382
825: s. Pi. O. 3. 53
826: Pi. O. 3. 30
827: GG 154 (136)
828: Hy. 30
829: E. HF 378
830: Ap. 2. 5. 3
831: Pi. O. 3. 26
832: Str. 5. 1. 9
833: Pi. O. 3. 31
834: GG 53 (46)
835: Ap. 2. 5. 3
836: Od. 6. 103
837: FGH 1. 6
838: Ap. 2. 5. 4
839: The. 7. 149 c. s.

840: GG 160 (146)
841: Ap. 2. 5. 4
842: s. The. 7. 149
843: D. S. 4. 12. 3
844: Ap. 2. 5. 4
845: Ap. 2. 5. 6
846: D. S. 4. 13. 2
847: Se. HF 243
848: Ve. A. 6. 311
849: S. OT 175
850: Pa. 8. 22. 7
851: Pa. 8. 22. 4
852: s. Ve. A. 8. 299
853: A. Rh. 2. 1036
854: D. S. 4. 13. 2
855: Ap. 2. 5. 6
856: Pa. 8. 22. 4
    D. S. 4. 13. 2
857: Ap. 2. 5. 6
858: A. Rh. 2. 10. 30
859: s. A. Rh. 1. 172
860: Ap. 2. 4. 5
    D. S. 4. 13. 3
861: Pa. 5. 1. 9
    s. Ve. A. 8. 299
862: Ap. 2. 5. 5
863: Pa. 5. 1. 9
864: Ap. 2. 7. 8
865: Ap. 2. 5. 5
866: Ath. 412a
867: Ap. 2. 5. 5
868: s. Ca. De. 102
869: Ap. 2. 5. 3
870: Er. C. 28
871: Ap. 2. 5. 5
872: D. S. 4. 33. 1
873: Hy. 33
874: s. Ve. G. 3. 267
875: E. HF 382

876: GG 206 (182)

877: Il. 11. 445

878: Se. HF 451

879: s. Pi. P. 4. 126

880: Il. 2. 763

881: Il. 2. 715

882: Ap. 1. 9. 15

883: Ap. 1. 9. 15

884: Ap. 1. 9. 15

885: GG 33 (28)

886: Ap. 1. 9. 15

887: E. Al. 24

888: E. Al. 476

889: E. Al. 1142

890: Pl. Sy. 179b

891: E. Al. 1140

892: Phr. 2 Nauck

893: D. S. 4. 15. 3

894: D. S. 4. 15. 4

895: Ap. 2. 5. 8

896: D. S. 4. 15. 4

897: GG 179 (159)

898: A. Rh. 1. 1275

899: The. 13. 75

900: A. Rh. 1. 1317

901: E. Al. 499

902: He. Sc. 319

903: He. Sc. 70

904: E. HF 591

     He. Sc. 479

905: He. Sc. 338

906: He. Sc. 120

907: GG 185 (163)

908: s. Il. 23. 347

909: Pa. 8. 25. 10

910: Ap. 2. 5. 11

911: Hy. 31

912: He. Sc. 477

913: Ap. 1. 7. 4

914: Pl. Phd. 84e

915: GG 110 (97)

916: Ap. 2. 5. 7

917: BKT 5. 2. 73. 24

     Ap. 2. 5. 7

918: BKT 5. 2. 73.

     26

919: Ap. 2. 5. 7

920: D. S. 4. 13. 4

921: Plu. Th. 14

922: Ap. 2. 5. 9

923: E. HF 409

924: Pi. N. 3. 38

925: s. Pi. N. 3. 64

926: Pi. I. 6. 28

927: Pi. N. 3. 37

928: Il. 5. 266

929: Il. 21. 448

930: Il. 21. 448

931: Ov. M. 11. 203

932: Il. 7. 453

933: Il. 21. 453

934: Il. 5. 640

935: s. Il. 20. 146

     Ap. 2. 5. 9

     s. Ly. 34

936: D. S. 4. 42. 3

937: s. Ly. 34

938: Il. 20. 145

939: s. Il. 20. 146

940: s. Ly. 34

941: Il. 5. 650

942: Il. 5. 642

943: S. Ai. 435

944: S. Ai. 1301

     Xe. Cy. 1. 9

     D. S. 4. 32. 5

     Ap. 2. 6. 4

945: Ap. 2. 6. 4

946: Ly. 337 c. s.

     Ap. 2. 6. 4

947: Pi. N. 3. 38

948: Ap. 2. 5. 9

949: Ap. 2. 5. 9

950: D. S. 4. 16. 4

951: A. Rh. 2. 966

952: Ap. 2. 5. 9

953: Plu. Th. 12a

954: Ath. 557a

955: Ly. 1329

956: Ap. ep. 1. 16;

     5. 2

     St. Th. 12. 534

957: E. HF 416

958: IG. 14. 1293 D

959: Il. 15. 30

960: Il. 14. 250

961: Plu. 304c.

962: Ap. 2. 6. 7

963: s. Il. 14. 78

964: Hsch.

965: Ap. 2. 7. 1

966: Plu. 304c

967: s. The. 7. 5

968: Il. 14. 256; 15. 18

969: GG 156 (138)

970: Th. 293

971: Th. 309

972: Ap. 2. 5. 10

973: Th. 287

974: GG 50 (44)

975: Il. 6. 328

976: Il. 5. 859

977: s. Th. 293

978: Th. 287

979: Ve. A. 6. 289

980: s. Th. 287

981: Is. 6. 19

982: s. Il. 11.690

983: Pa. 6. 25. 3

984: Il. 5. 392

985: s. Il. 11. 690

986: Pi. O. 9. 31

987: Il. 5. 394

988: He. Sc. 359

989: Il. 5. 397

990: GG 143 (126)

991: Il. 11. 690

992: s. A. Rh. 1. 159

    s. Il. 2. 336

993: Hy. 10

994: D. S. 4. 17. 4

995: Or. H. 41

996: Hsch.

997: Pi. P. 9. 105

998: Pi. I. 56

999: Ap. 2. 5. 11

1000: Ph. Im. 2. 22:

1: D. S. 4. 18. 1

2: s. A. Rh. 4.
    1396

3: s. Lu. ITr. 21

4: Ap. 2. 5. 11

5: D. Chr. 8. 32

6: Po. M. 1. 26;
    10. 105

7: Pi. N. 3. 21;
    4. 69
    s. Pi. O. 3. 79

8: Str. 3. 2. 11

9: Ath. 470 c

10: Ap. 2. 5. 10

11: GG 191 (164)

12: Ath. 470 f

13: s. A. Rh. 4.
    1399

14: Ath. 470 d

15: Ap. 2. 5. 10

16: A. fr. 74

17: Ath. 469 e

18: Plu. Ser. 9

19: Hdt. 4. 8

20: A. fr. 199

21: Ap. 2. 5. 10

22: Str. 4. 1. 7
    Po. M. 2. 78

23: Ve. A. 8. 194

24: Prop. 5. 9. 10

25: Ve. A. 8. 243

26: Ve. A. 8. 260

27: D. H. AR 1. 35.
    2

28: Ap. 2. 5. 10

29: GG 38 (33)

30: Pa. 3. 35. 2

31: s. Pi. N. 4. 43

32: GG 24 (26)

33: D. S. 4. 21. 5

34: Cla. RP 3. 184

35: Pi. I. 6. 32

36: Ap. 5. 6. 1

37: s. Pi. I. 6. 32

38: Pi. N. 4. 25

39: Su.

40: s. Pi. N. 4. 25

41: Ap. 2. 5. 10

42: Ap. 2. 5. 11

43: s. A. Rh. 4. 1396

44: GG 32 (28)

45: GG 54 (48)

46: Ath. 469 d

47: s. A. Rh. 4. 1396

48: Ap. 2. 5. 11

49: GG 187 (166)

50: Th. 529

51: Ap. 2. 5. 11

52: s. Il. 11. 1

53: A. fr. 192

54: GG 220 (195)

55: Th. 522

56: GG Pl. XI b

57: GG Pl. XI a

58: E. fr. 594

59: Ap. 2. 5. 11

60: A. fr. 195–8

61: s. Ve. A. 8. 299

62: Se. HF 324; 535

63: E. Hi. 742

64: E. Hi. 748

65: s. A. Rh. 4. 1396

66: GG 53 (47)

67: Hy. A. 2. 6

68: Ap. 2. 5. 11

69: Ep. fr. 11 Diels

70: Od. 1. 52

71: s. A. Rh. 4. 1396

72: Hy. A. 2. 6

73: Er. C. 2. 3

74: s. Ve. A. 4. 484

75: Od. 1. 50

76: GG Pl. II b

77: A. Rh. 4. 1396

78: s. A. Rh. 4. 1396

79: Ap. 2. 5. 11

80: Ap. 2. 5. 12

81: Od. 11. 603

82: Ap. 2. 5. 12

83: Ap. 2. 5. 12
    s. Il. 8. 368

84: h. C. 475

85: Euph. fr. 95

86: Ve. A. 6. 260

87: Ve. A. 6. 304

88: s. Ve. A. 6. 392

89: Ve. A. 6. 413

90: Se. HF 775
91: St. Th. 5. 401
92: Ve. A. 6. 392
93: s. Ve. A. 6. 392
94: GG 34 (30)
95: Th. 770
96: Th. 311
97: Th. 312
98: S. Tr. 1098
99: Ve. A. 6. 421
100: Th. 313
101: Ve. A. 6. 396
102: Ap. 2. 5. 12
103: s. Il. 21. 194
104: B. 5. 71
105: B. 5. 172
106: Od. 11. 633
107: Ap. 2. 5. 12
108: GG 126 (111)
109: Ap. 2. 5. 12
110: D. S. 4. 26. 1
111: E. HF 613
112: Ap. 2. 5. 12
113: Ap. 2. 5. 12
114: s. A. Rh. 101
115: Ve. A. 6. 617
116: Ap. 2. 5. 12
117: Pa. 2. 31. 2
118: Pa. 2. 35. 10
119: Euph. fr. 62
120: Ap. 11. 5. 12
121: Hsch.
122: Pa. 9. 34. 5
123: Archil. 119
124: Diog. Ep. 36
125: Ap. 2. 6. 4
126: Ly. 469
127: Ap. 2. 7. 7
128: Ap. 2. 7. 4

129: GG 153 (136)
130: Il. 2. 620
131: Ib. 2
132: Il. 23. 641
133: s. Il. 23. 641
134: Pl. Phd. 89c
c. s.
135: Pi. O. 10. 33
136: Pa. 8. 14. 9
137: Ap. 2. 7. 2
138: Pi. O. 10. 26
139: Pa. 5. 2. 2
140: Ap. 2. 7. 2
141: Pi. O. 2. 3
142: Pi. O. 8. 3.
11
143: Pa. 5. 14. 2
144: Pa. 5. 13. 2
145: Ap. 2. 7. 2
146: D. S. 4. 14. 1
147: Ap. 2. 4. 12
148: Pi. I. 4. 69
149: E. HF 526
150: E. HF 615
151: E. HF 575
152: E. HF 572
153: Pa. 9. 11. 2
154: E. HF 937
155: s. Pi. I. 4. 104
156: Ap. 2. 6. 1
D. S. 4. 31. 1
157: Ar. Th. 108
158: s. S. Tr. 354
Pa. 4. 33. 5
159: Od. 8. 224
160: A. Rh. 1. 88
161: s. Il. 5. 392
162: Pa. 4. 2. 2
163: Od. 21. 32

164: Od. 21. 15
165: Od. 21. 258
166: Ap. 2. 6. 1
167: s. S. Tr. 354
168: The. 24. 107
169: s. The. 13. 56
170: s. Ly. 50; 458
171: Ap. 3. 12
172: Ap. 2. 6. 1
D. S. 4. 31. 2
173: S. Tr. 268
174: Od. 21. 22
175: D. S. 4. 31. 2
176: s. Od. 21. 22
177: Od. 21. 26
178: Ap. 2. 6. 3
179: Od. 21. 28
180: Ap. 2. 6. 2
D. S. 4. 31. 3
181: s. Pi. I. 4. 104
182: Ap. 2. 6. 2
183: Od. 8. 226
184: Il. 1. 53
185: Plu. 557d
186: s. Pi. O. 9. 43
187: Ap. 2. 6. 2
Hy. 32
s. Ve. A. 8. 299
188: Pa. 10. 13. 8
189: Ap. 2. 6. 2
190: Pa. 3. 21. 8
191: Hy. 32
s. Ve. A. 8. 299
192: s. Ve. A. 8. 299
S. Tr. 275
193: Ap. 2. 6. 3
194: D. S. 4. 31. 6
195: s. Od. 21. 22
196: Lu. DD. 23. 2

197: s. A. Rh. 1. 1289
198: Plu. 301f
199: ICo. 36c
200: Plu. 304c
201: Hdt. 1. 7. 4
202: St. By.
203: D. S. 4. 31. 5
204: Ap. 2. 6. 3
205: D. S. 4. 31. 5
206: Hdt. 1. 93. 4
207: Ath. 516a
208: Ov. F. 2. 305
209: Ov. Her. 9. 73
210: D. S. 4. 31. 5
211: Hy. A. 2. 14
212: Ap. 2. 6. 3
213: Su.
214: Su.
215: GG 85 (74)
216: Eud. 72
217: s. Ly. 9
218: GG 21 (18)
219: Ap. 2. 6. 3
220: Hdt. 7. 216
221: s. Ar. N. 1050
222: Su.
223: Eud. 72
224: App. BC 5. 69
225: Ap. 2. 6. 3
226: FGH 26. 1. 17
227: Ap. 2. 6. 3 cum
      Tz. Chil. 2. 434
228: Hdt. 7. 115
229: Ap. 2. 6. 3 cum
      Tz. Chil. 2. 432
230: E. fr. 688
231: E. fr. 689
232: E. fr. 690
233: Ap. 2. 6. 3

234: Tz. Com. 3. 27
235: Philo II 461 M.
236: E. fr. 691
237: E. fr. 693
238: FGH 26. 1. 17
239: s. The. 10. 4
240: The. 10. 41
241: Pol. 4. 54
242: Su.
243: s. The. 10. 4
244: Ath. 415b
245: s. Ve. E. 8. 68
246: Sosi. fr. 2. 1
247: Sosi. fr. 3
248: s. Il. 24. 616
249: GG 159 (141)
      Pl. VIa
250: Ap. 1. 8. 1
251: Ap. 1. 8. 1
252: S. Tr. 18
253: S. Tr. 10
254: GG ill. on p. 57
      (50)
255: CG 56 (49)
256: GG 56 (50)
257: s. Il. 21. 194
258: S. Tr. 523
259: S. Tr. 21
260: S. Tr. 26; 516
      N. D. 43. 13
261: Ov. M. 9. 85
262: Ap. 2. 7. 5
263: S. Tr. 569
264: Il. 16. 115
265: Ap. 1. 7. 10
266: Str. 10. 2. 5
267: Th. 341
268: S. Tr. 559
269: Ap. 2. 7. 6

270: D. S. 4. 35. 4
271: D. Ch. 60. 1
272: Ap. 2. 7. 6
273: S. Tr. 565
274: S. Tr. 556
275: He. fr. 135. 19
      cum   PO.
      2075. 9
276: S. Tr. 38
277: S. Tr. 259
278: S. Tr. 354
279: S. Tr. 360
280: S. Tr. 1160
281: S. Tr. 750
282: Ap. 2. 7. 7
283: S. Tr. 1157
284: D. S. 4. 37. 3
285: S. Tr. 735
286: S. Tr. 780
287: S. Tr. 930
288: S. Tr. 1191
289: S. Tr. 1219
290: S. Tr. 1255
291: S. Tr. 200
292: Ca. Di. 159
293: Hdt. 7. 198
294: S. Tr. 1214
295: D. S. 4. 38. 4
296: S. Ph. 801
297: Ap. 2. 7. 7
298: S. Ph. 802
299: Lu. Am. 54
300: Lu. Am. 1
301: Ca. Di. 159
302: Li. 36. 30
303: Ap. 2. 7. 7
304: Il. 23. 252
305: D. S. 4. 38. 5
306: s. Ve. G. 1. 34

307: Ap. 2. 7. 7
308: D. S. 4. 39. 2
309: Pi. N. 10. 118
310: GG 98 (87)
311: Th. 950
312: Pi. I. 4. 67
313: PO. 2075. 16
314: Od. 11. 601
315: Er. C. 4
316: Arat. 63
317: Aristid. 40. 16
318: Hdt. 6. 52. 1
319: E. Her. 12
320: FGH 1. 30
321: Pi. P. 9. 80
322: s. Pi. P. 9. 137
323: E. Her. 6
324: Ap. 2. 8. 1
325: E. Her. 851
326: E. Her. 403
327: E. Her. 41
328: Pa. 1. 32. 6
329: GG 210 (185)
330: GG 124 (109)
331: Ap. 3. 14. 1
s. Ar. Ve. 438
332: s. Ar. Pl. 773
333: Ath. 555c
334: FHG 2. 319
Iust. 2. 6. 7
335: Su.
336: Str. 9. 20
337: Pli. NH 7. 194
338: GG 124 (110)
339: s. Pi. O. 9. 68
340: Ci. Le. 2. 63
341: Ar. Ve. 438
342: Ath. 555c
343: Aug. CD 18. 9

344: Pa. 2. 15. 5
345: GG 222 (196)
346: Ap. 3. 14. 1
347: s. Il. 17. 54
348: Hdt. 5. 82
349: Ap. 3. 14. 1
350: Ov. M. 6. 72
351: Ap. 3. 14. 1
352: Ap. 3. 14. 2
353: Su.
354: Pa. 8. 2. 3
355: Eus. PE 10. 9. 22
356: Su.
357: Athenag. 1
358: GG 124 (110)
359: Ap. 3. 14. 2
360: GG 124 (110)
361: E. Ion 496
362: Ap. 3. 14. 2
363: Pa. 6. 20. 2–5
364: GG 125 (110)
365: Hdt. 8. 41. 2
Ar. Ly. 759
366: GG 123 (109)
367: Ap. 3. 14. 6
368: Hy. A. 2. 13
369: Ap. 3. 14. 6
370: Ap. 3. 14. 7
371: Il. 2. 547
372: Od. 5. 8
373: E. Me. 824
374: IG. 12. 444. 24
375: Plu. 843 b
376: E. Ion 23
377: E. Ion 281
378: Athenag. 1
379: Pa. 1. 26. 5
380: Pa. 1. 5. 2
381: Thu. 2. 15. 1

382: Str. 9. 1. 17
383: Thu. 1. 20. 2
384: Ae. VH 12. 28
385: Ap. 3. 15. 8
386: FGH 328. 105
387: Su.
388: Hy. 46
389: Lycurg. 98
390: E. fr. 360
391: Ap. 3. 15. 4
392: Ap. 3. 15. 5
393: Hy. 46
394: E. fr. 357
395: Ap. 3. 15. 5
396: Art. 2. 12
397: GG 24 (21)
398: E. Hi. 30
D. S. 4. 62. 2
399: E. Me. 683
400: Pa. 2. 31. 9
401: Pa. 2. 33. 1
402: Pa. 2. 33. 1
403: Hy. 37
403a: Ap. 3. 15. 7
404: Ap. 3. 15. 6
405: Ap. 3. 15. 6
Plu. Th. 2c
406: s. E. Hi. 11
407: Ap. 3. 15. 7
408: Plu. Th. 2c
409: Ap. 3. 15. 7
410: Pa. 2. 32. 9
411: Ap. 3. 15. 7
412: Pa. 1. 27. 7
413: Plu. Th. 2e
413a: Pa. 1. 27. 8
414: Lu. Cy. 14
415: Ap. 3. 16. 1
416: Plu. Th. 4b

417: Ap. 3. 16. 1
418: Plu. Th. 4b
419: Pa. 2. 1. 3
420: B. 18. 20
421: Ap. 3. 16. 2
422: Str. 9. 1. 4
423: Pa. 2. 1. 3
424: Plu. Th. 4c
425: Pa. 2. 1. 3
426: Ap. ep. 1. 1
427: B. 18. 23
428: Pa. 1. 44. 8
429: Ap. ep. 1. 2
430: CG 114
431: s. E. Hi. 979
432: Plu. Th. 4f
433: Ly. 111
434: Pa. 1. 36. 1
435: Str. 9. 1. 9
436: GG 210 (186)
437: Ap. 3. 12. 6
438: Pl. Ap. 41a
439: D. S. 4. 59. 5
440: Pa. 1. 39. 3
441: Ap. ep. 1. 3
442: Pa. 1. 39. 3
443: Hy. 38
444: D. S. 4. 59. 5
445: B. 18. 28
446: Ap. ep. 1. 4
447: GG 85 (74)
448: B. 18. 27
449: s. Ve. G. 1. 399
450: Ov. Ib. 407
451: Pa. 1. 38. 5
452: Pa. 1. 38. 5
453: D. S. 4. 59. 5
454: S. fr. 19
455: Ap. ep. 1. 4

456: D. S. 4. 59. 5
457: Plu. Th. 5b
458: Ap. ep. 1. 5
459: Plu. Th. 5c
460: Pa. 1. 37. 2
461: Pa. 1. 37. 4
462: Plu. Th. 5d
463: Plu. Th. 17d
464: Plu. Th. 5d
465: B. 18. 30
466: Plu. Th. 5d
467: Pa. 1. 19. 1
468: Ap. ep. 1. 5
469: B. 18. 46
470: Ov. M. 7. 420
471: Plu. Th. 5e
472: Ap. ep. 1. 6
473: Ca. fr. 233
474: s. Il. 11. 741
475: Plu. Th. 5e
476: Ap. ep. 1. 6
477: Plu. Th. 5f
478: S. fr. 872
479: Hy. 244
480: Ap. ep. 1. 11
481: s. E. Hi. 35
482: E. Hi. 35
483: Ca. Di. 10. 21
484: Pa. 1. 27. 10
485: s. Ve. A. 6. 20
486: Ca. fr. 238. 15
487: Plu. Th. 6b
488: Th. 411
489: Ca. fr. 231
490: Ca. fr. 258
491: APal. 16. 105. 3
492: Ca. fr. 259
493: Ca. fr. 260. 4
494: Ca. fr. 262

495: Ca. Di. 11. 5
496: Plu. Th. 6b
497: Plu. Th. 6c
498: Ap. 3. 15. 7
499: Ap. 3. 15. 7
    D. S. 4. 60. 5
500: Ap. 3. 15. 7
501: GG 110 (97)
502: Ap. 3. 15. 8
503: Ap. 3. 15. 8
504: Ov. M. 8. 145
505: Plu. Th. 6c
506: Plu. Th. 7c
507: B. 17. 2
508: Ap. ep. 1. 7
509: Plu. Th. 7c
510: s. Ve. A. 6. 21
511: Pa. 1. 17. 3
512: D. S. 4. 72. 7
513: B. 17. 8
514: B. 17. 102
515: Hy. A. 2. 5
516: Plu. Th. 7d
517: Si. fr. 33
518: s. Ve. G. 1. 222
519: Hsch.
520: GG 269 (237)
521: Hy. 42
522: Ap. 3. 1. 4
523: Pa. 2. 31. 1
524: Hy. 255
525: Od. 11. 323
526: Ap. ep. 1. 8
527: Plu. Th. 8b
528: s. Od. 11. 322
529: Ap. ep. 1. 11
    Ov. M. 8. 188
530: Hy. A. 2. 5
531: s. Ve. G. 222

532: s. Pi. N. 5. 89
533: Plu. Th. 8 a
534: D. S. 4. 61. 5
535: D. S. 4. 61. 5
536: Od. 11. 322
537: Plu. Th. 9 a
538: Plu. Th. 8 f
539: Pa. 2. 23. 7
540: Plu. Th. 9 c
541: Il. 18. 591
542: DM. KN 205
    Palmer
543: D. S. 4. 61. 5
544: Pr. Chr. p. 322
    Bek.
545: Pl. XVI b
546: D. S. 5. 51. 4
547: Hy. 43
548: D. S. 5. 51. 4
549: s. The. 2. 45
550: The. 2. 46
551: Plu. Th. 9 c
552: Plu. Th. 9 d
553: Plu. Th. 10 d
554: Plu. Th. 9 e
555: Ap. ep. 1. 10
556: Plu. Th. 13 e
    Plu. Ro. 38 e
    Ath. 557 a
557: Plu. Th. 8 f
558: D. S. 4. 62. 1
559: Pa. 9. 35. 5
560: IG, 4^2 1. 128. 43
561: N. D. 14. 221
562: D. S. 5. 52. 2
563: GG 271 (238)
564: Ath. 557 a
565: Plu. Th. 14 e
566: Hy. 155

567: GG 154 (141)
568: Il. 14. 317
569: Hy. 14. 6
570: GG 160 (142)
571: s. Il. 1. 263
572: He. fr. 200
573: s. Il. 1. 264
574: A. Rh. 1. 59
575: Pi. fr. 150. 5
576: Ve. A. 6. 449
577: Ap. ep. 1. 21
578: Plu. Th. 14 c
579: Prop. 2. 2. 9
580: Od. 21. 295
581: Ov. M. 12. 210
582: Ov. M. 12. 227
583: Il. 1. 265
    Plu. Th. 14 d
584: Il. 2. 742
585: Plu. Th. 14 b
586: S. OC 1539
587: Plu. Th. 14 c
588: s. Il. 3. 144
    Pi. fr. 227
589: Ap. ep. 1. 23
590: D. S. 4. 63. 2
    s. Ly. 513
591: Is. 1c. 19
592: Pa. 1. 41. 5
593: Plu. Th. 14 f
594: Plu. Th. 15 a
    D. S. 4. 63. 3
595: Pa. 5. 17. 6
596: Il. 3. 143
597: Il. 3. 236
598: Pa. 2. 21. 6
599: s. Ar. Ly. 645
600: s. Il. 3. 242
601: s. A. Rh. 1. 101

602: Pa. 1. 17. 4
603: Plu. Th. 15 a
604: Ve. A. 6. 397
605: Hy. 79
606: Se. HF 662
607: Pa. 10. 28. 2
608: Ve. A. 6. 393
609: Ap. ep. 1. 24
610: Pa. 10. 29. 9
611: Ap. 2. 5. 12
612: Ap. ep. 1. 24
613: Hor. C. 4. 7. 27
614: Ap. 2. 5. 12
615: Ap. ep. 1. 24
616: Hor. C. 3. 4. 79
617: Pa. 10. 29. 9
618: s. Ar. Eq. 1368
619: Hy. 79
620: Ve. A. 6. 617
621: Ve. A. 6. 601
622: Hor. C. 4. 7. 28
623: D. S. 4. 6. 4
624: Hy. 43
625: Thu. 2. 15
    Plu. Th. 10 f
626: Plu. Th. 11 a
627: Plu. Th. 13 f
628: Plu. Th. 14 a
629: Pa. 1. 2. 1
630: Pa. 1. 41. 7
631: Pa. 1. 2. 1
632: Plu. Th. 12 a
    Pa. 1. 2. 1
633: Q. S. 13. 496
634: Ap. ep. 1. 16
635: Plu. Th. 13 a
636: Ar. Ly. 679
637: Plu. Th. 13 a
638: Pa. 1. 17. 2

639: Pa. 1. 15. 2
640: Plu. Th. 13 d
641: Ap. ep. 5. 2
642: Ap. ep. 1. 17
643: D. S. 4. 28. 4
    Pa. 1. 2. 1
    Plu. Th. 13 b
644: Ca. Di. 239; 266
645: D. S. 4. 62. 2
646: IG. 1². 310. 280
647: E. Hi. 31
648: E. Hi. 24
649: E. Hi. 953
650: Pa. 2. 32. 3
651: E. Hi. 72
652: Ap. ep. 1. 18
653: E. Hi. 888
654: E. Hi. 1197
655: Pa. 2. 32. 1
656: Pa. 1. 22. 1
657: Pa. 2. 32. 10
658: Pa. 10. 29. 3
659: Pa. 2. 32. 1
660: E. Hi. 1425
661: Ve. A. 7. 769
662: Pa. 2. 27. 4
663: Pa. 2. 32. 1
664: Ve. A. 7. 774
665: Plu. Th. 17 b
666: Plu. Th. 15 b
667: Plu. Th. 16 f
668: He. fr. 18
669: Ap. 1. 9. 16
670: A. Rh. 1. 232
671: He. fr. 19
    Pi. N. 3. 54
672: Pi. P. 4. 119
673: A. Rh. 1. 554
674: GG 113 (99)

675: Od. 12. 72
676: A. Rh. 3. 67
677: V. Fl. 1. 83
678: Hy. 13
679: Hy. 13
680: Hy. 12
681: A. Rh. 1. 12
682: A. Rh. 1. 5
683: s. Pi. P. 4. 133
684: Ap. 1. 9. 16
685: Pi. P. 4. 71
686: Pi. P. 4. 120
687: Mi. 11. 5
688: GG 194 (171)
689: Od. 10. 139
690: Th. 957
691: A. Rh. 2. 1194
    3. 191; 337
692: Acc. M. fr. I
693: s. A. Rh. 1. 4
694: A. Rh. 1. 19
695: A. Rh. 1. 551;
    721
696: s. E. Me. 1
    D. S. 4. 41. 3
697: E. Me. 3
698: Hy. A. 2. 37
699: Ly. 1319
    Ca. fr. 16
700: Ap. 1. 9. 16
701: Pi. P. 4
702: s. A. Rh. 1. 230
703: Od. 13. 59
704: A. Rh. 2. 596
705: s. A. Rh. 2. 596
706: A. Rh. 4. 786
707: Od. 13. 70
708: Pi. P. 4. 169
709: Th. 995

710: A. Rh. 112
    Ap. 1. 9. 16
    V. Fl. 1. 124
711: Ap. 1. 9. 6
712: A. Rh. 1. 109
713: A. Rh. 2. 854
714: Pi. P. 4. 171
715: A. Rh. 1. 137
716: A. Rh. 1. 151
717: Pi. P. 4. 176
718: s. A. Rh. 1. 23
719: s. Od. 19. 432
720: Pi. P. 4. 178
721: A. Rh. 1. 54
722: A. Rh. 1. 142
723: A. Rh. 1. 172
724: A. Rh. 1. 65
725: A. Rh. 1. 93–4
726: A. Rh. 1. 49
727: A. Rh. 1. 323
728: Ap. 1. 9. 16
729: Hy. 14
730: A. Rh. 1. 359
731: A. Rh. 1. 494
732: A. Ch. 631
733: Ap. 1. 9. 17
734: s. Il. 7. 468
735: Pa. 3. 24. 3
736: Phot.
737: Hdt. 6. 138. 4
738: s. A. Rh. 1. 769
739: A. Rh. 1. 635
740: A. Rh. 1. 855
741: Pi. P. 4. 253
742: Pi. O. 4. 30
743: A. fr. 96
744: A. Rh. 1. 861
745: V. Fl. 2. 367
    St. Th. 5. 460

745: Ov. H. 6. 56
746: A. Rh. 1. 850
747: A. Rh. 1. 886
748: Il. 7. 468
749: hyp. Pi. N.
750: D. S. 5. 49. 6
751: D. S. 4. 49. 8
752: A. Rh. 1. 917
753: Od. 10. 108
754: A. Rh. 1. 936
755: s. A. Rh. 1. 1117
756: A. Rh. 1. 1221
       GG 179 (159)
757: A. Rh. 1. 1317
758: A. Rh. 2. 1
759: The. 22. 27
760: s. A. Rh. 2. 178
761: s. A. Su. 317
762: Ap. 1. 9. 21
763: s. A. Rh. 2. 178
764: A. Rh. 2. 180
765: s. Od. 12. 69
766: A. Rh. 2. 191
767: A. Rh. 2. 194
768: GG 63 (56)
769: A. Rh. 2. 299
770: E. Me. 432
771: A. Rh. 2. 609
772: A. Rh. 2. 345
773: A. Rh. 2. 752
774: A. Rh. 2. 673
775: A. Rh. 2. 598
776: A. Rh. 2. 674
777: A. Rh. 2. 911
778: A. Rh. 2. 904
779: A. Rh. 2. 946
780: A. Rh. 2. 970
781: A. Rh. 2. 1007
782: A. Rh. 2. 1011

783: A. Rh. 2. 1018
784: A. Rh. 2. 1030
785: A. Rh. 2. 1231
786: GG 160 (142)
787: A. Rh. 2. 1235
788: A. Rh. 3. 598
789: A. Rh. 3. 245
790: Th. 960
791: s. A. Rh. 3. 240
792: A. Rh. 3. 957
793: A. Rh. 3. 445;
       834
794: Pi. P. 4. 244
795: A. Rh. 2. 465
796: s. Ve. G. 2. 140
797: Enn. fr. sc. 274
798: A. Rh. 2. 270
       Pi. P. 4. 224
799: Pi. P. 4. 232
800: Ap. 1. 9. 23
801: A. Rh. 3. 1182
802: A. Rh. 3. 1365
803: s. A. Rh. 4. 87
804: s. A. Rh. 4. 86
805: A. Rh. 4. 11
806: A. Rh. 4. 54
807: A. Rh. 4. 57
808: A. Rh. 4. 167
809: s. A. Rh. 4. 1053
810: A. Rh. 3. 862
811: D. S. 4. 45
812: A. Rh. 3. 1025
813: A. Rh. 3. 1013
814: A. Rh. 3. 845
815: A. Rh. 4. 245
816: Ap. 1. 9. 24
817: GG 254 (224)
818: s. A. Rh. 3. 1236
819: A. Rh. 3. 242

820: Pa. 5. 1. 3
821: s. A. Rh. 4. 223
822: E. Me. 1334
823: A. Rh. 4. 331
824: A. Rh. 4. 466
825: A. Rh. 4. 571
826: A. Rh. 4. 581
827: A. Rh. 4. 631
828: A. Rh. 4. 727
829: A. Rh. 4. 702
830: A. Rh. 4. 745
831: A. Rh. 4. 930
832: A. Rh. 4. 965
833: A. Rh. 4. 982
834: A. Rh. 4. 1104
835: A. Rh. 4. 1141
836: A. Rh. 4. 1234
837: A. Rh. 4. 1309
838: A. Rh. 4. 1324
839: A. Rh. 4. 1384
840: A. Rh. 4. 1396
841: A. Rh. 4. 1428
842: A. Rh. 4. 1446
843: A. Rh. 4. 1478
844: A. Rh. 4. 1551
845: GG 110 (96)
846: A. Rh. 4. 1670
847: A. Rh. 4. 1621
848: A. Rh. 4. 1691
849: A. Rh. 4. 1699
850: A. Rh. 2. 678
851: A. Rh. 4. 1709
852: s. A. Rh. 4. 1707
853: A. Rh. 4. 1730
854: A. Rh. 4. 1733
855: A. Rh. 4. 1765
856: Ca. fr. 198
857: GG 254 (224)
858: GG 254 (224)

859: GG 191 (169)
860: GG ill. on pl. 265
    (233)
861: Ov. M. 7. 159
862: s. Ar. Equ. 1321
    s. Ly. 1315
863: Pa. 3. 18. 16.
    5. 17. 9
864: Ath. 172d
865: Ap. 1. 9. 27
866: Pi. P. 4. 250
867: Hy. 24
868: Pa. 8. 11. 3
869: s. E. Me. 9; 19
870: Pa. 2. 1. 6
871: Pa. 2. 4. 6
872: s. Pi. O. 13. 74
873: GG 153 (136)
874: s. E. Me. 264
875: Pa. 2. 4. 6
876: GG. 206
877: s. Pi. O. 13. 32
878: s. Pi. O. 13. 74
879: Pa. 2. 3. 11
880: GG 236 (208)
881: A. Rh. 4. 869
882: s. Pi. O. 13. 74
883: s. E. Me. 264
884: s. E. Me. 19
885: E. Me. 383
886: E. Me. 230
887: E. Me. 476
888: Pa. 2. 3. 6
889: E. Me. 271
890: E. Me. 551
891: E. Me. 663
892: E. Me. 725
893: E. Me. 824
894: A. Rh. 4. 131

895: E. Me. 947
896: E. Me. 1141
897: E. Me. 1321
898: E. Me. 1382
899: Ap. 1. 9. 28
900: s. E. Me. 1387
901: s. E. Me. 9
902: Ap. 1. 9. 28
903: A. Rh. 4. 814 c. s
904: Ap. ep. 5. 5
905: Str. 1. 2. 39
906: A. Rh. 4. 812
907: GG 185 (164)
908: Si. 27
909: Ap. 1. 3. 2
    E. IA 1212
    E. B. 562
910: Ap. 1. 3. 2
    A. Rh. 1. 23
    Or. H. 24. 12
911: D. S. 4. 25. 1
912: Su.
913: Ov. M. 11. 8
914: s. Pi. P. 4. 313
915: Pi. fr. 126. 9
916: s. Ve. A. 6. 645
917: Ti. Pers. 234
918: Hy. A. 2. 7
919: E. B. 560
920: E. Al. 579
921: A. Rh. 1. 34
922: Or. A. 965
923: Ath. 597b
924: Ap. 1. 3. 3
925: s. Ve. A. 6. 667
926: Ve. G. 4. 317
927: GG 138 (122)
928: GG 142 (126)
929: Ve. G. 4. 460

930: Ov. M. 10. 8
931: Ve. G. 4. 460
932: Or. A. 42
    Ve. A. 6. 120
933: Or. A. 41
    Ve. G. 4. 457
934: Ve. A. 6. 892 c. s
935: Se. HOe 1072
936: Ve. G. 4. 471
    Hor. C. 21
    Ov. M. 10. 40
    Se. HOe 1067
    Se. HF 578
937: Ov. M. 10. 49
938: Ve. G. 4. 487
939: Ve. G. 4. 488
940: Ve. Cu. 299
941: Ov. M. 10. 56
942: Ve. G. 4. 493
943: Ve. G. 4. 502
944: D. S. 4. 25. 4
945: Ve. G. 4. 507
946: Ov. M. 10. 73
947: Ve. G. 4. 516
948: Hor. AP 391
949: Pa. 9. 30. 5
950: Ov. M. 10. 78
951: Ov. M. 10. 83
    Pha. fr. 1. 9
952: Er. C. 3. 26. 8
953: Hor. C. 3. 26. 8
954: Ma. S. 1. 18
955: Ve. G. 4. 521
956: FGH 26. 45
957: Pa. 9. 30. 5
958: Er. C. 24
959: Pha. fr. 1. 11
960: Ve. G. 4. 524
961: Ov. M. 11. 52

962: Ph. Her. 5. 3
963: Lu. Ind. 109
964: Ph. VA 4. 14
965: Pa. 9. 30. 6
966: Pa. 9. 30. 9
967: Pa. 9. 30. 7
968: Pa. 9. 30. 10
969: Thu. 2. 29
970: Ov. M. 6. 444
971: Pa. 1. 41. 8
972: Ap. 3. 14. 8
973: Th. 444
974: Ap. 3. 14. 8
975: Ov. M. 6. 565
976: Ov. F. 2. 607
977: Ov. M. 6. 521
978: GG 260 (229)
979: GG 254 (224)
980: Ov. M. 6. 648
981: GG 254 (224)
982: Hy. 45
983: Lu. Lex. 10
984: CIA 3. 900
985: Et. M.
986: GG 205 (181)
987: Pl. Phdr. 229 b
988: Ap. 3. 15. 4
989: Pa. 1. 38. 3
990: Ap. 3. 15. 4
991: h. C. 476
992: GG 200 (179)
993: Hy. 48
994: Hy. 189
995: Ap. 3. 15. 1
996: ALib. 41
997: s. Od. 11. 321
998: ALib. 41
999: Ap. 3. 15. 1
2000: ALib. 41

1: Ap. 3. 15. 1
2: Ov. M. 7. 713
3: S. OC 367
4: S. OC 770; 1356
5: S. OC 375
6: E. Ph. 71
7: A. Se. 664
8: s. E. Ph. 71
9: GG 261 (229)
10: Hdt. 2. 49. 2
11: Pa. 1. 44. 5
12: Ap. 1. 8. 5
13: Ap. 1. 8. 5
14: PO. 852 V 8. 9
15: E. Ph. 420
E. Su. 146
16: Ap. 3. 6. 1
17: Hy. 69
18: Pi. N. 9. 13
19: Hdt. 5. 67. 5
20: s. Pi. N. 9. 30
21: s. Od. 11. 326
22: s. Pi. N. 9. 30
23: Ap. 3. 6. 2
24: Od. 11. 326
25: s. Ve. A. 6. 445
s. St. Th. 3. 274
26: E. Su. 158
27: Pa. 8. 25. 8
28: s. Il. 23. 346
29: Hy. 242
30: A. Se. 572
31: Il. 4. 348; 5. 803
32: Il. 5. 802
33: Pi. N. 9. 18
34: Pa. 8. 48. 2
GG 265 (234)
35: Ap. 3. 6. 4
36: hyp. Pi. N.

37: Hy. 74
38: Pa. 2. 15. 3
39: Hy. 74
40: A. Se. 375
41: E. Ph. 1104
42: E. Ph. 1179
43: A. Se. 430
44: A. Se. 412
45: Ap. 3. 6. 8
46: s. Pi. N. 10. 12
47: Ap. 3. 6. 8
48: s. Il. 5. 126
49: E. Ph. 1156
50: Pi. N. 9. 24
51: Pa. 1. 34. 3
52: Ap. 3. 7. 5
53: Pi. O. 5. 15
54: E. Su. 16
55: Plu. Th. 14a
56: Pa. 1. 39. 2
57: Ap. 3. 7. 3
58: Hy. 71
59: Pa. 6. 20. 7
Ap. 2. 4. 6
60: Ap. 2. 8. 2
61: D. S. 4. 58. 2
62: D. S. 4. 58. 5
63: Il. 4. 381
64: Il. 2. 101
65: s. Il. 2. 105
66: Se. Th. 233 et 226
67: GG 264 (232)
68: Ap. ep. 2. 10
69: s. E. Or. 995
70: Ap. ep. 2. 11
71: s. E. Or. 998
Se. Th. 237
72: E. El. 726
73: A. A. 1583

74: Ap. ep. 2. 13

75: A. A. 1595

76: Se. Thy. 765

77: Hdt. 1. 119. 3

78: Ari. Pr. an.
　　3. 43

79: A. A. 1598

80: Hy. 88

81: A. A. 1605

82: GG 252 (221)

83: s. E. Or. 15

84: Hy. 88

85: Hy. 254

86: Mo. Chor. Pr. p.
　　294

87: Hy. 88

88: Hy. 87

89: Ap. ep. 2. 14

90: Pa. 2. 16. 6

91: Pa. 2. 18. 1

92: Tz. Ch. 1. 461

93: He. fr. 98

94: Tz. Ch. 1. 460

95: GG 225 (199)

96: GG 77 (67)

97: h. Ve. 256

98: h. Ve. 279

99: Il. 20. 92
　　Il. 20. 347

100: Il. 5. 309; 344

101: Il. 20. 318

102: GG 224 (198)

103: Pi. I. 8. 37

104: Pi. I. 8. 39

105: Il. 18. 433

106: Il. 24. 60

107: He. fr. 80

108: Pi. I. 8. 41

109: GG 210 (186)

110: Str. 9. 5. 9

111: s. Il. 16. 14

112: s. Ve. A. 4. 420

113: Ap. 3. 12. 6

114: Ap. 3 12. 6

115: Th. 1004

116: D. S. 4. 72. 6

117: Pa. 2. 29. 9

118: Ap. 3. 13. 1

119: Ap. 3. 13. 2

120: Hy. 273

121: Ap. 3. 13. 3

122: Pa. 1. 41. 3
　　s. A. Rh. 1. 517

123: Ap. 3. 13. 3

124: Ap. 3. 13. 3

125: Pi. N. 4. 59

126: s. Ar. N. 1063

127: He. fr. 79

128: Ap. 3. 13. 3

129: Pi. I. 8. 45

130: Cat. 64. 20

131: Al. 74. 7

132: He. fr. 81

133: Pi. I. 8. 48

134: E. IA 716

135: Il. 1. 538

136: GG 143 (126)

137: Pi. N. 3. 35

138: S. fr. 154

139: Pi. N. 4. 62

140: Pa. 5. 18. 5

141: s. E. An. 1265

142: S. fr. 561

143: Hsch.

144: Pi. N. 5. 22

145: Cat. 64. 305

146: GG 160 (141)

147: Ap. 3. 13. 5

148: Il. 19. 390

149: Pi. N. 3. 33

150: s. Il. 16. 140

151: He. fr. 82

152: Hy. 92

153: Pr. Chr. 102. 13

154: s. Il. 1. 5

155: Ap. ep. 3. 1

156: Hy. 92

157: Col. 59

158: s. Ve. A. 1. 27

159: s. Ly. 93

160: Hy. 92

161: GG 146 (128)

162: Pr. Chr. 102. 16

163: He. fr. 81

164: s. Pi. N. 4. 81

165: Et. M.

166: Il. 20. 74

167: Ap. 2. 6. 4

168: Ap. 3. 12. 7

169: s. Ly. 337

170: Il. 24. 495

171: Hsch.

172: Ap. 3. 12. 5

173: E. He. 1265

174: E. He. 1259

175: GG 37 (32)

176: Il. 24. 730 c. s.

177: Ap. 3. 12. 5

178: Pi. fr. 43. 11

179: Pa. 10. 12. 5

180: Hy. 93

181: E. An. 296

182: E. Tr. 921

183: GG 146 (129)

184: Ap. 3. 12. 5

185: s. Il. 3. 325

186: s. E. An. 293

187: Ap. 3. 12. 5
188: Ap. 3. 12. 6
　　Par. 4
　　FGH 23
　　Ov. H. 5
189: s. E. An. 276
190: E. An. 284
　　Hel. 676
191: Ath. 682e
192: Ov. H. 15. 67
193: E. Tr. 925
　　IA 1304
　　Ap. ep. 3. 2
　　Hy. 92
194: Il. 24. 29
195: Il. 5. 62
196: E. Hel. 631
197: Ar. N. 1068
198: s. Ly. 178
199: h. Ve. 291
200: Il. 348
201: Ap. 3. 13. 6
202: s. A. Rh. 4. 816
203: s. A. Rh. 4. 816
204: A. Rh. 4. 869
205: s. Ar. N. 1068
206: s. Ve. A. 6. 57
　　Hy. 107
207: Ap. 3. 13. 6
208: Pi. N. 3. 49
209: E. IA 927
210: Il. 11. 832
211: Ov. AA 1. 11
212: Pa. 2. 22. 3
213: E. IA 1150
214: He. fr. 96. 51
215: E. Hel. 109
216: Il. 3. 175
217: Ap. ep. 3. 3

218: He. fr. 94. 5
219: He. fr. 92
220: s. Il. 2. 339
221: He. fr. 94. 13
222: Ap. 3. 10. 8
223: Il. 2. 478
224: Il. 3. 169
225: Il. 1. 28
226: Il. 1. 113
227: Od. 3. 272
228: Od. 11. 411
229: A. A. 1125
230: s. Ly. 1123
231: Ap. 3. 10. 8
232: He. fr. 94. 21
233: He. fr. 94. 26
234: Ap. 3. 10. 9
235: E. IA 54
236: Pa. 3. 20. 9
237: Ap. 3. 10. 9
238: s. Pi. O. 9. 79
239: Od. 19. 403
240: Il. 10. 244; 279
241: Plu. 301d
242: Ap. 3. 10. 8
243: Il. 5. 860
244: Il. 5. 311
245: Il. 5. 127
246: Il. 5. 412
247: s. Il. 5. 412
248: Od. 3. 180
249: s. Il. 5. 412
250: s. Ve. A. 8. 9
251: Pi. N. 10. 7
252: s. Pi. N. 82
253: Pli. NH 10. 126
254: Str. 6. 3. 9
255: Ap. 3. 10. 8
256: He. fr. 96. 5

257: Il. 7. 208
258: Il. 17. 279
259: Il. 3. 229
260: Il. 7. 219
261: Il. 8. 331
262: Il. 7. 208
　　14. 410
263: s. Pi. I. 6. 67
264: Pi. I. 6. 35
265: s. Il. 23. 821
266: Od. 11. 546
　　Ap. ep. 5. 5
267: s. Ar. Eq. 1056
　　Plu. 337e
268: Od. 11. 547
269: Pi. N. 7. 25
　　s. Il. 11. 515
270: S. Ai. 127
271: Od. 11. 563
272: Pa. 1. 35. 3
273: Hdt. 8. 64
274: Ap. 3. 10. 8
　　Hy. 81
275: Il. 2. 528
276: Il. 13. 198
277: Il. 13. 703
278: Il. 12. 335
279: Il. 14. 521
280: Pr. Chr. 108. 3 4
　　E. Tr. 70
281: E. Tr. 324; 453
282: Ap. ep. 5. 22
283: Pr. Chr. 108. 4
284: Pa. 10. 26. 3
285: E. Tr. 77
　　Ve. A. 1. 39
286: E. Tr. 99
287: Od. 4. 500
288: s. Pi. O. 166

289: Ph. H. 8. 1

290: s. Ly. 1159

291: Ap. ep. 6. 20

292: s. Ly. 1159

293: Plu. 557d

294: Ap. 3. 10. 8

295: Il. 11. 508

296: He. fr. 96. 16

297: s. Ve. A. 3. 121
         11. 264

298: MVat. 1. 195

299: Hy. 78

300: Hdt. 6. 61. 4

301: Is. 10. 62

302: Od. 4. 563

303: Pa. 3. 19. 9

304: Il. 4. 181

305: Ph. Im. 2. 7. 2

306: s. Il. 4. 147

307: Od. 4. 12

308: Se. Tr. 70

309: Ap. ep. 3. 3

310: Il. 3. 232

311: Il. 3. 173; 420

312: Ap. ep. 3. 3

313: Il. 3. 445

314: Pr. Chr. 103. 12

315: Pr. Chr. 103. 17

316: Ap. ep. 3. 6

317: Pr. Chr. 103. 20

318: Il. 11. 769

319: Ap. ep. 3. 6

320: s. Il. 9. 668

321: A. A. 841

322: Hy. 96

323: Hy. 95

324: Od. 24. 115

325: Hy. 95. 2

326: Hy. 277

327: Alcid. 22

328: S. fr. 399; 438

329: Ap. ep. 3. 8

330: Hy. 96

331: Ap. 3. 13. 8

332: Il. 9. 668

333: s. Il. 9. 668

334: GG 264 (233)

335: Hy. 96

336: s. Il. 9. 668

337: E. fr. 682

338: Il. 19. 326

339: Od. 11. 508

340: Il. 11. 777

341: Il. 19. 407

342: Il. 9. 143

343: Il. 9. 145

344: s. Il. 9. 145

345: S. E. 157

346: Pa. 2. 35. 1
         Hsch.

347: Pr. Chr. 104. 12
         Ap. ep. 3. 21

348: Il. 2. 496

349: Pa. 9. 19. 6

350: S. E. 566
         E. IA 185

351: Ap. ep. 3. 21

352: s. Il. 1. 108
         s. E. Or. 658
         Pr. Chr. 104. 13

353: E. IT 20

354: S. E. 567

355: S. E. 568

356: S. E. 569

357: Ap. ep. 3. 21

358: Ap. ep. 3. 21
         Sabb.

359: S. E. 568

360: A. A. 192
         Pr. Chr. 104. 15

361: S. E. 564
         E. IT 15

362: E. IT 17; 209

363: S. E. 571

364: Hy. 98

365: S. An. 899

366: S. fr. 284

367: E. IA 610

368: A. IA 1366

369: E. IT 27

370: A. A. 239

371: Ar. Ly. 645

372: E. IA 1579

373: E. IT 26

374: E. IT 40

375: Hdt. 4. 103

376: E. IT 1462

377: Ae. NA 7. 39

378: Od. 4. 529
         11. 410

379: Od. 3. 172

380: Od. 11. 422

381: Pi. P. 11. 22

382: Se. Ag. 897

383: A. A. 1377

384: S. E. 12
         A. A. 881

385: Pi. P. 11. 34

386: E. IT 918

387: Ap. ep. 6. 24

388: s. E. Or. 268

389: Od. 3. 307

390: Od. 3. 311

391: Ap. ep. 6. 28

392: A. Eu. 179

393: A. Eu. 738

394: E. IT 970

395: E. IT 973
396: E. IT 977
　　Ap. ep. 6. 26
397: Ap. ep. 3. 18
398: Str. 13. 1. 69
399: Pa. 10. 28. 8
400: PO. XI. 1359
401: Pa. 1. 4. 6
402: Ap. 2. 7. 4
403: Pa. 8. 4. 8
404: Ap. 3. 9. 1
405: Pa. 8. 48. 7
406: Mo. Chor. Pr. p.
　　294
407: Pa. 8. 47. 4
408: E. fr. 265
　　Alcid. 15
409: D. S. 4. 33. 7
410: Ap. 2. 7. 3
411: Ap. 3. 9. 1
412: Ap. 2. 7. 4
413: E. fr. 696. 4
414: Ae. VH 7. 39
415: Hy. 99
416: Ap. 3. 89. 1
417: D. S. 4. 33. 11
418: Pa. 4. 34. 7
419: Hy. 244
420: A. E. 488
421: Ari. Po. 24
422: s. E. Rh. 251
423: Hy. 100
424: Ae. NA 3. 47
425: D. S. 4. 33. 12
426: Ph. Her. 3. 34
427: Od. 11. 521
428: Str. 13. 1. 69
429: s. Ly. 1249
430: s. Ve. A. 3. 680

431: GG 140 (124)
432: Pa. 9. 5. 14
433: Pi. O. 9. 72 c. s.
434: Pi. O. 9. 71
435: Il. 11. 787
436: Il. 23. 90
437: Il. 11. 831
438: Pi. I. 8. 54
　　Ap. ep. 17
439: s. Il. 1. 59
440: E. fr. 700
　　Pa. 9. 41. 1
441: s. The. 12. 25
442: Ar. Ach. 439
443: E. fr. 697; 698
444: Hy. 101
445: E. fr. 724
446: Pr. Chr. 104. 11
447: s. Od. 11. 520
448: s. E. Or. 1391
449: Pa. 5. 13. 3
450: Pa. 3. 26. 10
451: Ap. ep. 3. 18
452: Il. 2. 303
453: Pa. 9. 19. 7
454: Il. 1. 49
455: Il. 2. 720
456: S. fr. 353
457: App. M. 1. 77
458: St. B.
459: Pa. 8. 33. 4
460: A. Rh. 4. 1709
461: Il. 1. 37
462: Il. 1. 430
463: D. Chr. 59. 9
464: Ph. iun. 17
465: V. Fl. 1. 391
466: s. S. Ph. 194
467: S. Ph. 1327

468: Hy. 102
469: Ap. ep. 3. 27
　　Pr. Chr. 104. 22
470: s. Il. 2. 695
471: Ap. 1. 9. 12
472: GG 261 (230)
473: He. fr. 117
474: Il. 2. 701
475: Il. 2. 701
476: Batr. 303
477: APal. 7. 385. 1
478: APal. 7. 385. 9
479: Hdt. 9. 116
480: Pli. NH 16. 238
481: Ph. Her. 3. 1
482: s. Aristid. p. 671
483: Pa. 4. 2. 7
484: Cat. 68. 74
485: Hy. 104
486: Eu. Il. 325. 29
487: s. Aristid. p. 671
488: Hy. 103
489: Lu. DMo. 23. 3
490: Ap. ep. 3. 30
491: Hy. 104
492: s. Ve. A. 6. 447
493: Ap. ep. 3. 30
494: Hy. 104
495: s. Pi. I. 1. 83
496: Ph. Her. 3. 6
497: Il. 2. 674
498: Il. 1. 352
499: s. Pi. O. 2. 147
　　Thom.
500: Ap. ep. 3. 31
501: ALib. 12
502: Hy. 154
503: s. Ly. 237
504: s. The. 16. 49

505: S. fr. 500 Pearson
506: S. fr. 460
507: Ap. ep. 3. 31
508: Pi. O. 2. 83
    I. 5. 39
509: S. fr. 499 Pearson
510: Ap. ep. 3. 31
511: s. Ve. A. 3. 85
512: Ap. ep. 3. 32
513: GG 139 (123)
514: GG 140 (124)
515: Ap. 3. 12. 5
516: Pla. B. 953
517: Il. 1. 58
518: Il. 24. 257
519: Il. 9. 129
520: Il. 9. 664
521: Il. 1. 392
522: Hy. 106
523: Il. 19. 282
524: Il. 2. 690
525: Il. 19. 291
526: Il. 19. 298
527: Il .2. 691
528: Il. 1. 366
529: Il. 6. 414
530: Il. 6. 422
531: Il. 1. 425
532: Il. 1. 368
533: Il. 1. 14
534: Il. 1. 25
535: Il. 1. 49
536: Il. 16. 700
537: Il. 16. 785
538: Ve. A. 2. 319
539: Il. 16. 850
540: Il. 16. 96
541: Il. 18. 8
542: Il. 18. 96

543: Il. 18. 98
544: Il. 19. 258
545: Il. 18. 478
546: Il. 19. 21
547: Il. 22. 136
548: Il. 22. 203
549: Il. 22. 359
550: Il. 22. 385
551: Il. 23. 175
552: Il. 24. 560
553: Ap. ep. 5. 1
554: Il. 3. 189
555: Tz. Posthom. 14
556: s. Il. 3. 189
557: Il. 24. 670
558: Q. S. 1. 664
559: Q. S. 1. 594
560: Pa. 5. 11. 6
561: Prop. 3. 11. 15
562: Od. 11. 522
563: Pr. Chr. 106. 1
564: Pi. 2. 83
565: GG 32 (28)
566: Il. 22. 209
567: GG 33 (24)
568: Plu. 17a
569: Il. 22. 161
570: Il. 16. 857
571: GG 200 (177);
    Pl. VIII b
572: Pol. 4. 130
573: Pr. Chr. 106. 6
574: Pa. 10. 31. 6
575: Ae. NA 5. 1
576: EGr. 987
577: Pr. Chr. 106. 7
578: Ap. ep. 5. 3
579: Ve. A. 6. 57
580: E. Rh. 508

581: s. Ve. A. 3. 85
582: Il. 22. 359
583: s. Ar. E. 1056
584: Ap. ep. 5. 4
585: Ap. ep. 5. 4
586: Od. 24. 47
587: Od. 24. 47
588: Od. 24. 60
589: Il. 23. 91; 244
590: Od. 24. 81
591: Str. 13. 1. 32
592: Arr. A. 1. 12. 1
593: Pr. Chr. 108. 7
594: E. Hec. 37
595: Pr. Chr. 106. 14
596: Pi. N. 4. 49
    E. An. 1262
597: CIG 2. 2076
598: D. Chr. 36. 9
599: Pli. NH 4. 83
600: A. Rh. 4. 814
    c. s.
601: ALib. 27
602: Am. M. 22. 8. 34
603: Pa. 3. 19. 13
604: Pr. Chr. 105. 9
605: Od. 11. 467
606: Il. 6. 448
607: Ap. ep. 5. 10
608: Ap. ep. 5. 8
609: Ap. ep. 5. 10
610: Od. 11. 509
611: Ap. ep. 5. 11
612: Pr. Chr. 106. 30
613: Pr. Chr. 106. 30
614: Ap. ep. 5. 8
615: S. Ph. 1408
616: Pr. Chr. 106. 26
    Ap. ep. 5. 8

617: Ap. ep. 5. 8
618: Ap. 3. 12. 3
619: GG 122 (107)
620: Ap. 3. 12. 3
621: FGH 26. 34. 2
622: Od. 4. 244
623: Od. 4. 250
624: Od. 4. 261
625: Ap. ep. 5. 13
626: FGH 26. 34. 2
627: Pr. Chr. 107. 7
628: FGH 26. 34. 3
629: s. Ar. Ve. 351
630: s. Ve. A. 2. 166
631: FGH 26. 34. 4
632: Pr. Chr. 107. 2
633: Ap. ep. 5. 14
634: Od. 8. 493
635: Pa. 1. 30. 4
    5. 15. 6
636: Ca. LP 2
637: Pi. O. 13. 65
638: Ap. ep. 5. 15
639: Od. 8. 509
640: Pla. B. 953
641: Ap. ep. 5. 15

642: Od. 8. 501
643: Ap. ep. 5. 17
644: Ve. A. 2. 201
645: s. Ve. A. 2. 201
646: Hy. 135
647: Ap. ep. 5. 18
648: Ve. A. 2. 227
649: Pr. Chr. 107. 25
650: Pr. Chr. 107. 22
651: Ap. ep. 5. 19
652: Od. 11. 527
653: Od. 4. 274
654: Od. 11. 530
655: Ap. ep. 6. 12
656: Pa. 10. 24. 6
657: Pi. N. 7. 40
    fr. 40. 112
    Pa. 4. 17. 4
658: Ap. ep. 5. 21
659: Il. 6. 402
660: s. Lyl 1268
661: Il. 6. 455
662: Il. 24. 735
663: Od. 8. 517
664: s. E. An. 631
665: Ar. L. 155 c. s.

666: E. An. 630
667: Pr. Chr. 108. 1
668: Od. 3. 141
669: Od. 4. 1
670: Od. 4. 82
671: Od. 3. 299
672: Il. 2. 587
673: Od. 4. 83
674: GG 43 (38)
675: Od. 4. 772
676: Ste. 11
677: E. Hel. 31
678: GG 37, 59, 206,
    247 (32, 52,
    182, 218)
679: Od. 23. 156
680: Od. 14. 162
    19. 306
681: Od. 21. 258
    s. Od. 20. 155
682: Od. 21. 259
683: Ap. ep. 7. 36
684: Ly. 796
2685: Pr. Chr. 109. 23

INDEX

Numbers in italics refer to Plates
The letters A–L refer to the Genealogies

I

NAMES AND EPITHETS

Abas, A
Abderos, 156
Acheles, 197, 317
Acheloos, 198, 317
Achilleus (Achilles), 242, 275, 278, 309, 313, 315, 317, 318, 319, 323, 324, 328, 329, 332, 340, 347–61; *70, 72, 73, 75*; E
Admete, 159, 162
Admetos, 32, 74, 116, 139, 155, 156, 160, 247, 250, 253, 280, 282; C
Adrastos, 157, 295, 296, 297, 301, 304, 323; C
Aedon, 89, 287
Aeneas, *see also* Aineias, 179, 253
Aerope, 304; K
Agamedes, 138
Agamemnon, 8, 62, 238, 303, 305, 306, 319, 320, 321, 325, 326, 328, 329, 331, 332, 333, 334, 335, 347, 349, 350, 351; F, K
Agaue, 32, 91; A, D
Agenor, 27, 28, 40, 258; A, G
Aglauros, 212, 215
Agraulos, 212
Agriope, 281
Agrios, 63, 113; G
Aiakos, 75, 221, 253, 309; E
Aias s. of Oileus, 325, 360
Aias s. of Telamon, 228, 310, 315, 322, 323, 324, 325, 354, 358; *75*; B, E, K
Aietes, 87, 247, 250, 251, 253, 262, 263, 264, 265, 266, 267, 268, 274, 276
Aigaion, 216

Aigeus, 216, 217, 218, 219, 223, 224, 225, 226, 227, 234, 240, 276, 277; B, I, K, L
Aigialeia, 323; C
Aigialeus, 301
Aigimios, 184
Aigina, 75, 309; E
Aigisthos, 306, 334, 335; K
Aigle, 234
Aigletes, 272
Aigyptos, Aigyptiads, 40, 41, 42; A
Aineias, *see also* Aeneas, 110, 308, 309, 323, 327, 358; *16*
Aiolos, 69, 70, 71, 74, 75, 80, 85, 105, 247, 249, 250, 251; C, F
Aiolos Hippotades, 69
Aison, 74, 247, 250, 270, 273, 274; C
Aithalides, 253
Aithra, 217, 219, 238, 242; B, I, K
Aitolos, 113; G
Akamas, 242
Akastos, 247, 253, 274, 311, 314, 345
Akmon, 194
Akrisios, 45, 46, 47, 54, 81, 295; A
Aktaion, 33; A
Aktor, Aktorione, 184; E
Alalkomene, 322
Alalkomeneus, 57
Alea, 337, 338
Aleos, 338
Alexander the Great, 2, 354
Alexandros (Paris), 316
Alexidamos, 166
Alexikakos, 183
Alkaios, 55, 128, 136; A, B, H, K
Alkathoos, B, K

413

Alkeides, 128

Alkestis, 32, 155, 156, 166, 197, 247, 274, 282; C

Alkmene, 8, 55, 121, 126, 127, 128, 129, 131, 132, 133, 134, 138, 187, 188, 206; B, H

Alkyone, 122, 158

Alkyoneus, 170, 171

Aloadai, 146, 249, 274

Aloeus, 117, 274

Althaia, 106, 113, 114, 115, 120, 121, 198; G, H

Amaltheia, 199

Amisodaros, 82

Amphiaraos, 116, 294–301, 304; C

Amphiktyon, L

Amphilochos, 300

Amphion, 34, 35, 36, 37, 38, 57, 62, 67, 88, 89, 136, 279; B

Amphitrite, 229, 232, 309, 313; 54

Amphitryon, 68, 128, 129, 130, 131, 134, 135, 136, 138, 186, 188, 205; B, H, K

Amykos, 257

Amymone, 43, 44, 48, 143, 144, 253, 328

Amyntor, 184

Amythaon, 74, 247, 250, 295; C

Anaxo, B, H

Anchinoe, A

Anchises, 308, 317

Androgeos, 227

Andromache, 349, 359; 33

Andromeda, 52, 53, 54, 55, 251, 258; 7; A, F, H

Ankaios, 116, 119

Antagoras, 162, 166

Antaios, 162, 166, 167, 222

Anteia, 45, 81, 82, 83

Antigone, 99, 102, 301; D

Antikleia, 77, 219, 322; 9; C

Antiope, Theban, 35, 36, 37, 38, 39, 88, 89, 105, 136, 308; Amazon, 162, 235, 241, 242, 243; consort of Sun, 274

Antiopeia (Antiopethe Amazon), 241

Apaturia, Athene, 217

Aphareus, 43, 105, 107, 111; F

Aphidnos, 238

Aphrodite, 25, 31, 32, 33, 42, 64, 78, 109, 110, 118, 176, 180, 193, 233, 234, 243, 244, 255, 266, 274, 294, 308, 313, 314, 316, 317, 320, 323, 327, 331, 349, 352, 355, 359; A; Urania, 274

Apollo, 15, 26, 31, 32, 35, 38, 54, 66, 74, 75, 76, 81, 85, 91, 95, 104, 108, 109, 121, 135, 139, 145, 147, 148, 155, 157, 158, 159, 160, 165, 188, 190, 191, 202, 204, 219, 234, 235, 247, 249, 253, 258, 261, 262, 271, 272, 279, 280, 282, 284, 286, 297, 308, 313, 315, 334, 335, 339, 340, 342, 343, 347, 348, 349, 350, 351, 353, 361; 16, 27, 38; I; Agraios, 311; Aigletes, 272; Delphinios, 224, 226; Embasios, 254; Ismenios, 35, 136; Korythos, 339; Lykios, 42; Smintheus, 315; Thymbraios, 348, 349, 353, 358

Apsyrtos, 264, 267, 268, 276

Archemoros, 298

Areion, 157, 297

Arene, 107; F

Ares, 25, 29, 30, 31, 33, 63, 66, 76, 108, 114, 151, 155, 156, 157, 160, 164, 165, 168, 249, 264, 266, 287, 313, 320, 323, 324, 352; A, G

Arete, 269, 270

Argeia, 296

Argeiphontes, 79

Argiope, 27, 281, 339

Argo, 157, 179, 252, 253, 254, 256, 257, 260, 261, 263, 264, 266, 268, 269, 270, 271, 272, 277, 279

Argos, builder of the Argo, 252, 253, 257; s. of Phrixos, 263; Panoptes, 79

Ariadne, 31, 56, 230, 231, 232, 233, 234, 235, 238, 251, 273, 281, 308, 327, 329; 56; Ariadne Aphrodite, 233

Aridela, 230, 281
Arion, *see* Areion
Aristaios, 282; A
Artemis, 38, 66, 108, 109, 115, 116,
  117, 146, 147, 148, 155, 178, 190,
  191, 204, 230, 232, 243, 244, 245,
  268, 303, 304, 313, 314, 331, 332,
  333, 335, 338, 352; *38, 69*; Agro-
  tera, 311; Eukleia, 141; Kordaka,
  67; Orthia, 238; Orthosia, 146;
  Saronia, 244; Stymphalia, 151
Askalaphos, 178, 180
Asklepios, 15, 70, 125, 235, 245, 300,
  326, 341, 356
Asopos, 35, 76
Astakos, 299
Asterios, 230
Asterodeia, 267
Astyanax, 359
Astymedusa, 96
Atalante, 113–20, 254, 300, 310, 312,
  339
Ate, 132
Athamas, 85, 86, 247, 251, 263, 303,
  329; A, C
Athene, Pallas, 30, 43, 44, 48, 49, 50,
  51, 53, 54, 57, 81, 99, 109, 134,
  138, 139, 151, 157, 161, 165, 171,
  175, 186, 191, 194, 203, 209, 210,
  211, 212, 213, 214, 215, 216, 217,
  233, 252, 253, 261, 265, 294, 298,
  300, 306, 308, 314, 316, 317, 322,
  323, 324, 325, 326, 334, 335, 337,
  347, 351, 356, 357, 361; *16, 18, 27,
  46, 47, 52, 56, 75*; Alalkomene, 322;
  Alea, 337; Apaturia, 217; Hippia,
  81; Minois, 271; Polias, 212, 213
Atlas, 31, 58, 60, 173, 175
Atreus, Atreidai, 7, 8, 10, 57, 62, 68,
  89, 90, 129, 302–7, 319, 331; B, K
Atropos, 115
Auge, 187, 306, 337, 338, 339
Augeias, 151–3, 184, 185, 187, 253
Autolykos, 76, 77, 78, 135, 189, 247,
  322; C
Autonoe, 32; A

Axieros, 19
Axiokersa, 19
Axiokersos, 19, 20

Baal, 40
Bakcheus, 285
Balios, 313
Bateia, 106
Bellerophon, Bellerophontes, 45, 51,
  74, 75–84, 217, 244, 275, 311, 354,
  357; *12*; C
Belleros, 79
Belos, 40, 258; A
Benthesikyme, 290
Berekynthian Great Mother, 58
Bias, 295; C
Boiotos, 29, 69, 70; C
Boreas, Boreades, 69, 154, 253, 259,
  260, 290; *61*; I
Briareos, 216
Brimo, 267
Briseis, 349, 350, 351
Briseus, 349, 351
Broteas, 57; B
Bugenes, 15, 18
Busiris, 167
Butes, 1

Cacus, 169
Castor and Pollux, *see* Kastor and
  Polydeukes
Centaurs, *see* Kentauroi
Chalkiope, d. of Aietes, 87, 264; d. of
  Antagoras, 163
Chalkoarai, 186
Chalkodon, 162
Chariklo, m. of Teiresias, 99; w. of
  Chiron, 99, 249, 313; *67*
Charites, 34, 227, 235, 313, 316
Charon, 179, 182, 239, 282, 284
Charops, 182, 185
Charybdis, 269
Chelidon, 287
Chilon, 17
Chimaira, 82, 83
Chione, 77, 287, 290; I

Chiron, 70, 99, 149, 150, 153, 173, 236, 248, 249, 263, 278, 309, 310, 311, 312, 313, 318, 319; *67, 70*

Chloris, 67, 74; C

Choreia, 55

Christ, 303

Chrysaor, s. of Medusa, 51, 164; other name of Bellerophontes, 80

Chryse, 343

Chryseis, 320, 350

Chryses, 320, 350

Chrysippos, 68, 89, 90, 91, 92, 94, 97, 302, 303; B, K

Chrysothemis, 331; F, K

Chthonia, d. of Boreas, 258; d. of Erechtheus, 216

Chthonios, 30

Ciris, 227

Daidalos, 227, 231, 233, 311

Daktyloi, Daktyls, 12, 66, 93, 105, 126, 136, 137, 192, 203, 222; Daktylos Idaios, 126, 136

Damastes, 222, 223

Damnameneus, 222

Danae, 45, 46, 48, 49, 54, 74, 130; *3;* A, F, H

Danaids, daughters of Danaos, 41, 42, 43, 44, 45, 48, 143, 241, 254, 282, 328

Danaos, 25, 40–44, 45, 166; A

Daphnis, 197

Dardanos, 27

Deianeira, 114, 153, 180, 198–202, 205; *43;* G, H

Deidameia, w. of Peirithoos, 236; m. of Neoptolemos, 329; E

Deimos, 157

Deiphobos, of Amyklai, 190; of Troy, 357, 358, 359

Deipyle, 296

Delphyne, 81

Demeter, 12, 28, 59, 104, 126, 157, 166, 178, 181, 186, 215, 221, 223, 248, 275, 291, 313, 318; *67;* Demeter Chthonia, 186

Demonike, G

Demophoon, Demophon, s. of Theseus, 242; of Eleusis, 275, 318

Deukalion, s. of Prometheus, 69, 113; s. of Minos, 234; C, F

Dexamenos, 153, 164, 197, 198

Dia, 236

Diana, 245

Dikaios, 195, 196, 199

Diktys, 47, 48, 54; *3*

Diomede, 349

Diomedes, Thracian, 154–8, 282, 347; s. of Tydeus, 296, 301, 308, 322, 323, 333, 356, 357, 358, 360; C, G

Dione, 58

Dionysos, 12, 14, 15, 16, 17, 18, 20, 25, 26, 31, 32, 33, 37, 38, 39, 45, 52, 55, 56, 59, 81, 85, 88, 93, 97, 113, 114, 118, 125, 126, 128, 136, 143, 149, 158, 170, 189, 193, 198, 199, 230, 232, 233, 234, 235, 240, 248, 255, 262, 267, 273, 281, 284, 285, 286, 289, 295, 296, 298, 305, 313, 316, 327, 329, 345, 346, 349, 354; *46, 56, 67;* A; Dionysos Kadmos, 20, 88

Dios Kuroi, 105

Dioskuroi, 34–39, 55, 69, 88, 105–12, 116, 184, 238, 240, 241, 256, 274, 317, 319, 320, 321, 327

Dirke, 36, 37

Doris, 313

Doros, C

Dryads, 282

Echemos, 302

Echidna, 97, 140, 143, 174

Echion, Spartos, 31, 90; s. of Hermes, 253; A, D

Eetion, Samothracian, 27; f. of Andromache, 349

Eileithyia, 132

Elatos, Centaur, 149; f. of Kainis-Kaineus, 236

Elektra, m. of Kadmos, 27, 31; d. of Agamemnon, 334, 335; F, K
Elektryon, 55, 128, 129, 130; A, B, H
Elektryone, 27
Endeis, 309, 310; E
Endymion, 113, 291; G
Enipeus, 71, 72
Enyeus, 329
Eos, 84, 173, 229, 251, 287, 293, 352, 353
Epaphos, 25
Epikaste (Iokaste), 91, 96; d. of Augeias, 152
Epimetheus, 69
Epopeus, 36
Erechtheus, Erechtheidai, 209-46, 289, 290, 291; I, L
Erginos, king of Orchomenos, 138; Argonaut, 255
Eriboia, 228, 324; B, E, K
Erichtho, 258, 259; *60*
Erichthonios, 213, 214, 240, 288; I, L
Erinyes, 103, 121, 154, 164, 283, 315, 334, 335
Eriphyle, 296, 297, 300, 303; *66*; C
Eris, 314
Eros, 176, 283
Erysichthon, 213
Erytos, 253
Eteokles, 99, 102, 294, 298, 299, 300, 301; D
Eteoklos, 299
Eubule, 215
Euenos, f. of Marpessa, 108; s. of Jason, 255
Eukleia, 141
Eumenides, 103
Eumolpos, 178, 215, 216, 289-91; I
Euphemos, 253, 271, 272
Euphorbos, finds Oidipus, 93; *14*; Trojan, 350
Europa, Europe, 26, 27, 28, 32, 38, 83, 130, 131; A
Eurybatos, 194
Eurydike, 279-86
Euryganeia, 96

Eurylyte, 266
Eurymeda, 79
Eurymedon, 79
Eurynome, d. of Okeanos, 34, 309; m. of Bellerophon, 79
Eurypylos, of Kos, 162, 165; s. of Telephos, 339, 341
Eurystheus, 68, 129, 132, 133, 139, 142, 145, 146, 150, 152, 153, 154, 155, 156, 157, 158, 159, 161, 167, 171, 175, 177, 178, 182, 185, 186, 193, 195, 205, 245, 302; *28*; B, H, K
Euryte, 199; G
Eurytion, Peleus' father-in-law, 116, 119, 310, 311, 312, 343; Centaur, 153, 236; Geryoneus' herdsman, 164, 168
Eurytos, f. of Iole, 135, 153, 187, 188, 189, 190, 201; Centaur, 237; b. of Kteatos, 184

Galinthias, 132, 133
Ganymedes, 60, 89
Gelanor, 41
Gerapso, Geropso, *20*
Geras, *24*
Geryoneus, 153, 163-71, 181, 273; *35*
Giants, 135, 170, 171, 225
Glauke, 276
Glaukos the younger, 75, 79, 354; *75*; C; the elder, 75, 78, 79, 80, 106, 154; C; of Crete, 81
Gorge, 295; G
Gorgon(s), 49, 50, 51, 52, 53, 54, 55, 78, 154, 180; *56*
Gorgophone, 55, 105, 106, 107; F, H
Graiai, 50, 51, 53

Hades, *see also* Dead, Underworld, 16, 19, 20, 43, 74, 76, 96, 120, 165, 168, 177-82, 199, 220, 221, 239, 240, 251, 260, 264, 266, 271, 282, 285, 300, 310, 333
Haimon, 97; D
Haliai, 55

Harmonia, 19, 20, 25–33, 34, 88, 155, 251, 264, 278, 294, 296, 297, 300, 312; A, D

Harpinna, 63

Harpies, 63, 78, 89, 154, 164, 175, 258, 259, 260; *61*

Hebe, 204, 206, 327; *46*

Hekabe, 315, 316, 349, 355; *69*

Hekale, Hekaline, 226, 315

Hekate, 166, 226, 267, 281, 315

Hektor, 315, 347, 349, 350, 351, 352, 353, 355, 359; *69*

Heleios, 130; H

Helen, 106, 110, 111, 235, 237, 238, 240, 241, 242, 314, 317, 319, 320, 321, 322, 323, 325, 326, 327, 331, 335, 337, 355, 356, 357, 358, 359, 360; *57, 76*; F, K

Helios, 35, 87, 89, 93, 151, 168, 171, 174, 230, 235, 247, 251, 253, 258, 264, 265, 266, 269, 273, 274, 277, 348, 353; *34*

Helle, 85–87; C

Hellen, 69, 70; C, F

Heoos, 262

Hephaistos, 12, 32, 62, 163, 169, 214, 219, 265, 302, 324, 351, 352

Hera, 34, 43, 73, 85, 91, 94, 97, 100, 126, 127, 131, 132, 133, 136, 139, 140, 145, 156, 158, 161, 162, 163, 165, 171, 174, 175, 176, 186, 187, 192, 197–201, 203, 204, 211, 248, 253, 269, 270, 275, 277, 308, 309, 313, 314, 315, 316, 317, 321, 327, 330, 347, 360; *18*; Hera Akraia, 275, 277; Bunia, 275; Teleia, 204

Herakles, 1, 4, 8, 12, 41, 42, 51, 55, 63, 66, 74, 75, 106, 114, 116, 121, 125–206, 218, 219, 222, 225, 227, 236, 239, 240, 241, 245, 248, 253, 255, 256, 257, 262, 265, 268, 270, 273, 279, 281, 282, 291, 297, 302, 306, 308, 315, 324, 328, 337, 338, 339, 343, 347, 355, 356, 360; *18–40, 44–46, 59*; B, G, H, K; Herakles Kallinikos, 183–5

Hermes, 12, 26, 36, 37, 43, 49, 59, 62, 64, 65, 66, 75, 76, 79, 94, 100, 103, 107, 108, 131, 134, 137, 171, 174, 180, 192, 195, 198, 204, 253, 279, 280, 283, 288, 302, 304, 313, 314, 316, 322, 345, 360; *68*; C

Hermione, 327; F, K

Herophile, 315

Hesione, 160, 161, 197, 315; E

Hesperides, 50, 147, 148, 168, 169, 172–7, 252, 270, 314; *22, 26, 37, 38*

Hestia, 313

Hiera, 339, 341

Hilaeira, 109; F

Hippia, 357

Hippe, Hippo, d. of Chiron, 70; Amazon, 243

Hippodameia, d. of Oinomaos, 48, 62–68, 90, 94, 113, 217, 302, 303; w. of Peirithoos, 236, 237; *8*; B, K

Hippokoon, 106, 184

Hippolochos, C

Hippolyte, 159, 160, 161, 162, 192, 240, 241, 243, 352; *58*

Hippolytos, s. of Theseus, 118, 162, 240, 242, 244, 245, 311, 352; s. of Deiphobos of Argos, 190

Hippomedon, 299

Hippomenes, 118

Hipponoos, other name of Bellerophon, 79; s. of Adrastos, 297

Historis, 133

Homer, 306

Homonoia, 262

Horai, 34, 309, 313, 316

Hyades, 216

Hyakinthos, Hyakinthides, 26, 106, 215

Hylas, 157, 257

Hyllos, 197, 201, 202, 205, 302; H

Hymenaios, 65

Hypatos, 212

Hyperenor, 31

Hypermestra, 42, 43, 45; A

Hypnos, 162, 163, 171

Hypsipyle, 255, 298, 299

Iardanos, 192

Iasion, 27, 248

Iason, Ieson, Jason, 74, 87, 116, 157, 247–78, 281, 295, 303, 308, 343; *62, 63, 65*; C

Idas, 107, 108, 109, 110, 111, 116, 120, 253; F

Idmon, 253, 261, 266

Idomeneus, 326, 327, 360

Idyia, 264

Ikarios, 321

Ikaros, 231

Ilios, f. of Laomedon, 356

Illyrios, 33

Immarados, 215, 290

Inachos, 25, 40, 42, 43, 55; A

Ino, 25, 33, 85, 86, 87, 303; *13*; A, C

Io, 25, 27, 38, 40; A

Iobates, 82; *12*

Iokaste (Jocasta), 91, 92, 97, 99, 101, 102; D

Iolaos, 133, 138, 144, 145, 157, 160, 176, 187, 205, 206; H

Iole, 188, 189, 191, 201, 202

Ion, 1

Iphianassa, 331

Iphigeneia, 238, 331–6, 337, 355; *71*; F, K

Iphikles, 116, 131, 133, 138, 184

Iphiklos, 344; H

Iphitos, 188, 189, 191, 201

Iris, 108, 186, 259, 312, 328; *56, 67*

Ischomache, 236

Ismaros, 290

Ismene, 99, 102; D

Ismenos, 34

Itylos, 89

Itys, 89, 288, 289

Ixion, 58, 61, 85, 236, 239, 282

J, *see under* I

Kaaithos, 34

Kaanthos, 34, 35, 38

Kab(e)iroi, 12, 19, 107, 134, 194, 255, 328

Kadmilos, Kasmilos, 19, 26

Kadmos, 18, 19, 20, 25–33, 34, 35, 36, 62, 75, 85, 88, 101, 102, 125, 134, 145, 155, 251, 258, 264, 265, 278, 294, 311, 334; *1*; A, D

Kaineus, 236

Kainis, 236

Kalais, 253, 259, 290

Kalchas, 323, 332, 333, 342

Kallinikos, 183–5

Kalliope, 280

Kallirhoe, 164

Kalliste, 314

Kalydon, G

Kalyke, 62, 348

Kalypso, 176

Kandaules, 192

Kapaneus, 299

Kassandra, 315, 321, 325, 333, 358; *69*

Kassiopeia, 52, 53

Kastor, 35, 105–12, 116, 135, 184, 235, 238, 253, 327; *16, 17*; F

Kekrops, Kekropia, Kekropidai, 209–46; *47*; I, L

Kekrops II, I, L

Kentauroi, Centaurs, 67, 70, 71, 85, 99, 117, 149, 150, 153, 164, 178, 197, 198, 199, 200, 201, 202, 203, 235, 236, 248, 249, 250, 263, 309, 311, 318; *29*; *see also* Chiron

Kentauros, 85

Kephalos, 130, 287–93; I

Kepheus, 52, 53

Kerberos, 143, 144, 164, 174, 177, 179, 180, 181, 182, 186, 282; *39*

Kerkopes, 194; *40*

Kerkyon, 222; *50*

Keuthonymos, 181

Keyx, 158, 201, 205

Kilix, 26, 27; A

Kirke, 87, 251, 252, 260, 267, 268, 269, 361

Kisseus, title of Apollo, 285; f. of Hekabe, 315

Kleite, 256, 257

Kleopatra, 108, 120, 121; F
Klotho, 59, 115
Klymenos, of Kydonia, 126; of Kalydon, 199; G
Klytaim(n)estra, 106, 238, 319, 320, 331, 332, 333, 334; F, K
Komaitho, 130
Kopreus, 142
Korone, 235; 57
Koronis, m. of Asklepios, 15, 235; w. of Helios, 235
Koryne, 233
Korynetes, 219
Korythos, 339
Kranaos, L
Krenaie, 1
Kreon, various kings styled, 91, 97, 102, 128, 135, 138, 275, 276, 294, 301; D
Kretheus, 74, 247, 250, 263; C
Kreusa, 1
Kronos, 58, 63, 66, 95, 223, 236, 263
Kteatos, 184
Kychreus, 222
Kyklopes, Cyclopes, 45, 81
Kyknos, s. of Ares, 157, 158, 171, 347; s. of Poseidon, 347, 348; s. of Apollo, 347, 348; Ligurian, 348
Kynortas, 106
Kyparissos, 340, 348
Kytissoros, 263

Labdakos,. Labdakidai, 33, 88, 89, 288; A, D; *see also* Laios
Lachesis, 115
Ladon (serpent), 148, 174, 175, 270
Laertes, 78, 322
Laios, 33, 89, 90, 91, 92, 93, 94, 95, 96, 97, 99, 101, 104, 227; A, D
Laistrygonians, 256
Laodamas, 301
Laodameia, d. of Bellerophontes, 83; w. of Protesilaos, 342–6
Laodike, 331
Laokoon, 358
Laomedon, 89, 160, 161, 308, 315, 356

Lara, 288
Lares, 288
Leda, 35, 105, 106, 107, 110, 113, 238, 241, 308, 320, 327; 17; F, G
Leos, 215, 225
Lepreus, 152
Lethe, 239
Leto, 261, 282, 353
Leukippos, Leukippides, 105, 109, 110; F
Leukothea, 25, 85
Libye, 40, 270, 272; A
Ligyron, 317
Linos, 135
Lityerses, 196
Lykaon, 157
Lykomedes, 6, 245, 329
Lykos of Thebes, 36, 37, 89, 186; k. of the Mariandynoi, 261
Lynkeus, husband of Hypermestra, 42, 43; s. of Poseidon, 107, 109, 110, 111, 253, 271; A, F
Lyrkeus, 43, 45
Lysidike, 68; B, H, K
Lyssa, 186

Machaon, 326, 341
Maia, 36, 313
Makaria, 206
Makris, 270
Mania, 187; 40
Marpessa, 108, 120; F
Marsyas, 280
Mary, the Virgin, 133
Medeia, 32, 87, 176, 223, 224, 230, 247–78, 289, 303, 308, 318, 355; 63; C
Medos, 277
Medusa, 49, 51, 52, 53, 80, 81, 164, 180; 5, 6
Megapenthes, 46, 54, 55, 81, 295, 299; A
Megara, 138, 186, 187, 188, 201, 205
Melampus, 74, 247, 250, 295, 296, 344; C
Melampygos, 194

Melaneus, 188
Melanion, 119
Melanippe, d. of Aiolos, 69–74, 308; Amazon, 161; C
Melanippos, 299
Melas, f. of Eurytos, 188; s. of Phrixos, 263; eponym of Melantian Rocks, 271; G
Meleagros, 106, 108, 113–21, 149, 180, 198, 199, 254, 295, 345; F, G
Melia, 34, 35, 40, 257; A
Melikertes, 25, 78, 85
Memnon, 352, 353
Memphis, A
Menelaos, 110, 305, 306, 307, 319, 320, 321, 328, 335, 358, 359, 360; 76; F, K
Menestheus, L
Menoikeus, 91; D
Menoites, 168, 181
Menoitios, E
Mercurius, 288
Mermeros, 276
Merope, w. of Sisyphos, 76, 78; w. of Polybos, 94; C
Merops, 60
Mestor, 129; A, H
Michael, Archangel, 323
Midas, 197
Minos, 35, 81, 82, 83, 130, 158–9, 215, 226, 227, 228, 229, 230, 231, 232, 234, 260, 292, 304, 326, 327
Minotaur, 198, 227, 230, 231; 55
Minyad, 247
Minyas, 252, 289
Mnemosyne, 9, 10, 34
Moira, Moirai, 50, 59, 115, 132, 155, 172, 313, 328
Molionē and the Molione, 184, 185, 187
Molorchos, 141, 142
Molpadie, 243
Momos, 313
Mopsos, 253, 257
Musaios, 280, 281

Muses, 32, 34, 88, 98, 135, 280, 281, 285, 286, 313, 354
Mykene, 55
Mynes, 349
Myrtilos, 64, 65, 66, 217, 304; 8

Naiads, Neides, fountain nymphs, 49; 4
Nauplios, 44, 48, 253, 328, 338
Neaira, 264
Neilos, A
Neleus, 72, 74, 164, 165, 247, 253, 295, 328, 344; C
Nemesis, 107, 235, 238, 327; 8
Neoptolemos, 329, 356, 359; 74; E
Nephele, 85, 86; C
Nereids, 52, 228, 229, 269, 272, 354; 23
Nereus, 172, 310, 312, 313, 317, 354; 22
Nessos, 200, 201; 43
Nestor, 8, 9, 67, 74, 164, 165, 247, 328, 329, 354, 360; C
Nike, 176
Nikippe, 68, 132; B, H, K
Niobe, 38, 40, 57, 67, 74, 88; B, C
Nisos, 227
Nykteus, 35, 36, 89; B
Nymphs, 34, 40, 44, 50, 54, 58, 62, 106, 113, 157, 172, 197, 257, 263, 270, 276, 278, 282, 308, 316, 348; 1, 5

Odysseus, 18, 78, 101, 180, 188, 204, 219, 252, 256, 260, 269, 321, 322, 323, 324, 325, 328, 329, 330, 354, 355, 356, 357, 358, 359, 360, 361; 74; C
Ogygos, 29
Oiagros, 280, 281
Oibalos, 105
Oidipus, 2, 33, 88–104, 126, 128, 135, 136, 245, 283, 294, 300, 301, 332, 339; 14–16; A, D
Oidyphallos, 93
Oikles, 296; C

Oinatis, 146

Oineus, 63, 113, 114, 115, 116, 119, 180, 198, 199, 295, 345; G, H

Oinomaos, 48, 62, 63, 64, 65, 66, 67, 69, 108, 113, 188, 303, 304

Oinone, 316

Oinopion, 63, 113

Oistros, 277

Okeanos (Ocean), 34, 50, 163, 164, 168, 173, 194, 200, 263, 269, 273, 313, 320

Oklasos, D

Oknos, 2

Olos, 194

Omphale, 116, 163, 192–7, 219

Opheltes, 298

Ophiuchos, 193

Oreithyia, 290, 291; I

Orestes, 114, 331, 334, 335, 355; 71; F, K

Orestheus, 114

Orion, 12, 63, 113, 141

Orista, 114

Orpheus, 71, 243, 253, 254, 261, 269, 270, 279–86; 64, 65

Orsiloche, 355

Orthia, 147

Orthos, 97, 140, 164, 168, 174

Orthosia, 147

Osiris, 167

Paieon, 165

Palaichthon, 41

Palaimon, 25, 33, 85, 298; A, C

Palinurus, 253

Pállas, Pallantidai, 225

Pallás, companion of Athene, 356

Pallas Athene, *see* Athene

Pan, Panes, 176, 291

Pandareos, 60, 88, 287

Pandion, 225, 227, 287

Pandion II, I, L

Pandora, 1

Panopeus, 130, 234

Panteidyia, 106

Panthus, 350

Paris, 110, 316, 317, 319, 326, 327, 347, 353, 356, 357, 360; 68, 69, 75

Parthenoi, 215

Parthenopaios, 119, 299, 300, 339

Parthenos, 333, 338

Pasiphae, 87, 159, 227, 230, 231, 292

Passalos, 194

Patroklos, 340, 350, 351, 354; E

Pegasos, 51, 80, 81, 82, 83, 84, 85, 86, 164, 357

Peirithoos, 67, 116, 181, 235, 236, 237, 238, 239, 240, 241, 245, 254, 282; 57

Pelagon, 28, 29, 30

Pelargos, 65

Pelasgos, 41

Peleus, 6, 32, 116, 119, 253, 309, 310, 311, 312, 313, 314, 315, 317, 320, 327, 328, 330, 340, 343, 347, 354; 67, 70; C

Pelias, 32, 72, 73, 74, 78, 154, 155, 247, 248, 249, 250, 251, 253, 254, 274, 276, 310; C

Pelopia, 306, 320, 338; K

Pelops, Pelopidai, 57, 59, 60, 62–68, 83, 86, 89, 90, 93, 94, 129, 217, 236, 273, 302, 303, 304, 307, 310, 356; 8; B, H, K

Pelor, 30

Penelope, 73, 188, 321, 322, 328, 361; C, F

Penthesileia, 242, 352; 73

Pentheus, 36, 46, 54, 91, 285; A, D

Periboia, w. of Polybos, 94; Athenian virgin, 228

Perieres, 105; F

Perigune, 220

Periklymenos of Pylos, 165, 253; of Thebes, 300

Periphas, 65

Periphetes, 219

Pero, 295, 344; C

Perse, 251

Perseis, 251

Persephone, 14, 16, 19, 20, 28, 63, 76, 101, 108, 120, 125, 126, 180, 181, 206, 222, 235, 239, 241, 245, 248, 258, 262, 267, 279, 282, 283, 288, 306, 333

Perses, 55; A, H

Perseus, 2, 6, 7, 15, 16, 42, 45–56, 57, 75, 80, 93, 105, 128, 129, 130, 132, 133, 140, 143, 251, 255, 258, 279, 281, 295, 302; *3, 4, 5, 6, 7;* A, F, H

Phaethon, s. of Helios, 83, 348; Apsyrtos, 264, 267

Phaia, 220; *48*

Phaiakes, 269

Phaidra, 234, 242, 243, 244, 245

Phaistos, 126

Pheres, f. of Admetos, 74, 247, 250; s. of Medeia, 276; C

Philammon, 253

Philodike, F

Philoktetes, 203, 343, 344, 356

Philomela, 287, 288, 289, 291, 305; I

Philyra, 249, 263

Phineus, uncle of Andromeda, 53, 258; prophet, 258, 259, 260, 262; *60*

Phix, 97

Phobos, 157

Phoibe, d. of Leukippos, 109; Titaness, 312; F

Phoibos, *see* Apollo

Phoinix, s. of Agenor, 27, 228; tutor of Achilles, 120, 356; A

Phokos, eponym of Phokis, 38; s. of Telamon, 310

Pholos, 149, 150, 153; *29*

Phorkys, 49, 50, 51

Phoroneus, 40, 43, 57, 140, 211; A

Phrixos, 85–87, 247, 250, 251, 258, 263, 264, 303; *13;* C

Phrontis, 263

Phylakos, 344

Phyleus, 152, 185

Phytalos, 223

Phytios, 114

Pinakos, 88

Pittheus, 217, 218, 219, 228, 243, 277; B, K

Pityokamptes, 220

Pleiades, 58, 252

Pleisthenes, 306

Pleuron, G

Pluto, 58; B

Podaleirios, 326

Podarkes, earlier name of Priam, 161, 315; s. of Iphiklos, 344

Poias, 203, 342, 344

Polybos, 94, 97

Polydegmon, 48, 153

Polydektes, 48, 49, 53, 153

Polydeukes, 35, 105–12, 116, 184, 235, 238, 253, 257, 327; *16, 17;* F

Polydora, 345

Polydoros, 33, 88; A, D

Polygyios, 137

Polyidos, 81, 82

Polymede, 247

Polyneikes, 99, 102, 294, 295, 296, 297, 298, 299, 300, 302; *66;* D

Polypemon, 220, 222

Polypoites, 237

Polyxena, 355; *72*

Polyxenos, 129

Porthaon, G

Portheus, 199

Poseidon, 25, 40, 43, 44, 47, 48, 49, 51, 52, 59, 63, 64, 66, 69, 70, 71, 73, 78, 79, 80, 81, 82, 86, 102, 107, 118, 129, 131, 138, 158, 159, 160, 164, 165, 169, 170, 184, 187, 211, 212, 214, 215, 216, 217, 219, 220, 223, 228, 229, 231, 236, 237, 244, 247, 248, 250, 251, 256, 257, 258, 271, 290, 300, 308, 309, 313, 314, 320, 325, 330, 338, 348, 358; *53;* A, C, F, I; Poseidon Erechtheus, 214

Praxithea, 215, 216

Priam (Priamos), 161, 315, 316, 326, 329, 337, 341, 348, 349, 351, 355, 357, 359; *69*

Proitos, 45, 46, 54, 74, 81, 82, 83, 247, 295, 299, 344; A

Prokne, 89, 287, 288, 289, 290, 291, 305; A
Prokoptas, 223
Prokris, 130, 287, 291, 292; I
Prokrustes, 223; *51*
Prometheus, 12, 59, 60, 69, 150, 169, 172, 173, 174, 263, 267
Protesilaos, 342–6
Proteus, 360
Protogeneia, C, I
Psamathe, 310
Psylla, 63
Pterelaos, 129, 130
Pygmies, 166
Pylades, 334, 335; *71*
Pylaochos, 16
Pylartes, 16
Pylios, 178
Pyrrha, w. of Deukalion, 69; name of Pyrrhos disguised, 329
Pyrrhos, 329, 359; E
Pythia, 92, 191

Reitia, 147
Rhadamanthys, 83, 188
Rhea, Rhea-Kybele, 59, 110, 257, 263
Romulus and Remus, 71

Salmoneus, 69–74, 85, 247; *10*; C
Sarpedon, 83
Satyr(s), 36, 44, 203, 284
Schoineus, 117
Selene, 133, 140, 281, 291
Semele, 14, 15, 16, 18, 25, 32, 56, 88, 125, 126, 136, 284; A
Sibyl, 315
Sidero, 72
Silen(os), ∕oi, 47, 198, 248
Sinis, 220, 222; *48*
Siren(e)s, 98, 151, 175, 199, 269
Sirius, 113
Sisyphos, 69, 75–84, 85, 106, 137, 154, 219, 275, 282, 322, 356; *11*; C
Skamandrios, 359
Skiron, 220, 221, 222, 309; *48*

Skylla, sea-monster, 170, 269, 315; d. of Nisos, 227
Sosipolis, 213
Spartoi, 31, 299
Sphairos, 217
Sphinx, 91, 97, 98, 99, 140; *15, 16*
Staphylos, 114
Sterope, 67, 69
Sthenelos, 129, 130, 132, 262, 302; A, B, H, K
Stheneboia, 45, 82, 83
Strophios, 334
Stymphalos, 310
Sylea, 220
Syleus, 195, 196, 199

Talaos, 295, 296
Talos, 271
Tantalos, 38, 57–61, 62, 64, 69, 89, 192, 239, 267, 282, 289, 302, 305, 319; B
Tarchon, 339
Taurominion, 232; *55*
Tauros, 231
Taygete, 146
Teiresias, 92, 99, 100, 101, 133, 135
Telamon, 116, 160, 161, 162, 171, 183, 228, 253, 310, 315, 323; B, E, K
Telegonos, 361
Telemachos, 328, 360, 361; C
Telephae, 27
Telephanes, 337
Telephassa, 27, 28; A
Telephos, 187, 300, 306, 332, 337–41
Teneros, 35
Tereus, 89, 287–95, 305; I
Tethys, 34, 309, 313
Teukros, 315, 324; E
Teuthras, 337, 338, 339
Thamyris, 281
Thanatos, 76, 155, 156; *24*
Thasos, 27; A
Thebe, *1*
Theia, 194
Themis, 34, 172, 193, 309, 313
Theope, 215

Thersandros, 300

Theseus, 6, 41, 82, 103, 110, 116, 159, 162, 181, 187, 209–46, 251, 254, 272, 277, 279, 281, 282, 301, 308, 309, 317, 327, 329, 331, 352; *48–59*; B, F, I, K, L

Thespios, 137, 205

Thesprotos, 306

Thestios, 106; G

Thetis, 32, 110, 269, 275, 309, 312, 313, 314, 317, 319, 324, 327, 328, 347, 348, 350, 351, 354, 355; *67*; E

Thoas, f. of Hypsipyle, 255, 298; her s. by Jason, 256

Thyestes, 57, 62, 68, 90, 129, 302, 303, 304, 305, 306, 307, 319, 320; B, K

Thyreus, 199; G

Tiphys, 253, 261

Titan(s), Titaness(es), 12, 26, 58, 146, 169, 173, 174, 175, 194, 236, 263, 266, 267, 273, 277, 289, 319

Tithonos, 173

Tityos, 61, 249, 282

Tmolos, 192

Toxeus, 113, 199; G

Triptolemos, 277

Triton, 172, 199, 229, 271, 272; *53*

Troilos, 349, 355; *72*

Trophonios, 138

Tydeus, 295, 296, 297, 298, 299, 300, 323; G

Tyndareos, 105, 106, 107, 109, 184, 238, 307, 319, 320, 321, 338; *17*; F

Tyndaridai, *see* Disokuroi, 105

Typhoeus, 26

Tyro, 55, 69–74, 75, 247, 248, 250, 308; C

Tyrsenos, 339

Udaios, 30, 99

Urania, 135

Uranos, 95

Virbius, 245

Volcanus, 169

Xenodike, 195, 196

Xuthos, C

Zagreus, 76

Zetes, 253, 259, 260

Zethos, 34, 35, 36, 37, 38, 88, 89, 136, 287; B

Zeus, 15, 25, 26, 27, 31, 32, 33, 34, 35, 36, 37, 39, 45, 46, 47, 57, 59, 60, 62, 65, 66, 67, 69, 73, 74, 75, 83, 85, 86, 88, 89, 93, 97, 100, 101, 102, 103, 105, 106, 108, 109, 110, 111, 112, 115, 121, 125, 126, 127, 128, 130, 131, 132, 133, 134, 135, 139, 140, 141, 142, 146, 148, 150, 157, 160, 162, 163, 165, 167, 169, 172, 173, 174, 177, 181, 183, 185, 191, 195, 196, 200, 202, 204, 205, 212, 216, 221, 228, 229, 230, 235, 236, 237, 238, 241, 248, 250, 251, 252, 253, 258, 259, 260, 262, 263, 269, 271, 274, 275, 282, 283, 284, 285, 286, 289, 295, 298, 299, 302, 303, 304, 306, 308, 309, 310, 311, 313, 314, 316, 319, 320, 321, 324, 326, 342, 352, 356, 359, 360; *38*; A, B, E, F, H; Zeus Agamemnon, 321; Hekaleios, 226; Herkeios, 65; Laphystios, 86, 252; Meilichios, 223, 282; Phyxios, 87; Soter, 142

Zeuxippe, I

2

PLACES AND GENERAL SUBJECTS

Abas, Mt., 168
Abdera, 156
abstinence, 284
Achaia, 148
Acheles, 197
Acheloos, 114, 198, 199
Acheron, 150, 179, 181, 185, 239, 261, 262
Acherusian mere, 179
Adrasteia, 299
Adriatic, 147, 268
Aegean, 216, 234, 240, 327
Agnus, 225
Aia, 251, 252, 262, 263, 264, 272, 275, 277
Aiaia, 251, 252, 361
Aigina, 75, 160, 221, 272, 310, 323
Aigosthena, 295
aigle, 272
Aigyptos (Nile), 40
Aiolia, Aiolians, 69
Aisepos, 353
Aison, 247, 248
Aitolia, Aitolians, 63, 106, 108, 113, 115, 120, 188, 198, 295
aix, 216
Akarnania, 129
Akrai, 110
Akrokorinthos, 75, 79, 80, 274
Akropolis, 210, 217, 234, 240, 241, 242, 243, 246
Alalkomenai, 322
Alban Hills, 245
Albanians, 287
Aleion, 84
alke, 128, 134
Alkyonian Gulf, 171
Alpheios, 62, 69, 73, 149, 152
Amazons, 41, 44, 83, 159–63, 192, 225, 235, 240, 241, 242, 243, 254, 262, 349, 351, 352; *32, 33, 58*

ambrosia, 60, 252, 260
Amnisos, 232
Amyklai, 190, 215, 327
Amymone, 44, 143, 144
Anaphe, 272
anapto, 272
Anauros, 248, 249
Andania, 105
Anthedon, 94
Anthemos, 168
Antimacheia, 162
ants, 75, 165, 309
apate, 217
Apesas, 140
Aphidna, 110, 235, 238, 317, 331
apotheosis, 172, 204, 251, 326; *46*
Appennine peninsula, 269
apples, 118, 147, 148, 172–7, 270, 314, 316
Arabia, 41, 173
Ara Maxima, 170
Archon basileus, 114
Areia, 29
Ares, Island of, 262; Spring of, 37
Argonauts, 3, 53, 73, 74, 87, 110, 116, 151, 157, 160, 176, 179, 192, 251–74, 278, 279, 281, 290, 343, 361
Argos, 15, 25, 40, 41, 42, 43, 44, 45, 46, 54, 55, 56, 57, 62, 81, 83, 116, 128, 132, 139, 140, 142, 143, 146, 148, 154, 158, 163, 168, 182, 205, 211, 225, 232, 238, 244, 294, 295, 296, 302, 306, 321, 323, 335, 340
Aricia, 245
ari-bagne, 230
Arimoi, 140
Ark, *see* chest
Arkadia, Arkadians, 109, 116, 146, 148, 149, 150, 179, 190, 335, 337, 340

Armenia, 278
arrow, 82, 117, 120, 121, 144, 145, 151, 165, 168, 186, 190, 200, 204, 241, 326, 335, 350, 353, 354
Artakia, 256
Artemision, Mt., 146, 147
ash-trees, 34, 35, 40
Asia Minor, 45, 57, 64, 81, 82, 84, 86, 126, 159, 194, 196, 241, 308, 326, 337, 340
Asine, 324
Asopos, 35, 274
asparagus, 220
asphodel, 104, 355
Athamanes, 85
Athens, Athenians, 17, 102, 103, 114, 116, 119, 178, 181, 205, 206, 209–28, 232, 234, 235, 239, 240, 241, 242, 243, 244, 276, 277, 287, 288, 290, 291, 325, 335; 52; L
Atlas, 175
Attic, Attica, 4, 36, 44, 110, 130, 205, 209, 210, 211, 212, 213, 215, 225, 227, 235, 237, 238, 240, 245, 277, 287, 300, 302, 315, 333
aulion, 312
Aulis, 238, 328, 331, 332, 337, 340, 342, 343
Aventine, 169

Bacchantes, 284, 288, 290
Bakcheion, 286
ball, 46, 217
basket, 178, 213; 47
bear (for constellation, *see* star), 117, 316, 318; Bear Island, 256; Bear Fountain, 256
beasts, 17, 42, 70, 280
beauty, 34
Bebrykes, 257
beehive tombs, 9
bees, 165, 282
bird, 7, 88, 100, 107, 121, 150–1, 158, 164, 227, 279, 287, 289, 353
birthmark, 31, 59, 72
bisexuality, 209

Bistones, 155, 156
Bithynia, 257, 261
blind, blinding, (mental) blindness, 99, 100, 101, 102, 104, 113, 132, 258, 259
boar, 32, 115, 116, 119, 120, 148–50, 155, 182, 296, 318; 28
Boiotia, Boiotians, 8, 26, 28, 29, 35, 57, 69, 75, 85, 94, 99, 104, 128, 138, 182, 185, 188, 194, 252, 253, 263, 300, 322, 332
bomos, 4
Borysthenitis, 355
Bosporos, 257, 260, 269, 271
bow, 74, 135, 151, 153, 160, 168, 169, 171, 180, 188, 189, 203, 204, 261, 271, 335, 343, 350, 356, 361; 75
Brauron, 238, 333
bread, 136, 196, 197
bride-stealing, *see* abduction
bronze, 15, 46, 88, 107, 113, 142, 156, 162, 174, 201, 265, 271
brotoi, 57
brothers, pairs of, 45, 48, 63, 89, 109, 194, 199, 294; *see also* twins, Dioskuroi
buck-goat, *see* goat, 17
Budva, 33
bull, *see* steer
burial, 104, 210, 286, 301, 351
Buthoe, 33
Busiris (city), 167

Cadiz, 167
cattle, 75, 77, 81, 82, 109, 110, 129, 163–71, 181, 237, 269, 328, 354, *see also* cow
Caucasus, xxi, 173, 247, 251, 263, 267
cauldron, 59, 190, 201, 273, 289, 303, 318
cave, lair, earth, 26, 29, 36, 37, 51, 130, 140, 142, 144, 149, 150, 169, 170, 179, 249, 263, 265, 270, 284, 311, 318

celery, wild, 142, 298
Chalkidike, 171
Chalybes, 262
chariot, charioteer, team, 32, 33, 59, 64, 65, 66, 67, 73, 74, 108, 118, 135, 144, 174, 204, 224, 277, 300
chest, 47, 72, 93, 94, 255; 3
Chios, 113
Chryse, 343, 350, 358
clew, Ariadne's, 231, *see also* yarn
club, 98, 129, 137, 141, 144, 159, 168, 171, 186, 191, 193, 195, 198, 199, 200, 219, 232
cocks, 349
colours, black, 77, 230, 234, 240, 271; red (purple), 164, 173, 174, 224, 227, 229; saffron, 333; white, 25, 27, 72, 77, 105, 106, 109, 230
colt, *see* horse
contest, 63, 66, 67, 77, 108, 117, 126, 166, 185, 188, 189, 191, 196, 197, 199, 211, 212, 231, 255, 265, 266, 272, 298, 304, 310, 320, 346; 41
Corfu, 269
Corinth, Corinthians, 32, 35, 36, 62, 75, 78, 80, 81, 93, 94, 95, 140, 170, 219, 274, 275, 276, 323
corn, 12, 210
cow, cow-shaped, 25, 26, 29, 30, 32, 33, 42, 70, 129, 138, 151, 152, 163, 164, 169, 321, 342, 344
crab, 144, 145
crane, 220, 234, 297
Crete, Cretan, 9, 26, 35, 56, 60, 81, 83, 115, 117, 126, 130, 158, 188, 225, 226, 227, 228, 230, 231, 232, 233, 240, 242, 243, 248, 251, 260, 263, 271, 291, 292, 328, 360
Crimea, 333
Crau, Plaine de la, 169
cross-road, 194
cult, 3, 4, 5, 8, 10, 13, 14, 15, 18, 19, 273; cult-object, 178, 191
Cumae, 170
cup, *see* goblet
cypress, 340

Cyprus, 167, 232, 360
daimon, 65, 157, 180, 277
Danaoi, Danae, 45
dance, dancing-place, 148, 233, 234, 306, 312, 338
Danube, 174, 268, 355
Dardanelles, *see* Hellespont
Daulis, 287
dead, death, 14, 15, 18, 76, 116, 121, 141, 142, 144, 145, 150, 155, 156, 158, 175, 177, 183, 190, 197, 222, 223, 264, 265, 272, 282, 283, 332, 342, 353, 356, 361; cult of, 9, 10, 14; god of, 188, 356, *see also* Hades, Thanatos; realm of, 4, 14, 16, 17, 76, 101, 103, 143, 150, 170, 177–82, 185, 199, 245, 252, 258, 267, 281, 282, 283, 284, 285, 286, 355; *see also* Hades, Underworld
Delos, 234, 291
Delphi, 15, 28, 31, 33, 46, 86, 91, 92, 94, 95, 98, 102, 104, 128, 136, 148, 157, 190, 191, 193, 202, 203, 211, 216, 218, 250, 276, 306, 334, 335, 359
Delphinion, 224
deluge, flood, 52, 69, 140
destiny, Fate(s), 13, 14, 18, 157, 283, 320, 328, 347, 352, 356
Dia, 232, 233
Dindymene, 257
Dindymon, 256
Dion, 286
diphyes, 209
Dirke (spring), 37
discus, 54
disguise, 163, 192, 193
dismembering, 58, 59, 267, 268, 273, 274, 285, 303, 304; 65
divine child, 25, 26, 47, 54, 93, 134, 213, 214, 262, 273
Dnieper, 355
Dodona, 252
Doliones, 256, 257
dolphin, 229
Dorians, 183, 184, 205

double axe, 116, 192
dove, 252, 260
dragon, 26, 29, 30, 31, 81, 91, 174, 251, 262, 264, 265, 266, 270, 277, 299; *1, 62; see also* snake
dream, 49, 80, 233, 250, 272, 286, 315, 356; *see also* sleep
Drepane, 269
Drios, Mt., 233
duck, 321
dumbness, 288, 339
dwarfs, 166
Dyros, 202

eagle, 164, 165, 173, 227, 263, 324
ear, conception by, 133
Earth, 29, 30, 34, 36, 42, 61, 166, 170, 209, 214, 221, 236, 256, 309, 314; earth-goddess, 59, 174, 214
earthquakes, 103, 181, 244, 267
egg, 107, 184
Egypt, Egyptian, 166, 353, 360
Elaia, 338
Elaius, 145, 345
Eleusis, Eleusinians, 5, 177, 178, 181, 215, 222, 243, 275, 289, 290, 301
Eleutherai, 36
Eleutheron Hydor, 182
Elis, Elean, 14, 15, 62, 64, 71, 129, 148, 151, 152, 153, 184, 185, 187, 253
elm, 176, 291, 345
Elymoi, 170
Elysion, 277, 327
Emathion, 173
enagismos, 4
Encheleis, 33
Engonasin, 204
Enipeus, 71, 248
epaulia, 312
Ephesos, 194, 243
Ephyra, 75
Epidauros, 45, 244, 245, 323
epiphanies, 7, 271
Epirus, Epeiros, 179, 239, 359
Epope, 35

eranos, 48, 53
Erechtheion, 211, 213, 214, 215
erineos, 222
Erymanthos, 148-50, 182
Erytheia, 164, 167, 168, 171, 172, 174
Eryx, 170
eschara, 4
Eschatiotis, 290
Eteonos, 104
Ethiopia, Ethiopians, 52, 91, 97, 168, 173, 290, 352
Etruria, Etruscans, 169, 204, 222, 339
Euboia, 93, 188, 202, 325, 332
Euenos, 108, 198, 199, 200
eumolpoi, 289
Euripos, 93
Eurotas, 111, 326
eye, 50, 51, 269, 271, 315

Fate(s), *see* destiny
feasts, festivals, 67, 74, 138, 188, 203, 210, 213, 240, 272, 295, 361
fig-tree, 222, 223
fire, 15, 169, 170, 172, 187, 202, 203, 226, 265, 312, 315, 318
fish, 161, 279, 312
fisher, 47, 48, 49, 53
flower, 267; *46*
flute, pipe, 26, 138, 227
flying, 231; *see also* wings
foal, *see* horse
foundation, foundation-hero, 12, 15, 31, 45, 55, 62, 67, 68, 69, 71, 75, 105, 209, 216, 240, 291, 308, 339; *see also* towns
fountains, 55, 76, 182, 206, 348
fox, vixen, 70, 130, 291
friendship, 237, 334
fruitfulness, unfruitfulness, 39, 86, 174, 310
fulmar, *see* halcyon

Gabioi, 174
Gadeira, 167
gale, 132
Gargettos, 225
Genethlion, 218

Geraneios, Mt., 220

giant(s), 30, 107, 111, 146, 166, 167, 170, 171, 256, 271, 324

Gigantomachy, 171

girdle, 159–63, 241

Glauke, 276

goats, bucks, kids, 58, 82, 114, 216, 261, 305, 306

goblet, 102, 168, 174, 224, 273, 324

gold, golden, 31, 58, 59, 64, 68, 80, 89, 93, 101, 102, 118, 129, 130, 146, 148, 161, 163, 168, 172–7, 179, 192, 193, 204, 229, 247, 250, 261, 269, 271, 273, 277, 291, 292, 303, 314, 315, 324, 329, 341, 343, 352, 354; Golden Antlers, 27; Golden Fleece, 86, 87, 157, 247, 249, 250, 251, 255, 264, 265, 266, 268, 270, 274, 303 304; golden rain, 46, 48; 3; golden ram, 247, 303, 304, 306

Gorgopotamos, 202

grape, 114 116, 346; *see also* vine

grave, 7, 8, 9, 10, 15, 18, 33, 38, 45, 46, 47, 55, 57, 67, 78, 88, 103, 104, 109, 111, 135, 138, 139, 141, 142, 156, 166, 167, 196, 205, 213, 217, 226, 232, 233, 241, 243, 244, 245, 246, 262, 286, 287, 295, 300, 301, 306, 310, 327, 335, 345, 354, 359

Great Goddess, 7, 59, 139, 140, 178

Great Mother, 58, 93, 110, 194, 257

great year, 31, 41, 145, 155

Guadalquivir, xxi, 167

guinea-fowl, 121

Gytheion, 191

Hades, journey to, 179, 245, 279, 281

Hadou pylai, 165

hair, hair-style, 129, 130, 219, 227, 245

halcyon, fulmar, 158, 171, 257; halcyon days, 171

Haliartos, 8, 136

Halys, 267, 268

hammer, 223

hanging, suicide by, 101, 245, 257, 311

harpe, 51

hare, 119, 137

hart, hind, roe, fawn, buck, 44, 85, 119, 146–8, 172, 174, 190, 268, 280, 332, 333, 338; *26*

harvest, 196

hawk, falcon, 287, 289

head-covering, cap, etc., 30, 50, 52, 54, 107, 111, 224, 328, 340

heads, multiple, 82, 144, 163, 164, 180

heaven, journey to, 203, 233; king, queen of, 25, 34, 42, 53, 58, 60, 84, 88, 107, 111, 113, 134, 143, 145, 175, 198, 204, 226, 230, 232, 236, 239, 252, 254

Hebros, 286

hecatomb, 157, 343

Hekale (deme), 226

Hekatombaion, 223

Helene (island), 235

Helikon, 80, 100, 137

Hellespont, 86, 256, 271, 314, 345, 346, 354

herd, herdsman, 26, 29, 36, 37, 42, 47, 70, 72, 73, 74, 77, 82, 94, 100, 110, 114, 135, 136, 159, 162, 164, 168, 170, 171, 181, 197, 282, 286, 288, 304, 308, 316, 338,

herm, 26

Hermione (town), 182, 186, 323

heroes, cult and worship of, 5, 8, 9, 10, 11, 13, 14, 16, 17, 18, 19, 57, 67, 111, 125, 126, 133, 170, 185, 192, 202, 203, 214, 226, 245, 246, 277, 279, 295, 320, 321, 323, 325, 337, 345, 354

heros theos, 127

hetairai, 193

Hiera (island), 217

hierophant, 178, 215, 289

hind, *see* hart

hippos, 79

Hippukrene, 80, 100

Hittites, 339
homoerotic, 89, 90, 91, 284
honey, 81, 282, 354
hoopoe, 287, 289
horn, horned, antlers, 29, 77, 146, 148, 199, 338, 339; *27*
horse (colt, foal, mare, stallion, steed), 16, 36, 48, 49, 53, 63, 64, 66, 67, 69, 70, 72, 73, 78, 79, 80, 82, 83, 84, 86, 89, 95, 96, 99, 107, 108, 109, 110, 118, 154–8, 160, 161, 173, 184, 188, 189, 236, 243, 244, 297, 313, 314, 321, 328, 330, 349, 357; Wooden, 357, 358
hound, dog, bitch, 16, 60, 72, 97, 106, 113, 119, 130, 140, 143, 164, 168, 174, 177–82, 291, 292, 315
hundred-armed, 216, 315
hunt, hunters, hunting, 8, 12, 30, 37, 113–21, 137, 141, 146, 147, 225, 243, 248, 249, 261, 280, 291, 292, 310, 311, 318; *69*
Hydra, 143, 144, 145, 150, 164, 174, 180, 193
Hydrophoria, 272
Hyllos, 197, 202, 205
Hymettos, 225
Hyperboreans, 52, 147, 174, 185, 261
Hyria, 332

Iardanos, 192
Ida, Mt., Idaean, 58, 66, 126, 228, 308, 341, 316, 317, 358; *69*
Ikarian Sea, 231
Ilion, Ilios, *see* Troy
Ilissos, 290
Illyria, Illyrians, 19, 33
immortality, 134, 172, 227, 275, 277, 286, 291, 299, 318, 323, 353
Inachos, 25, 40, 41, 211
insanity, *see* madness
Iolkos, 74, 78, 155, 247, 248, 249, 250, 253, 270, 272, 273, 274, 275, 303, 310, 313, 314
Ionian, Ionians, 126
Ionian Sea, 268

Irasa, 166
Ischia, 195
islands, 232, 251, 254, 261, 270, 271, 272, 327, 343, 355; Island of Sunset-glow, 164, 168; Islands of the Blessed, 19, 33, 175, 278
Ismenion, 35
Ismenos, 34
Isthmus, 62, 63, 66, 68, 75, 77, 78, 159, 170, 171, 178, 184, 219, 220, 244, 277, 290, 298; Isthmian Games, 78, 142, 184, 187, 298
Istria, 147, 268
Istros, 174, 268
Italian, Italy, 170, 204, 245, 288, 360
Ithaca (Ithake), 321, 322, 328, 361
ithyphallis, *see* phallic, phallos
ivory, 59, 224
ivy, 88, 205, 315

Jaffa, 52
juniper, 266

Kabirion, *see* sanctuary
Kadmeia, Kadmeians, 20, 25, 29, 35, 96, 97, 139, 298
Kaikos, 340
Kallichoros, 262
Kalliste, 272
Kalydon, Kalydonian Hunt, 113, 115, 116, 119, 120, 121, 198, 253, 310
Kaphareus, Cape, 325
Karia, 83
Kelainai, 196
Kelenderis, 218
Kenaion, 202
Kenchreai, 220
Keos, 104
kephale, 291
Kephalos, 291
Kephissos, 223
ker, 352
Kerkyra Melaina, 268
Keryneia, 146, 172, 174, 190, 268
Keteioi, 339

kibisis, 50, 51, 52, 53, 54
Kilikia, 26
king, kingdom, 73, 74, 76, 114, 302, 303, 315
Kisthene, 50
Kithairon, 36, 92, 94, 100, 104, 136, 137, 295, 301
Kleite, 257
Kleonai, 141, 142, 184
klytopolos, 154
Knossos, 35, 226, 228, 230, 275
Kolchis, 74, 87, 157, 247, 251, 262, 264, 267, 268, 269, 276
Kolonos, 102, 103, 237
Korčula, 268
Korydallos, 222
Korykian, 267
Kos, 125, 126, 127, 162, 163, 165, 166, 171, 192, 193
kosmos, 31, 38
Kranae, 327
Krisa, 334
Krommyon, 220
Kuretes, 106, 115, 120 121
Kydonia, 126
Kyllene, 100
Kyrene, 166, 282
Kythera, 306
Kyzikos, 256

laas, laos, 210
Labyrinth, 226, 227, 230, 231, 233, 234, 240, 272, 275
Ladon, 147, 148
Lady of Wild Things, 7, 316
Laketer, Cape, 162
Lakonia, 105, 106, 107, 109, 110, 191, 238, 317, 327
lamb, *see* sheep
lance, spear, 64, 141, 158, 164, 165, 220, 314, 324, 325, 329, 341, 350, 352, 361
Lapithai, 67, 149, 184, 235, 236
Lapithos, Mt., 68
Larissa, 40, 43, 54, 81
Lechaion, 80

Lemnos, 254, 255, 298, 343, 356; Lemnian evil, 254
Leokorion, 215
leopards, 118
Lerna, 15, 16, 43, 44, 56, 143-5, 148, 164, 175, 180
Lesbos, 58, 286, 349
Leuke, 355
Libethra, 285, 286
Libya, 40, 41, 166, 167, 172, 270, 360
lightning, 15, 32, 66, 69, 74, 84, 88, 103, 111, 157, 191, 216, 226, 229, 284, 299, 314
Liguria, Ligurians, 169, 348
limping, 84
linden-tree, lime, 263
lion (not constellation), 32, 82, 97, 98, 117, 118, 136, 137, 140-3, 145, 146, 154, 155, 193, 195, 265, 280, 285, 296, 312, 318; 25
lion-skin, 137, 142, 167, 174, 181, 218, 324; *38*
lithos sophronister, 186
liver, 173, 263, 282
Lucus Nemorensis, 245
Lydia, Lydians, 38, 57, 58, 83, 89, 192, 193, 195, 196, 197
Lykabettos, 210
Lykia, 45, 82, 83, 261, 340, 354
Lykormos, 108, 199
lyre, 36, 38, 62, 234, 270, 279, 280, 282, 286
Lyrkeia, 43
Lyrnessos, 349

Macedonia, 157, 171, 195, 280, 284, 285, 286
madness, insanity, 32, 38, 45, 74, 85, 87, 91, 102, 118, 185-7, 188, 189, 190, 202, 236, 277, 283, 289, 295, 324, 328
Maeander, river, 197
maenads, 36, 37, 55, 176
magic, magician, 80, 87, 118, 176, 200, 223, 253, 264, 265, 266, 267, 268, 271, 273, 274, 276, 292; *63*

Magnesia, 249

meal, banquet, funeral feast, 48, 58, 59, 110, 120, 135, 210, 224, 255, 289, 305, 312, 313, 324, 335

Makaria, 206

Makris, 269

Malis, Malian, 202

Malea, Cape, 149

mallow, 104, 113

Marathon, 159, 206, 224, 225, 226, 228, 237

märchen, folktales, 5, 6

mare, *see* horse

Mariandynoi, 261, 262

Marmara, Sea of, 157, 256, 257, 353

marriage, wedding, 6, 19, 20, 28, 31, 32, 34, 43, 45, 48, 64, 68, 85, 108, 110, 118, 119, 130, 136, 153, 155, 163, 169, 193, 204, 217, 233, 235, 236, 243, 245, 267, 270, 290, 309, 312, 313, 314, 327, 329, 332, 338, 354; 58; god of, 126, 127; marriage chamber, 138, 321; 67

Mases, 323

Mauretania, 169

Medes, 277; Media, 278

Megara, 220, 221, 227, 241, 287, 290, 323

Melantian Rocks, 271

Meles, 285

Melos, 83

memory, 34

Memphis, 167

men, mankind, mythology of, 17, 70, 75, 99, 113, 173, 209, 308, 313, 314

Meropes, 163

Messenia, 105, 106, 107, 108, 109, 110, 111, 116, 188, 250, 253, 327

metal, 12

Metapontum, 71

Midea, 54, 68, 128, 129, 182, 302, 303

milk, 72, 134, 272, 346

Milky Way, 134

Minya, 252

Minyans, 138, 252

Molorchia, 141

Molossians, 239, 359

monkeys, 194, 195

monosandalos, 248

monster, 52, 91, 97–99, 160, 161, 264–6, 292, 342; 31, 55; *see also* sea

Monte Circeo, 269, 361

Monte Gargano, 323

moon, new moon, full moon, 26, 27, 28, 29, 30, 35, 41, 50, 109, 111, 113, 131, 133, 140, 241, 266, 267, 275, 281, 291, 292, 293, 312, 331, 338, 361

Mother of the Gods, 57, 118, 126, 263

Mossynoikoi, 262

mule, 97, 142

murder, fratricide, child-murder, 34, 42, 63, 71, 73, 82, 89, 90, 91, 94, 95, 111, 120, 188, 189, 190, 191, 201, 223, 230, 255, 268, 277, 303, 310, 333, 334, 339, 352

Mycenae (Mykenai), Mycenaean(s), 5, 6, 7, 8, 9, 10, 15, 25, 44, 45, 54, 55, 56, 62, 128, 129, 132, 133, 139, 140, 142, 143, 146, 148, 149, 150, 151, 153, 154, 156, 159, 162, 171, 177, 182, 206, 287, 302, 303, 304, 305, 306, 307, 314, 319, 321, 328, 334, 358

mykes, 55

Myli, 43

Myrmidones, 309, 350

myrtle, 64, 217, 244

Myrtoan Sea, 66

myrtos, 64

Mysia, 257, 337, 339, 340, 349

mysteries, 19, 20, 26, 28, 104, 105, 177, 178, 212, 214, 243, 256, 285, 289, 291, 305

myth, 5, 6, 10, 14

nativity, birth-legends, 14, 15, 17, 18, 19, 26, 46, 48, 80, 115, 125, 128, 129, 130, 131–6, 204, 213, 218, 227, 235, 262, 305, 306, 313, 329, 331, 338, 339

Nauplia, 44

Naxos, 232, 233, 291; *56*

Nea, 343

necklace, 32, 294, 296, 297

nectar, 60

Nemea, 90, 137, 139–43, 145, 146, 154, 265, 298, 299; Nemean Games, 142, 299

Nemi, Lake of, 245

night, 42, 50, 107, 131, 163, 173, 175, 238, 266, 267, 281, 312, 338

nightingale, 89, 287, 289

Nile, 25, 40, 167, 360

North Africa, 166

numbers: '3', 34, 44, 45, 49, 50, 54, 115, 118, 131, 143, 144, 161, 164, 168, 170, 175, 180, 270, 271, 283, 284, 313, 314, 316, 350; '4', 32, 41, 62, 67, 109, 154, 169, 175, 215, 313; '5', 30, 66, 144, 316; '6', 68, 101, 129, 216, 256; '7', 31, 35, 38, 45, 81, 100, 218, 228, 275, 284, 334, 350; '8', 31, 129, 145, 185, 292; '9', 34, 49, 82, 119, 144, 167, 227, 270, 342, 349, 350; '10', 134, 145, 327, 328, 342, 350, 360; '11', 352; '12', 64, 133, 140, 144, 145, 165, 185, 189, 212, 247, 351, 352; '13', 64, 68; '14', 228, 275, 276; '17', 354; '20', 184; '30', 141, 142; '48', 43; '49', 41, 42; '50', 4, 42, 137, 138, 144, 180, 225, 253, 264, 298, 302, 315; '100', 138, 144; in general, 329; *see also* Thebes

oak, 87, 111, 252, 264, 266, 344

oath, perjury, 77, 250, 257, 321, 328

odyssomenos, 322

Oichalia, 105, 188, 189, 191, 194, 201; *41*

oichomenoi, 188

Oinoe, 36, 146, 147

Oinone, 76

oinos, 113

Oita, 184, 201, 202, 203, 342

Olenos, 153

olive branch, tree, 137, 147, 185, 211, 212, 244; sacred olive, 47

Olympia, 63, 66, 67, 74, 83, 90, 126, 142, 147, 151, 152, 162, 175, 185, 213, 356; Olympic Games, 185

Olympos, 1, 74, 84, 111, 125, 132, 135, 158, 165, 170, 204, 260, 280, 282, 286, 302, 355; *45*

omphalos, 176, 193

Onchestos, 75, 138

onion, 220

Opus, 326

oracle, 28, 29, 30, 46, 52, 63, 85, 86, 91, 92, 93, 95, 98, 102, 128, 160, 167, 191, 201, 211, 214, 216, 218, 248, 249, 250, 274, 286, 296, 298, 300, 304, 306, 323, 328, 334, 339, 340, 355

Orchomenos, 138, 141, 234, 252, 263

order, rule, law, 34

Ormenion, 184

Oropos, 300

orphne, 281

Ortygia, 108

Otranto, 326

owl, 181, 265

paean, 226, 262

Paestum, 131, 198

Pagasai, 157, 247, 252, 272

palamai, 328

Palladion, 356, 357, 359

Pallene, 171, 210, 225

Palestine, 52

Panathenaia, 213, 240

Pangaion, Mt., 285

panther-skin, 249

Paphlagonia, 267

Paphos, 193

Parnassos, Mt., 77, 78, 262, 287, 334

Parnes, Mt., 226

Paros, 227

Parthenion, Mt., 117, 146, 337, 338, 339

Parthenon, 212 (temple), 329 (women's quarters)

Patara, 340
pege, 80
Peirene, 80
Peirithoidai, deme of, 237
Pelion, Mt., 149, 196, 237, 248, 252, 263, 309, 310, 311
Pellana, 106, 107
pēlogonos, 29
Peloponnesos, 5, 17, 57, 62, 66, 68, 71, 74, 83, 85, 129, 151, 154, 159, 164, 178, 184, 205, 217, 247, 282, 302
pelos, 309
Peneios, 152
penelops, 321
Pentelikon, 225
penthos, 352
Pephnos, 107
Pergamon, 341
Perkote, 256
perramos, 315
Perseia, 55
petrifaction, 53, 54
Phaistos, 35, 360
Phaleron, 234
phallos, phallic, 26, 126, 295
Pharos, 360
Pharsalos, 314
Phasis, 251, 262, 264, 267, 268
Pheneos, 190
Pherai, 155, 250
Phikion, Mt., 97, 98
Phlegraean Fields, 171
Phlegyes, 28
Phlius, 75
Phoenicia, 27, 40, 88, 125, 360
Phokis, 28, 38, 92, 95, 130, 334
Pholoe, 67, 149
Phrygia, Phrygian, 18, 58, 196, 315, 337; place on Mt. Oita, 202
Phthia, 310, 311, 312, 314, 318, 343, 344, 349
Phylake, 344, 346
Pieria, 280
pilos, see head-covering
pines, 252

Pisa, 62, 67, 69, 89, 90, 94, 236
Pithekusai, 195
Plakos, 349
Planktai, 252, 269
plants, 17, 42, 70, 220
Plegades, 252
Pleuron, 106, 115, 120, 198
Pnyx, 242
Po, 269
poison, 145, 150, 201, 202, 224
Polion, 57
politeia, 240
pomegranate, 16
Pontinos, Mt., 143
Pontos Euxeinos, 159, 355
poplar, black, 176; white, 185
Potniai, 78, 92, 95, 154
Prasiai, 255, 291
pregnancy, 70, 78, 80, 131, 315, 329
priamai, 161
primaeval man, 29, 30, 40, 43, 57, 76, 140, 141, 209, 210; primaeval woman, 35, 40, 106, 113, 308
pronymphios hypnos, 56
prophet, *see* seer
Propontis, 69, 256
prototype, 1
Psophis, 149
psychostasia, 353
Ptelea, 291
Pteleon, 291
purification, 81, 82, 165, 178, 187, 190, 203, 223, 269, 352
Pylos, 8, 9, 74, 164, 165, 168, 178, 190, 247, 253, 328, 360
pyre, 15, 187, 196, 202, 203, 205, 297, 301, 342, 351, 354; *44*

rain, 42
ram, *see* sheep; ram-marriage, 86
reaping-hook, *see* sickle
Red Sea, 173
Reggio (Calabria), 170
Rhamnus, 235, 238
Rhegion, 170
rhegnynai, 170

Rhipaian Mountains, 174
Rhodanos, 269
Rhone, 269
rhytor toxon, 188
ring, 229
ritual, 4, 15, 127, 204, 273, 285, 295
rocks, stones, 60, 76, 78, 79, 99, 103, 169, 211, 214, 218, 219, 220, 221, 239, 245, 252, 256, 260, 261, 264, 269, 271, 284, 325
Roman, Romans, Rome, 169, 245, 288, 308

Sacred Way, 223
sacrifice, 4, 16, 17, 29, 37, 43, 59, 66, 67, 70, 71, 73, 76, 81, 86, 87, 101, 102, 114, 118, 126, 128, 133, 140, 141, 142, 159, 163, 167, 185, 196, 202, 206, 215, 216, 223, 224, 226, 227, 228, 231, 234, 245, 248, 251, 261, 262, 267, 268, 273, 275, 281, 283, 302, 304, 305, 306, 310, 311, 312, 326, 332, 333, 335, 341, 342, 343, 344, 346, 348, 351, 354, 358, 360
saffron, 267
saga, 6, 13
Salamis, 116, 160, 221, 228, 290, 310, 315, 323, 325, 354
Salmona, 69
Samos, 116
Samothrace, 19, 20, 26, 27, 28, 31, 35, 256, 285
sanctuary, of Achilles, 355; of Amazons, 242; of Amphiaraos, 300; of Aphrodite, 233, 243, 244, 275; of Apollo, 35, 98, 148, 190, 224, 286, 348, 358; of Ares, 87; of Artemis, 141, 238, 243, 244, 268, 303, 333, 342; of Asklepios, 341; of Athene, 211, 213, 217, 271, 337, 358; of Demeter, 88; of Dionysos, 56, 233, 286, 345; of Hekate, 275; of Helen, 111, 326; of Hera, 44, 67, 131, 139, 162, 182, 198, 203, 275, 277, 307; of Herakles, 137, 183, 196; of

Hippodameia, 68; of Hippolytos, 245; of the Kabeiroi, 19, 35; of Memnon, 353; of Orpheus, 286; of Poseidon, 63, 277; of Tantalos, 57; of Zeus, 65, 66, 142
sandal, *see monosandalos*, shoe
Sangarios, 193, 315, 352
Santorin, 272
Sardes, 192
Sardinia, 137, 138, 205
Saronic Gulf, 76, 244
sceptre, 62, 68, 250, 302, 303, 307
scorpions, 292
Scythia, Scythians, 161, 169, 173, 174, 188
sea, sea-god, 16, 50, 72, 78, 79, 83, 85, 86, 94, 107, 112, 176, 216, 221, 227, 228, 229, 244, 260, 271, 272, 286, 289, 290, 309, 315, 317, 325, 339, 354, 358, 360; *23*; sea-monster, 52, 160, 161; *7, 31*; Black Sea, 151, 159, 242, 243, 251, 260, 303, 355
seal, 310
seer, seercraft, 70, 81, 82, 99, 101, 258, 260, 297, 299, 300, 342, 344; *see also* soothsayer
Sele (Silarus), river, 131, 312
Sepias Akte, 312
Seriphos, Seriphians, 47, 48, 50, 53, 54
serpent, *see* snake
sheep, lamb, ram, 16, 65, 67, 73, 85, 86, 87, 112, 125, 141, 142, 162, 163, 247, 274, 303, 304, 306, 344, 348, 354; *13*
shield, 45, 51, 164, 168, 324, 325, 329
shoe, one shoe, winged shoe, 49, 50, 51, 53, 192, 218, 219, 224, 248, 249, 274; *see also monosandalos*
Sicily, 110, 170, 269
sickle, sickle-shaped, 144, 161, 196, 269
Sigeion, Cape, 354
Sikyon, 36, 94, 126, 127, 296, 306
silver, 102, 184, 261, 264, 271, 312, 342, 343, 350, 361

sin, 59, 60, 66, 187–92, 232, 325, 332
Sinope, 262
Sipylos, 57, 58, 60, 64
Skaian Gate, 348, 353, 357
Skamandros, river, 314, 359
Skarphe, 104
sky, *see* heaven
Skyros, 245, 246, 329, 356
sleep, 162, 163; *see also* dream
smith, 222, 223
Smyrna, 57, 285
snake, serpent, 16, 19, 29, 30, 31, 33, 82, 88, 90, 97, 100, 101, 107, 134, 140, 143–5, 148, 155, 165, 172, 173, 174, 176, 178, 180, 182, 193, 198, 209, 212, 213, 214, 221, 239, 251, 264, 266, 270, 272, 277, 282, 292, 299, 312, 326, 339, 342, 343; *19*; snake-marriage, 155
Solymoi, 83
song, 88, 98, 158, 175, 196, 269, 279, 280, 282, 286, 289
soothsayer, soothsaying, 35, 92, 99, 101, 116, 167, 247, 253, 261, 266, 316, 332, 355
Sparta, Spartan, 8, 16, 33, 35, 55, 105–12, 138, 170, 184, 190, 205, 215, 224, 235, 238, 307, 321, 326, 335, 338, 360
spear, 82, 99, 111, 119, 286, 291, 292, 323, 329, 356, 358
sphaira, 217
Sphairia, 217
Sphettos, 225
spindle, spinning, distaff, 77, 193, 231, 356
spring, 29, 34, 36, 37, 44, 49, 55, 76, 80, 100, 106, 113, 143, 144, 157, 174, 194, 197, 206, 211, 214, 256, 257, 270, 276, 298, 316, 338, 342; *see also* fountains
stallion, *see* horse; stallion-wedding, 70, 86, 236
staphyle, 114
star, constellation, heavenly body, 53, 59, 111, 193, 198, 203, 204, 216,

230, 232, 245, 252, 264, 266, 286, 304
steer, bull, ox, 4, 25, 38, 39, 42, 70, 80, 82, 125, 158–9, 181, 195, 198, 224, 226, 227, 228, 230, 231, 232, 244, 265, 267, 268, 321, 344, 358; *50*; bull-wedding, 25, 26
Stoa Poikile, 242
stone, stoning, 30, 33, 38, 52, 54, 57, 60, 61, 78, 79, 111, 169, 171, 178, 179, 180, 181, 193, 210, 218, 219, 220, 232, 256, 265, 271, 276, 279, 282, 286, 300, 324, 325, 329, 342, 348; *see also* petrifaction
strings, string-music, 135, 318
Strophades, 259
Strymon, 284, 290
Stymphalos, 150–1, 179, 262; Stymphalian birds, *30*
Styx, 179, 318
sun, 38, 50, 54, 61, 100, 102, 151, 230, 231, 250, 251, 258, 273, 276, 277, 285, 304, 305; sun-god, *see* Helios; sun-child, sun-boy, 54, 89; sun's car, sun's cup, 168, 172, 174, 273; *36*
Sunion, Cape, 235
swallow, 287, 288, 289
swamp, 113, 117, 144, 148, 150–1, 179, 323
swan, 106, 157, 158, 290, 297, 348
swine, sow, farrow, 220, 225, 269
swing, 245
sword, 30, 51, 90, 134, 141, 164, 179, 180, 198, 200, 218, 219, 224, 232, 233, 259, 359
Syleus, 195
Symplegades, 253, 269
synoikia, synoikismos, 209, 240
Syrtis, 270

Tainaron, 178, 179, 239, 253, 282
talents, 58
Tangiers, 167
Tantalos (tarn), 57
Tantalos (mountain), 58

Taphians, 129, 130, 131
Tartessos, 167, 168, 172
Tauric peninsula, 333, 335, 355; *see also* Crimea
Taygetos, 106, 111, 146, 148
Tegea, 238, 302, 306, 337, 338
teirea, 99
Teleboans, 129, 130, 131
telete, 345
telos, 43
temple, *see* sanctuary
temple-burning, 35
Tempe, Vale of, 282
Tenedos, 347, 358
Teneros, 35
Teumessos, 130, 291
Thasos, 27, 125
Thebe, 349
Thebes, Egyptian, 353
Thebes, Thebans, 5, 8, 14, 18, 19, 20, 25, 26, 29, 31, 33, 34-39, 40, 46, 54, 57, 68, 69, 88, 89, 90, 91, 92, 94, 95, 96, 97, 98, 99, 102, 104, 105, 116, 125, 128-39, 140, 185, 186, 187, 191, 205, 227, 241, 245, 264, 274, 279, 285, 287, 288, 294-301, 302, 309, 322; Seven against, 3, 4, 5, 119, 294-301, 322
theft, robbery, 77, 96, 109, 131, 189, 190, 191, 195, 336, 344, 357, 361
Themiskyra, 161, 241
Thera, 272
Therapne, 111, 327
Thermodon, 159, 161, 262
Thermopylai, 194
Theseion, 215, 242, 246
Theseis, 219
Thespiai, 136, 138
Thesprotians, 239
Thessaly, 54, 67, 69, 71, 74, 81, 85, 116, 139, 149, 155, 157, 184, 188, 235, 237, 247, 250, 252, 263, 282, 309, 310, 317, 343
Thestia, 106
Thetideion, 314
Thorikos, 291

Thrace, Thracian(s), 19, 27, 28, 154-8, 163, 192, 215, 216, 254, 257, 280, 281, 282, 284, 285, 286, 287, 288, 289, 290, 347, 348; *64*
throne, 250
thunder, 74, 103, 283
thymbra, 348
Thynians, 257
Thynias, 261, 262, 271
thysia, 4
Tibarenians, 262
Tiber, 71, 169
Timavus, 147
Tingis, 167
Tiryns, 44, 45, 54, 62, 74, 81, 82, 83, 128, 129, 133, 139, 140, 143, 154, 160, 179, 182, 185, 189, 190, 201, 295
Tithoreia, Tithoreians, 38, 88
Tmolos, 58, 192
towns, foundation of, 5, 29, 38, 54, 55, 57, 71, 74, 85, 106, 141, 156, 191, 247, 356; *see also* foundation
Trachis, 184, 188, 200, 202
tragodia, tragedy, 17, 18, 32
tree, 38, 61, 148, 174, 176, 185, 270, 279, 280, 342, 344
Tremiti, le isole, 323
Tretos, 140
triad, trio, 35, 296; *see also* number, '3'
trident, 44, 82, 211, 214; *23*
Trikorythos, 302
Trinakria, 269
triple body, 164, 168
tripod, 136, 148, 190, 191; *42*
triselenos, 131
Tritonis, Lake, 51, 270, 271
Troizen, 181, 217, 218, 225, 243, 244, 245, 277, 323
Trojan War, 3, 74, 160, 161, 162, 254, 285, 296, 301, 302, 308-18, 319-30, 331, 337, 341, 342, 347-61; L
Troy, 58, 111, 160, 161, 162, 183, 203, 238, 241, 308-18, 319-30, 340, 343, 344, 345

trumpet, 56
turtle, tortoise, 220; *49*
twins, 34, 36, 37, 40, 45, 69, 70, 71,
72, 74, 105, 106, 107, 109, 111,
131, 133, 134, 137, 146, 184, 187,
247, 253, 259, 308
Tyrians, 125
Tyrrhenia, Tyrrhenian Sea, 169, 269,
361

underground, 15, 46, 102, 111, 113,
150, 152, 214, 230, 233, 250, 260,
267, 288, 345
Underworld, 1, 4, 9, 14, 15, 16, 17,
18, 19, 33, 43, 48, 56, 61, 74, 76,
78, 88, 97, 101, 102, 103, 113, 120,
121, 126, 132, 141, 143, 148, 151,
153, 154, 156, 160, 172, 176, 177–
82, 183, 186, 189, 197, 198, 201,
204, 216, 219, 220, 222, 223, 226,
232, 235, 236, 238, 239, 240, 245,
248, 252, 254, 258, 260, 265, 267,
272, 273, 277, 279, 281, 282, 283,
284, 285, 288, 291, 297, 298, 305,
310, 320, 325, 327, 345, 352, 355,
360; *2, 11*

Veneti, 147
vine, wine-grapes, 17, 88, 114, 195,
196, 257, 340, 341
vineyard, 75, 116, 195, 199
vintage, 116
Violet, 188
Vitalia, 170
vitulus, 170

vixen, *see* fox
Volo, 247

war-god, *see* Ares
water, waters, 42, 43, 44, 55, 61, 71,
72, 93, 114, 143, 172, 173, 200,
211, 212, 257, 272, 276, 282, 290,
312, 318
weasel, 132
wheel, 282
willow, 176
wind, 69, 85, 112, 154, 174, 290
wine, 12, 63, 102, 113, 114, 115, 149,
155, 176, 196, 236, 255, 285, 313,
354; wine-god, *see* Dionysos
wings, winged, 80, 83, 97, 98, 107,
112, 163, 164, 171, 259, 290, 352
winnowing-basket, 346
wolf, 36, 42, 77, 147, 261, 329
world, space of, 60
wound, wounded, invulnerability, 44,
54, 116, 150, 158, 164, 165, 180,
200, 238, 299, 300, 318, 324, 326,
340, 341, 343, 356
wreath, wreathing, crown, garland,
142, 176, 185, 210, 227, 229, 231;
54
wrestling, 135, 141, 156, 163, 166,
167, 170, 172, 179, 222, 232, 310,
311, 312

Xanthos, horse, 313; river, 314

yarn, ball of, 231

Zodiac, 143, 145, 198; *see also* star